D0780522

Sources Of American Spirituality

Alaskan Missionary Spirituality

Edited by Michael Oleksa

PAULIST PRESS
New York ♦ Mahwah

Library of Congress Cataloging-in-Publication Data

Alaskan missionary spirituality.

(Sources of American spirituality)
Bibliography: p.
Includes index.

1. Russkaia pravoslavnaia tserkov̂—Alaska—History—Sources. 2. Orthodox Eastern Church—Alaska—History—Sources. 3. Aleuts—Missions. 4. Aleuts—Religion and mythology. 5. Russkaia pravoslavnaia tserkov̂—Missions—Alaska. 6. Missionaries—Soviet Union—Correspondence. 7. Missionaries—Alaska—Correspondence. 8. Spirituality—Russkaia pravoslavnaia tserkov̂. 9. Russkaia pravoslavnaia tserkov̂—Doctrines. 10. Orthodox Eastern Church—Alaska—Doctrines. 11. Alaska—Church history—Sources. I. Oleksa, Michael, 1947- . II. Series.
BX497.A4A3 1986 281.9′798 86-16849
ISBN 0-8091-0386-9

Published by Paulist Press
997 Macarthur Boulevard
Mahwah, N.J. 07430

Printed and bound in the United States of America

CONTENTS

For Xenia

ACKNOWLEDGEMENTS

Chapter II: Letter of Archimandrite Ioasaph translated by Lydia T. Black, University of Alaska, Fairbanks.

Report to the Holy Synod translated by Lydia T. Black and Rev. Michael Oleksa, University of Alaska, Fairbanks.

Indication of the Way translated by Paul Garrett.

Chapter III: Letter from Father John Veniaminov to Archbishop Michael reprinted from ''Ivan Pan'kov'' in *Orthodox Alaska* and translated by Lydia T. Black.

''Missionary Oath'' reprinted from *Orthodox Alaska*.

Letter from Bishop Innocent Veniaminov to Metropolitan Filaret translated by Rev. Serge Bouteneff.

Address of Metropolitan Innocent Veniaminov to the Orthodox Missionary Society, and on the occasion of his enthronement, and Letter to the Ober-Procurator translated by Paul Garrett and reprinted from *St. Innocent, Apostle to America*, St. Vladimir's Seminary Press, Crestwood, NY.

Report on Education in Alaska and Report on School Work reprinted from the *American Orthodox Messenger*.

Chapter IV: Report from Hieromonk Makarii and Report from Hieromonk Gideon translated by Lydia T. Black.

All other documents from the *American Orthodox Messenger*.

Chapter V: ''Ivan Veniaminov'' reprinted from *Alaska Magazine*.

Map reprinted with permission from Barbara Smith.

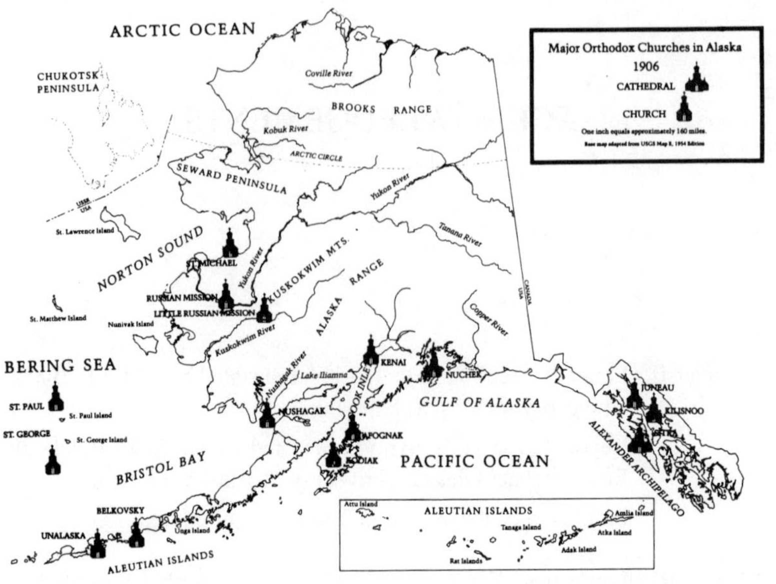

PREFACE

Many of the documents included in this book were translated by Lydia Black, professor of anthropology at the University of Alaska, Fairbanks, and by Paul D. Garrett, instructor of Church History and librarian at St. Vladimir's Seminary, Crestwood, New York. Without their encouragement, advice, and generous assistance, this collection would hardly have been possible.

Richard Pierce of Queens College, Kingston, Ontario, and editor of the Limestone Press graciously permitted the republication of many excerpts from books printed there. Perhaps these brief introductions to the writings of Alaskan missionaries will stimulate increased popular interest in the excellent translations and publications Pierce has produced over the last decade.

Barbara Smith, author of *Russian Orthodoxy in Alaska,* generously allowed reprinting of the beautiful map originally published in that volume. Her recent index to the Russian Orthodox *Messenger* should prove invaluable to Alaskan historians in the years ahead.

Finally, none of this could have been accomplished without the spiritual and theological education I received from the faculty of St. Vladimir's Orthodox Theological Seminary, especially the late Protopresbyter Alexander Schmemann and the present dean of the seminary, Archpriest John Meyendorff, or without the love and inspiration of St. Herman's own beloved flock, the Aleut people of Three Saints Parish, Old Harbor, Kodiak Island, Alaska.

FOREWORD

One of the goals of the *Sources of American Spirituality* series is to bring to light aspects of America's religious history that generally have been ignored by students whose methodological orientations have steered them in other directions but which are, nevertheless, valuable symbols of a people's religious experience. That goal is admirably met in this the sixth volume of our series.

Two decades after the thirteen British colonies declared their independence, there was one European power that was just beginning to develop its colonies in North America. That nation was Russia, and its religion was Orthodoxy. Though the standard pre-1960s histories of Alaska portrayed the period of Russian colonialism as one of exploitation of the land and native peoples which ended only in 1867 when Alaska became a U.S. territory, the real story was far different. Yes, it is true that the colonial practices did involve a degree of exploitation but it is evident that they did not inhibit the growth of vigorous Orthodox missions. Those missions achieved a success that was unparalleled in the rest of North America. The native peoples often accepted Orthodoxy and saw the relation between it and their own world view. They acquired literary skills in Orthodox schools that instructed them in their native languages, and they blended far more harmoniously with the Russian colonists than ever did the native Americans to the South with the land-hungry English. With the imposition of Protestant missions and an English-only education policy inaugurated by Shelton Jackson after the U.S. acquisition, the real story of suppression of the native culture began.

Many of the documents in this volume are published here in English for the first time. From them emerges the fasinating story of men like Father Herman, missionary to the Sugpiaq, or John Veniaminov, later St. Innocent of Alaska, who was named the first Bishop of Sitka in the 1840s, well before the center of Orthodoxy in America shifted to cities like San Francisco and New York. From the large number of missionaries' letters, reports to the Holy Synod, and devotional works like the classic *Indication of the Pathway into the Kingdom of Heaven* by St. Innocent, readers of this volume will be given a glimpse at over a century and a quarter of this singular history. There is much here that will challenge scholars of American religious and social history, much that will appear anomalous, much that will bring into question certain assumptions and interpretations and call for new attempts to integrate the data presented in these pages into the larger American story.

John Farina

INTRODUCTION

"THE PLACE GOD FORGOT"

"This is the place God forgot," summarized an Aleut mother at the end of a long, friendly conversation about the history of her village. Not only the Lord but missiologists, historians, and anthropologists have neglected or ignored the Aleutian and Kodiak archipelagos. Yet it was here that Orthodox Christian laymen and missionaries and the indigenous Alaskan peoples created a unique Aleut culture that blossomed and endured for generations after Alaska became U.S. territory. It was here that the secular business interests of the Russian American Company clashed directly with the evangelistic spiritual goals of the Russian Orthodox Church. It was here that bilingualism and literacy in Native Alaskan languages first emerged and Native Americans were first trained for positions of leadership within the commercial company and mission. It was here that Alaska's traditional societies first encountered the modern West, and polyglot Russia met the monolingual United States. And it was here that saints and martyrs walked the earth.

This story has been ignored by researchers "on the outside" and forgotten by most of those whose ancestors were directly involved "on the inside." So much of what happened here contradicts and overthrows existing stereotypes of Russia, the Orthodox Church, Native Americans, and even American social and educational policy that it is astonishing so few investigators have been attracted to the region. There are, on the other hand, serious obstacles. The records of Aleut achievement are difficult to locate and even more difficult to decipher. Many are inaccessible, stored in Soviet libraries and archives. Dozens of uncataloged crates lie in the basement of the Library of Congress. Still more untouched sources sleep in Kodiak, the site of the Alaskan diocesan seminary, and Syosset, the national headquarters of the Orthodox Church in America. Nearly all are in Russian script, fading on century-old paper. The letters, journals, and reports contained in this book were translated—many for the first time—from such sources. Fire, flood, shipwreck, and war have destroyed much. And with the passing of each articulate native elder, the rich oral tradition is further impoverished. The islands are remote, their population relatively small—and the local people know it. It seems to them, as to Mrs. Sophie Hapoff, an Aleut elder at Unalaska, Veniaminov's headquarters, that God—and the world—has forgotten.

PROMISHLENNIKI

The story of the evolution of the Aleut culture, beginning with Vitus Bering's first visit in 1741, however, is an exciting and inspiring one. The early years, during which Siberian frontiersmen and traders dominated the scene, appear to some modern experts to have been far more humane than the later published histories (financed by the Russian American Company monopoly) have indicated. There were, of course, occasional confrontations and outbreaks of violence. Certainly the Fox Island rebellion of 1761–1762 is no myth. But neither was the entire half-century between Bering's voyage and the formation of the Russian American Company one continuous bloodbath. The Promishlenniki were not all barbarians. Their journals reveal that many returned again and again, motivated not so much by greed (they often squandered or simply gave away several years' earnings in a few months and signed on for a new voyage as soon as they could) but by love for the land and its people. Many remained permanently in the islands, took native wives, raised families, and in baptizing their offspring, introduced Christianity. When Hieromonk Makarii, the first priest to reside at Unalaska in 1795, initially visited the region, he found the inhabitants already baptized. Children of "mixed" marriages were no longer classified as native (or "American") but assigned the status of "Creole" or "Townsmen," citizens of the empire. Since the Russian population never exceeded 800 employees in the entire territory, the tendency was for Creole youths to retain much of their native cultural heritage. Promishlenniki had no mail-order catalogs. Their food, clothing, lodging, and tools were local. When Captain Cook visited the region in the late eighteenth century, he found the Russians speaking the local dialects, virtually indistinguishable from the natives. These early frontiersmen enjoyed little technological superiority over the Unangan, who outnumbered them one hundred to one. They were armed, like the Natives, with knives and lances. The few muzzle-loading muskets they possessed had little military value. The Promishlenniki depended primarily on personal good will in this early, highly-competitive era. It was Shelikov who brought the first cannon to Alaska, and Baranov, who remained for nearly thirty years, who enslaved Alaskans.

Two centuries of intermarriage have served to reverse the camouflage: The Slavic surnames inherited from the Promishlenniki have tended to make the Aleuts indistinguishable from their Siberian in-laws, with the result that many Aleut achievements have been attributed to Russians by later historians. Once again, the Aleuts have been forgotten.

The very term *Aleut,* in fact, is the subject of some controversy. The Unangan-speaking people of the Aleutian Archipelago, logically enough, call themselves ''Aleut'' but so do their traditional enemies, the Sugpiaq of the Kodiak Archipelago and Prince William Sound. Even more surprisingly, some Yup'ik-speaking Eskimos in the Bristol Bay and Lake Iliamna regions insist that they too are Aleut. Early contact and some intermarriage with Siberians is a common factor, but not the only one. Some linguists and anthropologists have assigned the Unangan the exclusive right to the term *Aleut* and have attempted to persuade the Kodiak and Yup'ik Aleuts that they are simply mistaken, that they do not know, in fact, who they are. Certainly if the Unangan are the only genuine Aleuts, the others are, culturally and linguistically, ''imposters.'' And they themselves are perfectly aware that they are not Unangan. In particular, the Kodiak people fought with and enslaved Unangans in precontact times, calling them ''Tayaut,'' and the Unangan called their Kodiak area rivals ''Koniaga.'' That both rival tribes were the first to meet and marry Siberians would not, in itself, account for their assuming a common Aleut identity today. There is much more to the story than that, but this too, has been largely ignored or forgotten. This volume is intended to overcome some of this historical amnesia.

THE VALAAM MISSION

In addition to the contact with Promishlenniki and the exploitation that followed during the reign of Russian American Company manager Alexander Baranov, the Unangan and Sugpiaq share a more positive cultural heritage in which the Eastern Orthodox Church plays a central role. Beginning in 1794 and continuing to the present, the Orthodox Church aligned itself with the Alaskan native peoples. The original mission, recruited by the company founder, Gregorii Shelikov, arrived in Kodiak on September 24, having hiked, ridden, and sailed from Valaam Monastery, Finland. The first documents in this book are letters from Archimandrite Ioasaph (Joseph) and the lay monk Father Herman to their abbot describing their journey and the situation in Kodiak.

Conditions in the settlement were nothing like what Shelikov had described or promised. They found no chapel or supplies for celebrating services, but worse they discovered that the moral depravity of the Siberians and the brutal exploitation of Sugpiaq and Unangan peoples prevented any profound Christianization. Ioasaph's first message to Shelikov, dated 18 May 1795, describes in some detail the spiritual condition of Kodiak at the time of the mission's arrival. His report to the Holy Synod, together with that of Hieromonk Makarii and Cathedral Hieromonk Gideon a few years later, indicates that the Church rose immediately to the defense of the natives and opposed rather than cooperated with the company's oppressive policies.

The right and obligation of monastics to intercede with secular authorities on behalf of the poor and persecuted had been established in Byzantium and remained a permanent feature of medieval Russian society. In the fourteenth century, St. Cyril of Belozersk scolded the Muscovite Prince Basil I:

> Consider closely, my lord, what are your disputants rightful claims against you and then humbly make concessions; . . . And if they begin to ask pardon, my lord, you should, my lord, grant them what they deserve, for I have heard, my lord, that until this day they have been oppressed by you. . . . For, my lord, no kingdom nor any other power can rescue us from God's impartial judgment.

St. Cyril, a monk, advised the prince further:

> You should, my lord, judge right judgments as before God: without slander, without false evidence; the judges should not take bribes . . . there must be no murder or stealing in your domain . . . and also you, my lord, should restrain your subjects from foul words and abuse, for all this angers God. . . . You should abstain from drunkenness and give alms according to your means.

Few Russian subjects would dare address the ruler with such directness, but monastics enjoyed the legal privilege of doing so. St. Philip of Moscow was martyred for condemning the brutalities of Ivan the Terrible, but saner tsars heeded the counsel of the holy ascetics. This ancient tradition continued in Alaska even after the territory was ceded to the United States.

While the Valaam mission was condemning Baranov's injustices in reports to the civil and ecclesiastical authorities, they were also familiarizing themselves with the existing religious beliefs and traditions of the Sugpiaq people of Kodiak Island. Their own monastic community had been founded on the northwestern frontier of the empire at a time when the nomadic tribes of the region professed only a shamanistic religious identity. They themselves had crossed central and eastern Siberia, where monastic communities had been more recently established among shamanistic tribes. In transversing Asian steppes and forest lands, the Valaam monks reviewed the missionary history of the Orthodox Church from the Urals to the Pacific. They learned firsthand of the successful efforts that had preceded them, how monastics had ventured beyond the frontiers of the empire into the "wilderness" and established Christian communities whose goals included the conversion of the indigenous peoples of the region not so much by teaching and preaching, but by personal example. They came to Kodiak as representatives of a theological, liturgical, and missionary *tradition*.

A contemporary of St. Cyril of Belozersk, St. Stephan of Perm, devoted his life to the service of God and the Zyrians, a nomadic Finnish tribe of the Russian north. Stephan devised an alphabet for the Zyrians and taught them to read his translations of the Liturgy and the Bible. The beauty of Orthodox worship attracted the nomads, and St. Stephan imported fine liturgical vessels from European Russia, and painted the icons for his chapel at Ust-Vim himself. Worship aroused curiosity, but catechumens and the newly baptized required instruction. As bishop of Perm beginning in 1379, St. Stephan was able to ordain his students to create an indigenous Zyrian Church. From the beginning the goal of the Valaam Mission to Alaska was to do the same, to establish an *American* Church, respecting and employing the languages and artistic culture of Alaska within the community of the Orthodox churches. This had been the vision of SS. Cyril and Methodius, the Macedonian missionaries to the Slavs centuries earlier, and of SS. Hourg, Herman, and Barsanuphii, monastic missionaries and later bishops in the Kazan region, as well as St. Innocent of Irkutsk centuries later. Every successful Orthodox mission has had as its goal the creation of a self-governing "native" church, enjoying full administrative independence within the universal community of faith.

In order to realize this goal, however, every mission needs first to assess the religious traditions and spiritual milieu into which it hopes to bring the Christian Gospel. The Valaam Mission at Kodiak reported extensively on the traditional world view of the Sugpiaq, and the monastery published a compilation of these reports to commemorate the centennial of the mission in 1894. A translation of this publication is included in the second chapter of this book.

Traditional societies, as have existed since homo sapiens first appeared, have almost universally shared certain common attitudes toward fundamental human experience. They perceive time, space, and nature in ways remarkably different from those of the post-Renaissance West, but in close harmony with medieval and Eastern Christian world views. This idea requires elaboration.

Traditional Worldview

Before the introduction of written language, the invention of books, paper, and the printing press, human societies educated each successive generation in the ways of the world through a complex system of sacred stories, legends, songs, dances, artifacts, ceremonies, and celebrations. The goal of this educative process was to ensure that the next generation could carry on the traditions of The People and survive meaningfully. No society, no matter how "primitive," concerned itself exclusively with biological survival, but sought to give purpose and meaning to living humanly.

Every native Alaskan tribe considered itself and identifies itself (in its own language) as "the Human Beings." *Unangan* means "the people." *Tlingit* means "the people." *Yup'ik* and *Sugpiaq* mean even more: "the real People." When the world was made, or more importantly, when the first human beings appeared, they were given their own way to live appropriately, in harmony with the forces, spirits, and creatures with whom they share the cosmos. The beginning of each child's education is marked by this sense of self and collective identity. We are the human beings. We are the *real* people. *Our* ways are the ways human beings were from all eternity meant to follow. Any deviation—due to forgetfulness or carelessness—threatens to bring imbalance, and therefore catastrophe to the universe. To forget is to perish.

The stories of origins occupy a unique and prominent position within the entire corpus of sacred tales. They reveal the basic structures according to which all reality is governed. A Sugpiaq or Yup'ik traditional house is built according to a definite, fixed blueprint. The ground is leveled, a subterranean "basement" dug, a dome-shaped roof of driftwood and sod, with a smokehole in the center, erected according to the traditional model. Each procedure is done in the same sequence, for the work is not only a matter of providing housing for a family group. It is the re-creation of the world, each house being a microcosm, a replicate universe. The design never changes, for the shape of the world does not change. At certain times of the year, activities are appropriate inside the dwelling; at other times, the same activities are appropriate only outside the house. The cycles are fixed, the rhythms eternal. And the human beings must behave in harmony with the flow of the cosmos. Knowing how the world was made, being able to recite the events in the proper order, is essential information. You cannot build a home without it.

The notion of sacred space extends beyond the dwelling to the natural environment—the tribal homeland, where at the beginning of time, the eternally significant events, it is believed, actually occurred. Traditional societies live at the center. They must behave responsibly. The house is also a womb, the door the icon of birth. When the world was new, there was also free access to the spirit world, the world above, but this has been lost through human carelessness or forgetfulness. Now the journey is a one-way trip. To ascend through the central smokehole is to change dimensions, to enter a new form of existence. The dead are removed from Sugpiaq homes through the roof.

Time also is transformed. The time spent erecting a new dwelling is not chronological time—linear, irrepeatable time as the West experiences it, measures it, divides and manages it. The time spent behaving according to the eternal model, the hours spent building a microcosm in imitation of the act of creation, becomes contemporary with the Beginning, to That time, to Those Days. Sacred time cannot be radically separated from sacred space. Whenever one acts according to the eternal model as defined in the sacred stories, the myths of the people, one abolishes and transcends linear, chronological time. One is transported to That Time, to Those Days. One becomes contemporary with the Beginning and escapes the oppressive time modern man must "kill." Thus, traditional societies sought to fill time with meaning by supplying an almost limitless number of eternal models, the authentically human way to do *X*. The myths contained the fixed models, the paradigms for appropriate, genuinely human behavior. The legends reported the supposedly historical exploits of heroes who survived because they remembered and carefully lived according to those models, or those fools who perished because they forgot or were careless. Songs often served as reminders of the deeds of the mythic characters or of the legendary figures with whom all members of the group were familiar. The decorative art that constituted an integral part of every tool served to remind the user of the appropriate behavior. The world is ever watchful.

Basic to native Alaskan spirituality was a fundamental intuition that the animal world is intelligent and powerful. Together with hunting peoples throughout the world, Aleuts, Eskimos, and Indians attributed suprahuman powers to the animals they hunted. Each possessed abilities humans obviously lacked. Each had its "language" and in the Beginning human beings had been able to understand and communicate with them, as well as with the spirits in the upper world, but all this has been lost. A basic problem then arises: If one's prey is intelligent and either stronger or faster than the hunter, how and why does the human hunter ever succeed? And the answer throughout Alaska unanimously is *because they sacrifice themselves*. The animals allow themselves to be caught in order to feed the otherwise helpless people. But only if the people have shown the proper respect, have observed the appropriate rites, have not violated the eternal standards of protocol.

Good manners require much more than a few polite words of gratitude or respect. They include nearly everything the hunter and his household do. The hunting equipment and tools, the cooking vessels and storage containers must all be handled appropriately. The hunting season is inaugurated with special songs, dances, and festivities. The "blanket toss" of the northern Eskimo originated not as a game but a demonstration of respect, not so that the Inuit could spot the whales, but so that the whales could see them, as one elder expressed it. If the prey do not cooperate, if hunters are unsuccessful, it is not a matter of bad luck as understood in modern Western culture. It is an indication that something is out of balance; a relationship needs to be improved or restored. Perhaps someone has wasted food or treated meat carelessly. If so, that species will withhold itself from that community until proper apologies are made. To eat carelessly, to refuse food or throw it away, is unthinkable. It would mean that animal died for nothing, its sacrifice in vain. A hundred legends warn of the consequences of waste.

Even after the animal's skin has been tanned and its meat consumed, proper respect is extended to the bones. The *inua* or spiritual life-force of the prey remains, awaiting reincarnation. Improper disposal of the bones may inhibit this process, and therefore these must be treated respectfully, often returned to the tundra or river with the invocation "Come back."

To instruct, remind, and make visible or "real" the sacred stories and their characters, Sugpiaq, Unangan, Tlingit, and Yup'ik Alaskans developed an elaborate ceremonial calendar, according to which various events of the Beginning were commemorated and celebrated. At these festivals, the art, music, dance, and costumes served to reenact and make present (re-present) the eternally significant actions of Those Days.

The personification of this view of the world, the person whose powers to heal and prophesy confirmed the truth of this world view, is the shaman. The Angalkuq can deal with animal spirits who have been offended, or treat diseases among his neighbors, or find lost articles because he or she has recaptured to some extent the lost abilities of the Beginning, has, in other words, learned to communicate with at least some of the spirits and some of the animals. And the shaman learned this by visiting the Spirit World, by going to the Other Dimension, and then, of course, returning. To become a shaman requires the novice's spirit/soul to leave his/her body and go to the world beyond. It requires a death and resuscitation, a death and rebirth. In ritual or in reality (for traditional societies there is no difference), the shaman is one who has died and come back to life, and because he or she has "been there" the shaman "knows" from direct personal experience what the others only accept as the "way things are." Of course, not every shaman healed every sick person (but neither do modern doctors). And not every shaman was able to rectify a bad relationship between a village and a particular animal species. Each, it was believed, had different knowledge and powers that were personally communicated to the shaman at the time of his or her initiation. The power was personal and varied from shaman to shaman, but it "worked" often enough to provide an existential basis for the traditional world view. The existence and the success of the shaman verified the myths and affirmed the basic truths about reality as the People experienced them.

Shamanism dominated northern and central Asia as well as North America. Siberian missionaries had encountered it centuries before the Valaam monks set out for Alaska. The letter from Father John Veniaminov to his bishop dated November 5, 1829, represents a remarkable account of the attitude of an Orthodox missionary toward the indigenous religious tradition of the region. Together with the 1894 Valaam Description, the letter indicates the degree of tolerance the Orthodox displayed toward traditional cultures.

FATHER GIDEON

Formal schooling had always played an important part in missionary work, but the violent opposition the Valaam monks encountered from Baranov and his men prevented any effective educational effort for many years. Archimandrite Ioasaph complained of the difficulties the monks faced in Kodiak but adamantly opposed sending native children to Russia to school. In his first letter he recommended the establishment of a school at Kodiak, and after his visit to Irkutsk in 1797 and his consecration as bishop of Alaska there, the Church did plan to found a training school. With the shipwreck of the bishop's ship and the loss of all passengers, these early hopes were dashed. It was not until 1805 that the tsar appointed Cathedral Hieromonk Gideon to Kodiak with responsibility for starting a school as well as investigating the charges against the Baranov regime. In what appears to be an attempt to appear supportive of the Church and the mission, Baranov himself congratulated Father Gideon on his school's success, and to which Father Gideon replied (see Chapter 3). The Hieromonk, as the personal representative of the emperor, commanded at least token respect, but he was unable to win very many concessions from the company management, Count Nicolai Rezanov, or Alexander Baranov, as the letters printed in Chapter 4 indicate.

During his two-year sojourn at Kodiak, Father Gideon attracted over one hundred students, both boys and girls, to his school. He produced the first grammar of Sugpiaq (Kodiak) Aleut and began translation of biblical and liturgical texts. With his transfer back to Europe, however, this successful effort in formal schooling ended. Only a decade or so later did the only surviving member of the Valaam Mission, Father Herman, assisted by Mrs. Sophie Vlasoff and her husband, who were Creoles, begin his school a safe distance away from Baranov and his men, on nearby Spruce Island. Time, sacred space, and the sacredness of the cosmos were nothing new to them. The icon corner in each house (in some homes even today often covering an entire wall) as an extension of the iconostas in the church building, the saying of grace at meals, and the sumptuous traditional Orthodox banquets, especially at Pascha and Christmas, together with door-to-door caroling and intervillage visitations, allowed much of what the traditional Unangan, Sugpiaq, and Yup'ik peoples had practiced for centuries to continue in a new, ''baptized'' expression. The Alaskan *Slaviq* is the modern continuation of this synthesis of Eastern European and Native Alaskan religious culture.

FATHER HERMAN

The sole survivor of the original mission, Father Herman, represents the personification of the new, Christian world view in much the same way the shamans had authenticated the old. As a pious and devout layman, the Elder Herman became ''Apa'' (grandfather) to the Sugpiaq people. He continued to intercede on their behalf before the civil authorities, as his letter to Baranov's replacement, Simeon Ianovskii, in 1820 indicates. His life of humble service to the Kodiak people, his miracles of healing and his prophecies concerning the future of the land and the Church confirmed the Sugpiaq in Orthodox Christianity. The joyful character of his life shines through his own correspondence contained in Chapter 1. Descriptions of his pious life and his impact on the lives of others by his teaching and personal example appear in Chapter 2. The Tropar (Theme Hymn) to Father Herman, who was canonized as the first saint of the Orthodox Church in America at Kodiak on August 9, 1970, primarily due to the century-long veneration of his memory among the Aleut people of Alaska, furnishes this book with its chapter headings:

Joyful Northstar of the Church of Christ
Guiding All to the Heavenly Kingdom
Teacher and Apostle of the True Faith
Intercessor and Defender of the Oppressed
Adornment of the Orthodox Church in America
Blessed Father Herman of Alaska:
Pray to Our Lord Jesus Christ for the Salvation of our souls.

ALEUT ORTHODOXY

The ten men who had comprised the Valaam Mission enjoyed tremendous initial success. Thousands voluntarily accepted baptism on Kodiak Island, the Alaska Peninsula, the Aleutian Islands, and on the Alaskan mainland. With the Creole interpreter Osip Priannishnikov, the missionaries effectively communicated with the Sugpiaq in the Kodiak region, preaching to them the Christian Gospel without directly attacking the traditional shamanistic world view of the natives. They sought, as best can be determined from the archives, to present Christianity as the fulfillment of what the Alaskans already knew rather than its replacement.

In place of the sacred stories, the monks presented the Gospel history of Christ. The new paradigm, the new Eternal Model, would not be the sum of a thousand prehistoric behaviors, actions or persons, but the Person of Jesus Christ. To behave in an authentically human way is to act as Christ would have acted in any given situation or circumstance. There would be history now to replace the old legends, but with the same effect. The lives of the saints and the Bible stories would serve to reinforce the basic truths of the New Testament. The rich liturgical and festal cycle of the Orthodox year closely paralleled the ceremonial calendar of the traditional faith, so that native Alaskans, like traditional Russians, continue to date events before or after a given fixed feast of the Church. The cosmic dimension of Christianity receives special emphasis in the numerous rites of blessing conducted regularly throughout the liturgical year. When the priests explained that each January the homes of the believers are blessed as a sign of their dedication to God, that water is sanctified because all life depends on it, that God "in the Beginning" began the creation of the world "on the waters" and Christ began his earthly ministry by coming to waters of the Jordan, and that His mission was not only the sanctification of human souls but of the entire creation, the Alaskan natives understood. Three-fold baptismal immersion as initiation into Christ's death and resurrection, the celebration of the Divine Liturgy as participation in the Banquet of the

Kingdom that is to Come and in remembrance of the God-Man's Passion, the abolition of profane time as communicants partake of the Mystical Supper, the Upper Room, "Those Days" being accessible and present now, represented the Christian fulfillment of traditional religious consciousness. The Eternal Model and the paradigmatic events become historic, but the essentials of the world view remain.

Of course, Father Herman's spiritual life is itself the product of a long tradition stretching back hundreds of years to the ascetic fathers of the Egyptian desert and the Byzantine heritage of St. Basil the Great, St. Maximus the Confessor, and St. Simeon the New Theologian. Since Peter the Great's time a century before, the Orthodox Church in Russia had been tightly controlled administratively by a civil bureaucracy, and greatly influenced by Western liturgical art, music, and piety theologically. In a reaction against these alien influences, monasticism enjoyed a renaissance. A Ukrainian monk, Paisii Velichkovskii, revitalized traditional Orthodox monastic life with his translations of the ancient Greek Fathers into Church Slavonic and his reform of the monastic communities he headed. One of his disciples became Igumen (abbot) Nazarii of Valaam. Paisii declared in his basic principles that "the head of a monastery must be knowledgeable in the Holy Scriptures, just, capable of teaching his pupils, full of truly unhypocritical love for all, meek, humble, patient, and free from anger and all other passions—greed, vainglory, gluttony etc." He added that within the community there should be total obedience to the Elder (without whose permission nothing should be done), frequent confession of temptations and sins, a lifetime commitment to the monastic life, daily study of the Scriptures and the Holy Fathers of the Church, regular caring for the sick, weak, and old, strict observance of the liturgical order, and absolutely no private property. In all these things, as his biographers have noted, the monk Herman was completely faithful. Baranov, and indeed the entire Russian American Company, is gone and forgotten. The memory of the humble elder, the monk Herman, remains.

Despite the positive influence Father Herman exercised in Kodiak, the evangelical work of the Orthodox Mission by the end of the Baranov era in 1818 had otherwise practically ended. Archimandrite Ioasaph and several other members of the mission, including Hieromonk Makarii, had drowned. Father Gideon had returned to St. Petersburg. Hieromonk Juvenaly had been martyred. (A forged diary fabricated by a certain Ivan Petroff nearly a century ago served as the basis for a slanderous account of Father Juvenaly's death, also placing the scene of his murder at Lake Iliamna. The native oral tradition in the region, however, agrees unanimously that Father Juvenaly was killed near Quinahgak, at the mouth of the Kuskokwim River, together with his non-Yup'ik assistant, quite probably a Tanaina Indian convert or Creole from the Tyonek/Cook Inlet area. Other evidence substantiating the Kuskokwim site includes the appearance at the Nushagak Trading Post some years later of a man wearing a brass pectoral cross identical to the cross described in the Yup'ik accounts of the murder and in several priests' journals. Until 1837, Father Herman continued his life of prayer and service at Kodiak, but otherwise very little else was being done to serve the converts of the previous generation or to educate and evangelize others.

FATHER JOHN VENIAMINOV

Before renewing the Russian American Company's twenty-year charter, the Imperial Government added requirements that the monopoly transport and support clergy and finance the construction of chapels and schools. The government was especially anxious that the growing number of Creoles be trained for positions of leadership in the colony. Volunteers were needed from among seminary graduates to staff the churches and schools to be founded in Alaska. But there were few takers.

The talented twenty-seven-year-old priest John Popov, who had been awarded a new surname in honor of the recently deceased diocesan bishop Veniamin (Benjamin), with his young bride, his mother, and his brother requested permission to serve in Alaska. Although his bishop was anxious for volunteers, he only reluctantly gave Father Veniaminov his blessing. By 1824, the Veniaminovs were at Unalaska and his amazing lifelong career as a missionary priest, bishop, archbishop, and ultimately Metropolitan of Moscow had begun. A short biography, published by an Aleut Orthodox priest, Rev. Andrew P. Kashevarov, who served for many years as the curator of the Territorial Museum at Juneau, is included in the final chapter of this volume.

Veniaminov was certainly remarkable. He learned to speak Ungangan and together with the Aleut chief, Ivan Pan'kov, devised an alphabet for it. The two men translated a small catechism and the Gospel of St. Matthew, and Father John wrote the first Aleut book, *Indication of the Pathway into the Kingdom of Heaven,* which is included in a new English translation in Chapter 2 of this book. Predictably, the printers in St. Petersburg had considerable difficulty setting type in such an exotic language, and the finished product, after years of labor, was practically worthless. Father John then journeyed to Europe, rounding the tip of South Africa on the longest ocean voyage of his life. Arriving in the capital, he was introduced to the emperor, delighting the tsar with tales of the Alaskan frontier. He compiled and published his *Notes on the Unalaska District* (in two volumes), which included his scientific observations on the flora, fauna, and climate of the region, as well as his description of the Unangan culture and language. But while at St. Petersburg he received word that his wife, Katherine, had died at Irkutsk. The six Veniaminov children were anxiously awaiting their father's return.

The tsar intervened. His Imperial Majesty would see that the children would be properly cared for and attend the best schools. Father John would return to Alaska—but as Bishop Innocent Veniaminov. Crossing central Asia, the newly consecrated bishop was briefly reunited with his family before continuing to Unalaska and Sitka, the colonial capital. There he drew up plans for St. Michael's Cathedral and the "Bishop's House," which stands today as a National Historic Landmark, as his residence and the dormitory and classroom building for the All-Colonial School. The reader can catch a glimpse of Veniaminov as the newly installed bishop of Alaska in his letter to Metropolitan Filaret, written at Sitka in April 1842. His attitude toward native Alaskan culture and the missionary's approach to his work is perhaps best revealed in the "Instructions" he wrote for Hieromonk Theophan in 1853, and the speech he delivered to the organizational meeting of the Missionary Society in 1868 when he was already Metropolitan of Moscow. Certainly his acceptance speech delivered at his enthronement as Metropolitan reflects the deep humility of this extraordinary hierarch.

Wherever Veniaminov went, he founded schools. During his tenure as bishop of Alaska, the All-Colonial School trained clergy and ecclesiastical staff for the mission, but also accountants and seamen for service in the Russian American Company. Graduates of the school taught in village parochial schools, from which the best students were recruited to attend the Sitka school or other institutions in Siberia or even Europe. Several excellent candidates were sent to the naval academy at Kronstadt and returned to sail in Alaskan waters for many years. Aleuts were trained as navigators, cartographers, physicians, priests, musicians, and administrators. The Sitka seminary required six years of Russian, Latin, and native languages, with elective courses in medicine, trigonometry, navigational science, and astronomy, all at the "high school" level.

ALEUT IDENTITY

This is not the place to chronicle the accomplishments of every Aleut and Creole graduate of the Orthodox Mission school system, but a few important names require special mention. The archives included the names of scores of native and Creole students who served in various capacities in various parts of Alaska, Eastern Siberia, and even California. During Baranov's era, Aleuts were forced at gunpoint into company service. Hundreds were resettled on the Pribilof Islands, in the Kurile Islands, north of Japan, and at Fort Ross, north of San Francisco, as well as at Russian American Company posts throughout Alaska. Backed by company ships and cannon, Sugpiaq and Unangan warriors constituted most of Baranov's fighting force. With the spread of literacy—usually in both the native (Sugpiaq or Unangan) and Russian languages—and the promotion of natives and Creoles to responsible positions within the company hierarchy, the final components of the Aleut cultural identity appear. Throughout southern Alaska, native Alaskans professing an Aleut ethnic identity are laying claim to their rightful heritage as the descendants of those Native Americans who first encountered Russians and Siberians, and fought but also married them (the first priest to visit Kodiak, in 1791, performed dozens of marriages and baptisms, legitimizing those unions and making their offspring citizens of the empire). Modern Aleuts are also claiming that their ancestors attended the early bilingual schools founded by Father Gideon, Father Herman, Bishop Innocent, and their disciples, and that many of them served the Orthodox Mission and the Russian American Company with distinction during the final decades of "Russian" rule. In fact, the last years of the Russian period in Alaska's history were hardly Slavic at all. By that time, Aleuts were running the operation. Aleuts were sailing the ships, writing the books, keeping the accounts, engraving the maps, translating the Bible, exploring the coasts, navigating the seven seas, and populating Alaska's cities. At the time of the sale of Alaska to the United States, in 1867, Sitka, the capital, was 60 percent Aleut, and Kodiak, the second city, was 90 percent. The Russians did not stay. In fact, they were forbidden by law to remain. Unless they had married an Alaskan and had personal/family ties that forced them to remain permanently, Russian employees were legally obliged to return home. Alaska was becoming an Aleut province.

FATHER IAKOV NETSVETOV

Even during Veniaminov's ten-year stay at Unalaska, local Aleuts were displaying their talents. Ivan Kriukov had begun painting the icons that still adorn Holy Ascension Orthodox Cathedral there. Prokopii Mal'tsov had already graduated from the Kronstadt naval academy with a degree in naval architecture. Gerassim Zyrianov had become one of St. Herman's most promising students. Perhaps most significant of all was the 1828 ordination of the first Unangan priest, the Creole Iakov (James/Jacob) Netsvetov, who completed studies at the Irkutsk Seminary and returned to serve the parish at Atka, in the western Aleutians. Father Netsvetov's father, Igor, had served as company manager on the Pribilof Islands, and later on Atka, while his mother was a native of the region. Returning from school in Siberia, he learned the Veniaminov-Pan'kov writing system and began doing translation work of his own. Rather than render the Gospel of St. Matthew in the Atkan dialect, which is significantly different from the Fox Island language, Netsvetov furnished the Veniaminov text with footnotes, hoping in this way, as he expressed it, to develop a common Aleut literary language and bring the peoples closer together. Following the example of the Unalaska parish, Father Iakov also opened a school, where the four R's—reading, 'riting, 'rithmetic, and religion—were taught. Extracts from Netsvetov's journals, including his missionary voyages to distant islands in his district, are included in the third chapter of this book.

Netsvetov did not remain at Atka, but at Bishop Innocent's request accepted responsibility for missionary work among the Yup'ik-speaking Eskimos in the Kuskokwim-Yukon delta. There he learned his third language and devised a writing system for it. It is difficult to imagine the hardships Netsvetov faced in transporting supplies, providing for the basic necessities, and evangelizing nomadic peoples in so wide an area. His journals for these years are a remarkable testament to the devotion and perseverance of this Aleut apostle.

Netsvetov was succeeded by other Aleuts at both Atka and Russian Mission, his Yukon River headquarters. He was assisted by Constantine Lukin, the son of Simeon Lukin, the manager of the Russian American Company post on the Kuskokwim, near modern-day Aniak. Aleuts from the Pribilofs came to the Yukon to assist in constructing the church, and several remained in the region, generously contributing to its support. Father Zachary Bel'kov, the Aleut pastor, was succeeded by Rev. Vasily Changsak, the first Yup'ik Orthodox priest. Another Yup'ik, Archpriest Nicolai Epchook, originally from the Yukon delta, served at Kwethluk, on the Kuskokwim, while another Unangan Aleut from Unalaska, Matthew Berezkin, resided for many years at Napaskiak and continued the translation work Father Netsvetov had begun a hundred years before. Without exaggeration the village of "Russian" Mission was misnamed. It should have been called "Aleut Mission." The current pastor of St. Nicholas Orthodox Church in Kwethluk, Rev. Martin Nicolai, has recently published a collection of Orthodox festal hymns in Yup'ik, complete with the musical notation in the "Aleut" melodies, which have during the last century evolved into a distinctly Alaskan version of traditional Russian church singing. A selection from Father Martin's hymnal, the Tropar to St. Herman of Alaska, is included as an illustration in the final chapter. Father Netsvetov's work is being carried on today by three priests originally from Kwethluk, and five priests and one deacon who trace their family origins to the Yukon, as well as one newly ordained priest from Berezkin's base at Napaskiak.

ALEXANDER KASHEVAROV

The Russian American Company also benefited directly from the educational work of the Orthodox clergy. Alaskans trained in village schools maintained most of the company's posts after 1850. The Kashevarov family, originally from Kodiak, supplied the church with five priests, but also gave the company a sea captain who eventually rose to the rank of major general in the imperial military. Alexander Kashevarov received his elementary education at Kodiak and completed the course in navigation and cartography at the Kronstadt naval academy. Assigned to explore the north slope of Alaska, he took two ships, the other commanded by another Kodiak Aleut, Nicolai Chernov, to the area around modern day Point Hope. From there they proceeded along the coast, charting the shores as they went, paddling their kayaks until unreceptive Inupiat Eskimos forced them to turn back about forty miles east of Point Barrow. Kashevarov mapped several of the Marshall Islands in the South Pacific on one of his round-the-world voyages. Aleuts were regular visitors at Sydney, Australia, and Rio de Janiero, Brazil, by the middle of the nineteenth century. Baranov had dispatched Aleuts to Hawaii with the ill-fated Schaeffer mission; by the time of the sale of Alaska, many had been around the world several times.

ILARION ARCHIMANDRITOV

The Unalaskan Aleut Captain Ilarion Archimandritov enjoyed a particularly interesting career. His normal route included delivering supplies to most of the company's ports—Atka, Unalaska, Sitka, Kodiak, St. Michael's, and the Pribilof Islands—with occasional trips to San Francisco. Kodiak Aleuts were engaged in a relatively profitable ice trade with California. The freshwater lakes on Woody Island, near the city of Kodiak, froze each winter. A sawmill on the island produced very little lumber, but piles of sawdust, with which the huge chunks of ice were covered. The ice was then towed to San Francisco, where meatpackers purchased it by the ton in the days before electric refrigeration units existed.

One particular year during Archimandritov's long career had been especially unlucky. The ship aboard which he had served as a junior officer sank near Kodiak. Although Archimandritov had rescued many passengers and been commended for his heroism, a local native elder advised him to visit Father Herman's grave and request the local pastor to celebrate a short Molieben there for his safety. Ilarion agreed, but for one reason or another failed to visit Spruce Island. His next command was an ice-selling venture. He departed Kodiak on a clear, sunny day and within sight of the harbor struck a rock. A storm blew up rather suddenly and drove the wreckage of Archimandritov's ship toward Monk's Lagoon, the little harbor opposite Father Herman's burial site. There the ice kept the ship partially afloat until it reached the middle of the lagoon, where it sank, leaving only the center mast above water—forming a perfect cross. The company manager, a Lutheran who happened to be at Kodiak when this occurred, was so impressed he donated an icon to the Spruce Island chapel. He also assigned Archimandritov a new duty: Since he was so adept at locating heretofore unknown obstacles, he was issued paper, ink, a compass, and a kayak. Before long Archimandritov had produced the first accurate nautical charts, not only of Kodiak Island but of Cook Inlet and the southern shores of the Alaska Peninsula. After the Alaska Purchase, Archimandritov retired to San Francisco, where he married an American. They later traveled to Sitka and were wed in an Orthodox ceremony as well, and Ilarion ultimately returned to his hometown, Unalaska, where the villagers elected him to be their spokesman and liaison with the American officials because of his excellent command of spoken and written English.

ALEUT LITERACY

The development of Aleut literacy, especially in the Unangan-speaking area, provides another chapter in the evolution of Aleut culture. The literacy rate in the Aleutian Islands was, by the time of the sale, higher than that of European Russia. Innokentii (Innocent) Shayashnikov, Innokentii Lestenkov, Sergei Repin, Andrei Ladotchkin, and many others continued translating and publishing texts in Unangan. In the middle of the twentieth century, Sergei Sheratine, Vladimir (Walter) Melovedoff, and Innokentii Inga continued the work in churches on Kodiak Island, as did Father Nicolai Moonin and his sons on the Kenai Peninsula. An entire book could be written on the history and development of Aleut literacy and literature, which would include the production of dictionaries, grammars, liturgical texts, and entire books of the New Testament that have appeared in print, and numerous journals, diaries, and stories composed by Aleut people over the years. Today, Father Ismail Gromoff at Unalaska, Father Michael Lestenkof at St. Paul, Father Paul Merculief at Nikolski and Tyonek, and Moses

Dirks at Atka represent the current generation of Aleut language specialists and teachers who are laboring to perpetuate this rich tradition.

Veniaminov ended his days as Archbishop of Moscow in 1879, and was buried at Zagorsk. Almost a century later, at the request of the Orthodox diocese of Alaska, he was officially added to the canon (official list) of saints of the Church as "St. Innocent, Apostle to the Aleuts, Enlightener of America." Together with the martyred Kodiak Aleut Peter, who died under torture in California for refusing to renounce Orthodoxy after being captured by the Spanish; Father Herman, who is entombed within Holy Resurrection Church at Kodiak; and Father Juvenaly (and his anonymous assistant)—martyred, according to native oral tradition and the testimony of several Aleut priests, at the mouth of the Kuskokwim—Alaska is the home of four Orthodox saints who have been canonized by the Church. But anyone personally familiar with the pious elders and devout men and women in many Orthodox villages is well aware that there are many more. The anonymously composed *Akathist Hymn to St. Innocent,* a liturgical tribute to the Apostle to Alaska, appears in the final chapter of this book as evidence of the veneration and love with which Veniaminov is still remembered.

AMERICAN ASSIMILATIONISM

The years immediately following the transfer of Alaska to U.S. rule were relatively peaceful, except at Sitka, where the soldiers charged with responsibility to protect the town rioted and looted St. Michael's Cathedral. There was another tragic confrontation with the Tlingit at Angoon, during which the Indian community was actually shelled by a naval gunboat. For the most part, Alaska was much more the victim of benign neglect for several years, until Dr. Sheldon Jackson and Dr. S. Hall Young came to Alaska as Presbyterian missionaries. Dr. Jackson, using his family's social and political connections with the White House, was appointed the first Territorial Commissioner of Education. The twin goals of his term in this office were the Christianization and assimilation of the native population. Jackson felt that the only way to avoid the catastrophic experience of Indian wars, which had continued in the "lower 48" from the time of the Pilgrim Fathers until the age of Henry Ford, was to bring Native Americans into the public mainstream much the same way as public schools were doing with the millions of Southern and Eastern European immigrants flooding Ellis Island about this time. S. Hall Young wrote that an immediate first step had to be the eradication of the old Indian languages—the sooner the better. The Carlyle Indian School, a boarding program in Pennsylvania, provided Jackson with a ready-made model. Children would be removed from their homes and villages, sent to distant boarding homes where English and only English would be permitted. The cheapest and most suitable teaching staff for these institutions would be missionaries from various American Protestant denominations. Instead of a military confrontation on the battlefield, the war in Alaska would be fought in the classroom, with the full authority of the federal government backing the monolingual, English-speaking, Protestant missionary-teacher.

The main problem with the Aleuts was that they did not fit the expected stereotype. They were already educated, already literate, and already Christian. In fact, they had been teaching other tribes to read, and had sent missionaries to other regions for generations. Articulate enough and politically aware enough to resist Jackson's educational policies, they soon began to protest.

The article "Knock and it shall be opened to you" appeared in the *American Orthodox Messenger,* a monthly bilingual publication produced in New York City. The author's indignation stems directly from the sense of real injustice and blatant religious discrimination Alaskan Orthodox were experiencing at that time. The same issue of the *Messenger* contained the petition of the Orthodox residents of Sitka, most of whom were Aleut, asking the Russian ambassador to investigate their allegations that the provisions of the Treaty of Sale guaranteeing them civil and religious liberties were being violated. The petition of the Tlingit Chiefs and Bishop Nicolai's letter to President McKinley indicate that the Orthodox did not take this treatment without protest. Perhaps the most illustrative but also the most shocking report in this series is the published correspondence between Father Kedrovsky, the rector at Veniaminov's Unalaska parish, and Mrs. Agnes Newhall, the matron of the Jesse Lee Home, run by the Methodist mission there. The school reports, which conclude the chapter "Teaching the True Faith," were produced to present the Alaskan diocesan position on federal school policies in an attempt to alleviate what the Orthodox natives considered religious persecution. Ironically, the effect of this struggle in Southeast Alaska actually helped the Orthodox. Having resisted Christian missionaries for decades, the Tlingit finally decided to accept baptism, but seeing how rigid the local American Presbyterians were toward native language and culture, the chiefs at Killisnoo, Juneau, and Hoonah invited the Orthodox clergy to christen and chrismate them. The existence of Tlingit Orthodoxy can be directly attributed to an anti-Presbyterian backlash due to Sheldon Jackson's attitudes and policies.

As more and more immigrants arrived on the East Coast of the United States, the main centers of Eastern Orthodox Christianity shifted from Kodiak and Sitka to New York, Chicago, and Pittsburgh. The diocesan bishop moved the church headquarters first to San Francisco and then to Manhattan, with an auxiliary appointed to reside in Alaska and administer the mission. When the 1917 Revolution suddenly ended all financial support for the American Church, the situation in Alaska deteriorated rapidly. The mission school at Unalaska closed, and nearly all the bilingual Aleut schools were left without outside support as well. In some communities Aleut children continued to attend "Aleut School" until well into the twentieth century, using the old, well-worn primers published for their grandparents. The assimilationist policies of Young and Jackson won the battle by default, thanks to the Bolsheviks.

With the sudden and total loss of all financial support from the Mother Church in Russia, the American Mission was thrown into turmoil. Agents of the Soviet Government claimed and sometimes won title to church property in the United States. When for obvious political reasons the American Orthodox declared themselves administratively independent, the Moscow Patriarchate labeled them "schismatics." However, after fifty years of conflict, the Orthodox Church in Russia eventually recognized the American Mission as the self-governing (autocephalous) Orthodox Church in the Orthodox Communion. The original goal of the 1794 Valaam Mission was fulfilled with the Tomos of Autocephaly signed by Patriarch Alexei in 1970, creating the *Orthodox Church in America,* which includes Romanian, Bulgarian, Albanian, and Mexican dioceses as well as the original Alaskan Mission.

Alaskan history, like all history, is written from a particular point of view. Seen from the perspective of the dominant Anglo-American culture, the Aleuts are an insignificant minority inhabiting a remote and inhospitable region. They retain characteristics of an alien and "un-American" culture, which uninformed visitors to the state think should have been abandoned long ago. The history of the Russian colonial period is simply stated. The Russians (being, as everyone knows, inherently wicked and brutal people) invaded Alaska, devastated the fur seal, sea otter, and Aleut populations in a century-long massacre that ended only because the fur market profits fell abruptly or the fur seals were extinct. The Aleuts, according to this version, were exploited, demoralized, enslaved and decimated. Liberty and justice for all arrived in 1867, after which the real history of the territory began with the gold rush, the rise of the salmon industry, the arrival of the military during World War II, and finally the battle for statehood and the construction of the oil pipeline. Aside from a chapter on the settlement of the native land claims (which was necessary before the pipeline could be built), the natives contributed virtually nothing. They were victims or spectators in the real history of Alaska. If a text discusses the Russian period in any greater detail, the focus is inevitably on Alexander Baranov and his supposed achievements. The Valaam Mission is almost never mentioned, and the contributions of Veniaminov receive little or no coverage. Father Herman and Father Netsvetov, Major General Alexander Kashevarov, Capt. Ilarion Archimandritov, Simeon Lukin and his sons, and the host of Aleut authors, teachers, missionaries, and explorers are ignored. The Aleuts have been omitted—forgotten again.

The effects of Sheldon Jackson's educational policies remain. Young children were required to abandon their first/home language in order to succeed in school, but no one was there to interpret or instruct in the home language. Students were expected to learn English by "immersion," which is, of course, quite possible, given enough time and a reasonable approach to teaching the second language. Instruction in arithmetic, social studies, reading, and the rest, however, began immediately in English. Students who failed were labeled "dumb." The obvious unfairness and mental cruelty of a half century ago translates today into adult human beings who are convinced that they were the ones who failed in school, that it was their fault—for being Aleut, "dumb Aleuts." At the same time, Eskimo and Indian children were dropping out of school at an early age, having learned some English and much more self-hatred.

The feelings of anger and bitterness might even then have had some positive effect if they could have been channeled into some constructive expression. This is how the first generation had responded, with their petitions in 1897. Students who succeeded in the primary grades went off to high school boarding programs, and some even managed to earn high school diplomas. But on returning to their villages they found themselves strangers in their homelands. As one Eskimo mother put it, "When these kids come home they are strangers to us. But worse than that, they are strangers to themselves." Caught between the traditional life of a rural Alaskan Native community and the outside world but fitting comfortably into neither, several generations have had their self-esteem and positive self-identity systematically destroyed. The resulting social problems are predictable: Alcoholism, drug addiction, violent crime, suicide, and domestic violence have become increasingly common in the past two decades, and as these self-destructive and antisocial behaviors spread, the community and the regional governments solicit more outside expertise. Professionals with degrees in social work and law enforcement come to help. But this help is nonreciprocal and addictive itself. It is unlike the meaningful personal assistance one neighbor renders another. Public assistance and the courts "help" but they, together with missionaries and teachers, also represent a new and deeper level of dependence, which produces a new cycle of bitterness, anger, and frustration, leading to a rise in antisocial and self-destructive behavior. The native people of Alaska are literally being helped to death.

The Aleuts have been in this situation before. At the end of the Baranov era, thousands had died or been impressed into the service of the commercial company. When Father Herman met Simeon Ianovskii, the Aleuts were in a desperate state. Within a generation their condition was considerably improved because without being forced to abandon their traditional culture, without any radical overthrow of their world view, without loss of their language and self-esteem, they were at the same time becoming productive members of a new society, a culture in which they themselves soon came to play an important and even determining role. Father Herman, Father Gideon, Father Iakov Netsvetov, and Father John Veniaminov had little of the technology and knowledge the modern world has. They had a vision, however, of what *could* be. The fact remains that with extremely limited resources and personnel they produced native leaders and professionals whose contributions have been almost completely ignored or unappreciated for a hundred years.

CONCLUSION

The spirituality exemplified by the nineteenth-century Alaskan Orthodox missionaries derives directly from a consistent theological vision, in which the writings of St. Maximus the Confessor (+662) and his contemporary, St. Isaac the Syrian, are of central importance, and from an integrated liturgical/sacramental experience through which this weltanschauung is communicated to the members of the Church. Several specific aspects of the Orthodox theological/liturgical tradition corresponded directly to the pre-Christian beliefs and customs of the indigenous peoples and facilitated their conversion to Orthodox Christianity.

The proclamation of the Kingdom of God is fundamental to all Christian mission, as it was to the earthly ministry of Jesus Christ. The Orthodox Church understands the twin objectives of all her work to be the restoration of humankind to its original condition in the "image and likeness of God" and the transformation of the created universe into His Kingdom, the *telos* toward which all history moves. Christ came, and His Church comes to "make all things new,"[1] not by replacing or annihilating the "old" but by completing and fulfilling it: to be "perfect as your Heavenly Father,"[2] to attain to the "fullness of the measure of the stature of Christ,"[3] and to "love one another as I have loved you"[4] or to become a "new creation." The "old person" that must "die to sin" and "live to God"[5] after baptism is the *un*natural (fallen) being, born into a world unnaturally separated from the Creator, the Source of Life, and thus unnaturally mortal. Becoming citizens of the Heavenly Kingdom means attaining to humanity's natural condition.

The Alaskan missionaries came to announce the Good News that God as Father, Son, and Holy Spirit has revealed Himself and made His Ekonomia, His saving plan, known so that those who believe and are baptized into this new life, His Mystical Body, the Church, can become "partakers of Divine Nature,"[6] can become, in the words of the ancient Greek Fathers, "gods by grace."

The ultimate sign of the new godlike humanity, of spiritual "perfection," is overflowing, all-embracing love, as St. Isaac of Syria writes:

> The perfect person has "a kindling of the heart for all creation—for humanity, the birds, the animals, the demons, the whole universe. And whenever he thinks of them or contemplates them, tears pour from his eyes because of the strong sympathy which possesses his heart. And his heart feels itself touched and possessed and he cannot endure to see or to hear of any creature suffering any hurt or even the slightest pain."[7]

The new humanity to which Christ calls His disciples sees the world differently. Salvation requires godlike love, for the Creator Himself, for all other human beings—the biblical "neighbor"—and for the entire creation, the world that "God so loved." The visible universe is itself a means of contact with God, since it is His self-expression. St. Anthony the Great (+356) writes that the whole creation was his book, lying open before him whenever he (a desert ascetic) wanted to read the Word of God.[8]

Native Americans share a similar apprehension of the visible world as the "sign" of ultimate reality, as constituting a sacramental unity through which the spiritual is experienced and communicated. The "inua" as an indestructible life-force that enlivens all animate beings represents the fundamental component of the traditional Eskimo world view. The essentially spiritual relationship between the hunter and his prey, between consumer and food, between the residents and their dwelling, imposes a system of protocol that fills life with beauty and meaning. The traditional Alaskan understands that while the survival of his people requires the constant taking of animal lives, this killing, dictated by biological necessity, defiles him and violates the ideals of harmonious cooperation required of interpersonal relationships. The ceremonies, household traditions, festivals, and artistic motifs of nearly all precontact cultures signify their constant desire to restore peace and balance between themselves and the animals upon whose deaths their lives depend. The Eskimo must kill to live, but he kills and eats apologetically.

The intrinsic unity of spiritual and physical realms extends to human language and the names of each living thing. As some Indian tribes in the Alaskan interior explain:

> The animal and its spirit are one in the same thing. When you name the animal, you are also naming its spirit. That's why some animal names are hutllaanee ("taboo")—like the ones women should not say—because calling the animal's name is like calling its spirit. Just like we do not mention a person's name after they die . . . it would be calling their spirit.[9]

Eastern Christians likewise affirm the spiritual significance of the created universe and affirm the intimate link between a person and his or her name. At baptism each initiate is buried/immersed and risen again to new life—a central motif of all shamanistic initiations—and is given the name of a spiritual ancestor whose Christian perfection has been officially recognized by the Church. Orthodox Christians traditionally celebrate their name's day, the annual commemoration of the saint whose name they bear, with greater festivity than their birthday. The hesychastic tradition, based on constant invocation of the Name of Jesus and introduced into Alaska by the Valaam Mission, especially St. Herman, offers another parallel between the indigenous Alaskan spiritual tradition and that of the Orthodox Church.

Theologically, of course, the Church does not affirm the existence of immortal inua, for while the spiritual and material worlds exist (the former, the realm of God and the spiritual powers He created—angels and demons—and the latter the visible universe) the two are united only in humanity. Each human person is, according to the Greek Fathers, especially St. Maximus the Confessor, "microcosm and mediator." Yet St. Maximus also expressed what became at the Sixth Ecumenical Council the official dogma of the Universal Church the Orthodox teaching on the eternal significance of the physical world:

> We believe that the logos of the angels preceded their creation [we believe] that the logos of each essence and of power which constitute the world above, the logos of all human beings, the logos of all that to which God gave existence—and it is impossible to enumerate all things—is unspeakable and incomprehensible in its infinite transcendence by being greater than any creature . . . but this same logos is manifested and multiplied in a way suitable to the good in all the beings who came from Him . . . and He re-

> capitulates all things in Himself. . . . For all things participate in God by analogy, insofar as they came from God.[10]

In accepting and ratifying this understanding of the cosmos, the Church rejected the classical Platonic notion that all things eternally exist in themselves, of necessity. There is, in Christianity, no ontological necessity for the created universe. It is brought "from nonexistence into being" as the Eucharistic prayer in the Liturgy attributed to St. John Chrysostom states, according to God's Divine Plan. All that exists originated in Him, each creature a divine "idea" (logos) that has no "necessary" existence in itself, but that God brings into existence because of His love. Each created being preexisted, so to speak, in the "mind" of God, and the many logoi share a common origin, participating in Him as their origin. Christ, the Divine Logos, through whom all things were made, contains within Himself all the logoi that did, now do, or ever will exist. He thus "recapitulates all things in Himself." The inua as logoi do exist. They are not in themselves the immortal "souls" of various creatures, but insofar as they are alive and constitute part of the Creator's plan, they participate in God. Their personal identity is a revelation the Eskimo could never have guessed, for if the inua are logoi, they are contained and summed up in Christ.

The scriptural basis for this cosmic vision is found not only in the Prologue to the Gospel according to St. John, but in the first chapter of St. Paul's Epistle to the Colossians:

> In Him all things were created—all things were created through Him and for Him. He is before all things and in Him all things hold together. He is the head of the body, the Church. He is the beginning, the first born of the dead, that in everything He might be pre-eminent, for in Him all the fulness of God was pleased to dwell, and through Him to reconcile to Himself all things.[11]

The fall and its consequences are understood here not in legal terms, in the Anselmian sense that Adam violated a divine injunction and was justly—though perhaps harshly—punished, but as the rejection of the original and "natural" vocation of humanity as "microcosm and mediator." Sin is not only a personal but a cosmic catastrophe, for it disrupts the fundamental unity between Creator and creation, introducing mortality not as a legal penalty for disobedience, but as the "natural" consequence of estrangement from Life. Having no eternal ontological basis in themselves, created beings separated from the Creator who freely created them because of His love simply die.

Human existence becomes enslaved therefore to mortality, as the traditional Alaskan world view well understood. The continued survival of one requires the death of another, meaning that all life as biological survival alone depends on the killing of other creatures, and all food constitutes communion with death. Nomadic hunters recognize this more clearly than anyone else. Their life as *bios,* as biological survival, required the continuous killing, or what they perceived as the constant cooperation and self-sacrifice of their prey. Their entire culture aimed at mitigating the inherent spiritual insecurity and defilement they recognized as intrinsic to the human condition. It is no accident that members of the Whale Hunter Society, whose skills and techniques fed their Kodiak Island communities, were also treated as untouchable outcasts.[12]

The Orthodox missionaries realized they were not entering a spiritual vacuum as they arrived from Siberia. The inua as the inner life-force of every creature did exist, according to Christian doctrine, but not conceptualized in exactly the same way as the traditional Alaskans had conceived of it. The intrinsic link between the visible and spiritual worlds also existed, the created universe being God's self-expression, a sign of His love. The ambivalence an Arctic hunting society "naturally" felt toward their prey and their attempts at stabilizing and purifying their relationship with the creatures on whose deaths their lives depended were readily intelligible from the Orthodox theological perspective. The intimate relationship between the name and the person in traditional Alaskan cultures echoed an ancient biblical theme. What the mission came to contribute was the personal identity of the One who is *the* inua of all things: Jesus Christ. As the Way, the Truth, and the Life, He also liberates humanity from biological determinism, abolishing the terrifying sense of instability and defilement traditional peoples have always known. Without destroying their positive reverence for life, the mission set the whale hunters free, nourishing them, in the Eucharist with Living Bread and Living Water.

Christianity claims to make accessible a new life, an existence in which the human person rises above the limitations of life as bios and participates in the uncreated and eternal life of God, *zoë*. Human beings were intended from all eternity to participate in both, but as self-centered egos, they have become isolated individuals. Through baptism the individual as "the hypostasis of biological existence," in the phrase of John Zizioulas, is transformed into "the hypostasis of ecclesial existence," that is, a being capable of becoming a fully human person, in the image of God. Individual commitment and faith bring the believer into a community whose collective vocation (*leitourgia*) is the renewal of the world in preparation for the coming of the Lord and His Kingdom, in which they already participate. Individual repentance and struggle to overcome all that remains of the "old person'' enslaved to biological necessity and the whims of a self-centered ego do not produce ''individual salvation.'' Indeed, to be ''like God'' requires interpersonal love in the image of the Tri-Hypostatic God, Father, Son, and Holy Spirit.

The Trinity is not a doctrinal abstraction but the Eternal Model, the Divine Paradigm according to which human beings are created. Father, Son, and Spirit are all equally divine, each fully and completely eternal, omnipresent, omnipotent, omniscient, all-loving, transcendent, and so forth. Each possesses all the characteristic attributes of the Perfect Being defined as God. Christians nevertheless insist that they confess *one* God, not three. The Trinitarian experience of God reveals that the three are one, a unity in plurality constituted in and by total and absolute love.

The Father, Son, and Holy Spirit so completely love one another that there can never be any division or separation between them. The Son and the Spirit always and eternally fulfill the Will of the Father, not because the Father is ''more'' almighty or all-knowing—that is, out of compulsion (a logical impossibility if all Three Persons are divine)—but in loving obedience and humility. Submission to the Will of the Father, the source of the Godhead, as revealed in perfect, self-sacrificial love, is the eternal and divine—and not just the temporal or human—attribute of the Son. To accomplish the Will of the Father in humility and love is to live according to the divine model revealed in Christ. Being restored to the ''image and likeness of God'' requires community, for God is a unity of persons. One Christian is no Christian.[13]

In practical human terms, believing and being baptized are the temporal beginnings of an infinite and eternal process, which requires constant struggle and effort in this fallen world. St. Maximus writes:

> Do you want to be righteous? Give to each part which constitutes you what it deserves—I mean your soul and your body—to the reasonable part of your soul give readings and contemplations and prayer; to the irascible part, spiritual love and the adversary of hatred; to the concupiscible part, chastity and temperance; to the flesh, food and clothing, which alone are indispensable.[14]

In traditional native Alaskan culture, ''righteousness'' included a cosmic and, one might say, ''ecological'' dimension that required every individual to know his or her proper place and function within the family or village unit. Consider what one modern anthropologist calls the ''legacy'' of the Koyukon Indians:

> We often remember ancient or traditional cultures for the monuments they have left behind—the Megaliths of Stonehenge, the

> temples of Bangkok, the pyramids of Teotihuacan, the great ruins of Machu Picchu. People like the Koyukon have created no such monuments, but they have left something that may be unique—greater and more significant as a human achievement. This legacy is the vast land itself, enduring and essentially unchanged despite having supported human life for countless centuries. Koyukon People and their ancestors, bound to a strict code of morality governing their behavior toward nature, have been the land's stewards and caretakers. Only because they have nurtured it so well does this great legacy of land exist today.[15]

To preserve the environment itself for uncounted centuries as an inheritance for each succeeding generation required a commitment of the entire society. The collective structure of traditional society and the holistic, cosmic vision on which it is founded served as the basis for the Alaskan Orthodox understanding of "Church." To the ancient methods of establishing an increasingly wider network of personal and family ties (such as the Eskimo practice of naming newborn children after the most recently deceased elders of the community regardless of biological relationships) was added the institution of sacramental sponsorship—godparenthood. Receiving a new—and holy—name represented an important achievement. The Church as "mother," establishing a common brotherhood/sisterhood with a common Divine Father and divine "adoption" as His sons and daughters, reinforced the traditional communal orientation of native Alaskan life and added a universality unknown in earlier times. The liturgical use of the indigenous languages, together with Church Slavonic and even Greek, further enhanced the Catholic—all inclusive—understanding of the Church.

The earliest monks fled to the desert not only to escape the temptations of society but to assault Satan on his home ground, for the wilderness is primarily the biblical symbol of death, the region where the Evil One reigns. Father Herman's relocation to Spruce Island represents not only an exile from Kodiak with its dangers, but an invasion of "enemy-occupied territory"—the "reclamation" of another tiny portion of the created universe in the name of the living God. St. Herman's monastic life-style there and his lifetime of loving service to the Aleuts confirmed and encouraged the newly baptized natives in their new faith, and continues to do so nearly two centuries later. St. Seraphim of Sarov, a contemporary of Father Herman and himself the spiritual son of the same elder, Igumen Nazarii, advised, "Save yourself and a thousand others around you will be saved." The proverb is certainly fulfilled in the example of St. Herman, but what is probably more significant is that the elder "saved"—that is, lived according to the example of Christ—himself in service to his people. The process of salvation is never individual, even for a hermit living in solitude, but always as a member of the community, the Church.

Orthodox missionaries came to Alaska to announce and begin an eternal process of growth toward godlikeness, understood in Trinitarian terms. It was not therefore necessary or wise to inaugurate this infinite pilgrimage with lengthy condemnations of the insufficiency or corruption of "heathenism." Nor would it have been consistent with Orthodox theology or missionary practice to threaten potential converts with hellfire and damnation should they have refused the invitation to accept baptism. Salvation as *theosis,* acquiring godlikeness, is a positive transformation, bringing humankind to its next and final level of "evolutionary" development, with the crucial difference that unlike all previous developments, this final stage requires the free assent and cooperation of the participants. Coercion and intimidation had no place in evangelization. Baptism represents the temporal start of the eternal pilgrimage, a journey undertaken in this life only with struggle, pain, suffering—the cross—but in the Kingdom that is to come, the transformation "from glory to glory" will constitute the very joy of heaven.

Within the Orthodox tradition, in fact, heaven and hell are understood as essentially the same reality, as St. Isaac the Syrian writes:

> Those who find themselves in hell will be chastized by the scourge of love. . . . For those who understand that they have sinned against love undergo no greater suffering than those produced by the most fearful tortures. The sorrow which takes hold of the heart which has sinned against love is more piercing than any other pain. It is not right to say that sinners in hell are deprived of the love of God. . . . But love acts in two ways, as suffering of the reproved and as joy of the blessed.[16]

During a millennium of Orthodox Christianity, Russian culture was profoundly influenced by this spiritual vision. The iconography and architecture of even the earliest Christian centuries reveal a national consciousness of the Trinitarian and cosmic dimensions of Orthodoxy. Eugene Trubetskoy wrote of this at the turn of the century:

> The architecture of the interior (of an ancient Russian church) expresses the ideal of the all-embracing church where God Himself resides and beyond which there is nothing. Naturally the dome represents the highest extreme limit of the universe, the crowning celestial sphere where the Lord of Hosts reigns. The outside is a different story: There, above the church, is the real sky, a re-

> minder that the earthly church has not yet reached the highest sphere. To reach it, a new surge, a new fervor are needed. That is why the same dome assumes on the outside the mobile form of an upward-pointing flame.
>
> Need I say that the interior and the exterior are in perfect harmony? It is through the flame that heaven descends to earth, enters the church, and becomes the ultimate completion of the church, the consummation in which the hand of God covers everything earthly, in a benediction from the dark blue dome. God's hand, vanquishing the world's discord, leading to universal community, holds the destinies of humanity. . . .
>
> Thus the church affirms the inner communal unity destined to overcome the chaotic divisions and enmity in the world and in man. A SOBOR (''cathedral'' ''council'' ''assembly'') of all creatures as the coming universal peace encompassing angels and people and every breathing creature of the earth—that is the basic idea of the church which dominated both ancient Russian architecture and religious painting. St. Sergius of Radonezh himself expressed it quite consciously and in a remarkably profound way. [He] ''erected a church to the Trinity, as a mirror for those he had gathered into a community, so that the sight of the Holy Trinity might vanquish the fear of the world divided by hate.'' St. Sergius was inspired by the prayer of Christ for his disciples, ''That they may be one as we are one'' (John 17:22). His ideal was the transfiguration of the world in the image of the Holy Trinity, that is, the inner union of all beings in God. All of ancient Russian religiosity, including icon painting, lived by this ideal. Overcoming hateful discord, transforming the world into a church uniting all creation as the Three Persons of the Holy Trinity are united in one Godhead—to this basic theme everything in old Russian religious painting was subordinated.[17]

Nor was this vision lost in the more secularized post-Petrine age of the Alaskan mission. Through his fictionalized ''Elder Zossima'' in *Brothers Karamazov,* Fyodor Dostoyevsky seems to paraphrase St. Isaac:

> Love man even in his sin, for this is a love like the love of God, the highest form of love on earth. Love all God's creation, the whole universe, and every grain of sand. Love every leaflet, every ray of God's light; love the beasts, love the plants, love every creature. When you love every living thing you will un-

> derstand the mystery of God in created things. . . . Kiss the earth and love unceasingly, insatiable. Love all, love everything.[18]

At each celebration of the Divine Liturgy, when the congregation has been summoned to "love one another, so that with one mind we may confess [our Faith]" and the people respond "Father, Son and Holy Spirit, the Trinity, one in Essence and Undivided," and when the celebrant elevates the chalice and diskos (paten) exclaiming, "Thine own of Thine own, we offer to Thee, on behalf of everyone and for everything," this Trinitarian and cosmic vision is proclaimed, affirmed and celebrated. At every baptismal rite and each time the Great Blessing of Water is performed, the same weltanschauung, the same vision of reality becomes immediate and accessible—not by replacing "regular" or profane water with supernatural or sacred water, but by revealing once more the essentially sacramental nature of the cosmos. At every Pascha, the eternal Passover "from death to life and from earth to heaven," the Banquet Feast of the Bridegroom whose Kingdom is "to come," becomes present, and the closed doors of the Upper Room of Those Days are open. Within the context of the Liturgy, the Last Supper has never ended, but the "Bridal Feast of the Bridegroom" that is, of the Parousia, has already begun. Ultimately it was and is this joy, the joy of knowing the Divine Ekonomia, understanding what it means to become a human person and struggling to fulfill that eternal vocation—to become saints, immortal creatures sharing even now in the Divine Life, participating here and now in the Kingdom that is to come—that served as the inspiration, the means, and the goal of Alaskan Orthodox missionary spirituality.

Notes

1. Revelation 21:5.
2. Matthew 6:48.
3. Ephesians 4:13.
4. John 13:34.
5. Romans 6:8–11.
6. 2 Peter 1:4.
7. Isaac the Syrian, Homily 48, quoted from Nicholas Arseniev, *Mysticism and the Eastern Church,* St. Vladimir's Seminary Press, 1979, p. 52.
8. Bishop Kallistos (Ware), *The Orthodox Way,* St. Vladimir's Seminary Press, 1980, p. 54.
9. Richard Nelson, *Make Prayers to the Raven,* University of Chicago Press, 1983, p. 22.
10. Quoted from John Meyendorff, *Christ in Eastern Christian Thought,* St. Vladimir's Seminary Press, 1969, p. 102. The consistent Orthodox Christian op-

position to abortion arises precisely from this doctrine: life begins *before* conception.

11. Colossians 1:16–20.

12. Margaret Lantis, *Alaskan Eskimo Ceremonialism,* University of Seattle, 1971, p. 33.

13. John 17; Hebrews 12:40. Orthodox parish censuses have traditionally considered the family or household as the basic unit.

14. Meyendorff, *Christ in Eastern Christian Thought,* p. 104. Also see L. Thunberg, *Man and the Cosmos,* and J. Zizioulas, *Being as Communion* (both St. Vladimir's Seminary Press, 1985).

15. Nelson, *Make Prayers to the Raven,* p. 246.

16. Thomas Hopko, *Spirituality,* Department of Religious Education, Orthodox Church in America, Syosset, N.Y., 1976, p. 134.

17. Eugene Trubetskoy, *Icons: Theology in Color,* p. 18–19.

18. Quoted in Arseniev, *Mysticism,* St. Vladimir's Seminary Press, 1979, p. 51.

I

O JOYFUL NORTH STAR OF THE CHURCH OF CHRIST

Editor's Note: A letter about the voyage to America written by Archimandrite Ioasaph (Bolotov) and Simeon Ianovskii's letter to Igumen Damascene of Valaam several decades later describe Father Herman's joyful character. Joy is a constant theme of the Gospel. The archangel greeted the Virgin with the exclamation "Rejoice" and other angels brought the shepherds near Bethlehem "tidings of great joy." The Apostles returned to Jerusalem from the Mount of Olives "with great joy, and were continually in the temple, praising and blessing God." The most frequently celebrated service in honor of St. Herman of Alaska, the "Akathistos Hymn," contains the command "Rejoice!"[1] nearly one hundred times. It is altogether proper, then, to begin with this theme of joy, the heavenly joy originating from the Good News of salvation itself.

The authors of these reports knew Father Herman at very different times. Father Ioasaph was his monastic superior, a fellow member of the Valaam community, who entrusted supervision of the mission in Kodiak to Father Herman when he departed for Siberia to report on conditions in the colony directly to government authorities in 1797. Together the two ascetics had labored and worshiped at Valaam. Together they traveled across Russia and sailed across the North Pacific. Together they faced the opposition and persecution of Alexander Baranov, the Russian American Company manager. Ioasaph was to be named bishop of Kodiak and sent back with authority to correct the situation there, only to perish on his return voyage in 1799 when the *Phoenix* went down in heavy seas.

Baranov's temporary replacement, Simeon Ianovskii, arrived at Kodiak nearly twenty years later. A well-educated member of the aristocratic Westernized elite, he probably suspected that the rumors accusing Father

Herman of sedition contained some truth. When he met the elder and became well acquainted with him, however, Ianovskii's life was irreversibly transformed. Although he spent less than two full years in Alaska, he himself entered a monastery in Russia after the death of his wife and composed this report about Father Herman for the igumen of Valaam, who was at that time conducting an inquiry into the life and deeds of the blessed Starets. Letters from Father Herman himself exhibit how the joyful personal character of Alaska's first saint shines through his correspondence.

LETTER FROM ARCHIMANDRITE IOASAPH TO IGUMEN NAZARII, MAY 1795

[*The letters following this introduction are taken from The Russian-Orthodox Religious Mission 1794–1837, Kingston, Ont.: Limestone Press. Reprinted by permission of Richard Pierce, publisher.*]

I set off from Moscow in 1794 on the twenty-second day of January. We celebrated Easter in Irkutsk. There we remained for a month. From Irkutsk we travelled along the Lena River for more than 2,000 versts, sailing calmly and at our pleasure. From Irkutsk to Okhotsk we covered more than 1,000 versts on horseback, with the other brothers; and our belongings were carried on 100 pack horses. Although river travel had been enjoyable, it was even better on horseback. We were able to see everything as we traversed forests, mountains and bivouacs. The pastures were everywhere lush, and the best season was May, June and July: but one had to beware of bears; we saw many of them—although they were friendly, our horses would take fright. We arrived in Okhotsk on 13th July, the town is on the very coast, and we then sailed past Kamchatka, cross the Kuriles and along the Aleutian chain. God allowed me to see things I had barely even heard of: sea whales, swallows, and otters. Beside our very ship the whales swam on the surface and played, so that we could get a good look at them. They were not large animals, perhaps 15 sazhens long, with heads 5 sazhens long. Beginning at Iakutsk everywhere we found willing Iakuts and baptized them; whenever we came to a river we would stop to do this. Although there are preachers locally, they charge much money to baptize. When we had travelled along the Aleutian chain by sea for only two days we came to the island of Unalashka—there we baptized more than one hundred people: they had been willing to be for some time, for they had been living constantly in the company of Russian hunters.

I have been living on the island of Kadiak since 24th September 1794. I have, praise God, baptized more than 7,000 Americans, and celebrated more than 2,000 weddings. We have built a church and, if time allows, we shall build another, and two portable ones, but a fifth is needed. We live comfortably, they love us and we them, they are a kind people, but poor. They take baptism so much to heart that they smash and burn all the magic charms given them by the shamans. You frightened us by saying they would be naked but, thank God, they have some conception of good sense; although they are not finely dressed they are at least not naked, and they walk around more neatly dressed than the Russians; although the clothes they wear are not expensive, made from birdskins, they are long, down to the heels and with the bottom unhemmed, like a surplice; there is only one aperture, where the head goes through; the smarter ones wear otter-skin clothes. Their diet consists of fish and various roots.

Father Herman works in the mill together with me and Father Ioasaf, formerly Koz'ma Alekseevich; Father Makarii Konevskii is very useful here, contrary to all expectations. I had not thought that he would make the journey here, but he has travelled round half the island almost alone, baptizing and wedding, and on the ship bearing this letter he has set off for the island of Unalashka and the surrounding islets to baptize the natives there. Afanasii is learning his way here and is mostly responsible for the allotment, digging the ground. Father Nektarii, and the good Hierodeacon Iuvenalii (the hieromonk and preacher-martyr) is quite sensible, while his brother, Father Stefan, who was made hierodeacon in Irkutsk, is, although a young man still, very kind, simple, helpful and wise, that if one had to choose from the brothers at Valaam it would be hard to find any more fitted to local conditions. As a result of your holy intercession I have been granted by God fellow-missionaries who are both kind and affectionate: I could not tell beforehand how God would strengthen me, all is well. I would describe to you everything that we are doing here but, forgive me, time will not permit it. There is such a press of people waiting to be baptized or married, or who have come to learn God's laws, and we do not want to grieve or hurt anyone by refusing them. In addition the Russians here have various needs of their own: they wish to talk to us and for us to hear confessions. When a ship is sailing I send off a report to His Grace (in Irkutsk), and send letters to Russia to the Company about various shortcomings here and any needs that we might have, and so on, and so on. In these short lines to you I seek only one favor from you, that you do not exclude us from the beloved brotherhood of Valaam, but that you still think of us as your own and keep us in your holy prayers. So far we have only been here for a short while and thus we have had little opportunity to look around. This coming spring, however, I intend to travel with Iuvenalii to the mainland of America, to Kenai Bay, and from there to Chugatsk, to the Ungalikhmiuts, and further to Yakutat, and I hope that God grants us success in our preaching of the Gospel.

I shall attempt to provide you with more detailed information with the next ship. I beseech all the brothers of Valaam, beloved brothers, not to forget us, savages, in their prayers, while we are amongst the world's tribulations constantly.

LETTER FROM THE MONK HERMAN TO IGUMEN NAZARII, MAY 1795

By the Grace of Almighty God and the help of your devout prayers we reached the shores of America safely, all ten of us; time does not allow for a full and detailed account of such a long journey; we were under way for almost a whole year; the episodes worthy of note were few, apart from our impressions of new places and means of transport: if you like, for the lovers of simple conversation, one can say that on the road to Okhotsk, as we rode on horseback, we were attacked by bears, and that at sea we came across various sea animals: whales, sea-cats, sea-pigs, seals and others in great numbers. There were no great storms except for one.

The Americans come very eagerly to be baptized, just under 7,000 have taken the faith. On Unalashka, during our journey through the Aleutian Islands, we were driven against our will into one bay by unfavorable winds, and the Aleuts there caused us great amazement by their kindness to us in distress and their willingness to be baptized. At the present time Father Makarii is setting out to preach and baptize on the Aleutian, Fox and Andreianov Islands and, soon after this, Father Iuvenalii will go to the mainland and, beginning at Kenai Bay, he will visit the Chugach and the Alegmiuts, the distant Kolosh, and many other tribes, as far even as Chilkhat. O! Here I am, anguished in spirit, with all the scarcity of time. To go on with the story, I must break the bounds for the very briefest moment, to add one detail. Caught as I am between the devil and the deep blue sea, joy and anguish, plenty and need, satiety and hunger, warmth and cold, with all my tribulations, I must relate something which amused me when I hear conversations between the brothers about preaching, and the various divisions of labor, in this activity, especially the debate between the hieromonks Makarii and Iuvenalii, for they set off to sail round Kadiak in one of the smallest skin-covered boats, heedless of all the dangers of the sea; the Father Archimandrite took leave of us in the harbor, as though we were small children. On one occasion I happened to be with the same two hieromonks as they developed their ideas along the same lines; we were walking about our harbor and went up on a hill facing south; we sat down facing the ocean and began to discuss who should go in which direction to preach, because the time of departure of the ships which we would have to travel upon was approaching. An argument then arose between them which I, in my humble way, found cheering and amusing. On Cook's charts there is one location marked to the north showing that Russians live along one of the rivers. We had heard various tales about them and these were referred to during this conversation; we all expressed the desire to meet them. Father Makarii began by saying, "I intend, if God wills it, when I am on the Aleutian Islands, to make my way to Aliaska whence I have been invited by the Aliaskans, and as this is near to where these Russians are supposed to live I shall seek ways of finding out more about them." But Father Iuvenalii, having heard the word Aliaska, in his eagerness to speak, broke in eagerly with, "Aliaska really belongs to my area, so I would ask you not to interfere there. When this next vessel leaves for Iakutan [Iakutat?] I shall begin preaching from the south. Then I shall go north along the coast, cross Kenai Bay, and from the port there I shall, of course, cross to Aliaska." When he heard this Father Makarii was very much saddened and, looking glum, said pleadingly: "No, Father, do not press me; you know yourself that the Aleutian chain is linked to Aliaska, therefore it must obviously be in my area, and the whole shore to the north also. You may have the whole of southern America if you like; there's enough there for the rest of your life." I, however, listening discreetly to such an argument, was overjoyed. Hieromonks Father Makarii and Father Iuvenalii are always so fervent, almost like madmen wanting to rush off in all directions. Father Afanasii stays with us, so that we should not be without a hieromonk, and to carry out the celebrating of the services and the baptizing of those who come to us.

LETTER FROM THE MONK HERMAN TO IGUMEN JONATHAN OF VALAAM, 13 DECEMBER 1819

Your Reverence, kind sir, respected Father Ionafan, we wish you and your brothers may enjoy the love of Christ and the Lord.

To our great surprise your much desired and extremely kind but unexpected letter, dated 8th November, 1818, arrived here 10th November, 1819 and acted as a streak of joyous lightning in the midst of our troubles. It filled us with the light of joy, humble as we are and so far away, living for so long in darkness and covered in oblivion.

We have no adequate means by which to show our gratitude for your love, apart from this humble, insignificant letter, by means of which we give heartfelt thanks for your first letter, and we would ask of you from your side, if it be possible, that you favor us with another written visitation like this present one and to inform us for what reason Father Nazarii left Valaam for the Sarovsk Settlement, whether he was sent there or went of his own free will, and also in what year and month he died, also how many hieromonks and hierodeacons there are in your Holy Valaam Monastery, and who they are, whether they are from among my former acquaintances or all are newcomers.

We also beg you, as you have been so kind as to remember us and write to us, to remember and pay heed to our humble state, before almighty God, in your holy prayers. We are not on the storm-tossed waves of the sea, but are suffering amongst the tempting and tempestuous world and on a pilgrimage of the Apostolic word. Although we do not have the grace which the Holy Apostles enjoyed, yet our battle is with the same fleshly and worldly powers, with the spirit of darkness in the world in this age, with all the evil spirits under heaven, who try to seize all those on their pilgrimage to the heavenly kingdom and hold them back and not allow them in the words of St. Peter: 'because your adversary the devil, as a roaring lion, walketh about, seeking whom he may devour'; in such cases we are weak and powerless and naturally need to seek aid from your Holy prayers.

Do not forget our most esteemed Holy Fathers, do not forget to mention our poverty before the Almighty King of Heaven; we ask this of all those in your sacred monastery.

We have the honor to report to you on the country and place we live in and on our conditions. The country you know is America.

The main island is Kadiak and on it are the company harbor and the church of the resurrection of Christ; we have been given a house here by the company, which was given us as soon as we arrived. The country is cold, though the winters are not so cold but they are changeable with rain and snow mixed. The summers begin late and with a cold spell. Amongst the garden vegetables there are only turnips, radishes and potatoes and nothing else will ripen. Grain will not germinate and so no one sows it, and there are only small supplies of imported grain. Amongst the self-sown vegetables there are the root crops, the first of which is called sarana and tastes rather bitter, though it is widely used here. It is just mixed with berries after it has been boiled and in this form it is called *shiksha*—which is eaten with helpings of whale fat and is in these parts considered a delicacy. Another root is called *makarsha* and is very difficult to gather. It is eaten both raw and cooked—it has a rather nutty flavor, but it is in short supply. There are also raspberries, not like the Russian ones, but a different species. There are also bilberries and whortleberries, but very few blackberries. Sufficient quantities of berries are available each year and a suitable quantity of shiksha especially can be laid in. In winter whale blubber is prepared: and in fact it does occur at Valaam Hermitage but is called *voronitsa* and is not eaten. There are extraordinarily large quantities of different species of fish—but whales are considered the best. There are also other sea animals here and they are also eaten. There are few people here on Kadiak and on the other islands. They are called Aleuts. They are peaceful and very poor. Many speak Russian and are kindly disposed towards us and have friends amongst us. The mainland is forty versts away from us to the north. On the eastern side there are other tribes known as the Kenai, the Chugach, Kolosh and many others that we know quite well.

We, all the men of Valaam, the three of us that you know about, do not live together. Father Afanasii lives forty versts from the church on the island of Afognak which is separated from Kadiak by a narrow strait. Father Ioasaf, whom you mention as your lay-brother, lives in the harbor at the church in the house of which I made mention above. He looks after the library and the vestments and on Sundays, together with some of the boys from the school, he conducts the services in the church. I live ten versts away from the harbor on a special little island, which is called New Valaam. Near my dwelling is the tiniest of streams which in summer contains reasonable quantities of fish. I live alone. Some two versts away are three families of Americans, and with great love they help me in my labors. Father Ioasaf often comes to see me in one of the little American boats made of leather, which are here called *baidarki*. We have plots here containing vegetables. The Americans living near are natives and help us in everything.

As for the remaining brothers I believe you heard about them in the first year after our arrival. Two hieromonks, Father Makarii and Father Iuvenalii who had been an assistant in our monastery and was a former officer called Iakov Fedorovich and when he entered the monastery in St. Petersburg given the name Iuvenalii, set off to preach, Makarii to the Aleutian Islands of the Fox Chain and from there he returned to Russia, and Iuvenalii went to the eastern coast of the mainland, first of all to Chugatsk Bay where he baptized all the people. Then he set off northwards along the coast, crossing the mountains to Kenai Bay where he spent the winter baptizing the natives. Then he went further north and crossed Alaska. There he was killed by some of the tribesmen, though rumors vary as to in what manner, and by exactly which tribe. There is still no reliable information. After this our Father Archimandrite was summoned to Russia to be made an archbishop. He accepted this honor in the town of Irkutsk and returned, in the company of the above-mentioned Hieromonk Makarii, and they were already off Kadiak, judging by the pieces of ship washed up, when the ship was wrecked in an unknown place. And so now there are only three of us left alive, thanks to Almighty God. For all our somber circumstances and adventures we live happily and peacefully on our own; our only worry is togain entry to the Kingdom of Heaven. For this we pray and beseech you, kind Reverend Father, to help our humble selves with your holy prayers—in hope of which I remain

Your Reverence's
Obedient servant and fervent subject
Humble Herman

I also ask you to bear witness to my heartfelt respect for Father Iakov, formerly Ivan Alekseevich, the brother of our monk Ioasaf, although I did not have the chance to know him personally, and also for Gavriil Terent'-evich—I rejoice many times over for them and thank God.

Humble Herman

13th December, 1819
America, Kadiak Island

LETTER FROM THE MONK HERMAN TO SIMEON IANOVSKII (YANOVSKY), 20 JUNE 1820

Your Honor
Gracious Sir
Semen Ivanovich

I have had the honor to receive your kind, pleasant and gracious letter containing its interesting news, and the packet with it. I offer my heartfelt gratitude—I have nothing else to give you. I thank Almighty God for keeping you well and protecting you from all misadventures on land and on the sea, but even more for having in his incalculable ways shown you the true path by following which we may all achieve eternal joy, and by thus fulfilling the duty of our existence we shall fulfil the will of our Creator, who brought us into life for this sole purpose!

I had already been assured of your good disposition towards my humble self even before I met you personally. And I hope to retain this affection in future. So that now be gracious and without disdaining my unworthiness show more and more of the milk of human kindness to my humble self as I am making myself more and more unworthy before you, hoping that you will not only not be angry at my ignorance and coarseness, but that you will be generous in forgiving them, for it is not because I like the role of teacher, but because I feel that to do so, and to help others is my duty. My opinions are based on the teachings of the Holy Scriptures, and they are aimed at those who are thirsting and searching for His eternal Kingdom in Heaven.

Faith and love of Christ make a true Christian. Our sins in no way hinder our Christianity, as we can tell from the words of our Saviour himself. He stated that he had not been called to judge the righteous but to save the sinful—there is more joy in Heaven at one sinner who repents than at ninety-nine righteous men. And he also said to Simon the Pharisee, about the woman who was a sinner and washed his feet: much is forgiven to those who love and much is asked of those who have no love. Such thoughts should give the Christian hope and joy and not lead to utter desperation. This is where the shield of faith is needed.

A sin for a person loving God is nothing more than an arrow fired by an enemy during battle. The true Christian is a warrior, fighting his way through hosts of unseen foes to his place in Heaven. For, in the words of the Apostle, Our Kingdom is in Heaven, and about the warrior he says: our battle is not with flesh and blood, but with ideas and authorities.

The empty acceptance of this wish makes the Kingdom more distant; and love for it and habit clothe our soul with a kind of dirty garment, called by the Apostles the outer man. We, on our journey through life, must call on God for help, and we have to shed this filth and clothe ourselves in new desires and new love for the coming ages, and thereby come to know our nearness or distance from our Heavenly Father. But it is impossible to do this quickly; but we must follow the example of the sick who, wishing to be of sound health again, seek every means to effect a cure. I am not explaining very well because I am hurrying, there is not enough time. But I hope that you, with your sharpness of intellect, and your ardent wish for joy in Heaven, may discover the path to Holy Truth, not only for yourself but for others.

Now I shall talk about matters of another kind.

When you left Kadiak, either through God's wrath or His holy workings for our good, the epidemic which we had continued for some little while. It caused the death of many of the young women and left their children orphans. Amongst the dead were the godmother of Leont'ii Andreianovicha and Anna Aleksandrovna, the wife of Khristofor the employee at the Church, but it did not touch my late daughter's five young children. To the Glory of the holy mystery of God He has recently, through his unfathomable workings, shown me something which in all my twenty-five years here on Kadiak I had never seen before. Just after last Easter a young woman of no more than twenty who spoke good Russian and who was previously unknown to me and whom I had never seen, came to me and heard about how the Son of God was made flesh, and about eternal life and she was so filled with love for Jesus Christ that she would not leave me, but she pleaded with me with great conviction, against my inclination and my love of solitude and in spite of all the obstacles and difficulties I brought up, to take her on, and she has been living with me now for more than a month and is not bored. I have observed this with great amazement, recalling the words of the Saviour that what is hidden from the wise and clever is revealed to babes. There are other women who see her and wish to do the same. But the trouble is that I have not the strength to build a separate dwelling for them. There are also many young men who would like to come but there is no room for them.

Eremei who lives on Katmai came to see me with his children, and with a toen who had a complaint to Eremei about Epifanov. But this toen, who had previously been an interpreter with the Russians, told me himself that the complaint had been made in anger to Epifanov about Eremei by the present toen but in vain, and Eremei himself told me that, concerning the sea otters, he had given Ershev 680 pelts, and Ershev had given Epifanov 300, and that he had for a great many years been a faithful servant to various baidarshchiks, for which he had received a medal from Aleksandr Andreevich [Baranov], and that there were now surplus otters against the company goods, and only Ershev was short, and where could he have put so many—it all seemed an obvious lie.

Please be so kind as to despatch my letter to Valaam whenever you are able.

Farewell, farewell, our kind benefactor, time does not allow me to write more. Forgive my bad writing, even it is carried out in conditions of great hardship, for my eyes almost refuse to serve me. Forgive me also that in return for your kindness and blessing I can pay nothing but gratitude from myself and my colleague Ioasaf. We accept your gracious kindness not only with feeling but with surprise. It is with wholehearted gratitude that I remain

Thanking you
Your Obedient Servant
Humble Herman

I tender my respects to your noble and kind wife, Anna Aleksandrovna, and your kind little son Aleksandr Semenovich. Humble Herman.

LETTER FROM SIMEON IANOVSKII (YANOVSKY) TO IGUMEN DAMASCENE OF VALAAM, 22 NOVEMBER 1865

Your Reverence,
Most Worthy Father Damascene.

I enclose, in the original, two letters written by my unforgettable benefactor, the Holy Elder, the monk Herman. I would like, when you have taken copies of them, to have the originals returned to me so that they may remain as a treasured memento in my family; but if you should wish to keep them then I would most humbly beg you to return at least one to me, as you see fit.

Calling God to my aid, and mentally seeking your blessing, I shall describe to you everything I know about Father Herman with whom I first became closely acquainted in 1819. He often told me himself how from his very earliest years he had been very eager to serve God, and how he had entered the monastery at the age of 16, first the Troitsko-Sergiev hermitage, near St. Petersburg, and then subsequently Valaam. In the Sergiev hermitage the following incident involving him took place: A swelling came up on the right side of his neck under his chin. It gave him terrible pain and had soon grown to such an extent that it disfigured the whole of his face. It made it difficult for him to swallow and gave off a terrible odor so that people began to give him a wide berth. He could no longer go to the refectory and even in his cell he could only down a few spoonfuls of thin soup or mushroom bouillon. In such grievous condition, expecting any moment to die, he did not have recourse to any earthly doctor, but addressed himself with fervent prayers to the Heavenly Mother. He locked himself up in his cell and wept and prayed all night. Then he took a clean towel, wet it and with it he wiped the icon of the Mother of God and then bound the same towel around the boil on his neck. He continued to pray and weep until he collapsed into slumber there on the earthen floor. And he dreamt that he saw the Mother of God curing him! When he awoke he got up and saw to his great amazement that he was completely well and that the swelling had gone down without coming to a head and bursting; just a small mark on the skin remained as a sign of the miracle that had taken place! The doctors to whom he related this subsequently would not believe him, saying the boil must have burst or been lanced. But the Lord knows better. When he was at Valaam, Father Herman would often go off into the forest with two or three companions and live there, spending the time in prayer until those in the monastery came out to find them and accompany them home. In the last years of the reign of the Empress Catherine II the Monastery was asked to provide volunteers to preach and to convert the idol-worshippers to the Orthodox faith. He then volunteered, together with the other monks and hieromonks. And a party of them set out already in the time of the Emperor Paul. They were directed first of all to Irkutsk. In Irkutsk they wished to make Father Herman a hieromonk, or even an archimandrite, but he refused and remained a simple monk. It would seem that they arrived in Northwest America in 1794, at the island of Kadiak, at Three Saints Bay. The complete mission consisted of 12 hieromonks and monks. Soon after their arrival they built a small wooden church and cells, and the resulting monastery they named New Valaam. At that time the Aleuts were all idol-worshippers of the Shaman sect and made human sacrifice, even of children. All the Aleutian Islands and Cape Aliaska had been subdued and annexed to Russia by Shelekhov and the merchant Baranov. But the inhabitants were all pagans. Thus our missionaries eagerly set about preaching the word of God, and after a short while, some ten years, they had succeeded in baptizing almost all the Aleuts and many of the peoples on the mainland. Some of the missionaries had suffered for the faith, had been tortured or killed because they preached against polygamy; and others had died. When I arrived in America at Sitkha Island in 1817, in July, there remained of the total mission one hieromonk, Ioasaf, and one hierodeacon, Iona. Father Herman, when I first came across him, was leading a strictly ascetic life. He lived alone, one and a half versts from the port, on a small wooded island known as Spruce Island. He had a cell, i.e., a rough hut, a garden, nets and he did his own work. He sowed potatoes and cabbage, dug vegetable patches, caught fish and stored them for the winter. Aleuts of both sexes with their children often came to visit him—for advice, with complaints against the authorities, seeking his protection, and with various other needs; sometimes they brought him fish and helped him with his work. He always welcomed them, pacified them, and helped them as best he could. On Sundays and feast days many people came to him to pray. Father Herman told the hours, the Acts and the Gospel, and sang and preached. He would give the children biscuits or bake them cracknels. The children loved him and he loved them. But because he revealed many as leading a life of drunkenness, as being revoltingly sinful and oppressing the Aleuts, he made many enemies, and brought upon himself much unpleasantness and slander. He suffered all this and bore his heavy cross in silence.

I have already mentioned that in the year of 1817 I had arrived in America at the island of Sitkha, the site of the main administrative office for all the colonies of Northwest America. In the following year I married the daughter of the Chief Manager of the American colonies, Baranov, and shortly afterwards, in the same year, I was appointed by the government to take over the administration, and Baranov returned to Russia. Sitkha is situated some 1,500 versts east of Kadiak, separated from it by open ocean. I must confess that I myself heard such slanderous tales about Father Herman that I had begun to write back to St. Petersburg about him, even before I had met him. It was reported to me that he was encouraging the Aleuts to rise in rebellion against the authorities there. But in the following year, 1819, I set off by boat to make a tour of inspection of all the colonies, and in November I arrived at the island of Kadiak. Father Herman immediately came to see me. He explained local conditions to me, how poor the Aleuts were, in what need they were, and how they were in various ways oppressed, and he asked me to protect them. I promised to look into all this and do what I could. And so I set to work, that is, a detailed revision of everything: I received complaints, made inspections; there was much to be done, so that I was busy for the whole day. I invited Father Herman to join me for dinner and evening tea, at seven.

At this juncture I must give you some details about myself. I was thirty. I had been educated at the Naval Academy. I was acquainted with many sciences and had read a great deal; but unfortunately the science of sciences, i.e. God's Law, I knew only superficially and even then only in theory, without applying it to life; and I was a Christian in name only, but in my soul and in fact I was a free-thinker, a deist, like almost all the others who had been educated in the academies and in government institutions. What a pity that little attention is given to this fact: that God's Law is taught only superficially, even in the seminaries; and indeed even the religious academies produce pupils, even magisters, who are very learned, but who have no real faith in their hearts, and because of this they do not lead Christian lives.

Not only did I fail to recognize the godliness and sanctity of our religion but I had read many godless works by Voltaire and other eighteenth-century philosophers. Father Herman noticed this at once and wished to turn me away from it. But it was not easy! I had to be convinced: the sanctity of our religion had to be proved to me, and this took a great deal of time, knowledge and the ability to argue persuasively. To my great surprise the simple, uneducated monk Father Herman, inspired by God's Grace, spoke so skilfully, forcefully and convincingly, and offered such proof, that no learning or earthly wisdom could stand against it! In fact, Father Herman had a great natural intellect, much common sense; he was well read in the writings of the holy fathers; but the main thing was that he had God's Grace! But as in the short winter days I had absolutely no time to be with him, he came to take evening tea with me every day, and sometimes at supper, and he and I would sit talking until midnight, and sometimes later. He would never stay the night. Neither rain, nor blizzard, nor storm could prevent the enthusiastic elder from visiting me and then making the half-verst journey home alone at midnight! He would come to see me every day dressed in an ancient habit without a topcoat, I would warm him with tea, and we would have endless discussions: about God's love, about eternity, the salvation of the soul, the Christian life, and so forth. The sweet words poured in an endless, intriguing stream from his lips. Then, at midnight or later, the elder would return home alone, leaning on his staff, whatever the cold, and however stormy the weather. No one went with him along the slippery, stony path; but the angels accompanied him and looked after him—"For the Angel of the Lord shall protect you and keep you wherever you go." And he was warmed by Christian love, the love which burned in him for the salvation of others. With such constant discourses and the old man's prayers the Lord brought me completely onto the true path, and I became a real Christian. For all this I am obliged to Father Herman; he is my true benefactor!

During my stay on the island of Kadiak there was brought there a contagious, fatal epidemic disease, or plague. This began with a fever and a heavy cold, a cough, shortness of breath, choking, and three days later death followed! There were neither doctors nor medicines there; the sickness quickly spread throughout the whole settlement and soon crossed to all the nearby islands. The energetic elder Father Herman ceaselessly, tirelessly and at great personal risk visited the sick, not sparing himself in his role as priest—counselling those suffering to be patient, pray, repent and prepare themselves for death. I, in the course of my duties as administrator and out of sympathy for human suffering, visited them all every day, and took all possible measures to help. I gave advice, gave people tea with elder or camomile, as it came, and issued food—many people were helped by eating warm food—but many were dying. The epidemic affected everyone, even babes in arms; my family: my wife and young babies were also ill, as was I myself. The death rate was so high that after three days there was no one to dig the graves and the corpses lay around unburied. It was good the weather was frosty, because there was no smell.

I can imagine nothing more somber and terrifying than the spectacle which greeted me when I visited the Aleut *kazhim!* This is a large barn or barracks with board partitions, in which the Aleuts live with their families. In it were almost one hundred people. I visited them all, talking to them, questioning, advising, cheering them up and comforting them. Some were lying already dying, their bodies growing cold, next to those who were still alive; others were already dead: groans and screams tore at my heart. I saw mothers already dead, on whose cold breasts hungry children crawled, crying and trying to find food for themselves, but in vain! My heart contracted with pity, struck with horror, when I saw this melancholy picture of death. No artist could convey in sufficient colors this picture for the illumination of those who are wallowing in luxury, forgetful of death.

Finally I myself grew weak and prepared for death; but merciful God had decided to spare me. At night I drank elder-tea, wrapped myself up and sweated, and then I began to feel better. It would seem that only Father Herman was not affected; for everyone else was, and a good third had died! When the sickness and mortality began visibly to decrease I had already accomplished the business of my visit and I was in haste to return to Sitkha, to the port of Novo-Arkhangel'sk, where my permanent residence was and where much important official business awaited me. Now when I bade farewell to Father Herman, I was doing so to a friend, to my mentor and benefactor. I asked him to pray for me, and set sail.

Several years ago he even converted a certain naval captain G. from the Lutheran faith. This captain was very well educated; in addition to many sciences, he knew languages: in addition to Russian he knew German, French, English, Italian and a little Spanish, and he was well-read, yet with all this he could not withstand the convincing proofs offered by Father Herman; he changed to the Orthodox faith and accepted the sacrament. When he left the island the Elder said to him as they took their leave of each other: "If your present wife should die, take care under no circumstances to marry a German. If you do she will undoubtedly persuade you to forsake the Orthodox faith." He gave him his promise that he would never do so, but he did not keep it. The far-sighted Elder had warned him. Several years later his wife died and he married a German woman and he probably left or grew less attached to the Russian faith. He soon died without repenting.

This is the way in which the Elder was gifted with spiritual wisdom: Once he was invited to dine, aboard the frigate which had arrived from St. Petersburg, with Captain G., who had been sent, on Imperial instructions, to inspect all the colonies. Captain G. was a very intelligent and educated man. At his table there were some 25 officers, chosen from the best in the fleet, all well educated and learned. And in such a company of educated men, together at table with them, sat a simple monk, a small man, wearing threadbare clothes, ill-educated. And he put to them questions which stumped them all, which they could not answer. Captain G. told me this himself: "We had no answers, we were like fools in front of him!" He put to them the question, "What do you love most and dearest of all? What would make you happy?"

Many wishes were expressed in answer to this: one wanted riches, another fame, another a beautiful wife, another a splendid ship to sail on, and many other things.

Father Herman said: "Is it not true that of all your answers and desires one thing may be concluded: each of you gentlemen requires that which he thinks best and loves most?"

They all answered that that was so. Then he said to them, "What could be better, higher, more worthy of love and more splendid than Our Lord Jesus Christ himself, who created the firmament, and adorned everything, gave life to everything, who keeps everything, feeds everything and loves everything—who is himself love, more splendid than all men! Should you not love God above all things, wish for Him and seek Him?"

They all answered: "Of course we love God; how can one not love God!"

At this he sighed, let fall a tear, and said: "I, poor sinner, have been trying to learn how to love God for more than forty years, and I cannot say even now that I love him properly." And he showed them how one should love God: "If we love someone, then we think of him always. We try to please him day and night, our heart and mind are full of the object of our love. So then, gentlemen, do you love God? Do you turn to Him often? Do you remember Him always, always pray and perform His will, his Holy Scriptures?"

They had to admit that they did not.

"For our good, for our happiness," he said, "let us make a vow: at least that from this day, this hour, this very minute, we should try to love God above all else and carry out His teachings."

This is how intelligently and beautifully he spoke in the company of those who would remember what he said for the rest of their lives!

Once I asked him: "Father Herman, how can you live on this island, alone in the forest? Do you not get lonely?"

He replied, "No, I am not alone, God is there, just as He is everywhere, and the Holy Angels are there also. How can I be lonely? With whom is it better and more pleasant to speak—people or angels? Angels, of course!"

Others have told me how in winter they had seen bears near his dwelling, how he would feed them and then they would wander off again. It should be noted here that the employees of the American Company issue from the stores grain and other supplies for the up-keep of the monks, but sometimes there is no grain. No wheat is sown there and it will not grow, but rye is brought by transport the ten thousand versts from Irkutsk, which makes the local price for rye flour 12 rubles paper per pud; or wheat is brought the two thousand versts from California, which then puts a price of 5 rubles paper per pud on wheat flour; but sometimes the boat is shipwrecked or is late, which then creates a shortage of grain. So then they eat fish, of which there is a plentiful supply of a variety of species in the summer. In addition they eat the flesh of all sea-animals—sea lion, walrus, seal, sea otter, and many shellfish. Whenever Father Herman dined with me he would eat what was served to him, for example: thin soup with pork or chicken, but would never eat the flesh; or he would take only bouillon, gruel and potatoes. At that time I did not know that monks did not eat meat, but he once said to me himself: "I think you are surprised to find me eating a meat dish?"

When I said that I was not, he himself explained to me: "Monks are forbidden to eat meat or meat dishes; but here, because of the poverty and local food shortages, particularly of grain, the Synod has permitted the consumption of meat."

He tried to pacify everyone, especially in cases of family dissension. If he did not succeed in placating a couple then he would separate them for a short while. This he told me himself: "Better that they should live apart than fight and row all the time. If not separated there have been cases where husbands have killed their wives, or wives have murdered their husbands!''

It seems to me that this simple rule might be applied to us as well, because our cruel peasants, especially when drunk, beat and kill their wives. I know this from my experience as a landowner.

Father Herman loved children and was very kind to them. My little son Aleksandr, then a year old, and who is now the Hieromonk Kristofor, was always being carried in his arms and comforted, so that he would go to him willingly. He once said to me: ''You are going to Russia, to St. Petersburg. Do not take with you there your wife, who was born here and who has not seen the wide world, its captivating luxuries, its temptations and its sins. Better to leave her with your mother in the Ukraine, while you yourself go about your business in St. Petersburg!''

I gave him my word, but I did not keep it. She did not want to be without me on any account. I took her with me and within a year I had lost her. She died in St. Petersburg. He even tried to persuade me to remain in America but I had already applied for a replacement. In 1821 I left America.

I shall continue with my narrative about Father Herman: I had in all four letters from him, it would seem; it does not seem likely there were any more because post from those in Kadiak arrives only once a year. But only two of these letters have been preserved. One I received in Sitkha, in answer to one of my letters; and the second in Sitkha also. There was also a letter which I received in St. Petersburg, but this has been lost. And so it is these two letters that I am offering you.

After my period of office Father Herman was subjected to great pressure and persecution, so that he carried his cross to the end. In my letters from other sources I was told that after I had left a priest arrived from Irkutsk with wide-ranging powers from the bishop. This priest despatched Hieromonk Iosaf back to Irkutsk; the hierodeacon was already dead. He harried Father Herman, inventoried and took away everything he had, which came to the sum of eight thousand paper rubles. This money and other items had been collected for the building of a new church to replace the whole of the old rickety structure. He had himself told me how he was making this collection. Other people looked upon it as Father Herman's 'personal fortune', but this cannot have been the case. It is true that he never refused to accept offerings, be they food, money or other articles: but he also gave out again many things to those who had nothing, while the money was put aside for the reconstruction of the monastery. He himself always wore no shirt, having next to his bare skin a deerskin *kukhlianka*—a kind of shirt which, as he himself told me, he had not taken off or changed for eight years. As a consequence the fur had already rotted and gone thin, and the skin itself was stained. In addition he wore canvas breeches, *bashmaks* or shoes, an undervestment, an ancient threadbare habit, patched and darned in many places, and a cowl. Wearing these clothes he would appear before me in all kinds of weather—rain, blizzard, storm or cold! This is what Christian love means—far different from earthly! What did he expect of me, what was he looking for? He only wished to save the soul of someone in error! May God remember him in Heaven, and may he enter into the joy of the Lord! And so the priest from Irkutsk was harsh and rude to him in many ways and even wanted to send him back to Irkutsk; but my successor would not let him do this and protected the Elder. After many labors and great tribulations he passed peacefully to the Lord there on Kadiak Island in 1825, in which month I cannot recall.

He was of medium height, his face was round, pleasant-featured and happy, with a ready smile. His speech was not loud, always pleasant and what he said was always interesting, instructive and useful. He liked to talk and spoke wisely, in a businesslike way, to the point. More than anything he liked talking about eternity, salvation, the next life, and God's miracles, the Holy Martyrs; here he never said an empty word. He related many episodes from the lives of the saints and the *Prologue*. He was very pleasant to listen to and the ordinary Aleuts and their womenfolk loved to do so. There were few grey hairs on his head, and he wore a small beard. His face was pale and lined, his eyes grey-blue and twinkling. When I knew him he was 65, and he was 70 when he died. He loved me as a son, and was overjoyed at my conversion to the true Faith. One day I recited to him Derzhavin's "Ode to God". He was amazed and full of praise and asked me to read it again. I did so and he asked: "Was this a simple or a learned man who wrote this?" I told him it was written by a learned poet. "It was inspired by God!" he replied.

Once I related to him how the Spaniards in California had taken fourteen of our Aleuts prisoner, and how the Jesuits* had tortured one of them, to try and force them all to take the Catholic faith. But the Aleuts would not submit, saying: "We are Christians, we have been baptized," and they showed them the crosses they wore. But the Jesuits objected, saying "No, you are heretics and schismatics; if you do not agree to take the Catholic faith we will torture you." And they left them shut up two to a cell until the evening to think it over. In the evening they came back with a lantern and lighted candles, and began again to try and persuade them to become Catholics. But the Aleuts were filled with God's grace, and firmly and decisively answered, "We are Christians and we would not betray our faith." Then the fanatics set about torturing them. First they tortured one singly

*Since Jesuits were not active in California at this time Ianovskii either errs through ignorance of Roman Catholic religious orders or refers to any Western clergy as "Jesuit."

while the other one was made to watch. First they cut off one of the toe joints from one foot, and then from the other, but the Aleut bore it all and continued to say: "I am a Christian and I will not betray my faith." Then they cut a joint off each finger—first from one hand, then the other; then they hacked off one foot at the instep, then one hand at the wrist. The blood poured out, but the martyr bore it all to the end, maintaining his stand, and with this faith he died, from loss of blood! On the following day it was planned to torture the others, but that same night an order was received from Monterey that all the captured Russian Aleuts were to be sent under guard to Monterey. And so in the morning those remaining alive were sent away. This was related to me by an Aleut who was an eyewitness—a colleague of the man put to death—and who later escaped from the Spaniards. At the time I reported all this to the Head Office in St. Petersburg.

When I had finished telling him this, Father Herman asked me, "What was the name of this tortured Aleut?"

"Petr," I replied, "but I cannot remember the other name."

Then the Elder stood before the icon, devoutly crossed himself and said, "Holy, newly-martyred Petr, pray to God for us!"

I have finished my narrative about my beloved elder and mentor Father Herman. I have written as best I am able; or as God has seen fit to guide and help me. But with all my soul I have tried to compose this as well as possible so as best and most faithfully to reflect the worthy Elder. If some parts are infelicitous, please forgive me! I have done what I could. I am a feeble old man—I am 77—and am on the edge of the grave: Know therefore that the Lord has borne my life in patience so that I might convey information about the life of the Holy Elder.

II

GUIDING ALL TO THE HEAVENLY KINGDOM

Editor's Note: To lead others to Christ, as Metropolitan Gabriel had reminded the Valaam mission as it set out for America, is to perform an Apostolic ministry. The personal character and example of the missionary is central to this work. When the monks from Finland arrived in Kodiak, however, they recognized that the success of their evangelical efforts was jeopardized by the immoral conduct of their countrymen, and by instructions from their superiors they thought would be counter-productive. The first report dispatched to Siberia about conditions in Alaska contains many accusations and complaints, directed somewhat naively to Gregory Shelikov, the founder of the colony. Archimandrite Ioasaph hoped that Shelikov would soon intervene and remove his manager Baranov, whom Ioasaph personally blamed for the corruption he discovered at Kodiak.

Perhaps more importantly, Ioasaph is willing to overlook many serious shortcomings, and while threatening to report these to more powerful secular and ecclesiastical authorities, he instead awaits Shelikov's intervention—except in one instance. Ioasaph is willing to tolerate many of the indignities and inconveniences he describes, but will not permit children to be removed from their homeland. He suggests that the hierarchy reconsider its directive to send students to Russia for training, and that a school be established at Kodiak instead. A few years later, Ioasaph will argue and win this point with his superiors at Irkutsk, and gain support for an indigenous seminary, only to have these hopes dashed with the sinking of the *Phoenix* with Ioasaph, his faculty, and his books on board. It is obvious from his 1795 report, however, that from the very beginning the Valaam monks intended to conduct a traditional Orthodox mission, in the spirit of St. Stephen of Perm and the Siberian missionaries who followed him, in providing a personal example of Christian life within their community and in educating native leaders for service in the Church, teaching and worshiping in their own language.

Ioasaph's second report indicates the extent to which the Valaam Mission studied the traditional religious beliefs of the Kodiak people, and arrived at a rather positive assessment of them. His third report, taken from the minutes of the Holy Synod in 1798, contains further information on pre-Christian Aleut religion. Any competent teacher must first assess the student's level and establish realistic educational goals on that basis.

Simeon Ianovskii is again the main source for the biographical details of St. Herman's later years. In these letters, Ianovskii describes the impact the elder's personal example and piety had on those who knew him. A Kodiak Aleut, Constantine Larionoff, also knew Father Herman personally and gathered his biographical data at the request of church authorities.

At the end of this section, the *"Pathway Into the Kingdom of Heaven"* is reproduced in a new translation by Paul Garrett, author of *St. Innocent, Apostle to America,* a biography of Veniaminov. The "Pathway" was first published in Unangan (Fox Island dialect) Aleut, and was subsequently translated into several European languages. This work, together with Veniaminov's catechism and *Gospel of St. Matthew,* constituted the beginning of native-language literacy in Alaska. Veniaminov, however, was always careful to credit his assistant, the Aleut leader Ivan Pan'kov, with guiding and assisting him with every aspect of the translation, and Pan'kov's name appears together with Veniaminov's on the title pages.

John Popov was born in Siberia in 1798, raised by his uncle, and educated at the Irkutsk seminary. After marrying his wife, Katherine, and accepting ordination, he volunteered for missionary service in Alaska, where he arrived with his brother, mother, wife, and infant son in 1824. Having been awarded the name of a recently deceased and highly respected bishop, Veniamin (Benjamin), for his superior academic performance, Father John enthusiastically undertook to learn all that he could about his flock and their traditional culture as well as their natural environment. He took careful notes of the weather, tides, flora, and fauna of the region and compiled a grammar of the local language. One of his first tasks was to construct a church building, for which a local self-taught Aleut man, Ivan Kruikov, painted some original icons.

Since the Aleutian Islands had been visited by Hieromonk Makarii (1795–1798) and Hieromonk Gideon (1807), Father Veniaminov found the entire Aleut population already baptized, but requiring instruction to deepen their commitment to and understanding of the faith. It was for this purpose that he began work on his sermon, the "Indication of the Pathway," reproduced here.

In the library of Orthodox spirituality, the work is hardly a classic. Veniaminov studied theology in a small rural secondary school and, despite his brilliant academic career, lost his opportunity to continue his studies on the university level (at a theological "academy") by marrying and volunteering for duty in America. The essay echoes much Westernized legalism, especially in its emphasis on Christ's suffering and agony, not characteristic of traditional Orthodox piety. The section on interior crosses originated from a book banned by ecclesiastical censors as inconsistent with Orthodox doctrine, but Father John, far removed from the intellectual centers of the empire, could not have realized this. Certainly these defects are more a matter of style and emphasis than of dogmatic significance, and the booklet became quite popular not only in the original Aleut, but in later Russian and German translations. As an example of the first Aleut book specifically written to "guide all to the Heavenly Kingdom" the "Pathway" represents a major contribution to the development of Orthodox Christian spirituality in nineteenth-century Alaska.

LETTER FROM ARCHIMANDRITE IOASAPH TO GREGORY SHELIKOV, 18 MAY 1795

[*Translated by Lydia Black, University of Alaska, Fairbanks.*]

Benevolent Sir, Gregory Ivanovich [Shelikov]

Dear Friend and Patron! The love, respect and affection I have for you I can feel better than I can express the same on paper. I do not think that it is even necessary to do so, as it is not flattery and therefore does not require much proof. Thus leaving aside empty compliments, I shall talk to you about the following:

Having departed from Okhotsk August 13, we arrived in Kodiak safely on the 24th of September [1794]. Throughout the winter there were many visitors who came voluntarily—inhabitants of Kodiak and also Alaskans [from the Alaska Peninsula], Kenai people and Chugach. We did baptize many.

We as yet have no church. We asked for a tent of the manager, Alexander Andreevich [Baranov], but so far without result. Though Alexander Andreevich himself arranged for the construction of a small church the cornerstone was laid the 21st of November [for a 4 sazhen church, with a $1^1/_2$ trapeza], the building stands to this day unfinished. I decided not to report about the field church to the Metropolitan. Since my arrival at the harbor, I find nothing whatsoever that should have been done in accordance with your good intentions accomplished. My only delight is in the Americans who are coming from everywhere to be baptized. The Russians not only do not aid them in this but on the contrary employ all possible means to scare them off. The reason for this is their dissolute life which is put to shame by the good conduct of the Americans. I was barely able to convince some of the promishlenniki to get married. The rest do not want to hear of it, but openly keep women, even more than one each, which constitutes a great insult to the Americans. You know how Baranov likes women, and he will chase them in the face of any kind of danger! I am unable to ascertain what enraged Mr. Baranov more—our arrival here itself or our impassioned reprimands of him. All signs indicate he agitates the promishlenniki and sets them against us. Besides constant intrigues, he tries to pursuade everyone to agree in writing that everything is company property, not the property of the company investors. He tells them that settlers are harmful to the interests of the company and all these state interests [matters of state] he presents to them in a perverted way. He tells them that it is a burden on the company, and has ordered that no less than 30 people would be assigned to become settlers; that from this the resources decrease because of taking the settlers along the coast for 500 versts; that the promishlenniki who arrive newly hired are incompetent and useless, that only a few investors will get rich and not the entire company, that the dead [illegible] and also the economic profits do not belong to members of the company in any way, etc. etc. You can learn more of this from those who have returned to Okhotsk, including those who left against their will, and also from company records here.

In terms of economics, nothing good can be noted. Since our arrival, there was hunger all winter. We ate rotten three-year-old dried fish, to the last bit, although when we arrived here, fish were still running but not harvested. The herring run was also there later, but the catch was conducted only two or three times. The Aleuts were not ordered to take halibut and it was said that since the settlers do not work, in putting up food supplies, it is not needed. The seines lay on the shore all winter long. The cows which were brought by the ships are only skins now, and most died. Two calves (besides those few born here) were eaten by dogs. Many mountain sheep have also been attacked. Only two goats remain, and recently the dogs feasted on one for their good health. Phillip will elaborate on this.

Under our parkas, we are always half naked, and those parkas get very dirty. In the daytime, we feed the people. At night we [the clergy] collect wood and bring it out of the forest ourselves. It is laughable that a household may not put up one single stick of wood, but whenever Baranov wants his tea pot heated, he sends men out for wood. They break corners off of buildings, or rob the coal from the metalsmith. I have never seen these things done in an economically sensible way. He spends his days inventing various schemes. He did not make any attempts to grow any vegetables. Phillip planted potatoes and turnips, but he was alone in this, but the crop was good. Sokozhnikov says that he experimented with barley at his bay. He sowed one pound and harvested one and a half. I have advised that in spring we should plant something here in Kodiak, but I do not know if it will happen. I would like to see some potatoes, cabbages and some other vegetables planted here. But here is an obstacle: I have asked for a few hoes or adzes and a few spades, but I do not know if I will be able to get them. Right now, we are working the ground with sharpened wooden sticks we have fashioned ourselves.

We have only five students whom we are teaching. The older students are living in their settlements without any supervisions [the students of Shelikov's earlier school]. They do not show any difference from any other Aleuts. One of them, for the sake of Baranov's woman, has been forced to run the gauntlet. His head and his eyebrows were shaved, the front of his parka was cut off, and he was banished to Yedrishnikov settlement where he is under guard. I do not know how to teach the five I have. Our room is always filled with people. Some are being baptized, some married, some visit. Besides we do not have a church, so that the services can not be conducted.

Of all the books which you sent for us, I received only a few, not more than twenty. Ten of these are sluzhebniki [service books] and they all have rotted and can not be used. The rest I have not seen yet. I baptized the Americans, creating no difficulties for the company. An indentured servant remains indentured, a hostage remains a hostage. And a hunter remains at his post—it should not interfere, that he is now baptized. But everytime obstacles are created for me, I was able to baptize people in the settlements, or to marry Aleuts with the partner with whom they were living, but this resulted in such situations that as soon as they were married, the women were taken away from their spouses and given to others or became indentured servants or hostages, and I am sure only to disturb me. I am being patient, awaiting a resolution from you of this situation.

In one settlement I married an Aleut to his girlfriend. She was sent to me with an interpreter, and I was told that this woman had been kidnapped some time ago, when they used to attack one settlement against another. She was taken prisoner first by one chief then another and finally by a Russian. When the Russian abandoned her, she returned to the chief with whom I married her. I was asked for what reason I baptized and married a prisoner who at one time was the wife of a chief. I excused myself as ignorant of the past situation. Then they found another reason: they say that the chief who had first taken her prisoner is indebted to the company for one bird parka and a metal container, so he should pay by means of this woman. If not, the debt should be settled by the Aleut who married her. Otherwise he must return her to the first chief. I agreed to pay the company, although it should not be done. But Alexander Andreevich said that if I am permitted to do so we will suffer terrible losses. Do you see what small matters are inflated and contrary to common sense?

I would like to cite another example and write you about it. There are even sillier instances. I would suffer it in silence myself but there are outsiders to our brotherhood who will speak instead of myself bringing testimony of their immoral deeds. They are exploiting in every possible way and one must testify about their barbarous treatment of the Americans. Recently I do not marry a single Aleut without reporting to him. But one can not satisfy him. He always tries to agitate the promishlenniki. He started rumors that there are no reasons to be shamed by me and that the promishlenniki have nothing to fear. Baranov claims he has orders from you to keep the clergy firmly under his control.

We are told we must use local food, local boats, etc. Without any orders from you, our need will indeed teach us to be used to the local food! There is no chance that we will use too much of the provisions. We regularly go to the beaches to collect sea snails and mussels and we have only some leftover bread which will not last long. Mr. Baranov and his colleagues do not experience hunger. For him they hunt sea lions and seals. From the Alaska Peninsula they bring caribou meat, and he always has milk. During the winter we were kept well by Phillip. There were two cows then. At the very least we had milk for the tea, but now the cows are gone and we get for the ten of us no more than a tea cup each day, excluding the fast days. With great difficulties we obtain whale oil. We have neither the time nor the means to produce handicrafts for sale. As the day dawns we think about food. We walk five versts to get snails and mussels, as near the harbor they are not available. Actually there are some mussels at the harbor, but they are food for the workers and therefore not enough. We must haul fire wood and do our sewing and laundry. There are over 100 women laborers here, but not one is assigned to assist us.

The windows of our quarters were not sealed and were very poor; we barely survived the winter. It is true initially he honored me. He reserved a pretty good room for me, but the brethren were placed in the barracks, where the men lived with their prostitutes. I did not want to live apart from the brothers, and moved with them to other quarters. Besides the prostitutes, they used the barracks for games and dances that lasted all night, so that even major [religious] feast days were not observed. Sometimes they stage these parties even on ordinary days. He would come to me and say that they are having a party because of bad weather. His only pleasures are women and dancing. That is the kind of men he and his closest advisors are.

He is not ashamed to use profanity publicly, nor to argue with me about morality. He says that we are hypocrites who do not want to understand anything, that all those moral rules are for the ignorant. He and Yakov Igorovich [Sheilds] have taught many French free-thinking which he himself accepts. He has ordered the baidarshi to keep their women without fear, and not only the old voyagers can do so. Nowadays, the one who keeps women is honored. It has happened that the day the woman is baptized, she would be taken from her settlement to promishlenniki by force. They kept changing them very often very young, ten year old girls. Some may be convinced to marry, but Mr. Baranov says that anyone who marries becomes a poor promishlennik. Another will get married but loses his credit, and is forced to leave for Russia.

I observe that the men do not travel from one settlement to another without their women, so that if they would have wives, they would be more reliable for the company. Those who are married would buy more goods from the company store and the others who follow their example would take provisions for their lovers. Prior to our arrival, not a single woman had anything but a parka. Nowadays each has a shirt and blouse. When they have children they will not want to return to Russia. (Regular family life will bring social and economic stability to the colony).

If I were to describe all his actions to you in detail, I would have to write an entire book, and not a letter. About his loose life, even so, I should according to the instructions His Eminence gave me, I should report to him and to the Holy Synod, but my affection and respect for you convinced me to refrain from this for the time being. I am hoping that you in your wisdom will take measures to alleviate the situation. But wisdom does not find home in an evil soul. Wisdom does not take abode there where sin is active either. So that if you want to write to Mr. Baranov, I am convinced that nothing will come of it except more evil, especially if he finds I have written you. If he remains as manager here, evil will not cure evil. Even so, he is entering in his books 1500 roubles for the church and the clergy, but it would be better for me if he had taken as much *from* me but acted here with greater decency. I am mentioning all this because I fear there will be worse consequences if he learns that I am writing. According to his custom, he would be forced to denigrate me further, and I might lose my patience and raise my voice to him and express my own dissatisfaction. I did not express my opinion about Baranov until I learned that he told his friends that he is against me. I would like to counsel you to send here Ivan Iosipovich, or someone as good as he is. I could at least take counsel in private with a trusted man, and bring some order to some matters where it might be possible. I am not one who demands that everything be repaired immediately, but I do trust that in the long run God will set things right. It is not possible to take counsel with Baranov—he has his own. I am too timid to.

He sells his tobacco at exorbitant prices while there is in the storehouse, twenty pud of company tobacco. When there are murmurs against his price, he blames you. You can look into this matter better than I, and I will attend to others.

Children born to Russian fathers with the permission of the manager are taken from their mothers—one or two years old—and try to take them to Russia. I do not like this at all. This kind of transport will be seen as cruelty and evidence of our dishonor. For the children it will be catastrophic. It would be better to bring them up here in the Russian manner. They should be taught to read, and then according to their abilities educated in other liberal arts. Then we could have people here as good promishlenniki instead of importing them from Russia. The state interest would also be served better. I see that there is an opportunity to raise them here if there were a good manager. In the meantime, they should leave the children here, and not allow them to take them to Russia. In all of this, I would like instructions from His Eminence, the Metropolitan, but in the meantime I want to know what you think about it and if we are in agreement.

The French free-thinking which is popular here gives me reason to think a lot. Here in the harbor there are robbers disturbing the peace, but also many good people, but the others are vulgar. When one passes a group of them they loudly curse me as an agent of the distant members of the company, while they openly swear at married companions and their wives in the market place. The prekrasniks are also persecuted. Hoping for Baranov's protection, I don't see how I can go to Yakutat. Baranov always makes difficulties for me and Ivan Gregorievich. He keeps apart from him and refuses to speak to him. He says let them go and settle with Archimandrite. In the fall he promises to give some planks, but now he says he remembers nothing about them. He has used all the lumber himself, and he told me that he would send me beyond the company possessions before Sheilds goes, while he will proceed along the coast with a party . . .

REPORT OF ARCHIMANDRITE IOASAPH TO THE HOLY SYNOD, 1797

[*Translated by Lydia Black and Michael Oleksa, University of Alaska, Fairbanks.*]

There are no missionaries from other nations on any islands nor are there any on the mainland shore nor were there ever any. The allegiance of the local inhabitants to any nation cannot be ascertained. They always prefer the strongest one.

IV Aesthetics

On Faith

QUESTION: Do the inhabitants besides those who have already accepted Christian Faith have any understanding about God, His Name, and do they have any services or are they idolaters? If so, what are the idols? What are their names? What kind of sacrifices do they offer, and what is the object of these sacrifices? Are they divided into any kind of sects [in their aboriginal faith]?

ANSWER: They acknowledge a supreme being and call Him ''Agayun,'' or a Good Spirit, who teaches people such things as how to make kayaks, who helps them in hunting animals, and in all human needs. But they make no sacrifices to Him, nor do they worship Him, because they know that this being never causes any evil. The Evil Spirit is called ''Elan'' and this spirit attempts to harm people in every possible way. For this reason, to appease him, they make sacrifices, at which time, they put on special clothing, masks, and some even engage in shamanism. But they do not have any kind of idols.

QUESTION: Do they have any concept of ''dobriedyetel'' [conduct conducive to goodness] or of wrongdoing, and how do they define it?

ANSWER: Behavior conducive to goodness is understood as all that is done in accordance with customs. Whatever is contrary to custom is called wrongdoing.

QUESTION: What are their thoughts about the future life and happiness? How do they imagine it?

ANSWER: They acknowledge that there is a future life, but their understanding of the new life is based on sensory imagery. They believe that good people in the next life will have a life of plenty, in terms of successful hunting. The wicked will be poor, beggars suffering hunger. For this reason, before they were enlightened, people of status were buried with all their military and hunting equipment, and they also killed a good and beloved prisoner. He was buried with his master to serve him in the next life.

QUESTION: Are they hospitable? Are they kind? Do they possess charity [love of their fellow man]? What are their major moral faults?

ANSWER: The dominant wrongdoing among them is lack of charity (love of humanity) [probably cruelty toward prisoners] and prodigality [literally poor household management, not saving provisions for future needs].

QUESTION: Do they accept the faith and Christian conduct readily? Are they constant in these, and are they respectful toward the holy services?

ANSWER: All without exception accept Holy Baptism. It is remarkable that the elders, who are fossilized in their previous errors, accept it as they look at the younger people, as they believe it is dishonorable not to be baptized. The respect toward the sacred services, and the constancy in Christian conduct is more noticeable among the younger people, especially among those who have prolonged contact with the Russians.

QUESTION: Are the newly converted Christians ostracized, and if so, why does this occur?

ANSWER: No kind of ostracism or disrespect toward the newly baptized has ever been observed.

QUESTION: Are they adept in learning, and is there hope that they can be educated as conditions require?

ANSWER: We have every reason to hope that in time they will be enlightened.

QUESTION: What are their inclinations—to the verbal or visual arts?

ANSWER: The Native inhabitants have aptitude toward both verbal sciences as well as toward the arts. However, they are by nature rather lazy and they have to be weaned away from this. One must take wise measures to teach them diligence. As the arrival of the missionaries has not made the faith of the Natives more difficult, but on the contrary makes it easier, care for them is evident. Also we assist them in their needs as much as we can. They have good thoughts and opinions of the missionaries.

QUESTION: How are they treated by our countrymen? What is the basis for extending our sovereignty over them?

ANSWER: Russian forces, spread over incredible distances and numerous tribes, cannot subjugate them. Only well-instituted order within the company and care, kindness, and various political means intended to accomplish this will restrain their inclination to barbarism and fratricidal warfare. These evils were common prior to the arrival of the Russians. There was constant warfare. But no one can rule over them despotically, because as soon as they feel themselves oppressed, they will either decide to liberate themselves by killing their oppressors, or, if this is not possible, they will retreat into the interior of the island, and after regrouping will conduct frequent raids.

QUESTION: Are they unduly burdened by work demands, taxes or yasak?

ANSWER: Yasak has not been collected since 1794. However, the company cannot function without workers recruited from among the local inhabitants or from the hostages. This is true for both Kodiak and the American [Alaskan] mainland. The hostages are taken as a pledge that the tribe will be faithful to the Russian customs and restrain their natural habits for future benefit. Through the hostages, so educated, their fathers and relatives are attracted, because they come to visit our Russian harbors and observe our activities, and the mutual interconnections are increasingly reinforced. However, only a very small number of hostages are taken on Kodiak. They were handed over when it was necessary, as a precaution. The workers at the company outposts, and the women are taken with the chief's permission, usually from the solitary people. And many are former prisoners of war, who have been ransomed by the Russians from their captors. These are helping the company in preparing food supplies which are used by everyone, without exception, including the Americans [Native Alaskans] who come to visit. Often provisions are issued to villages suffering food shortages. Also, these supplies are issued when someone is leaving a company outpost, and on other occasions as the company management determines. Such distribution is needed because in many settlements, when people perform their hunting duties or sail, the Russian promishlenniki cannot spend the time to put up the food supplies. Besides, additional food supplies are necessary as a constant precaution at harbors and forts, and among the artels, where they always keep a certain number of guards. Within the Kodiak region, and on various islands, as well as on the mainland, there are more than 10,000 inhabitants, and these have not yet forgotten their barbarous customs, which were natural to them, and often when the occasion arises, without warning, they can turn on the promishlenniki, of whom there are seldom more than 200. Usually there are no more than 200 in the region. Therefore it is necessary to seek assistance and service of the hostages and Native employees of the company.

The hostages and these others are maintained with food, clothing and boots. Those who are diligent and intelligent often replace Russian promishlenniki whose contract of service expires. Those receive the same kind of conditions. The intelligent hostages are admitted to the school which has been established on Kodiak. They are not forced to attend classes. They are admitted on the basis of their own voluntary request.

QUESTION: To what does the company give priority, the enlightenment of the aboriginal peoples or their own profits?

ANSWER: The company became interested in these localities initially to make quick profits. The enlightenment of the Natives occurred almost imperceptibly through intercourse with individual Russians. Consequently, the company even now will not consider sacrificing its benefits for the welfare of the Natives.

QUESTION: Are there churches on Kodiak or on the coast? How many are there, and where?

ANSWER: On Kodiak, the local wooden church was consecrated in 1796. At other locations, along the coast, there are two field churches. [NOTE: This indicates that Makarii and Juvenalii had Antimens.]

QUESTION: What is the basis for the establishment of churches and parishes?

ANSWER: Churches can be established with the approval of the company, because they must be built and equipped by the company. The Natives are not able to aid the church in any way. On the contrary, as far as possible the church is supporting them. They ask, in their poverty, for our help.

QUESTION: How far along the coast has Christianity spread?

ANSWER: Beginning at the Aleutian Islands, along the Alaska Peninsula, and the Gulf of Alaska all the way to Yakutat and Chilkat, a considerable number of inhabitants have been baptized.

QUESTION: Who performs the liturgical services and meets the sacramental needs of the people?

ANSWER: These are conducted by the hieromonks assigned to the mission.

QUESTION: Are there Americans who have learned Russian, who could be ordained to the priesthood?

ANSWER: Those who have been educated and fostered by the Mission under its special care are capable of becoming clergy and priests, but they are all still minors. Those who have been educated by the company and taught to speak and read Russian, prior to the arrival of the Mission, have more inclination toward the study of navigation and similar courses. Therefore, according to their aptitude, they have been employed in many such positions, from which they get many benefits.

QUESTION: Does the church need wine, incense, candles, and what kind of difficulties prevent the mission from obtaining them?

ANSWER: Everything the church needs, including flour for baking communion bread, can only be obtained from Russia via Okhotsk. Even if vessels arrive safely and on schedule at Kodiak, we need a minimum of three years' supplies. The money appropriated for the support of the Kodiak clergy needs also to be allocated three years in advance.

QUESTION: What books are needed for teaching the children and how many books do you need?

ANSWER: Although the Holy Synod has ordered that the hostages must be sent to Irkutsk for schooling, doing so would be very difficult. Not only is the voyage hazardous, but the change in climate, the danger of smallpox infection, and other diseases kill them prematurely, even before they reach Yakutsk. Therefore to prevent this, it would be much better and much less costly to appoint the teachers appointed by His Grace. Bishop Veniamin of Irkutsk, to serve at Kodiak as choir members. Then we can select the youngsters from the school we have established to study all the sciences and arts that are taught in Russian seminaries. If the Holy

Synod will agree, I will be able to determine the books we will need for the projected school.

QUESTION: What are the methods and what kind of help is needed to propagate the Christian religion, and what kind of administration [for the Native population] is needed in the colony?

ANSWER: To facilitate the spread of Christianity, a missionary must require no payment from the people for his work, and he must be diligent. The mission must be self-supporting, and not use anything from the Natives for themselves or for the church until such time as they become devoted to the Gospel, to the Church, and to the commandments. The evangelists can accomplish this by treating the local inhabitants with kindness and assisting them whenever they are in need. We cannot advise what kind of government should be instituted among them. In time, perhaps, this can be determined if we succeed in educating them in their natural aptitudes and gifts, and as they are introduced to animal husbandry and farming.

QUESTION: How can one avoid difficulties in transport from Yakutsk to Okhotsk?

ANSWER: The government and private companies have been trying to alleviate the difficulties of this journey for a long time, but even at great expense, they have not succeeded.

DESCRIPTION OF THE TRADITIONAL RELIGIOUS BELIEFS AND PRACTICES OF THE KODIAK PEOPLE, COMPILED FROM VALAAM ARCHIVES, 1894

[*The following text and the letter from Bishop Petr are taken from The Russian-Orthodox Mission 1794–1837, Kingston, Ontario, Limestone Press, 1978. Reprinted by permission of Richard Pierce, publisher.*]

We have only very sparse information about the religious beliefs and ideas of the Kadiaks. They, like the Aleuts, believed in the immortality of the human soul and in life after death. This belief of theirs is indicated by two lines from a song noted down by Hieromonk Gedeon.

> Enough of weeping! This world is not immortal: Aknak [the name of the deceased] has died as a person and will come to life again.

And so, according to the Kadiaks, this world is not immortal: the dead will be reborn, but where and how man will live when he is reborn, as the Kadiaks understand it, about this we know nothing.

The Kadiak people also believed in a Creator of the Universe: but this belief of theirs was extremely ill-defined, vague and in part naive. About the creation of the world they have the following idea or, to put it more precisely, opinion. There was a certain Kashshakhiliuk [wise man or clever man]. At that time there was neither day nor night. He began to blow on a straw. This caused the earth gradually to grow out of the water and imperceptibly to spread. Then, while he was still blowing, the heavens opened and the sun appeared: and after dusk the stars came out, and the moon rose. Finally men and beasts appeared. This is all that we know about the religion of the Aleuts and the Kadiaks. We should add that both the former and the latter have all possible kinds of superstitions, but amongst them there is none which is persistent or especially harmful, with the exception of the savage custom, mentioned above, of killing kalgas [slaves] over the graves of their masters. Neither the Aleut shamans, nor those of the Kadiaks, had the status of a powerful caste of priests and any powerful religious or moral influence; their role was more that of witch-doctors, or magicians, who had dealings with spirits.

Let us allow ourselves to direct the reader's special attention to some of the religious concepts and moral rules of the Aleuts and the Kadiaks. These concepts and laws have sometimes a very distant and sometimes a very close similarity to the message preached in the Holy Scriptures:

(a) "The place where the first people came from was warm; there there were no winters or storms, but always gentle healthy breezes. To begin with people lived in peace and knew no want. The first people were gifted with long life," and so forth [the Aleut belief about man's origins and subsequent development which we quoted above in full]. What do we find in these ideas? In the distant past people led a peaceful life in a beautiful place where eternal Spring reigns—a life without enmity or want. This is the biblical paradise, the innocent and blessed condition of the first men, reflected, of course, not with literal exactness, but in a certain, very similar way. The longevity of the first people is the longevity of the patriarchs of the Bible. Later, so the Aleut belief goes, need and enmity arise—this is the story of man, from its natural side and development, after the Fall, and it does not contradict the Biblical account. The essential difference is that in the Aleut account the causes also are shown to be only natural, and not the darkening of man's nature through his transgression against God's teaching through the Fall, as happened in fact.

(b) According to the Kadiak account of the Creation there was a certain Kashshakhiliuk [wise man], i.e. [to put it into more readily intelligible terms] there was a certain all-knowing and at the same time personalized principle, a Creator. This is not to say even then that there actually was anyone, or anything; in other words, apart from the all-knowing Creator, there was nothing and no one. But can this unenlightened idea of the human condition, distorted by many centuries, be an idea of the eternal, ever-present God? At that time, according to Kadiak belief, there was neither day nor night; and the Bible says the same. He [Kashshakhiliuk, the wise man] began to blow on a straw; and this is how the land gradually rose out of the waters and grew. The Bible also relates a similar gradual process, with the land appearing from the depths of primeval chaos. And so, the wise man, the all-knowing Creator, created the Earth simply by the blowing of his breath. In the 32nd psalm [*sic.* Ps 19:1] the King and Prophet David says: ''The heavens declare the Glory of God; and the firmament sheweth his handiwork''; in other words, ''By the word of the Lord were the heavens made; and all the host of them by the breath of his mouth'' [Ps 33:6]. Are the heavens not higher than the land? ''And all the majesty of the heavens is created by the Voice of God'': such is the limitless force, the boundless might of Him who is without beginning and without end. Does not the naive *straw* of the legend point to the Glory of the Creator and the pettiness of the Earth by comparison with Him? He, the Creator of the world, is so immeasurably great and powerful by comparison with his creation, that for him the act of breathing alone is sufficient to create the Earth, for there was nothing there before. Then, while he [the wise man] was still blowing (in other words while the creation was still taking place), the sky opened, the sun appeared, and after dusk the stars appeared and the moon rose. This, according to the Bible, was on the fourth day of the Creation. Finally, animals and people came. If by 'animals' we understand all species without distinction, then this is the fifth and sixth days of the Creation according to the Bible story. There are omissions, there are distortions by comparison with the Bible, but the actual sequence of the Creation has not been lost at all. The wise man went on blowing throughout the whole process of creation. This blowing, this breathing of the breath of life, however naively it is expressed in the beliefs of these savage people of Kadiak, becomes for us an intelligible [although doubtless distorted] reflection of the Holy Truth—when we compare it with the words of the psalmist. In the Bible we read: ''And the Lord God formed Man of the dust of the ground, and breathed into his nostrils the breath of life'' (Gn II:7). Here again we find—breathing, breath of life. In the half-savage Aleuts or Kadiaks we can see only too clearly a half-understanding of God; and for us, Christians, enlightened by the Son of God to the fullness necessary for a man of Holy Revelation [for the Lord has revealed to us only that which we are capable of understanding], God is an unreachable Being—''God is not a name, but an idea, deep-seated in the nature of man, about something which cannot be explained,'' said the holy martyr Justin, the philosopher (Apologia 2:6).

(c) The detailed moral laws about respect for one's parents and for older people in general, with the promise in return of a long life and other earthly reward (. . . in *Notes on the Island of the Unalashka District,* part II, pp. 136–137), are they not the same moral injunctions which are present in the fifth commandment of the laws of Moses: "Honor thy father and thy mother: that thy days may be long upon the land . . ." (Ex 20:12)?

(d) "We are all born from one father and mother, and are all brothers one of another" (*Notes,* Chap. 22, p. 142). Here are expressed both the moral concept of the brotherhood of all peoples one of another, and the conviction about the origin of all peoples from one pair, which is what the Holy Scriptures tell us.

In general the pure and elevated moral ideas of the Aleuts and Kadiaks and their religious views are in essence similar to the Bible stories, although they are fragmented and obscured by the continuing moral condition of these peoples, and they lead us to the very instructive conclusion quoted below. The legends of these peoples confirm the origins of all people, of all the human race from one pair of progenitors. Otherwise how would we be able, in the case of the Aleuts and Kadiaks, living at an enormous distance from the places and people amongst whom the Bible came into being, and several thousand years later, to come across conceptions of the creation of the world and the beginnings of the life of man similar to the Bible stories? The incomplete and fragmentary nature of the religious views of the Aleuts and Kadiaks can simply be explained by the fact that they have been too long, like many other peoples, removed from the direct influence of God's Revelations, which alone can communicate to people in all its fullness the knowledge they need to have about God and the World, whereas originally God's Revelation was limited in all its purity to the European peoples alone. It must be noted that in accordance with God's Holy Revelations the Aleuts and the Kadiaks were not completely bereft of God's Grace, as a result of which there remained with them a sense of morality which prevented them from falling into ultimate sin.

The unity of man's nature, for us, is not a matter for question; it is a firm conviction. But let us also note that anthropology, from that time [on], since more attention has been directed to studying various peoples from a psychological point of view, cannot now but recognize that "the basic traits of human psychology appear to be similar in people with different colored skins." True science only confirms the Holy Scriptures. And although mistakes are unavoidable in every human endeavor, we must, however, be careful not to accept frivolously as science that which only calls itself by that great name.

Moral laws can only be firm, effective, can only have a binding force when they are based upon religion, when they flow out of a religion which is sacred to the people, not only in words but in deeds, or—when the very moral laws themselves are as sacred as religion. This latter we can observe in the case of the Aleuts and the Kadiaks. They had no strict system of concepts about the true God, the Creator and the Founder of the world. The moral laws, which they respected as religion, replaced this latter for them, up until that time when merciful God was so good as to send them the light of His true knowledge.

LETTER FROM BISHOP PETR OF YAKUTSK TO IGUMEN DAMASCENE OF VALAAM, 9 SEPTEMBER 1867

Your Reverence
Most Deeply Respected Father Abbot!

I do not know whether the Kadiak creole, Gerasim Zyrianov, will provide you with any information about Father Herman. I for my part have commissioned the priest on Kadiak and a native of Kadiak, the creole Konstantin Larionov, to write giving me all the information they have or can find out from others about Father Herman. What I have been able to acquire I am sending to you with this letter. If you need still more information then contact His Eminence Pavel who has taken my place in Novoarkhangel'sk, for I have in the meantime been transferred to Yakutsk. I wish you all good fortune from the Lord and, seeking your holy prayers, with complete respect I have the honor to be

Your Reverence's
Most obedient Servant
Petr, Bishop of Yakutsk,
Vicar of the Kamchatka Diocese
9th September 1867
Yakutsk

INFORMATION ABOUT FATHER HERMAN, COMPILED BY ALEUT CONSTANTINE LARIONOFF, 1867

Information about Father Herman collected from various people.

(1) When Father Herman settled on Spruce Island there was during the early years a flood or flood tide [doubtless caused by an earthquake], and the people there, the inhabitants, were frightened and came to tell the Elder. He left his cell and went to his pupils' house, where he celebrated service every Sunday because there was no chapel or church. He took the icon of

the Mother of God from its place and carried it out into the meadow where the tide had earlier been and, placing the icon on the ground, he began to pray to God. When he had finished his prayers, he told those who were present that they should not be afraid, saying: "The sea will not come further or higher than where the holy image stands." And this is in fact what happened. And this was confirmed by those who heard it.

When it was necessary to carry the icon back, after the people had been instructed, Father Herman is reputed to have said to Sofia Vlasova (who was then supervisor of the girl pupils) that if the waters began to rise again she should place the icon on the beach, and he promised that the sea would not go beyond that point where it stood. This icon of the Mother of God is still to be found to this day on Spruce Island in the place called New Valaam.

Since I wished to hear about this event from other sources I asked the following:

Pelageia, the wife of Stepanov, says that as a girl she had heard of it, but that she does not remember a great deal.

The colonial citizen, the creole Petr Gavrilov, says that he heard about flooding at St. Pavel Harbor while Father Afanasii was there, and that the latter stayed all night on the fields beside the sea because of the danger. But he does not know whether Father Herman was living on Spruce Island at that time.

The Aleut Ignatii Alig'iaga says that at the time when Father Herman settled on Spruce Island he was sent as part of his duties from Igak Bay to Father Herman, and that he had heard no one talk about the alleged events, so that he very much doubts them.

Because I thought that I must have heard a lie, God sent as it were a comforting sign—the Aleut Vasilii Gagarin who arrived from Orlovsk village with his wife Irina came to visit me, and I asked him about Father Herman and whether he had heard of great floods during the Elder's lifetime. To this both answered that they had heard it from such good and old people who could never have been lying, and the man (Vasilii) said that he thought he had heard Father Herman once say that it was more likely something dangerous would happen on Kadiak than on Spruce.

(2) The tale of the old woman Pelageia, wife of the creole Stepanov, an eyewitness to the events when she was in service with the administrator Nikiforov.

The former chief managers of the colony Messrs. Chistiakov and Murav'ev once rowed out to Spruce Island secretly at night together with the former administrator of Kadiak Nikiforov and the priest Frument'ev. They came ashore on the island at a point where they would not be noticed and they hid in the forest as though waiting in ambush and kept watch on what Father Herman was doing. Since they were not noticed they returned quietly the same night without, of course, having seen anything prejudicial and so they could not blacken or calumny the Elder.

(3) In 1825 when the priest Frumentii Mordovskii arrived on Kadiak, for what cause or reason I do not know, he went to Spruce Island and began to investigate (so they still say now) the way Father Herman lived! With him was the Administrator Nikiforov and Russian employees of the company. When they found nothing of value amongst his possessions then one of the Russians, Ponomar'kov, took an axe and began to tear up the floorboards (presumably with the permission of his superiors). Then it seems Father Herman said with a sigh, and in a spirit of resignation: "Oh, unfortunate man, you should not have picked up that axe." And he explained to him that it was by means of such a weapon that he would lose his life. And so, shortly afterwards people were needed to carry out duties at Nikolaevsk redoubt and so some Russian employees were sent from Kadiak, amongst them Ponomar'kov. There some short time later some Kenais cut the man's head off while he was asleep. Thus did the offended Elder's prophecy come true.

(4) In 1834, during the time that chief manager F. P. Wrangell was on Kadiak, Father Herman came to visit him by invitation (this is what Wrangell's predecessor had done, for the Elder was eloquent and tireless in instructive discussion). A bed was made up for Father Herman in the study, but when the servants arrived in the morning they found it unslept in and the Elder still awake!

At this same time Father Herman asked Wrangell one day to write something for him (which I subsequently heard described as a letter to a Metropolitan, but I do not know which one) and he asked him not to use any eloquent phraseology but just to write down what he said. When the letter was finished he asked for it to be read back, and when he found that it was true to what he had dictated, the Elder stood up and said in thanks: "For your true work, Ferdinand Petrovich, I congratulate you on your appointment to the rank of Admiral." Wrangell leapt up, visibly shaken, and said with a bow, "What do you mean, Father?" To which Herman repeated that he would be made an admiral. When Wrangell later returned to St. Petersburg the prophecy was fulfilled! Maybe this good man is still alive and can still recall this occurrence.

I also heard that a year before the receipt of the news on Kadiak Father Herman foretold the death of the Moscow Metropolitan; he explained it to the Aleuts saying that their great leader had quit this earthly life.

He is also said to have foretold the events of 1812.

(5) Father Herman paid frequent visits to the harbor during the time of the administrator V. Ivanovich Kashevarov whom he loved and respected. The latter was the cause of the old man's journeyings and indeed Kashevarov himself often visited Spruce Island, especially when the first chapel was being built there.

One day, in the middle of a conversation Herman said to Kashevarov, "Dear fellow (Father Herman had accepted from the font Kashevarov's only son) I am sorry your transfer will be unpleasant." Kashevarov was replaced a year or two after Herman's death, and the prophecy came true because Kashevarov was transferred to Sitkha bound as a prisoner!

Petr Gavrilov will also testify to the truth of this. He says that he himself heard and saw how it happened (he was at the time on Kashevarov's staff): when Kashevarov was on Spruce Island for the last time in the middle of a conversation as he was conducting Kashevarov to his baidarka, Father Herman stopped opposite the chapel and prophesied that Kashevarov's next posting would be an unpleasant one. And Father Herman spoke of other things to Kashevarov but Gavrilov could not hear it all, first because he was supposed to be busy and he was too afraid of his superior to stop and listen, and also Kashevarov's family were waiting on the beach.

Others said that Herman had foretold a shameful posting for Kashevarov because he had inhumanly punished some of his men, and it was true that if Kashevarov wanted to break someone of some particular sin he would give them something to think about, and as a result the men respected and feared their superiors.

(6) Once during my time on Spruce Island, K. Larionov visited the old man's cell; with me was the Aleut Petr, known as Shtuluk. When we arrived at the cell, as we had been instructed we said a prayer before entering, namely: "Lord Jesus Christ the son of God, have mercy on us," and we heard an answering "Amen". Then we entered the cell where we found the Elder seated on the floor cutting up potatoes into a tub with a knife (which I later discovered was for bread). This was in 1835, when I was hardly more than twelve years old. He told me to take down a book from the shelves and made me find the articles which had to do with his discourse. As I was not reading fluently at that time, he told me or showed me the pages and explained the Church script to me. He himself, it would seem, was blind, but apparently he recalled the contents of the books by heart, because he was seated some distance away from us.

In between his stories he put a question to me—which I shall reproduce verbatim: "My son, what do you think? Will the chapel we have built be left in the future?'' To which I answered, ''Apa (a term used by all of us inhabitants of Kadiak, and which means in translation 'uncle' or 'father') I do not know.'' And at that time I really did not understand the significance of the question. But he sighed and after a brief silence said, ''My child, remember, in time on this spot there will be a monastery,'' and he asked me to translate this for my companion Stepan, who was somewhat younger than I. I carried out his request word for word.

I do not know to this day why such an aged, grey-haired Elder honored me with such a prophecy or could see in his time that, although unworthy, I would be a purveyor of his words.

The Elder also visited our house once shortly after our arrival from Sitkha, while my mother was still alive. I was then very small and of course do not remember clearly, but I can recall holding some piece of paper in my hand and going up to the old man (as my parents told me afterwards), placing the paper on his knees and lisping something to him. Father Herman looked at me for a long while and then is said to have told my parents: ''Take good care of your son. I can see that something will come of him.'' Maybe the Lord had mercy on me as a result of his prayers.

(7) Once there was a fire on Spruce Island as a result of a bonfire for the gardens. When Father Herman was told he set to work straight away, together with Ignatii who had gone to tell him—the work was of the following kind: they scraped away the moss which grew thickly amongst the trees, leaving a bared strip no wider than an arshin, and this strip stretched to the foot of the hills. It was more like a boundary mark, so Ignatii said. Then Father Herman is alleged to have said that the fire would not cross this line. And on the next day the fire came rushing up, and Father Herman went to his cell, to a sure refuge, before the mercy of God. The fire reached the turned-back moss, ran along its length, and finding no way of crossing, for all that it raged, it could not reach the thick wood and it turned again, i.e. went back! Yes, this was truly a miracle.

A former co-worker, Ignatii Alig'iaga, is still alive and bears witness to the fact that they would all have perished [if the fire had crossed].

(8) Father Herman made a prophecy to the Aleuts in which he is alleged to have said that shortly after his death there would be an epidemic and that many people would die, after which the Russians would gather the Aleuts into one community. This prophecy came to pass shortly after Herman's death—some six months later, it would seem; it was a smallpox outbreak and many Aleuts died so that only a few children were left in some settlements. When this came to the notice of the colonial authorities, who acted in collaboration with the arch priest Petr Litvintsev (he was at that

time priest on Kadiak), out of 20 villages some 7 were created and Father Herman's prophecy was fulfilled to the letter.

(9) According to Ignatii, who lives on Spruce Island to this day, Father Herman once told him that all the people living on Spruce would die and that he, Ignatii, would be left alone, and would grow old and poor, and that people would remember Father Herman and thirty years after his death Ignatii would still be alive. He is amazed at this saying: "How could a man like us know something like this so long in advance; he must have been a very special man because he could read our thoughts, which we involuntarily revealed to him, and [Father Herman] would use these thoughts to teach us things."

Herman also said that although a long time would go by after his death, he would not be forgotten and the place where he had lived would not be empty. He also said that another monk like himself, escaping from social fame, would come and live on Spruce Island, and Spruce would not be without people.

He also prophesied that the earth tremors on Kadiak would be frequent and increasingly severe, and that comets would appear—one of which would be terrifying.

(10) There is also Herman's request shortly before his death, a story which is confirmed by Ignatii.

Father Herman asked those around him as he was dying not to tell the administrator of his death until they had buried him (obviously an attempt to avoid ceremonial), saying that none of those at the harbor would see his face. But the inhabitants of Spruce did not carry out his request because, according to them, they were afraid of the Russians.

As soon as Kashevarov learnt of the death of a man who had been so widely respected, he took steps to have a coffin made ready and this, to Kashevarov's credit, was done in the best possible fashion. Only the wind which blew up prevented Kashevarov and the priest who had made ready from travelling themselves (even though it was only two hours' ride from the harbor), and the coffin was transported with great difficulty a month later in the care of the skilled veteran, Koz'ma Uchilishchev.

As soon as those on Spruce received the coffin they placed our worthy Elder's remains in it and committed them to the earth, and at once the wind dropped and the sea became like a glass! and so Father Herman's last prophecy had been fulfilled. The old man's request was of the following nature, according to Ignatii:

Towards the end of his life he told them to wash his body and lay it on a simple board, placing both his hands on his chest, to dress him in nothing but his mantle, to take a strip a hand's breadth wide from the hem and to wrap him in it and to cover his face with its folds. If anyone wished to bid him farewell, to place on their head for confession the cross which he wore (perhaps with a rosary or some such, I could not understand Ignatii at this point). They were to kiss this cross—but he ordered that no one should be shown his face.

He asked to be buried under a tree or tree stump and to be covered with his old 'blanket'; no one knew of this blanket apart from the old men Ignatii and Isai—it was as long as Father Herman and was—a board! Ignatii adds at this point that the Apa led a hard life which no one else could imitate.

After his death Herman was kept for exactly a month in his pupils' house where it was warm, but Herman's face did not change and there was not even any smell, although those living in the house kept expecting this. Ignatii adds that they went against his last wishes even then.

Even before his death he had left as a legacy or given instructions to the inhabitants gathered around the chapel or to his pupils that when he should quit this life they should kill a large bull for the funeral breakfast. Isai died after Father Herman.

And Father Herman's soul had hardly departed when this bull marked down for the slaughter went berserk and began to charge and as it did so crashed into some trees and fell dead! so that the people had to cut it up and eat it. Those who saw it, and Ignatii himself, related this with amazement. Of course these people would have carried out his request, but not until after the local administrator had been informed, but it may be that this did not suit the Elder. This was also worthy of his attention, for nothing happens by chance—everything is in accordance with the Will of God.

(11) According to an eyewitness account by the old woman Anna, the widow of Vologdin, and on her evidence there is also still alive the old Aleut woman Anna Nytsmyshknak whom I cannot visit now because she lives so far away.

During our stay in the village of Katani (on Afognak) one evening, we could see an unusually bright column of light rising into the air above Spruce Island—then experienced old men and Anna's husband the creole Gerasim Vologdin said: "It looks as though Father Herman has left them," and they straightway began to pray to God. When they subsequently learnt of Father Herman's death they found that it had occurred on the very night of the vision [in the margin at the bottom of the page is written in the Very Reverend Petr's hand: "Father Herman died 13th December, 1837"].

I have heard of this from many sources, people who saw it from various places, and others who saw it while at sea in their baidarkas.

On the same evening from other villages and also from Afognak a figure was seen in the sky below the clouds over Spruce.

(12) A scene from his life in his cell.

During my visits to Father Herman's cell I had the honor to see his so-called litter or "bedchamber"; a bench less than 3/4 of an arshin wide and covered with deerskin without the fur—I do not know why, maybe as a result of age. There was no blanket. I, sinner that I am, sat on it, which I consider more than happiness. This bench was right next to the stove, and on top of the stove lay the board of which no one knew the meaning or purpose as I noticed. Only two people, Ignatii and Isai, knew about the board.

At the head of the bench there were two bricks in place of a pillow, covered also with bare skin or chamois! This too was not noticed by many visitors.

Not far from the cell there flowed a stream with a swell always running where it flowed into the sea. Father Herman, when the river fish appeared in the spring, would start digging in the sand so that the fish could only just get past and as soon as the fish made for the shore they would come into this trap. Then the Elder would adopt the following procedure, as related by Ignatii: The Apa (elder) would order the fish to be caught and stunned and then gutted and cut into two strips—of these he would take a very small portion for himself and order the remainder to be placed on a board and cut into strips to feed the birds which were constantly around his cell, and, what was even more remarkable, the mink which lived and had their litters under his cell! It is strange that it is normally impossible to approach this little animal when it has pups, yet Father Herman would feed them by hand. Was what we saw not miraculous, Ignatii would ask. After Herman's death the birds and animals left. And if a stranger took over the running of Father Herman's allotments on their own nothing would grow there, Ignatii assures me.

Father Herman wore metal fetters which were discovered some time after Herman's death in the chapel behind the icon of the Mother of God; others said they had fallen from behind the icon by themselves. They are even now housed in this same chapel.

[signed] The creole Konstantin Larionov

P.S. In the summer Father Herman would busy himself in his garden: he would turn over the earth himself, sowing turnips and radishes. He would plant potatoes and garlic without plowing the earth, but he would simply make a heap of soil and drop the potatoes into a hole made in it; the garlic was sown in trenches. He would set horseradish, and he gave his pupils the means of increasing the gardens, and the people lived on the produce derived therefrom. He taught them to read and write and sing the litanies, when Father Herman used the girls and boys to replace reader and choir. They sang very well as I know because I have been to several services—matins in Holy Week and the hours.

INDICATION OF THE PATHWAY INTO THE KINGDOM OF HEAVEN

[*by Rev. Priest John Veniaminov, translated by Paul Garrett, St. Vladimir's Orthodox Seminary, Crestwood, New York.*]

Introduction

Unlike animals which after death disappear, human beings were created for more than life on earth. We were created for a life with God and in God, a life which would last not just a hundred or a thousand years, but for all eternity. Only those, however, who are Christians are capable of this life with God. That is, only those WHO RIGHTLY BELIEVE IN JESUS CHRIST.

Without exception human beings desire and seek for themselves prosperity and happiness, and to desire that which is good and seek prosperity and happiness is neither sin nor vice. Rather, it forms an innate part of our human nature. We must be aware, however, that true and perfect happiness and prosperity have never, do not now, and indeed never will exist on this earth. These can be found in God alone, and without God (or outside of Him) will no one ever find true happiness or perfect prosperity.

In God alone can our hearts be filled and the desire we feel in this world be completely satisfied. Kindling wood and oil can never extinguish fire; water alone is capable of doing so. No more can the good things of this world ever satisfy the desires of the human heart, for the grace of God is alone able to quench our thirst's desires.

The things which we desire please us only until we have obtained them; once they are in our possession, they quickly tire us. Only that which we still lack seems good and attractive to us; those things which we actually possess—even those which are truly of the highest quality—never seem good or attractive to us. KING SOLOMON offers us the best example of this. As we know, he was so rich that in his palaces everything was made of solid gold. His wisdom was such that kings came to visit him, and he was so glorious that his enemies stood in terror before him. He was wiser and mightier than all his contemporaries, yet he could never satisfy all his wishes and desires. There was scarcely a thing in this world which he lacked and could not obtain, yet his heart could not be satisfied. Indeed, far more than any ordinary man, the desires of his heart wearied and tormented him. And ultimately, having tried everything in this world he wrote, "Everything in this world is useless and nothing can satisfy our desires" (Eccl 1).

This is precisely the case. There is no earthly pleasure capable of satisfying our hearts. As strangers on this earth, pilgrims and wanderers, our home, our country lies in heaven, in the Kingdom of Heaven, and nothing on earth can fully satisfy our desires. If a person were to own the whole world and everything in it, this might suffice to hold his interest for a moment, so to speak, but never would his heart be satisfied. For nothing short of the love of God can fully satisfy and fill the human heart and soul, or quench the thirst of our desires.

And so, my brothers, if you wish to live with God in the Kingdom of Heaven, be true ORTHODOX CHRISTIANS. If you desire prosperity and happiness, seek these in God. If you wish your heart to be fully satisfied—turn to God from Whom you have been separated by your sins.

You should know however, that no one can on his own, without Jesus Christ, turn to or draw near to God, for our sins stand as a high wall preventing us from approaching Him. Were it not for the fact that in His mercy towards us Jesus Christ came down to earth, took upon Himself our human flesh, and by His death destroyed the wall separating us from God—all mankind would have perished; not a single soul could have drawn near to God or lived with Him, for everyone is a sinner, born into sin from his mother's womb (Ps 51:5). Indeed, sin exists, as a seed, even in children who have as yet no knowledge of the world, who have as yet committed no evil.

Jesus Christ is, therefore, our Redeemer, our Savior, our Deliverer, and our Benefactor. He has now made it possible for all who so desire to return to God and enter the Kingdom of Heaven. One must be aware, however, that there is but one path leading into this Kingdom of Heaven, and this is the one which Jesus Christ Himself followed during His life on earth. There is no other way—never has there been, nor will there be—for Jesus Christ has told us, "I am the Way" (Jn 14:6) and "If anyone wants to come with me, he must forget himself, carry his cross, and follow me" (Mk 8:34).

And so, for every Christian—indeed, for every human being it is critically important to know what kind of way this is, how one can find it, and how he can follow it. And so it is that I wish to speak with you about THE WAY, knowing that while I shall prove incapable of indicating it to you as fully as I ought, I shall do my best, trusting in Jesus Christ Who can turn even mud into something capable of healing and curing.

Those who happen upon my book and desire to read it will find in it but a poor and feeble explanation of the PATHWAY INTO THE KINGDOM OF HEAVEN. But let him read it through with prayer to Jesus Christ, that He, our Almighty God, may through these words of mine enlighten and warm the reader's heart.

I divide my work into four parts:

(1) On the benefits granted us by Jesus Christ through His death.
(2) How Jesus Christ lived on earth and how He suffered for us.
(3) The Pathway by which we must enter the Kingdom of Heaven.
(4) How Jesus Christ helps us to follow this path and how we can receive His Help.

O Lord Jesus Christ, I call to You—hear me, Your unworthy servant! Enlighten my mind and grant that with truthfulness and clarity I may describe the pathway which leads into the glorious Kingdom which in Your mercy You have granted to us. Grant also that those who read and listen to my words may be filled with love for You, enlightened by coming to know You, and strengthened through Your power. If Your Spirit will but warm our hearts, we shall joyfully and fervently follow the pathway which you have indicated for us.

Part One

The Blessings Granted to Us by Jesus Christ through His Death

Before beginning to speak on this subject, let us first examine the blessings which Adam before he sinned possessed in Paradise, and the evil which befell him—and all humanity with him—as a result of sin.

The first man, being created in the IMAGE AND LIKENESS OF GOD (Gn 1:26) was blessed with these until by his own self-will he obscured his resemblance to God. For God, Who knows no end and is eternal, created Adam to be immortal; God, Who is supremely righteous created Adam sinless and righteous; God, supremely happy, created Adam with a happiness which should have increased more and more daily into all eternity.

In PARADISE, that garden supreme in beauty which God Himself planted for him, (Gn 2:8), Adam was content in every way. He enjoyed perpetual good health, never experienced disease of any sort. He never knew fear, for all animals and birds obeyed him as their king. He experienced neither cold nor heat, and although he was assigned to labor and work in Paradise (Gn 2:5), he did so with pleasure and enjoyment, being neither burdened nor physically exhausted by his work.

His soul and heart were filled with knowledge of and love for God. He was perpetually happy and at peace, knowing or seeing no unpleasantness, no trouble, no pain, no sadness. His intentions were all pure, true and in good order. His memory, intellect and all his other spiritual faculties were perfect. And being innocent and pure, he lived continually with God. He spoke with Him and was loved by Him as His own beloved son. In brief, Adam was in Paradise and in Adam WAS that paradise.

Now, had Adam obeyed his Creator's command, he and all his descendants would have remained happy forever. But Adam sinned against God by breaking His law—a law which was exceedingly light—and was in return expelled from Paradise (Gn 2:16) since it is impossible for God to abide with sin or a sinner (Gn 3:23).

Thus Adam found immediately that the prosperity he had enjoyed in Paradise was lost. His soul was darkened, his thought and desires grew muddled, his imagination and memory were clouded. Instead of joy and spiritual comforts he encountered sadness, sorrows, afflictions, poverty, tormenting labors, and troubles of every variety. In the end a diseased old age and ultimately death awaited him. Worse yet, the Devil, who takes comfort in human sufferings, was able to gain control over Adam.

The very elements of nature—air, fire, and so forth—which before had served to satisfy Adam, now stood in opposition to him. He and all his descendants would thereafter experience cold and heat, changes in wind and weather—and their adverse effects. The animals too grew savage and began to look upon human beings as enemies—and prey. Mankind began to suffer disease, both from outside and from within, and as time passed these grew more varied and severe. Human beings forgot that they are brothers and began attacking, hating, deceiving, torturing, and killing one another (Gn 4:8–9). And now, at the end of all their bitter labors and anxieties they had, as sinners, to face death. Hell was their portion, where they would suffer unceasing torment throughout eternity.

What Adam lost no one could then (or now) restore by his own efforts. What, then, would have become of us had Jesus Christ in His great mercy not Himself redeemed us? What would then have become of the human race? But God, Who loves us even more than we love ourselves, did indeed send to us His Son Jesus Christ to become a man like us entirely (except He was sinless).

Through His TEACHINGS Jesus Christ routed the darkness of ignorance and the errors of the human mind to illumine the whole world by the light of His Gospel. Now anyone who so desires can know the will of God, and the path and means which lead to bliss.

Through His LIFE Jesus Christ showed us that path into the Kingdom of Heaven which Adam lost, and at the same time demonstrated to us both that we ourselves must seek it and how we are to follow it.

Through His SUFFERINGS and DEATH Jesus Christ paid the debts we owed to God—and which we ourselves could never have repaid. By Himself bearing the torments which as transgressors of God's Will we ourselves ought to have endured, He transformed us from slaves to the Devil and sin into children of God. Through His death He delivered us from the privations and torments which lay before us, and from eternal death.

Through His RESURRECTION, Jesus Christ destroyed the gates of hell and opened to us the doors of Paradise which since Adam's transgression had remained locked to us. He conquered and destroyed the power wielded by our enemies, the Devil and Death. Therefore, those who now die with faith and hope in Jesus Christ pass through death from our present deceitful, corrupt and fleeting life into a radiant, incorrupt, and never-ending one. Now, as aids in defeating and routing the devil we have His CROSS and PRAYER.

Through His ASCENSION Jesus Christ glorified our humanity, for He ascended into heaven bearing the body which He will wear throughout eternity.

Finally, through the GRACE and MERITS of Jesus Christ we are now about to enter the Kingdom of Heaven and receive both support and help along the way. That is, we can truly and unhindered receive the Holy Spirit and be filled with Him without whose help no one can follow the path which Jesus Christ took.

Had Jesus Christ not lived on earth no one would be able to enter the Kingdom of Heaven. Now, however, each and every one of us can enter it with ease—but by no other path than that which Jesus Christ Himself followed during His earthly life.

No one can describe or imagine all that the Lord has prepared for us in heaven (1 Cor 2:9) and we are able to say nothing more concerning this than that those who believe in Jesus Christ and keep His commandments will after death live with the angels, the righteous and all the saints in heaven. They will see God face-to-face. They will rejoice with pure joy, ceaseless and eternal, knowing neither tedium nor sorrow, nor worry, nor torment, nor suffering—and at the end of this age they will be raised up with their bodies to reign eternally with Christ.

Jesus Christ grants these good things not to just one nation but to all—without exception—who desire them. The path to them has been shown to us. It has been arranged and, inasmuch as possible, smoothed and leveled for us. Furthermore, Jesus Christ is Himself prepared to help us follow His path. He wishes, so to speak, to lead us by the hand if only we will not oppose Him—not become stubborn—but rather surrender ourselves fully to His Will. May He indeed lead us where and as He wishes!

Thus, you see how Jesus Christ loves us and what good things He gives to us! But what if He were to appear to us, suddenly, right now, and ask, "My children, do you love me in return for all I have done for you? Are you thankful to Me in your hearts?" Who among us would fail to respond, "Indeed, Lord, we love You and are thankful"?

But if you truly love Jesus Christ and feel thankful to Him, do you also do the things He commanded you to do? For if one person loves another and is thankful to him, surely he will do everything in his power to please that person. Now Jesus Christ, your Benefactor, wants from you just one thing: THAT YOU FOLLOW HIM INTO THE KINGDOM OF HEAVEN.

Jesus Christ did everything for us. Can it be that we will now fail to do the one thing He asks of us? In order to save us, Jesus Christ came down from heaven to earth; are we not willing for His sake even to desire to follow Him up to Heaven? For our sake He endured all torments, all sufferings; can it truly be that for His sake we have no desire to suffer and endure just a little? Blessed—exceedingly blessed—is anyone who throughout his life follows Jesus Christ, for he will surely find himself where Jesus Christ dwells.

Happy is anyone who cares and who tries to imitate Jesus Christ, for he will receive His help. But how unhappy are those who lack the desire to follow Jesus Christ, those who say, "It is so hard to follow Him," or "I lack the strength for it." SUCH PEOPLE DEPRIVE THEMSELVES OF THE GRACE OF GOD, and as it were, spurn the helping hand of Jesus Christ.

How horrible for those who oppose Jesus Christ and stand as it were, in stubborn opposition to Him! Their lot will be the lake of fire and sulfur (Rv 20:10).

Part Two

Jesus Christ's Life on Earth and His Sufferings for Us

Everyone ought to obey God's law, a law composed of two commandments: 1) Love the Lord your God with all your heart, with all your soul, with all your mind and with all your strength, and 2) Love your neighbor as you love yourself (Mk 12:30–31). Each person's reward will depend on how he has fulfilled these.

No human being has ever fulfilled these two commandments to perfection. Jesus Christ alone did so with no deficiency. In this respect, the saints—even the greatest—are but lights while Jesus Christ is the sun in all its brightness and splendor. And just as no one can look at the sun and describe it fully, so no one is capable of describing all the good deeds of Jesus Christ. Therefore I shall attempt no more than to speak in brief about those aspects of His life and virtues which can be seen in the Gospel.

No human being—indeed, no angel—has ever loved God as fully as Jesus Christ did (and does). Jesus Christ prayed constantly to God His Father, particularly at night and while alone. At every feast, at the Passover in particular, He travelled to the Temple in Jerusalem despite the fact that His home was not near-by. Likewise, every Sabbath day He gathered with the people for prayer and instruction. In everything He did, Jesus Christ glorified God's Name continually, offering Him praises both inwardly and openly in the sight of others.

Throughout His life, Jesus Christ truly respected, obeyed, honored and loved His Mother and Joseph, the man people supposed to be His father. In like manner He respected authorities and elders and paid the taxes He owed to the earthly king.

Willingly and without murmur, conscientiously, zealously and lovingly, Jesus Christ fulfilled His ministry, the work for which He came into the world.

Jesus Christ loved every person, desired good for all, and did good to everyone. To assure true happiness for the human race He did not even spare His own life.

With unspeakable meekness and love did Jesus Christ endure every insult. He never complained to those who offended Him, or grew angry at even the worst of His enemies, those who slandered, mocked, and sought to kill Him. A single word from His mouth would have sufficed to kill and annihilate all His enemies and opponents, yet such was not His desire. On the contrary, He wished them well, did good to them, prayed for them, and wept when He saw that they were nonetheless perishing.

In brief, from birth to death Jesus Christ never sinned at all in word, deed, or thought, but in all things and at all times did good to all people.

Now let us look at how Jesus Christ suffered on earth.

Despite the fact that He was the Son of God—indeed, He was GOD—Jesus Christ accepted a human body and soul to become a perfect person (without sin). And despite the fact that He was all-powerful, He appeared to us as a Servant. Although He was truly King both of heaven and earth, He was born in poverty from a poor Mother in a cave. He slept in a manger (Lk 2:7). The man supposed by all to be his father was a lowly carpenter (Mt 17:55).

Although He was Himself the supreme Lawgiver, Jesus Christ in order to fulfill all that the Law required, poured out His most-precious blood at his circumcision on the eighth day following His birth (Lk 2:21). Later, His most-pure Mother brought Him to the Temple and paid the redemption price for Him—the Redeemer of the world (Lk 2:22–24). Jesus Christ still lay in the cradle when Herod sought to kill Him, and He was forced to flee into Egypt, a foreign land (Mt 2:13–18). (Never think that even in childhood

Jesus Christ was unaware of the things which were being done to Him. No! For although he was indeed fully human, Jesus Christ was also fully divine, and as such He saw and knew everything which was happening to Him.)

Being Himself God Almighty, Whom Heaven, earth, and the myriads of angels all obey, Jesus Christ in His earthly lifetime had nowhere to lay down and rest (Mt 8:20). Jesus Christ, the King of the whole universe, paid taxes to an earthly king (Mt 17:24–27).

Jesus Christ, Whom the angels and all creation serve, Himself served others and even washed His disciples' feet (Jn 13:4–11) (and those whom He had chosen were indeed simple, untaught people).

As He preached, Jesus Christ received countless insults from His enemies. They accused Him of being a sinner, a transgressor of Moses' Law, and derelict, a carpenter's son, the friend and companion of gluttons, drunkards, and tax collectors. Once the malice and fury of His enemies reached the point that they were about to hurl Him over a cliff. Another time they wished to stone Him to death. His holy doctrine they labelled lies and deception, and when He healed the sick or raised the dead, His enemies even dared to charge that He did so with Satan's help, suggesting that He Himself possessed a devil.

In short, from birth to death, Jesus Christ suffered, experiencing sorrows and outrages from all sides. He suffered at the hands of those whom He wished to save. And the sorrow He felt came not only from the people's failure to hear Him, or even from their insults—but from the fact that even while they were perishing, they had no desire to turn from their perdition. Jesus Christ suffered, so to speak, both visibly and invisibly, for not only had He to encounter and endure open insults and offenses at the hands of others—but He had also to see all the evil thoughts and intentions which His enemies entertained towards Him in secret. He saw likewise that even those who seemed to love Him warmly and listen to Him in fact either failed to believe or were indifferent to their own salvation.

Who brought the greatest sufferings to Jesus Christ? The Jewish high priests and scribes. That is, those scholars and leaders of the people who knew of and awaited the Savior's coming, but who wished neither to receive nor to hear Him. Quite the contrary, they were the ones who condemned Him to death as a deceiver and a criminal. Then, when the Jewish nation as a whole was at the point of having Jesus freed from the sentence of crucifixion, the leaders convinced them to ask freedom instead for Barabbas, a thief and rebel, thereby betraying to death the Holiest of Holies. O God! the lengths to which human envy and malice can go! Most horrible of all, however, was the fact that Jesus Christ was betrayed by one of His own disciples, one who had known Him, eaten with Him, drunk with Him—one whose own eyes had beheld His life, His miracles, and the power of His doctrine! And how was He betrayed? By the treachery of a kiss. And the price? Thirty pieces of silver.

For whom did Jesus Christ suffer? For ALL those who sinned or would sin from Adam until the end of the world. He suffered even for those who were tormenting Him, those who had betrayed Him to such torments, and those who, in spite of the countless blessings they had received from Him had not only failed to thank Him but had indeed openly hated and persecuted Him. He suffered for ALL OF US who day-after-day offend Him through our lies, our wickedness, and our horrible indifference toward the sufferings He bore for us. He suffered for us who even now, by our ingratitude and vile sins, nail Him to the Cross.

In the final days of His earthly life, Jesus Christ performed one of His greatest miracles by raising Lazarus, a man who had already lain buried four days and begun to decompose, from death. This miracle caused many of the multitude who witnessed it to believe in Jesus Christ and to acknowledge Him as indeed the One Whom God had sent. But not so the high-priests and scribes, for rather than accepting and believing in Him, and convincing the masses that this was truly the Savior of the world, they gathered in council in Caiaphas' house to decide what was to be done with Jesus. They sought accusations against Him and finally determined that JESUS CHRIST, WHO HAD RAISED THE DEAD, WAS HIMSELF TO BE BETRAYED TO DEATH.

Now, Jesus Christ's sufferings that final night—from the time of the Last Supper until His betrayal into the soldiers' hands—can scarcely be imagined. His inner sufferings were so terrible that no one but He could have endured them—and even He sweated blood. His soul endured cruel agony, profound sadness, and horrible sufferings. His soul was covered with shame and terror because of the sins which He took upon Himself for our sake—all the sins which mankind from Adam until the end of the age would commit.

At that moment Jesus Christ was also able to foresee that soon, even among Christians, hypocritical disciples like Judas would appear, many of whom would not only fail to imitate Him but would surrender themselves to vices and vile and abominable sins. He foresaw too that there would appear those who would deny the faith and His doctrine, and moreover those who would distort it by false interpretations and seek to lead others in accordance with their own ideas rather than surrendering to God's wisdom.

On the one hand, love for God His Father demanded of Jesus Christ that He destroy this criminal and thankless human race. But on the other, His love for these same people, fallen and perishing, urged Him to suffer for their sakes in order that through His sufferings they might be delivered from eternal perdition. Such sufferings were for Him so terrible and so great that He declared to His disciples, "the sorrow in My heart is so great that it almost crushes Me" (Mt 26:38).

After His betrayal, Jesus Christ was bound and led like an evildoer before His enemies to stand trial and be condemned to death. The Apostles—for whom His love was greater and more special than anyone else—abandoned Him and fled. When Pilate asked, "which one do you want me to set free for you—Jesus Barabbas or Jesus called the Messiah?" (Mt 27:17) His evil and malicious enemies incited the senseless crowds to DEMAND BARABBAS, a bandit, and to CRUCIFY JESUS, the Righteous and Holy One (Jn 18:40). Therefore, they handed Him over, placing on His head a crown of thorny branches, stripped Him of His clothing, nailed Him to a cross, and lifted Him up in a shameful place between two bandits, as an evildoer and criminal. Even while He hung on the cross their cruel malice and envy never spared Him; even there they taunted Him as a deceiver and for His thirst they gave Him vinegar and gall to drink.

Finally Jesus Christ DIED. He died the DEATH OF THE CROSS in torment and shame.

Never think that Jesus Christ suffered because He was unable to deliver Himself or escape these tortures. No! He surrendered and offered Himself to such a sacrifice willingly. Otherwise, no one would ever have dared to touch Him, or even to consider this, for as we know, when those who were sent to arrest Him were asked, "Who is it you are looking for?" and replied "Jesus of Nazareth," His words—"I am He"—caused them to fall to the ground (Jn 18:4–7).

We can say no more than this concerning the suffering which Jesus Christ in His unspeakable love for us endured for our sake, but must—in order to understand as fully as possible just how great His love for us is and how great His sacrifice was—remind ourselves WHO Jesus Christ IS. Jesus Christ is truly God, the almighty Creator of the universe, the great King of angels and the human race, the powerful Master of all creation, the fearful Judge of both the living and the dead—this is the One who accepted all these things on behalf of the human race!

Part Three

The Path Which Leads into the Kingdom of Heaven

Jesus Christ is Himself the pathway into the Kingdom of Heaven, and only those who follow Him are on it. Now, if you want to know how to follow this path, listen to the words of Jesus Christ: "If anyone wants to come with Me, he must forget himself, carry his cross, and follow Me"

(Mk 8:34). And just what it means to forget oneself, carry one's cross and follow Jesus Christ will now be told.

Jesus Christ said, "If anyone wants to come with Me." These words signify that Jesus Christ will not compel or force anyone to follow Him. He does not want reluctant disciples or those having no particular desire. He wants a person willingly and with no compulsion to surrender himself wholly to Him. Therefore, only those who personally desire to enter the Kingdom of Heaven will do so. O Christian! Your salvation—or perdition—depends on your own will. In His unspeakable wisdom and love, the Lord has given you the gift of freedom to do as you like, and He has no desire now to take back from you this most precious gift. If you truly wish to follow Jesus Christ He will show you the path into the Kingdom of Heaven, and indeed stands ready to help you walk down it. If, however, you wish not to follow Him—that is up to you. No one is forcing you or will force you. But beware, for you are despising the will of Jesus Christ and His mercy. In His great goodness Jesus Christ will knock for a long, long time at the door to a person's heart (Rv 3:20), trying to awaken his soul and arouse in it the desire for salvation. But how horrible it will be for anyone whom He finally abandons and casts out as a child of perdition!

Thus, in order to follow Jesus Christ one must first of all have the desire and the resolve to do so. But to have this desire one must know WHERE TO GO and WHAT WILL BE REQUIRED FOR THE JOURNEY. But how can one have certain knowledge of something which he really does not wish to know, or of which he has heard but superficially, perfunctorily? No, before following Jesus Christ you must do the following:

1) Study diligently the foundations upon which our Orthodox Christian faith is built, that is, the actual books of Holy Scripture. You should know WHERE THEY CAME FROM, WHO WROTE THEM AND WHEN, HOW THEY HAVE BEEN PRESERVED AND HANDED TO US, AND WHY THEY ARE CALLED "DIVINE," "HOLY" and so forth. But when studying the Holy Scriptures you must do so in simplicity of heart, without prejudice, inquisitiveness or bias. Never exceed the limits of your own mind. That is, never seek to penetrate and understand things which God in His Wisdom has concealed from us. If you study the faith in this way, you will never find yourself going counter to the faith, and it is indeed the binding duty of every Christian ONCE HE HAS REACHED MATURITY TO KNOW HIS FAITH THOROUGHLY, since those who fail to know their faith thoroughly will remain cold and indifferent to it and will frequently fall into either superstition or disbelief. How many Christians (or better put: how many of those who have received baptism in the name of Jesus Christ) have perished and are even now perishing simply because they do not and did not wish to pay attention to the foundations of

our Orthodox faith? Anyone who despises this duty will have no defense at the fearful Judgement.

Not everyone is capable of studying to the same degree, but everyone is obliged to undertake it according to his own abilities, intelligence and degree of education. The scholar, for example, must personally consider how historical events are relevant to the origins and development of the faith, discern the spirit of the Holy Scriptures, etc., whereas the simple and uneducated are obliged to consult with and learn from the pastors and teachers of the Church—those who have promised and dedicated their entire lives to teaching the faith, having studied since childhood for this very purpose.

2) When you know and are convinced that OUR ORTHODOX FAITH IS FOUNDED UPON THE HOLY SCRIPTURES rather than on fiction or mere speculation, and that the HOLY SCRIPTURES ARE TRULY THE WORD OF GOD REVEALED TO US BY THE HOLY SPIRIT THROUGH THE PROPHETS AND APOSTLES—pry no further into the things which have not been revealed to us. Believe unconditionally, without doubt or speculation, in all that the Scriptures teach. Listen to no human explanations or interpretations of those things which transcend the human mind. If you proceed in this way your faith will be true and proper and it will be imputed to you as justification and merit.

3) Finally, strive to possess and stir up within yourself the desire to do what the Holy Scriptures teach. If you presently lack such desire, fall down in fervent prayer before our Savior Jesus Christ and ask Him to grant you this. And once grace calls you to the way of salvation, never resist it.

All that we have been saying concerning faith we will now explain using a parable. Let us say that you hear of an enormous, magnificent building whose top reaches the heavens. Its entrance, however, is obscured such that it requires special instructions for people to locate it, but there has been provided a multitude of attendants for this purpose and as further guides. These serve also as physicians of the sick and crippled and as dispensers of the food needed along the way. For the ascent there are provided such a multitude of ladders that almost everyone has one of his own. But these are steep and narrow and poorly lit, such that without direction and outside help one can scarcely take a step—especially at the beginning. This building was erected by the very wisest Architect, and exists for the express purpose of leading mankind to heaven, into Paradise itself.

Having heard this, you will doubtless desire to go to where this building leads. But how should you proceed? First of course, you must locate the building, examine it carefully, question the attendants well, and so forth—learning about the BUILDING ITSELF: ITS PURPOSE, HOW AND WHERE TO ENTER etc. And the attendants will gladly tell you all you need to know. If you are a person of learning, examine the actual construction, considering it from every angle: are THE FOUNDATIONS STRONG? ARE THEY CAPABLE OF SUPPORTING THIS VERY HEAVY BUILDING AS WELL AS ALL WHO WILL ENTER IT? If you are indeed very learned you may examine the materials which went into the building. Measure them, study them, learn all you can with your own eyes and through the use of whatever instruments you may require. Then, when you have seen and convinced yourself that THIS BUILDING IS INDEED STRONG AND SOUND, AND THAT IT SERVES ITS PURPOSE FULLY, abandon further searching, and leave at the door all the tools you have used in your investigations—for inside they will be of no further help to you and can henceforth serve only to hinder you. Next, enter the building without the slightest trace of doubt. Do not hesitate or begin to fear the climb—though difficult it indeed will be, particularly at the outset; the ascent to heaven IS difficult, but it leads directly to where all human beings should aspire, to that for which we ought throughout our lives to seek.

Once inside the building, you will find companions who will proceed hand in hand with you. They are physicians to aid you should you stumble and be bruised; dispensers of the food you will need along the way; guides, directors and teachers to tell you all you will need to know. You will continue to encounter such people all the way along your path until finally the MASTER OF THE HOUSE, THE CREATOR OF THE BUILDING HIMSELF will come to greet you. But in order all the more quickly and surely to reach the end of your path, you must SURRENDER yourself as fully and trustingly as you can to the will of the Builder and Master of the house.

Now tell me, should it happen, for whatever reason: pride, self-reliance, or stubbornness—that a person decides that he wishes to examine not the FOUNDATIONS of the building (that is, those things which our eyes are capable of seeing) but the very TOP, which normally the clouds and that vast expanse of space between heaven and earth keep hidden—would this not be unreasonable? Would it not indeed be foolishness for him to choose to pass judgement and draw conclusions on the building as a whole on the basis of those remote parts of the building which he is incapable of examining as fully as he should? Or to find fault and excesses at heights so extraordinary that the building itself is scarcely visible? Would it not likewise be foolish on his part—indeed criminal—to begin criticizing some detail or other without a full examination? Indeed, having scarcely entered the precincts of the building, has he the right to persuade others that the BUILDING IS UNSOUND OR IN SOME WAY DEFICIENT? Or, if he were to begin suggesting his own instructions and ideas as substitutes for the laws and instructions issued by the Master Architect Himself? Certainly the biggest fool would be anyone who, having scarcely bothered to enter the area, abandons all desire not only to enter the building but even declines to give it a full examination.

Those who sincerely desire to be where this building leads will find it sufficient simply to convince themselves that it is soundly built and firmly grounded, made not by the hands of ordinary artisans and workers but by the Great Architect Himself, Whose own blood established and purified the way, and that He Himself first walked through it. It suffices to convince oneself of THIS and all else (for instance, why it was built in such a manner and not otherwise, or why it is located here rather than elsewhere) will cease to be any of one's business. One's SOLE concern will then become surrendering to the Master's will and desire, and hoping in His help. With love for Him in your heart now walk towards Him. Go as He commands.

Now let us apply this PARABLE to Christianity. The BUILDING set upon the earth and reaching to heaven is our Orthodox Christian Faith. The ARCHITECT and Master of the building is Jesus Christ. The ATTENDANTS are the Church's pastors and teachers. Now, let us examine the PATHWAY along which we must follow Jesus Christ. He has told us that anyone wishing to be with Him must 1) forget himself, 2) carry his cross, and 3) follow Him.

Thus, the FIRST duty of a Christian (that is, a disciple and follower of Jesus Christ) is to FORGET HIMSELF. To forget oneself means to set aside all one's evil habits, to root out of one's heart everything that binds us to this world. It means not entertaining evil desires or thoughts, but rather quenching and suppressing them. It means avoiding all occasions for sin, doing and desiring nothing which stems from self-love, but only those things which result from love for God. To FORGET ONESELF means, in the words of the Apostle Paul, TO BE DEAD TO SIN AND THE WORLD, BUT ALIVE TO GOD (Rom 6:11).

The SECOND duty of a Christian (one who follows Jesus Christ) is to CARRY HIS CROSS. By "cross" we mean all sufferings, sorrows, and annoyances. CROSSES can be both external and internal, and TO CARRY ONE'S CROSS means to accept and bear without complaint whatever annoyances, sorrows, sadnesses, difficulties and distresses might befall us in life. Thus, should anyone offend or laugh at you; should anyone weary, sadden or annoy you; should anyone for whom you have done good rise up to cause you trouble rather than offering you thanks; should you fail in your desire to do good for someone; should some misfortune happen to befall you (should you, your spouse or children, for example, happen to fall sick); should you find yourself in want or need despite your work and tireless labors; even should poverty and misery overwhelm you, or any other sort of annoyance come upon you—bear all things without malice, without grumbling, without criticism, without complaint. Never hope to receive your reward on earth, but endure all things with love, joy and determination.

TO CARRY ONE'S CROSS means not only to bear those crosses which others impose upon us, or those sent to us by God's Providence, but to take up and carry crosses of our own—indeed, even to impose crosses upon ourselves. This means that a Christian can and should make and keep vows and promises which seem burdensome and difficult to him. (These promises should, however, conform to the Lord's Word and will, rather than to one's own ideas and fancies.) Thus, for example, one can and should make and keep vows expedient for his neighbors, such as MINISTERING TO THE SICK, ACTIVELY HELPING THOSE IN NEED, SEEKING OPPORTUNITIES TO CONTRIBUTE TO THE SALVATION AND WELFARE OF OTHERS in patience and humility by deeds, words, advice, prayer, etc.

And as you bear your cross in accordance with the Word and intention of the Lord, should proud thoughts arise within you (that unlike other people you are firm, pious, better than your companions and neighbors)—strive as hard as you can to root these thoughts out, for they can undo all your virtues.

Although we mentioned above that crosses can be of both external and internal types, we have thus far spoken almost exclusively about the external ones—and happy indeed is anyone who can bear these wisely, for the Lord will never allow such a person to perish, but will send the Holy Spirit to strengthen, instruct, and lead him forward. But for one to be made holy in the likeness of Jesus Christ, external crosses alone will not suffice, for in the absence of interior ones, these are no more useful than external prayer without inner. Such is the case because the bearing of external crosses, sufferings imposed from without, is not limited to the disciples of Jesus Christ alone. Rather, each and every human being must endure these. That is, while no one in this world is free from suffering or enduring wrongs at the hands of others, those who wish to be true disciples of Jesus Christ and numbered among his followers must certainly bear interior crosses as well.

INTERIOR CROSSES can be found at any time, even more readily than external ones. One has only to be attentive to oneself and in repentance to examine one's own soul in order immediately to find thousands of interior crosses. For example, consider your coming into this world: why do you exist? Do you live as you ought to? And so forth. Pay due attention and you will see right off that as a creature of Almighty God you exist in this world SOLELY IN ORDER THAT THROUGH ALL YOU DO, BY THE TOTALITY OF YOUR LIFE, YOUR ENTIRE BEING—GOD'S GREAT AND HOLY NAME MAY BE GLORIFIED. You, however, not only fail to glorify Him but, indeed, offend and dishonor him through your lawless life. . . .

Next recall and consider WHAT AWAITS YOU BEYOND THE GRAVE: WILL YOU FIND YOURSELF TO CHRIST'S RIGHT OR LEFT AT HIS DREAD JUDGEMENT? If you ponder these things and more, you will involuntarily grow alarmed, disquieted—and herein lies the BEGINNING OF YOUR INTERIOR CROSSES. If you never allow yourself to banish such thoughts from your mind; if you never seek diversion from them in worldly pleasures and vain amusements; if instead you examine yourself all the more carefully—you will discover additional crosses still. For example, HELL, of which you perhaps had hitherto not been mindful (or had kept it in mind with indifference at best) will become manifest to you in all its horror. PARADISE which the Lord has prepared for you—but about which you gave no thought (or considered little more than in passing)—will now appear to you vividly, as it truly is—a place of pure, eternal joys, of which you through carelessness, stupidity, and so forth are depriving yourself. And if, in the face of all the pain and inner suffering which these thoughts will cause you, you will firmly resolve to endure them rather than seek consolation in anything of this world, and will pray fervently to the Lord for your salvation, surrendering completely to His will—He in turn will begin to reveal to you precisely the condition of your soul, thus allowing you more and more to sow and nourish fear, affliction, and sorrow in yourself—and thereby purify yourself all the more.

TO GRASP THE STATE OF OUR OWN SOULS when they stand completely naked, and to sense vividly the danger we are in always remain impossible for us UNLESS THE LORD GRANTS US HIS SPECIAL MERCY AND HELP. For the interior of one's soul remains ever hidden from him through self-love and false wisdom; the passions, cares and deceptions of this world. And if, at times, we feel ourselves capable of seeing the condition of our soul—we see no more than externals, no more than our own intellect and conscience are able to reveal.

Our enemy, the Devil, knowing that EXAMINATION AND KNOWLEDGE OF OUR SOUL'S TRUE CONDITION CAN LEAD US TO SALVATION, and fearing that we will be converted and begin to desire that we may be saved, first uses all his wiles and cunning to prevent our seeing this reality. Next, however, should he sense that his cunning has not availed, but that a person has, with the help and grace of God, rather begun to SEE HIMSELF, the Devil tries a different, more cunning trick—he himself hastens to reveal to that person the true condition of his soul—but very rapidly, and from the worst possible angles in order thereby to strike terror in him and bring him to the point of despair. Were the Lord always to permit the Devil to make use of this ploy (showing us our soul's most dangerous sides), very few of us would survive, for indeed, the state of a sinner's soul (and particularly the unrepentant) is a terribly dangerous and horrible thing. (Indeed, not sinners alone, but even the most holy and righteous people could never, for all their righteousness, find sufficient tears to weep over their souls.)

When the Lord finds proper to reveal to you the condition of your soul, you will begin to see clearly and FEEL VIVIDLY, despite all your virtues, just how corrupt and perverted your heart is, how filthy your soul is; how you are nothing but a slave to sin and to passions which hold you in complete control and prevent your approaching God. You will then begin to realize that there is no true goodness in you, and that what few good deeds you may indeed have done are all mixed with sin and represent not the FRUIT OF TRUE LOVE, but merely a result of various passions, circumstances and so forth. At this point you will surely suffer. Fear, sorrow, misery and so forth will seize you: FEAR that you are in danger of perishing; SORROW AND MISERY over the fact that for so long and with such stubbornness you have shut out the Lord's gentle voice calling you into the Kingdom of Heaven; that you have so long and so brazenly angered Him through your sins.

The more the Lord reveals to you the condition of your soul, the more your inner sufferings will increase. This is the meaning of the interior cross!

Now, since not all people share the same virtues and sins, their interior crosses are not all the same. For some they are more oppressive than for others. For some they are more prolonged than for others. For some they come in one form, for others in another. All of this depends on the condition of the individual soul, in the same precise way that the duration and course of treatment for disease depend upon the patient's condition. The physician is surely not to blame if drastic, long-term treatment is required to cure a chronic and dangerous disease which the patient himself has perhaps irritated and worsened. Those who wish truly to be healthy must consent to endure all things. For some their interior crosses will form such a burden that they find no consolation anywhere. This could well happen to you also. But no matter what position you find yourself in, no matter what spiritual sufferings you may have to endure, never despair and never think that the Lord has abandoned you. No! He will be with you always, strengthening you invisibly even when you feel yourself to be on the very brink of perdition. No! He will never allow you to be tempted beyond what He sees fit. Never despair! Never fear. But in complete submission and devotion to Him BE PATIENT AND PRAY. For He never ceases to be our Father, a Father Who loves His children deeply. If He allows someone who is devoted to Him to be brought to hard testing, it is only thereby TO DEMONSTRATE TO THAT PERSON AS PERSUASIVELY AND CLEARLY AS POSSIBLE HIS OWN IMPOTENCE, WEAKNESS AND INSIGNIFICANCE IN ORDER TO TEACH HIM BOTH THAT HE MUST NEVER RELY ON HIMSELF ALONE, AND THAT WITHOUT GOD NO ONE CAN DO ANY GOOD. If the Lord brings suffering on a person or places crosses on him, THIS IS STRICTLY IN ORDER THAT HIS SOUL MAY BE HEALED, AND THAT HE HIMSELF MAY BE MADE TO CONFORM TO JESUS CHRIST. The Lord does these things in order to purify this person's heart completely so that He Himself may dwell there as He wishes, together with His Son and His Holy Spirit.

In your sorrows—no matter how profound they may be—never seek consolation in others (unless the Lord indicates to you specifically that you should and sends you someone He has chosen) for "normal people"—those inexperienced in spiritual matters—always make the worst comforters, even when sadness is of the usual sort, while should you find yourself in sorrow and sadness FOR THE LORD—something about which they simply have no conception—they will sooner ruin you than bring you comfort or ease your sufferings. The Lord, your Lord, is your Helper, your Comforter, and your Guide—so run to Him alone, and in Him alone seek comfort and help.

Happy—a hundred times happy—is anyone whom the Lord allows to bear such interior crosses, for these serve as true spiritual medicine, a sure and reliable means of becoming like Jesus Christ. Hence, these crosses mark also a special manifestation of the Lord's favor and visible concern for a person's salvation. No less happy is this person because he is now in a condition which he could never before, without the aid of God's grace, have attained—or even have considered necessary for his salvation.

If you bear your sufferings meekly and with loyalty to the Lord's will, and if you refrain from seeking consolation anywhere or in anyone other than the Lord, He in His mercy will never abandon you or leave you comfortless. He will touch your heart with His grace and communicate to you the gifts of His Holy Spirit. As you suffer—even, perhaps at the very outset—you will begin to feel in your heart an inexplicably sweet joy such as you have never felt before. At the same time you will begin to experience within yourself the strength and ability to pray to God in true prayer, to believe in Him with true faith, and your heart will begin to burn with pure love for God and your neighbor. All of this is a gift from the Holy Spirit and, should the Lord grant you such a gift, you must never consider it a reward for your labors or sorrows, nor think that you have attained perfection or holiness. Such thoughts are but an inspiration of that inner pride which has so deeply penetrated our soul and taken such firm root there that it can manifest itself even in those who possess the power of performing miracles.

The comfort of being touched by the Holy Spirit is not REWARD but the Lord's mercy granted to you in order that you might taste the good things which God has prepared for those who love Him, that having tasted these you may seek them with greater fervor and zeal and thereby be prepared and strengthened to endure new sorrows and sufferings. Nor is the love which you will then begin to feel as yet that perfect condition which the saints attain on earth. It is simply an indication of it.

The THIRD duty of each disciple of Jesus Christ is TO FOLLOW HIM. To follow Jesus Christ means to imitate His deeds and actions in your every deed and action. We ought to live and act just as Jesus Christ lived and acted on this earth. For example, Jesus Christ always thanked, glorified and prayed to God His Father. So too must we—no matter what the circumstances of our life may be—thank, love, and praise God (openly and in secret), pray to Him and keep Him continually in our minds and hearts.

Jesus Christ respected His most pure Mother, His supposed father, and all authorities, and remained ever obedient to them. Likewise must we listen to and respect our parents and teachers, never irritating or offending them by our deeds. We must respect our rulers and all powers, obeying and fulfilling their orders without complaint.

Jesus Christ, the King of the Universe, paid taxes to an earthly king, and though He was indeed Judge both of the living and the dead, He had no desire to exercise any civil authority as judge or arbitrator (Lk 12:14). So too ought we to pay our taxes without complaint and seize for ourselves no power which is not rightly ours—to judge, for example, or criticize those in power. Jesus Christ fulfilled willingly and with zeal and love the duties which He accepted by coming into the world. So ought we also willingly and without complaint to carry out the duties which God and the State have assigned to us, no matter how difficult—or menial—they may be.

Jesus Christ loved everyone and did good to all. So too ought we to love our companions and inasmuch as possible, do good to them in word, deed, and thought.

Jesus Christ offered Himself up to save the human race. So too ought we never to spare labors or health to achieve good for others. If for the salvation and defense of our nation and its ruler (he being the father of society) we are not expected to spare even our life, how much more ought we for the sake of Jesus Christ, our Redeemer and Benefactor, like the holy martyrs never spare the comfort of our soul and body, but for His sake endure all tortures and even death.

Jesus Christ offered Himself WILLINGLY to suffer and die. So too ought we never to avoid the sufferings and tribulations sent to us by God, but in humility and with devotion to God to accept and bear these.

Jesus Christ not only forgave all that His enemies had done to Him; He indeed returned good to them and prayed that they might be saved. So too ought we to forgive our enemies, repay with good the evil that they do us; bless those who curse us—in full faith and hope in God our fair and omniscient Judge who must give His consent for even a single hair to fall from our heads (Mt 10:29–30). When you have endured insult in love rather than with complaint or revenge then you have acted as a true Christian!

Jesus Christ, the King of heaven and earth, lived in poverty, personally labored to earn the things necessary to sustain His life. So too must we be industrious and without slough to seek the things we need. We should be satisfied with our status and never desire wealth, for as the Savior has said, it is harder for a rich man to enter the Kingdom of Heaven than for a camel to go through the eye of a needle (Mt 19:24).

Jesus Christ, Who was gentle and humble in spirit (Mt 11:29), never sought or desired praise from others. So too ought we never to boast to others or seek their praise. For example, if you do good to someone, if you give alms, if you live more piously than others, if you are more intelligent than many others or in general surpass those around you, never boast of this before others—or yourself—for nothing of what you find good and praiseworthy in yourself comes from you, but is rather a gift of God. Only sins and weaknesses are truly your own. All else comes from God.

TO FOLLOW JESUS CHRIST means, furthermore, to obey His word. We must, therefore, listen to, believe in, and do all He has told us to do through His Apostles in the Gospel—and to do so without guile, in simplicity of heart. Whoever listens and attends to the word of Jesus Christ is entitled to CALL HIMSELF a disciple. Those, however, who not only listen but DO what His word says (in simplicity of heart and complete devotion)—they ARE INDEED His TRUE AND BELOVED DISCIPLES.

This, then is what it means to forget oneself, take up one's cross and follow Jesus Christ. These are the true qualities and virtures of a disciple of Jesus Christ. This is the true and straight path into the Kingdom of Heaven—that which Jesus Christ Himself followed on earth, and which you, O Christian, must yourself also follow. There has never been—nor is there now—any other path than this.

This path, as we know, is neither smooth nor wide nor free of thorns (and particularly at the beginning is this the case), but it does lead directly and surely into Paradise, the Kingdom of Heaven, eternal bliss. It leads to God, the Source of all happiness. And if indeed this path is filled with sorrow, we can state that for every step we take a thousand rewards await. The sufferings along this path will not last forever; indeed, they are just momentary. But the rewards for them are unending and eternal, just as God Himself is unending and eternal. And day-by-day these sufferings will decrease and grow lighter while the rewards will increase more-and-more, hour by hour, without end throughout the life to come. So never fear this thorny and uneven path which leads to heaven; fear rather the smooth and even one which has its end in hell.

Many confused individuals ask WHY THE PATH INTO THE KINGDOM OF

HEAVEN IS SO DIFFICULT AND WHY THE CHRISTIAN MUST BEAR SO MANY WEIGHTY CROSSES. And the Christian answer to these and similar questions must always be simply that such IS THE WILL OF OUR GOD, a wise and loving God Who knows what He is doing—and must do—with us. Now, if we wish to be TRUE disciples of Jesus Christ (that is, submissive, obedient and devoted), surely we must unquestioningly "commend ourselves, each other and our WHOLE life to Christ our God." Yet since there exist several clear and easily understood lines of reasoning concerning the inevitable difficulty of following the path to salvation in the Kingdom of Heaven, we may without fear consider these:

1) The Kingdom of Heaven is SUPREME HAPPINESS, SUPREME GLORY AND HONOR, AND INEXHAUSTIBLE WEALTH. Since even petty trifling wealth can never be attained on earth except through great efforts and cares, how can such an unspeakable treasury be received except through labor?

2) The Kingdom of Heaven is a REWARD—indeed, the very greatest of rewards—and are rewards ever granted for free, for nothing? No, if on earth we must work and struggle to receive mere temporal rewards, how much more must we labor to receive an eternal reward in heaven?

3) Since we call ourselves (and truly desire to be) Christians, disciples, followers and members of Jesus Christ, we must bear our crosses, for as the Teacher, Leader, and Head is—so too must His disciples, followers and members be. And since it was through suffering that Jesus Christ entered His glory, so can we enter our glory in no other way than by suffering.

4) All people bear crosses; in varying degrees each and every human being must suffer and endure wrongs—hence it follows that it is not the exclusive lot of Christians to bear crosses. And indeed it is not! Christians and nonchristians alike must bear them, with just one difference. For SOME these crosses serve as medicine, a means of inheriting the Kingdom of Heaven, while for others they bring only chastisement, penalty and punishment. For some their crosses with time grow lighter and sweeter, until ultimately they are transformed into eternal crowns of glory; for others they grow progressively heavier and more oppressive until in the end all the crosses in the world will unite to form that single monumental burden of hell under which they will suffer eternally and without rest. But why this difference? Because SOME bear their crosses with faith and devotion to God, while others complain and blaspheme. And so, O Christian, never shun your crosses or grumble about them—quite the contrary! Indeed, give thanks to Jesus Christ for having sent them to you. Thank Him day and night for having allowed you to be numbered among those who bear His cross, for had He not suffered for the world, no amount of individual suffering or torment would ever have sufficed to bring anyone into the Kingdom of Heaven. For then our suffering would have been just punishment meted out

on those condemned and rejected for having transgressed God's Will. Such sufferings can hold no hope, no comfort. But now, though our sufferings are quite real, we suffer—and CAN suffer—for salvation's sake, for deliverance's sake, with hope and comfort, and in order to receive our reward. O merciful God! How great are your benefits towards us! For our sake You transform the very evil of this world into benefits, profits, and salvation. O Christian! Thankfulness and love for Jesus Christ, your Benefactor, alone oblige you to follow Him. For your sake Jesus Christ came down to earth. Is there anything, then, on earth which you can hold more dear than Him? For your sake Jesus Christ drank the last drop from the cup of suffering. Can you truly lack the desire to down a single drop of sorrow for Him?

5) By His sufferings and death Jesus Christ redeemed us and we, therefore, by right of redemption belong to Him. Hence we are no longer our own, but His, and must, if we wish not to be rejected by Him, carry out all He commands. Now, one thing only does Jesus Christ demand of us—and this solely for our own good: that we FOLLOW HIM INTO THE KINGDOM OF HEAVEN!

6) Jesus Christ did not suffer and die to enable us to do whatever we please. No! May God preserve us from even thinking such things!

7) Finally, let us state why we cannot avoid the narrow path before us which leads into the Kingdom of Heaven. Because SIN exists in everyone, and sin is like a wound which cannot be healed without medicine. In some people this wound is deep and dangerous, and to cure it requires cauterization or excision. Therefore, no one can be cleansed of his sins without spiritual sufferings. In God's sight sin is more horrible filthiness and vileness and no one who is vile, filthy or unclean can enter the Kingdom of Heaven. For a person suffering internally from disease or weighed down by deep depression, it matters little where he goes, for even in the most magnificent of palaces his suffering will continue, since his pain and depression accompany him everywhere, continually. Now the same is true of the unrepentant, uncleansed sinner: since sin, the cause of his sufferings, nests in his heart. For a sinner, everywhere is hell.

On the contrary, those who feel joy at all in their hearts will rejoice in a mansion or in a hovel—indeed, even in prison—for there is joy in their hearts. So too with the righteous person whose heart is filled with comfort by the Holy Spirit: no matter where he goes will be Paradise, for THE KINGDOM OF HEAVEN IS WITHIN US (Lk 17:21). Regardless of how many branches are pruned from it, a live tree will not die but put out new shoots. To destroy it completely one must tear it out of the ground by the roots. Likewise, sin can never be destroyed in a person's heart through pruning or abandoning certain vices or habits. Anyone who wishes to destroy sin must tear out its very roots—roots which lie deeply and firmly planted in the heart. This can never be a painless process, but it is at least now possible since the Lord sent to us the great Physician, Jesus Christ. Had He not come nothing anyone might have done would ever have availed to destroy the root of sin; all attempts to do so would then have remained absolutely futile.

Thus you can see for yourselves, my brothers, that WE MUST SURELY FOLLOW JESUS CHRIST. We cannot avoid the path He Himself took. You see also that NO ONE CAN ENTER THE KINGDOM OF HEAVEN WITHOUT SUFFERING—for this is the path which all the saints who have ever pleased God have taken! Some ask, HOW CAN WE—WEAK SINNERS—BE LIKE THE SAINTS? or, how can WE, living in this world, having responsibilities and so forth—BE SAVED? My brothers! Not only is this a falsehood—it indeed offends and blasphemes our Creator as well! To excuse yourself on such pretexts is to accuse your Creator of inability to create us any better than He did. No! This is an empty and blasphemous excuse—but no reason. Look at the saints. They were not all desert hermits. They began like us. They weren't sinless. They had earthly tasks, concerns, duties. Many of them had families. But as they went about performing their duties in this world they never forgot their Christian duties. While living in the world they followed the path into the Kingdom of Heaven, and often succeeded in leading others in as well. So too can we (if we wish) be good citizens, faithful spouses and good parents—as well as good and faithful Christians. NEVER HAS TRUE CHRISTIANITY ANYWHERE INTERFERED WITH THIS. On the contrary, it has always proved beneficial in all things. A true Christian is simply one who believes in Jesus Christ and imitates Him in all things; the SPIRIT OF CHRISTIANITY IS PURE, UNSELFISH, SPIRITUAL LOVE—love which only the Holy Spirit can give. People may call many things "love," but not everything is indeed CHRISTIAN LOVE.

Thus, my brothers, if you wish to find yourselves in the Kingdom of Heaven, you must follow the path which Jesus Christ did. Otherwise you will perish—irrevocably.

Here we must state, however, that should anyone following the path of Christianity hope in his own strength alone, he will never succeed in taking a single step. Had Jesus Christ, our great Benefactor, not given us HELP to follow this path, no one would be capable of doing so. Even the Apostles, when deprived of this help, were able to do nothing. They were too fearful and terrified to follow Jesus Christ. But once this help came to them they followed Him joyfully and happily, and no labors or suffering—even death included—could terrify them.

Now, what kind of help does Jesus Christ offer those who follow Him? It is the help of the Holy Spirit, Who is given to us by Jesus Christ. He is always with us, surrounding us, drawing us to Himself. Anyone who so wishes can receive Him and be filled with Him. And HOW does the Holy Spirit help us? How can we receive Him? This we shall see below.

Part Four

How Jesus Christ Helps Us Follow the Path into the Kingdom of Heaven and How We Can Receive This Help

Just like the Father and the Son, the Holy Spirit—Third Person of the Holy Trinity—is God Almighty. He vivifies, animates and empowers all creatures. He gives life to animals, intelligence to human beings, and higher spiritual existence to Christians. That is, the Holy Spirit gives a person reason and helps him to enter the Kingdom of Heaven.

The Holy Spirit is granted not on merits, but as a gift. Through God's mercy is He sent for the salvation of mankind, and He helps us in these ways:

1) When the Holy Spirit comes to dwell in a person, He grants him FAITH and LIGHT. Without Him, no one can have a true, living faith. Without enlightenment by the Holy Spirit even the wisest, most learned person is totally blind to God's works and plans, while even the most unlearned and simple person can, through the Holy Spirit, receive an inward revelation and direct demonstration of God's work—a taste of how good the heavenly Kingdom is. Anyone who receives the Holy Spirit within himself will sense in his soul an unusual LIGHT which hitherto he had never known at all.

2) By coming to dwell in a person the Holy Spirit brings to his heart TRUE LOVE. True Love in the heart is like pure fire, a warming heat: it is like a root from which all good deeds will grow within a person. For those moved by true love, nothing can prove too difficult or terrifying or impossible. No laws or commandments are difficult. All are easily fulfilled.

The FAITH and LOVE which are granted to a person by the Holy Spirit are such great and effectual means that those who possess them can easily, properly and with joy and comfort follow the path which Jesus Christ took.

3) Furthermore, the Holy Spirit grants a person the POWER TO RESIST THE DELUSIONS WHICH THIS WORLD PRESENTS TO HIM. Thus, those who possess the Holy Spirit, though indeed they make use of the good things of this world, do so as though they were temporary visitors, without developing attachments to them in their hearts. (On the contrary, those who lack

the Holy Spirit no matter how learned or sensible they otherwise might be, are always to a greater or lesser extent, slaves and worshipers of this world.)

4) The Holy Spirit grants wisdom to a person. We see this in particular in the holy Apostles, who before receiving Him were the simplest, most unlearned of men. Afterwards, however, who could resist their wisdom and the power of their words (Acts 4:13)? No less does the Holy Spirit grant us wisdom in works and deeds. Thus, for example, those who possess the Holy Spirit in themselves will always find the time and means to be saved—even amidst the turmoil of the world. In everything necessary they will turn within themselves—something the "normal" person will find impossible, even standing inside the Temple of God.

5) The Holy Spirit grants true JOY, GLADNESS of heart and unspeakable PEACE. Those who lack the Holy Spirit within themselves can never know true joy or pure cheer; they will never experience this delightful spiritual peace. True, they may from time-to-time be happy and cheerful—but with what joy? Momentary and impure. Their joy is always empty and impoverished, and their boredom will seem in its wake all the more overwhelming. It is likewise true that although such people at times find calm, it is not the calm of true spiritual peace, but that of spiritual sleep, stupor. How horrible for those who fail to be aroused, who have no wish to awaken from this sleep!

6) The Holy Spirit grants true HUMILITY. Even the wisest person, if he lacks the Holy Spirit within himself, can never know himself as he ought to, for as we have already said, without God's help one can never see the inner condition of his own soul. If he does good to others and acts honorably, such a person comes to think of himself as a RIGHTEOUS PERSON—perfect, indeed, in relation to others. Therefore, he THINKS THAT HE HAS NO NEED OF ANYTHING . . . Oh! How many people have perished because of false confidence in their own honesty and righteousness! That is, they perish because the hope they place in their own righteousness prevents their giving any thought at all to the true spirit of Christianity and help which comes from the Holy Spirit—which help they so desperately need! And since the Holy Spirit is given only to those who ask and seek Him—and such people not only fail to ask and seek, but indeed consider doing so superfluous—He is not given to them. They remain in their error and perish.

But when the Holy Spirit has indeed made His home in a person's heart, He shows to him his inner poverty and weakness, the corruption of his soul and heart, and his isolation from God. He demonstrates to him, despite all his virtues and righteousness the depths of his sins: his laziness and indifference to the salvation and good of others, the greediness which lurks even in his seemingly most unselfish virtues, his coarse self-love—even where he would never think of it. Briefly stated, the Holy Spirit shows everything as it truly is. A person then begins to grow humble with true humility; he considers himself the worst person in the world, and by growing humble before Jesus Christ—Who alone is Holy to the glory of God the Father!—he begins truly to repent. He decides henceforth to sin no more, to live more carefully, and if indeed he does possess any virtues, he now realizes clearly that nothing of what he has done (and is doing) is without God's help. Hence, he comes to hope in God alone.

7) The Holy Spirit teaches true PRAYER. No one can pray in a way truly pleasing to God until he has received the Holy Spirit. Thus, those who begin to pray without having received the Holy Spirit within them find their souls distracted on all sides, from one thing to the next, and are unable to focus their thoughts on one thing. They know neither themselves nor their needs as they ought, nor how or what to ask of God. Indeed, they scarcely know Who God is. But anyone in whom the Holy Spirit is at home knows God and realizes that He is his Father. He knows how to approach Him, how and what to ask of Him. When He prays, his thoughts are orderly, pure and aimed at just one object—God. Through prayer such a person can literally do everything, including moving mountains from place to place.

Such is our brief presentation of what the Holy Spirit grants to those who possess Him within themselves! You see how without the help and cooperation of the Holy Spirit it is not only impossible to enter the Kingdom of Heaven, but it is indeed impossible to take a single step down the path which leads there. Hence, we must surely seek and ask for the Holy Spirit, in order like the holy Apostles to possess Him within ourselves. But HOW CAN WE RECEIVE OR FIND HIM? This we shall see directly.

Jesus Christ said that the HOLY SPIRIT LIKE THE WIND BLOWS WHEREVER HE WISHES (Jn 3:8), and though people hear Him they never know where He has come from and where He is going. These words mean that although the Holy Spirit's presence in our hearts—His touching them—can be heard, felt, and sensed, we can never determine the moment or the circumstances of His arrival.

We see also that it was from Jesus Christ that the holy Apostles received the Holy Spirit. They received Him more than once and never at a time foretold to them or which they might have somehow determined or established for themselves. They received Him at a time which pleased Jesus Christ. Only the solemn descent of the Holy Spirit at Pentecost was foretold to them at a given time and place. But even here they received Him not because of any special merits of their own, but freely through FAITH and HOPE. The single-minded prayer in which they remained from the Lord's ascension until the descent of the Holy Spirit (Acts 2:44) served not so much as a means towards their receiving the Holy Spirit as a preparation for this. Hence, no one can state for sure that HE RECEIVED THE HOLY SPIRIT at such-and-such a time or in such-and-such a manner. The Holy Spirit is God's gift, and gifts are granted unexpectedly and at the pleasure of the Giver. He grants them to whomever He wishes. Therefore, those who think they have received the Holy Spirit in just such a way and at just such a time are quite mistaken, while those who invent means of their own for receiving the Holy Spirit will not only fail, but indeed will bring terrible sin upon themselves.

Before speaking about how the Holy Spirit can be received, we must state that he can be received BY NONE OTHER THAN THE TRUE BELIEVER, that is, by those who confess the Orthodox Catholic Faith correctly, with no additions, subtractions or changes—just as it has been transmitted to us from the holy Apostles as defined and confirmed by the Holy Fathers at the Ecumenical Councils. Any doubt or criticism of this faith amounts to insubordination and the insubordinant can never serve as temples or homes of the Holy Spirit.

The authentic channels for receiving the Holy Spirit as recognized by the teaching of the Holy Scriptures and the experience of the great saints are: 1) purity of heart and chastity, 2) humility, 3) attentiveness to the voice of God, 4) prayer, 5) daily self-denial, 6) reading or hearing the Holy Scriptures, and 7) the sacraments of the Church, Holy Communion in particular.

The Holy Spirit fills every faithful soul, provided it is purified of sin and not blocked or closed to Him through self-love or pride. For the Holy Spirit, Who surrounds us continually and wishes to fill us, is prevented from drawing near—and is indeed repelled—only by our evil deeds which surround us like a strong stone wall or evil guards. Any sin will suffice to remove the Holy Spirit from us, but in particular He takes offense at PHYSICAL IMPURITY AND SPIRITUAL PRIDE. As the ultimate in purity, the Holy Spirit naturally cannot dwell in those defiled by sins. Indeed, how COULD He live in hearts filled and blocked with various cares, desires and passions? Therefore:

1) If we wish the Holy Spirit (Whom we received when we were baptized) not to depart from us—or if we wish to receive Him once again—we must become PURE in heart and guard our bodies against unchastity, for these must serve as His temple. And the Holy Spirit will indeed enter and take possession of a person's heart and soul provided his heart is pure and his body undefiled—and providing this person does not rely upon his own good deeds or revel in them (that is, as long as he never feels that he has a

RIGHT to receive the gifts of the Holy Spirit or to receive these as a reward owed to him).

If you, however, have been unfortunate enough to defile and corrupt your soul and body, attempt to cleanse yourself through repentance. That is, stop sinning and with contrite heart, confess to God, your loving Father, that you have offended him. Turn from your sins and become more careful about how you live. Then you will be able to receive the Holy Spirit.

2) One of the most reliable means of receiving the Holy Spirit is HUMILITY. Even if you are good, honest, just and merciful—if, in a word, you fulfill all of God's commandments—you must still consider yourself an ordinary servant (Lk 17:10), simply an instrument whereby God is at work. And if indeed we were to examine more closely our "good deeds"—even the very greatest of our virtues—how many of them will prove worthy of being CHRISTIAN virtues? How often, for example, when giving alms or aiding our needy brothers, do we do so either out of vain-glory or self-love (like Pharisees) or out of self-interest—like money lenders whose hope is to receive from God hundreds or thousands in exchange for the mere penny we give to the poor! Of course good deeds will always remain good deeds—so never stop doing them. Indeed, multiply the good deeds you do! Any good deed is like gold, and even tarnished gold is of value. One has only to bring it to a goldsmith for it to be given once again its full worth. So too will your good deeds receive their true value if with full trust you surrender them to the will of the Great Artist. Thus, continue being honest, good, just and merciful—faithful keepers of the Law—but if you wish your virtues to have true value, never boast of them or consider them to be as yet pure gold—worthy of heavenly treasures. For you are no goldsmith; you are not qualified to evaluate them. TRUE VALUE comes to gold through ART, and to virtues through LOVE alone. This love, however, must be CHRISTIAN love—that is, pure, unselfish love which only the Holy Spirit can give. Nothing done without Christian love (that is, without the Holy Spirit) represents true virtue. Hence, despite all virtues those who lack the Holy Spirit will remain indigent and poor.

HUMILITY is another factor. That is, you must with patience and without complaint endure all the troubles, sorrows, and calamities which befall you, and consider these just PUNISHMENT FOR YOUR SINS. Never say, "How unfortunate I am!" Rather say, "Considering all my sins, this isn't much at all!" And ask God not so much for deliverance from adversities as for the strength to endure these.

3) The Holy Spirit can be received through careful ATTENTION TO GOD'S VOICE. God speaks clearly, distinctly and intelligibly, and can be

heard everywhere and in all things. We have simply to have "ears to hear" in order to do so. Since the day of your birth, God, your loving Father, has spoken to you in every way He could—and He continues to do so even now. He calls you to Himself. He warns you. He instructs you. He teaches you. He enlightens you. Therefore, for example, if you are happy or offended; if one of your relatives dies, or you yourself fall ill; if you grow sad or depressed for no obvious reason (a common occurrence with us all)—discern in all of this God's voice telling you to COME TO YOUR SENSES and turn to Him in repentance, rather than to anyone else in search of help or consolation through diversions or amusements. In God alone must we seek comfort and help.

Or, on the contrary, let us suppose that you are prospering. You not only enjoy all you need to live on, you have a surplus. If indeed, in everything you do, all the circumstances of your life are as good as they could be; if you know no sorrows, no griefs; if in fact you are often happy—at times even spiritually so—this too is God's voice telling you to LOVE HIM WITH ALL YOUR HEART FOR HIS HAVING BEEN SO VERY GOOD TO YOU, AND TO THANK HIM AS FULLY AS YOU CAN. He is telling you that while enjoying the good things of this world you must never forget to bring joy to the least of Jesus Christ's brothers (that is, the poor), nor forget the true good things and joys which await in heaven—and indeed, Him Who is the source of all good things and joys. Who among us has not heard—and indeed does not hear—God's voice speaking through all the things which happen to us? Indeed, we all do hear, and hear clearly and distinctly. But more than a few of us fail to understand and do the things which God commands us. Usually, in our sorrows and griefs we seek distraction in vain pursuits and amusements rather than entering more deeply into ourselves. Indeed, rather than accepting such visitations from God as a source of great healing and applying them in this spirit to our souls, we seek to be delivered from them, sometimes grumbling and losing our tempers. At the very least we seek comfort not in God, the Source of all comfort, but in this world and its pleasures. On the other hand, when things are going well for us and we prosper, we tend to forget God rather than loving Him more and more as our Benefactor, and we use all the good things the Lord has given us not for the common good (to aid our neighbors in need), but at our own whim, to satisfy our own utterly extravagant desires. If it is criminal and horrendous to show inattention and laxity in obeying the decrees of an earthly king, how much more sinful and horrible it is to fail to be attentive or heedful to the voice of our Heavenly King! After incessant calls and summonses from God, such negligence and inattention will ultimately result in our being rejected as stubborn children. Turned out by God to do whatever we wish, we will find our minds darkening little by little until even the most vile and horrible sins will appear to us as little more than the inevitable weakness of our human nature. This is why it is such a useful and saving thing to be attentive to God's voice—and so destructive and horrible to fail to heed, or even to reject it.

4) The Holy Spirit can be received through PRAYER. This is the simplest and most reliable means of which everyone can avail himself at any time. As we know, there are two kinds of prayer: external and internal. That is, those who pray and prostrate their bodies at home or in church are praying externally, whereas those who within their souls and hearts turn to God and strive always to keep Him in mind—pray inwardly. All of us know which of these kinds of prayer is better, more effective, and more acceptable to God. And you all know as well that you can pray to God at any time and in any place, even while sin holds you in control. You can pray both at work and while idle; on feast days and ordinary ones; standing, sitting or lying down—this all of you know. We need state here only that while inner prayer is the mightiest means to receiving God's grace, one ought not to abandon external prayer (especially prayer in the community). Many ask, "Why should I go to church? I can pray at home. In church you end up sinning more than praying!" Now what do you think—what causes people to talk like this: fairness? prudence? Certainly not! Rather laziness and pride cause them to say such things, for while it is unfortunately true that people do indeed sin in church, this is not at all caused by their COMING to church. Rather it results from their coming in an INAPPROPRIATE SPIRIT, and standing in church not to pray, but to do other things entirely. Now consider those who avoid coming to church for the reasons given. Do THEY pray at home? Of course not! And if a few of them do indeed happen to pray, it is for the most part like the Pharisees—for all their prayers can be expressed in the very words which the Pharisee used: "I thank You God that I am not greedy, dishonest or an adulterer, like everybody else" (Lk 8:11). Therefore, do attend the community's prayers and pray on your own at home before the holy icons. Do so no matter what "clever" people in their philosophizing might say—that unless you possess the Holy Spirit within yourself you cannot offer true prayers to God. Indeed, this is completely true: it DOES take a lot of work before you can offer truly holy prayers to God, nor can you suddenly or quickly reach the point where you are able to lift up your thoughts and heart to God. But we ordinary people are not the only ones who at times find that when we wish to turn our thoughts to God they are scattered in all directions, preoccupied with all sorts of other matters. Many people who have devoted their whole lives to prayer have found themselves in the same condition. You might wish to think about God but think rather of things quite different—even horrible.

Yet true prayer brings to the heart comfort so sweet that many holy fathers spent whole days and nights standing in prayer, oblivious to time or the length of their prayer because of this ecstasy. For them, prayer was pleasure, not work. But to attain such a state is no easy matter, especially for those who from childhood have given free rein to the passions and whose consciences have never pressed them. But does ANYTHING in this world come easily, quickly, or without labor?—any science or art—or comfort? So pray. Even if in prayer you find just work, no comfort or pleasure at all—pray. And pray diligently, with as much zeal as you can muster. Teach yourself to pray and talk with God. Try as hard as you can to gather and master your scattered thoughts, and little-by-little you will begin to feel it becoming easier and easier—and at times you will indeed experience sweet comfort. And if you really care about this, the Holy Spirit will see your efforts and the sincerity of your desire and will quickly come to your aid. He will enter you and teach you to offer true prayer.

It is easier for us to pray when misfortunes and adversities befall us. Therefore, never let such opportunities go by, but make full use of them. Pour out your sorrow to God in prayer.

Jesus Christ commands us to pray at all times (1 Thes 5:17). Now, many ask "How can you pray at all times if you live in the world? If we occupy ourselves exclusively in prayer, when will we attend to our duties and do our work?" Of course, one cannot pray EXTERNALLY at all times (that is, spend all of our time standing in prayer). We must attend to our other duties and work. But anyone who truly senses his inner poverty will never stop praying even while attending to all his other activities. Those who wish to enter the Kingdom of Heaven will find time and opportunity to pray both inwardly and externally. Even in the midst of the most difficult and demanding work they will find time to utter a word to God and worship Him. Only those who actually have no desire to pray will fail to find time to do so.

It has also been said that GOD DOES NOT LISTEN TO SINNERS. That is, that sinners do not receive from God what they ask for. This too is true. But WHICH sinners does God refuse to hear? Those who pray to Him without thinking about their conversion. Or who ask Him to FORGIVE THEIR SINS but are unwilling to forgive others for anything. Of course, God will never hear such sinners or fulfill their requests. So when you pray to God for forgiveness or the wrongs you have done, you must forgive others the things they have done and be resolved to abandon your own sins. When you ask God for mercy you must yourself at that very moment be merciful to others—and then God will listen to you.

Some think that YOU CAN ONLY PRAY FROM BOOKS, and it is, of course, good to pray and glorify God in Psalms and sacred songs (Eph 5:19) if you are able. But if you cannot read, it is enough that you know the most important prayers, and especially the Lord's Prayer ("Our Father") since in this prayer given to us by Jesus Christ Himself we find all our needs set forth. But when circumstances will not allow you to pray at length, offer simple prayers such as "Lord have mercy!" or "God help me!" or "Lord cleanse my sins!" or "Lord Jesus Christ, Son of God, have mercy on me a sinner!"

5) A certain holy Father once said, "If you wish for your prayer to fly to God, give it two wings: fasting and alms."

Before speaking about what FASTING is, let us look at WHY IT WAS INSTITUTED. The goal and intent of fasting are to humble and lighten the body, thereby rendering it more obedient to the soul, for a well-satisfied and fattened body requires peace and comfort; its disposition to laziness interferes with thinking about God. It binds and constricts the soul like a self-willed, spoiled and capricious woman who rules her husband.

WHAT, THEN, IS FASTING? There are various types. For individuals raised in comfort fasting can mean one thing, while for those brought up in simplicity and coarseness it means another. The one can eat coarse food and remain healthy—he can even go several days without food, while the other will find any large change in diet significant, even harmful. Thus as a general rule FASTING MEANS PRIMARILY ABSTINENCE AND STRICT MODERATION in the use of food: eat moderately and above all bridle your physical desires. Do not cater to any whims which serve to further more than the preservation of physical health and the maintenance of life. Then yours will be a true fast.

But while fasting BODILY you must also fast SPIRITUALLY. That is, you must refrain from speaking evil. You must say nothing bad or unnecessary. Moderate your desires and root out the passions. For example, TODAY should it enter your mind to do anything indecent or unnecessary—don't. TOMORROW, should circumstances cause you to become angry at anyone, control yourself and never let your heart or tongue yield to your desires. THE DAY AFTER TOMORROW, should you wish to have a good time (especially where you might see or hear anything indecent)—don't go. And so forth. Continue in this way to gain control over yourself, and AFTERWARDS begin to seize control over your thoughts and organize them in order to prevent their wandering where they really ought not to go—for much evil comes of such thoughts. We must be frank here: nothing is harder than controlling and organizing your thoughts, and to organize and cleanse them QUICKLY is impossible—as impossible as pacifying and taming in a short time a wild horse which has never known the bridle. So too will those who their whole lives have given full rein to their thoughts find organizing them impossible. Moreover, as a "normal" person, occupied with worldly cares and able to give little thought to your Christian duties, you think that your thoughts are ALREADY in order (and even pure). But if you will just begin to think about your salvation and grow concerned, you will begin immediately to be stirred up like a stagnant swamp whose waters normally seem clear and clean—until stirred up. But as it is drained the waters become murkier and murkier. So too are one's thoughts. Ultimately the Devil himself will be dredged up. Nevertheless, fight your thoughts. Be strong and brave. Never despair, and never think that you may fail to draw a halt and purify your thoughts. Struggle as hard as you can and seek God's help. Then, seeing your true desire, the Holy Spirit will abide in you to help you.

WHAT ARE ALMS? Normally by "alms" we understand the giving of things to the poor. But alms ought to encompass all deeds of mercy and charity, such as FEEDING THE HUNGRY, GIVING DRINK TO THE THIRSTY, CLOTHING THE NAKED, VISITING AND HELPING THE SICK AND IMPRISONED, PROVIDING LODGING FOR THE HOMELESS, CARING FOR ORPHANS, etc. (Mt 25:35–36). But for your alms to be true they must all be done without boasting, with no desire to be praised by others for what you have done—or indeed to be thanked by the poor. Just do as Jesus Christ Himself told us, "Never let your left hand know what the right hand is doing" (Mt 6:3). Then your Heavenly Father Who sees in secret will reward you openly.

6) The Holy Spirit can be received by READING and HEARING the Holy Scriptures as the true Word of God. The Holy Scriptures are a treasury from which mankind can draw both light and life: that light which can enlighten and wisen all, and that life which can vivify, comfort and delight all. The Holy Scriptures are one of God's greatest gifts to mankind, and anyone who wishes to can avail himself of them. The Holy Scriptures are Divine Wisdom—a miraculous wisdom which even the simplest, most untaught person can understand and comprehend—and indeed by reading or listening to them many simple folk have become pious and received the Holy Spirit. Others, however (learned people included), have read the Holy Scriptures but gone astray and perished. This is because SOME have read it in simplicity of heart, without philosophizing or sophistication, seeking in the Scriptures not erudition but grace, power, and the Spirit; while others, on the contrary, by considering themselves wise and all-knowing have sought neither the power nor the spirit of the Word of God, but worldly wisdom. And rather than humbly accepting all that Providence has found worthy to reveal to us, these people have tried to penetrate and learn things which are held secret. Therefore, they have fallen into disbelief or schism. No! Better to float out to sea in a tiny cup than to try to comprehend the full wisdom of God!

Therefore when reading or listening to the Holy Scriptures, lay aside all philosophizing and submit yourself to the Word and will of Him Who is speaking to you through the Scriptures. Ask Jesus Christ to grant you wisdom, to illumine your mind, and to instill in you the desire to fulfill all that you have read in the Scriptures.

There are many books in the world said to be of use in saving one's soul, but only those which are based on the Holy Scriptures and in agreement with the doctrine of the Orthodox Church are truly worthy of this claim. One can and should read such books, but care must be exercised in selecting them in order that having found one which you think will help save your soul, you have not, in fact, gotten one capable of destroying it.

Jesus Christ said, "Whoever eats My flesh and drinks My blood lives in Me and I in him . . . and he has eternal life, and I will raise him to life on the last day" (Jn 6:56, 54). That is, those who partake WORTHILY of the Holy Mysteries are mystically united with Jesus Christ—which is to say that those who in TRUE REPENTANCE, WITH A PURE SOUL AND WITH FEAR OF GOD AND FAITH partake of the Body and Blood of Christ receive at that moment the Holy Spirit, Who enters to prepare in them a place where Jesus Christ and God the Father can be received. Such people in this way become temples and homes of the living God. Those, however, who receive the Body and Blood of Christ UNWORTHILY (that is, with impure souls, a spiteful, vengeful, or hate-filled heart) not only fail to receive the Holy Spirit, but become like Judas the Traitor—crucifying, as it were, Jesus Christ for a second time.

Christians living in the first centuries sensed the importance and spiritual value of the Holy Mysteries, and so received the Body and Blood of Christ every Sunday and feastday. Thus they were as it says in the BOOK of the ACTS "one in mind and heart" (Acts 4:32). My God, what a difference between them and us! How many of us have gone years without receiving Communion! How many of us never give this any thought!

For God's sake, let us desire to receive the Holy Mysteries AT LEAST ONCE A YEAR—every one must do this without fail! For those who are worthy, the Body and Blood of Christ are TRUE MEDICINE to heal all their ailments and diseases—and who among us is completely healthy? Who wouldn't like to receive healing and relief? The Body and Blood of Jesus Christ are PROVISIONS FOR THE PATH LEADING INTO THE KINGDOM OF HEAVEN. Can you set out on a long and difficult trip without provisions? Of course not, and the Body and Blood of Jesus Christ are something VISIBLY SACRED which He Himself left us to bring us to true holiness. Who wouldn't like to partake of such sanctity and become holy? Do not be lazy, then, about approaching the Cup of Life, immortality, love and holiness—

but do so with fear of God and faith. Those who do not wish to do so, who have no such zeal—lack also love for Jesus Christ and will never receive His Holy Spirit. And neither, then, will they enter the Kingdom of Heaven.

Such, then, are the means whereby we can receive the Holy Spirit (namely: purity of heart, chastity of life, humility, careful attention to the voice of God, prayer, self-denial, reading and hearing the Word of God, and Communion in the Body and Blood of Christ). Each of these in isolation is, of course, capable of bringing to us the Holy Spirit, but how much better and surer it is for us to make use of them all together. Then surely we will receive the Holy Spirit and be made holy ourselves.

Finally, we must state that should any of you have once been found worthy of receiving the Holy Spirit but later fallen into sin (thereby losing for yourself the Holy Spirit)—such persons ought never to despair or think that they have lost all. Rather, with even greater haste and zeal they must fall down before God in repentance and prayer. Then the Holy Spirit will return to them once more.

Conclusion

My brothers! I have tried as best I could to indicate to you the pathway into the Kingdom of Heaven, and now you are able to see for yourselves that 1) without faith in Jesus Christ no one can return to God and enter the Kingdom of Heaven; 2) even though they believe in Jesus Christ, none can be called His disciple—and hence live with Him in heaven—unless they act and live as Jesus Christ did on earth; 3) without the Holy Spirit none can follow Jesus Christ; 4) anyone who wishes to receive the Holy Spirit must make use of the means given to us for this purpose by the Lord.

Once more I repeat that the pathway into the Kingdom of Heaven which Jesus Christ opened for us is the only one; there is not, has never been, and will never be any other path than that which Jesus Christ has indicated to us. Naturally, this path is difficult and dangerous, but it leads straight and true to authentic and eternal bliss. The path into the Kingdom of Heaven is difficult, yet along it—and indeed, at its very beginning—one finds comforts and pleasures such as can never be found along any of the pathways of this world. The path into the Kingdom of Heaven is difficult and dangerous indeed, but all along it the Lord's help is constantly available; the Lord Jesus Christ Himself is prepared to help us along this way: imparting to us His Holy Spirit, sending angels to preserve us; providing teachers and guides. Indeed, He Himself is ready, so to speak, personally to take us by the hand and support us. The pathway into the Kingdom of Heaven is difficult indeed, and the labors required along it can be bitter, but until one has seen and experienced some bitterness he can never appreciate the value of sweetness. The path into the Kingdom of Heaven is difficult indeed, but suffering here on earth helps us to pray to God at all times, and in prayer to find comfort and reinforcement. In this life God is ready at all times to hear our prayers, but should we die as non-christians this will no longer be the case (even if after death we were able to pray He would no longer hear us). The pathway into the Kingdom of Heaven is difficult indeed, but the sufferings and torments of all eternity will be incomparably greater and more oppressive than those we now experience on earth. Our sufferings here—even the most oppressive—are, by comparison with those prepared in hell for the Devil and his angels (Mt 25:41), a mere drop in comparison with all the waters in the ocean. The pathway into heavenly bliss is difficult indeed, but are the paths to earthly happiness easier? Look how hard those who gather riches and seek earthly honor and glory must work and sweat. See how often we are willing and happy to accept labors and heartaches to achieve some empty satisfaction! And what do we get, in fact? Instead of getting satisfaction we simply waste our time, spend our money, ruin our health, and destroy our soul. Therefore, the more attentively we examine ourselves, the more clearly we will see that our failure in moving towards the Kingdom of Heaven lies not in the DIFFICULTY OF THE PATH, but in our lack of zealous desire and inclination towards taking it. We simply have no real desire to be concerned with it. No one who possesses the fervent desire for something will ever fail to find it no matter what difficulties and obstacles may stand in his way. Now, while none of us desires NOT to be in the Kingdom of Heaven, our desire to be there is weak and results solely from our innate desire for well-being. And while some of us might even work towards attaining the Kingdom of Heaven, very few do so with full faith and devotion to God and with the self-denial this requires! How many of us, however, think that no matter how we have lived on earth we will have only to repent at life's end in order to enter the Kingdom of Heaven . . . How horribly wrong are those who think this! Of course, the Lord's mercies are great and limitless, and Jesus Christ did indeed take into Paradise a criminal who repented only at the point of death (Lk 23:39–43). But did THIS man succeed in entering without suffering and sorrow? No indeed! He hung from a cross. He had been condemned, imprisoned, perhaps even beaten. True, his sufferings came as punishment for the evil deeds and crimes he had committed—but who among us has never transgressed the law—either of God or of man? And if none of us is literally a murderer—how many have nonetheless killed others through words, cruelty or carelessness about the well-being and salvation of others? Of course, the Lord's great and unspeakable mercies can come upon us as well. He can indeed change our final death agonies into merit and cleansing, some measure of effort toward following the pathway into the Kingdom of Heaven.

(This is particularly true if, at the same time, like the criminal on the cross, we repent of our sins and in faith receive Holy Communion as a final token along the way.) But who among us can be certain that sufferings will accompany his death, or that if so he will have time to repent? How many people die unexpectedly and with no sufferings! How many die without repentance or the Sacraments!

Thus, my brothers, if you wish not to perish for all eternity, you must turn attention to your soul. You must care about the portion which will be yours in the future. For we know that beyond the grave there is no middle ground—either one thing or the other awaits everyone: either the Kingdom of Heaven or HELL, eternal bliss or eternal torment. Beyond the grave there will be only TWO opposite conditions to which here on earth there are but two corresponding paths. The one is wide, smooth, even and easy—and many follow it. The other is narrow, difficult, and infested with thorns—but happy—a hundred-fold happy!—is anyone who follows that narrow path, for it leads into the Kingdom of Heaven. And how few there are who take it! My brothers, if we haven't been and aren't now travelling down this difficult path, and should we die without being cleansed or repenting at all—what will become of us? To whom shall we then run? To the Lord? Surely if here we have had no desire to listen to Him He will not hear us there! Here He is our merciful Father, but there He will be our righteous Judge. Who then will defend us from His righteous anger? O my brothers! WHAT A TERRIFYING THING IT IS TO FALL INTO THE HANDS OF THE LIVING GOD! (Heb 10:31). So be diligent now about salvation, while the time is still right. Work towards your salvation while it is still daytime, for the night will come when no one will be able to do anything (Jn 9:4).

Go, then. Don't allow yourself to procrastinate day after day; death WILL come, and it will be too late for you to enter the Kingdom of Heaven. So hurry now, while you are still able. Advance at least part of the way—just be sure to MOVE toward the Kingdom of Heaven, even if your movement is slow. This way, in the end you will at least find yourself closer—just as anyone going anywhere finds himself closer to his destination with every step he takes.

Those who wish to follow Jesus Christ will find this additional advice useful:

1) Never look at others—at those who are defiled, at how they live. Never justify yourself by their example. Don't be like many others who say, "What can I do? I'm not alone in the way I live. I'm not the only person who fails to live by Christ's commandments—almost no one does." Even if you knew for sure that everyone around you—even those who ought to serve as examples of virtue and piety—were failing to live like Christians,

what good would that do you? THEIR perdition won't save YOU. At the fearful judgment you will find no defense in the argument that you weren't the only one on earth who lived badly. So you have no business looking at others, as to whether or not they are following the pathway into the Kingdom of Heaven. This is none of your business. Your only task is to know yourself and to worry about yourself and those whom God has given you to teach. In addition, it is quite often the case that we can be mistaken about which of our neighbors are following Christ's path and which are not, since we frequently notice it when others are sinning, we almost never see them repenting and being cleansed of their sins.

2) When you follow this path, many people (perhaps even those closest to you, the members of your own family) will mock you. But don't pay attention to this. Don't be upset. Remember that even Jesus Christ was laughed at! But did He quarrel with such people? No, He remained silent and prayed for them. You do likewise.

3) In the opinion of many learned people the pathway into the Kingdom of Heaven indicated to us by Jesus Christ the Son of God isn't as it ought to be. YOU DON'T NEED (they say) THIS PATH TO REACH THE KINGDOM OF HEAVEN; THIS IS THE PATH FOR JUST A FEW, NOT FOR ALL . . . etc. If you should be approached or stopped by such people wishing to dissuade you—don't listen to them. Even if an Angel should come down from heaven and begin to tell you that YOU DON'T NEED TO FOLLOW THE PATH WHICH JESUS CHRIST DID—pay no attention to him (Gal 1:8). Yet never argue with such deceivers and enemies. It is better to feel sorry for them and pray for them.

4) When you find yourself carefully following the path of Jesus Christ you may happen to meet people who will say evil things about you for the sake of the Lord's word, or who will slander, insult, or scorn you. Be patient and endure these things. Rejoice and be glad when you are offended in any way for Christ's name—for your reward will be great in heaven (Mt 5:11).

5) When you are on this pathway the Devil himself will surely rise up to oppose and tempt you in various ways. He will inspire in you evil thoughts, doubts about the faith and its manifest truths—blasphemies against holy things and so forth. But have no fear of him, for the Devil can do nothing to you unless God allows it. You have only to pray to the Lord and like an arrow the Devil will go flying from you!

6) We must note that nothing truly useful and just will ever hinder the true Christian. These things include first INDUSTRIOUSNESS, which not only

never hinders salvation but indeed advances it. We know that IDLENESS is the MOTHER OF VICES. (Why, for example, do people become drunkards? Because they have nothing to do. Who becomes a thief or a robber? Those who are idle.) Indeed, one can state positively that those who do nothing, who occupy themselves with nothing are—no matter how good they may seem—bad Christians and poor citizens, and if they are not in addition terrible sinners, this is only because of God's special providence for them. Therefore, be industrious. Grow accustomed to labor. You must labor and work and do everything your job and duties to the state and your nation require.

Now if idleness is the mother of all vices, industry can surely be termed the father of all virtues. This is the case, first because lacking the time to do or even think of evil (being continually at work or tending to one's duties, or occupied with one's salvation and other Christian duties) the industrious person surely commits fewer sins. Second, because those who grow accustomed to industry will more readily consent to follow the pathway into the Kingdom of Heaven than those who lead an idle life, and will do so more easily. Thus, it is always and everywhere useful to be industrious. But to do so one must from childhood learn and grow accustomed to working.

7) There is another form of perfection just as useful and necessary for those who wish to enter the Kingdom of Heaven, and one which must be learned and assimilated even earlier in life than industriousness. This is PATIENCE and FORBEARANCE. Without this one cannot take even a single step down this path, for at every step cruelty, rough treatment—patches of thorns—are encountered. But if you get used to being patient—first physically then spiritually—you will find it easier to be an industrious member of society, a good friend, a good employer, a good citizen—and a good Christian!

And so, my brothers, I can tell you no more than this about the pathway into the Kingdom of Heaven. I will add only that those who zealously follow it will, for every effort, every sadness, every victory over themselves, every act of abstinence, every deed—indeed, every good intention and desire—receive in reward seventy times seven, even in this world, while what awaits them THERE cannot even be imagined. Thus, my brothers, never fear. To follow Jesus Christ is nothing awesome. He is our mighty Helper—so follow Him. Hurry. Don't dawdle. Enter before the doors to the Kingdom of Heaven slam shut on you. And your Heavenly Father will come a long way down this path to meet you. He will kiss you and return to you the clothing which originally belonged to you. He will adorn you with a ring (Lk 15:20–22) and lead you into the palaces where He Himself abides with all the holy prophets, apostles, bishops, martyrs, and every righteous soul. There you will truly rejoice for all eternity. But if the doors of the Kingdom of Heaven should shut on you—should you die without repenting and performing good deeds—you will never be admitted, no matter how you have sought to go there. Then you will begin to knock at the doors crying, "Lord let us in! We know you. We were baptized in Your Name. We bear Your Name and have even worked miracles through it!" (Mt 7:23, 25:11, 30)—but Jesus Christ will answer you, "I do not know you. You are not Mine. Go away from Me into eternal fire prepared for the Devil and his angels." And there will be crying and gnashing of teeth.

III

TEACHER AND APOSTLE OF THE TRUE FAITH

Editor's Note: In a sense, of course, all Christians teach, and all are apostles, for Christian instruction is as much if not more a matter of example than of conducting seminars or preaching sermons. Nevertheless, there are those whom the Christian community selects and even ordains specifically to preach and teach, and this chapter is devoted to a few exceptional teachers and apostles who served heroically in Alaska.

The Valaam monks attempted to organize a school but conditions in Kodiak during the first years of their stay prevented the development of any cohesive educational plan. Ioasaph reported that students feared for their safety and hardly attended classes, while the monks remained in their quarters unable to function well in the face of Baranov's harassment. Only when Cathedral Hieromonk Gideon arrived did education begin in earnest at Kodiak.

Gideon had been sent by the Emperor himself to investigate conditions in the colony, and neither Baranov nor Rezanov, Shelikov's son-in-law, dared to oppose him too directly. Gideon organized a school that drew nearly a hundred Aleut and Creole students before his return to Russia in 1807, when he placed Father Herman at the head of the mission. He began compiling a Kodiak Aleut dictionary and primer and trained local Kodiak Aleut students to continue this work. Since he had been sent to inspect the colony, however, he had to return to the capital to report directly to the Metropolitan and consequently his impact on life in Kodiak was short-lived. Nicolai Rezanov, also an influential figure, filed his own report with the company's board of directors on the situation in Alaska that contradicted and neutralized Gideon's. Thus, Baranov was free for another decade to continue his oppressive rule of the colony without significant interference from the government.

Ianovskii reported on the educational work of St. Herman and his collaboration with Mrs. Sophie Vlasov to prepare young native and orphaned children for productive, meaningful lives.

However, all these sporadic attempts to organize formal schooling in the colony bore little fruit. Some native students were sent to Europe for training, and in 1812 Prokofii Mal'tsov had already completed the course in naval architecture (shipbuilding and design) at the Kronstadt naval academy. He too was the victim of a shipwreck, however, drowning when the *Neva* sank near Sitka in 1813. Others who traveled with Hieromonk Makarii even earlier either died en route or perished with the *Phoenix*. The earliest attempts to send native students to Siberia or Europe for training, as Archimandrite Ioasaph had predicted, failed. Therefore, with Father John Veniaminov, a new era of literacy began, as he together with Ivan Pan'kov created an Unangan Aleut alphabet, devised a primer for the teaching of reading, and produced the first books in the Fox-Island dialect.

This educational work continued in the Western Aleutians during the pastoral ministry of the first Aleut priest, Father Iakov (James) Netsvetov, born of an Atkan mother and a Russian father at Unalaska and raised on St. George Island, who had successfully completed his theological studies at the Irkutsk seminary and returned to Atka in 1829. There he too began translating the New Testament and in 1833 organized a school.

The natural environment of the Aleutians is both magnificent and brutal. Volcanic islands convered with emerald-green foliage in summer, the archipelago is often enshrouded in fog or battered by hurricane force winds the rest of the year. The difficulties entailed in making regular pastoral visits to villages scattered across a thousand miles of stormy seas can hardly be appreciated in the jet age, but both Veniaminov and Netsvetov traveled extensively throughout the region in tiny skin-covered kayaks. Some hint of what missionary work in southwestern Alaska in the early nineteenth century was like appears in the official journals of Father Netsvetov.

There were human as well as climatic obstacles to the preaching of the Gospel. Christianity did not arrive to fill a religious vacuum, but encountered opposition from traditional spiritual leaders. Shamanism based on an oral tradition in which all living things were understood to possess a spiritual reality or power, and therefore all creatures were believed to be intelligent, dominated the religious outlook of Siberian as well as Alaskan tribes. Hunting societies needed to attend carefully to the various protocols established "in the beginning" in order not to offend the spirits of their prey. Any violation of this etiquette might have disastrous consequences for the community. Entire species might withhold themselves from capture, humans would starve. If infractions did occur, those who had special personal powers, the shamans, were summoned to remedy the situation. Not only bad luck in hunting, but all diseases and calamities were attributed to voluntary or involuntary offenses to the spiritual realities that dominated the natural world. It was the shaman's function to communicate and, if his or her personal powers could manage it, correct any imbalances caused by human transgression. Shamans served as both prophets and healers in most traditional Alaskan societies.

On Kodiak Island and on the Alaska Peninsula, modern oral tradition relates that the shamans at the time of the arrival of the Valaam mission advised their people to meet the monks and do what they asked, although the shamans themselves, apparently, did not participate. Shamanism survived in this region until the early twentieth century, in fact, when shamans reportedly continued to use their powers to avenge wrongs and harm their opponents. One community on the mainland opposite Kodiak Island was deserted in one afternoon because the villagers became convinced their local shaman was performing some sort of witchcraft, resulting in several deaths. The belief in the existence of good and evil spirits, while biblically based, remains a powerful element in religious life throughout rural Alaska. The belief that various men and women had the power to manipulate these forces for their own good or evil purposes certainly existed at the time Christian missionaries arrived.

Veniaminov reported to his bishop an extraordinary account of his meeting a baptized elderly man whose familiarity with spirits earned him the title ''shaman'' in his village. What is remarkable about his letter, however, is not that Veniaminov investigated this case, but his positive assessment of Smirennikov and his spiritual condition, and Veniaminov's own humility when presented with the opportunity to meet these spirits himself. In his total lack of pride and arrogance of assumed spiritual superiority, Veniaminov personifies in his encounter with the Aleut shaman some of the finest qualities of a Christian missionary.

In 1840, after the death of his wife, Veniaminov took monastic vows and received the name Innocent. As the tsar's favorite candidate, he was promptly elected bishop of Alaska. He spent the first years at his residence in the colonial capital, New Archangel (Sitka), organizing and building a school and designing and constructing St. Michael's Cathedral there. Bishop Innocent issued instructions to his clergy, which are included here as another indication of Veniaminov's cultural sensitivity and superb pastoral judgment. The ''Missionary Oath'' all Alaskan Orthodox missionaries had to sign before beginning their labors also dates from Veniaminov's time, and his letter and sermon dated soon after his arrival at Sitka as the new bishop provide further insight into the personality of this remarkable man. His son-in-law, Elia Petelin, was sent to the Nushagak as missionary priest, while his former colleague Netsvetov was transferred to the Yukon delta to begin the evangelization of the Yup'ik Eskimos.

Actually, oral tradition among the native people of this region today indicates that Netsvetov was the second Orthodox priest to venture into that region. Hieromonk Juvenaly reportedly visited the Kenai Tanaina, and with a guide crossed to the western shore of Cook Inlet and entered the Iliamna/Kuichak drainage. There the local Indians and Eskimos proved largely unreceptive to his message, and he fled northwestward, arriving, according to modern oral accounts, at the mouth of the Kuskokwim, near the present site of the village of Quinahgak, where he was killed immediately by a hunting party. The local shaman removed his brass pectoral cross and began attempting some sort of incantation, but instead of producing its desired effect, the shaman found himself being lifted off the ground. Three times he tried the same spell, before concluding that there was spiritual power greater than his own present here. He admonished his companions to treat any other visitor wearing similar garb well, to welcome him cordially. Father Juvenaly's Indian guide, in the meantime, attempted to escape, and nearly succeeded because of his extraordinary swimming ability. (Yup'iks traditionally did not and do not swim, while the Tanaina on the shores of Cook Inlet still swim in the icy North Pacific when hunting whales.) The oral traditions of both Eskimos and Indians in both the Kuskokwim and Iliamna Lake regions are further corroborated by the written reports of later visitors to the area. The Nushagak trading post officer reported a decade later meeting an Eskimo from the mouth of the Kuskokwim wearing a brass cross. Members of a later exploratory expedition mention seeing the Kuskokwim shaman "healing" someone by mimicking the Orthodox rite of chrismation (confirmation). Fathers Netsvetov and Bel'kov record being taken to Juvenaly's gravesite. But, understandably, the present-day residents of Quinahgak deny all knowledge of these reports. The next missionary to visit them nearly a century later was a Moravian, whose denomination they all joined.

As was expected of all clergy and civil servants of the time, Netsvetov kept a daily journal of his activities, which was submitted to the bishop at the end of each year. Consequently, a rather complete account of missionary life on the lower Yukon would exist if all these annual reports were extant. Unfortunately, the church archives of the Orthodox Mission in Alaska have been divided among several archives, and scholars have never been granted access to much of what is stored in the Soviet Union. Certainly Netsvetov's ethnographic notes would be of considerable value to anthropologists and historians, should these ever appear. What is known about Netsvetov's activities from the pages of his surviving journals, however, presents an inspiring and even astonishing account of the devotion and perseverance that marked the character of this Aleut missionary. The excerpts included here from his years on the Yukon do not exhaust the remarkable accomplishments of this pastor, teacher, and apostle, but they do provide a clear profile of the man and his life among the Yup'ik Eskimo and Ingalik Indian at mid-century.

As his mission grew, Netsvetov asked for relief—hoping for a transfer to a more comfortable climate, but settling for an assistant to cover some of his vast territory. The first monks sent to the Yukon Delta proved more of a burden than a help. When the order to recruit more missionary clergy for Alaska was issued, some diocesan officials apparently decided to use this opportunity to rid themselves of troublesome or incompetent clerics. Netsvetov found his difficulties increased with the "volunteers" he had welcomed so enthusiastically. One had to be physically restrained and returned to Russia, another spent his time leveling ridiculous criminal accusations against Father Iakov, before his insanity was verified and he too shipped home. But tragically, the new bishop, Peter, who only recently had arrived from the capital city, knew little of Netsvetov's condition or reputation and decided to summon the Yukon missionary to Sitka for questioning. Although eventually cleared of all charges, Archpriest Iakov Netsvetov died there, and was buried under the porch of the Tlingit chapel, very near the present-day bishop's residence, in 1865.

Veniaminov, with characteristic vision and enthusiasm, welcomed the 1867 sale of Alaska as a new opportunity for the Church to extend her mission to other parts of the United States. His letter on this topic is included here together with his opening speech to the organizational meeting of the Orthodox Missionary Society, which he founded after being elected Metropolitan of Moscow. As a country boy from rural Siberia, John Popov had risen from obscurity to occupy the throne of Russia's ancient patriarchs by serving with energy, enthusiasm, commitment, and humility in what was, especially in his day, the most difficult and remote region of the world. He was buried at St. Sergius-Holy Trinity monastery at Zagorsk, near Moscow, in 1879, and glorified as "St. Innocent, Enlightener of the Aleutians and Apostle to America" nearly a century later.

After the sale of Alaska, the Orthodox diocese continued its educational work, although this effort was hardly recognized by federal authorities coming to the territory to organize public schools a decade later. The need to document and justify the presence of Orthodox schools was met by the editorials published in the *American Orthodox Messenger*. The last section of this chapter includes a report on the school work of the Orthodox mission for 1900, and an editorial in the *Messenger* articulating an Orthodox missiology, specifically renouncing cultural assimilation as a valid missionary goal. The distinction between evangelization and cultural imperialism, and the rejection of the more widespread identification among Western missionaries of Christianity with European culture, is perfectly understandable within the full context of Orthodox missionary tradition.

LETTER FROM ALEXANDER BARANOV TO CATHEDRAL HIEROMONK GIDEON, 23 APRIL 1807,

[*The following letters are taken from* The Russian—Orthodox Mission 1794–1837, *Kingston, Ontario, Limestone Press, 1978. Reprinted by permission of Richard Pierce, publisher.*]

Your Honor, Dear Sir!
Father Gideon.

As an expression of my recognition of the basis laid for the education of the local youth gathered here in the Kadiak school, of the impression made by your guidance, and feeling this success all the more deeply in my heart because in the course of my period in office the long-desired enlightenment and organization for the public good in these areas so distant and yet belonging to the one all-Russian scepter has been established, I have the honor to send you from my own profits, five hundred rubles to your Honor and an additional two hundred rubles towards the upkeep of those pupils who show aptitude in the study of the rules of science which you teach them, and who are able to teach others because of the level they have reached by their own endeavors. I leave it to you to divide these rewards in accordance with achievement as you see fit and in what quantities—they may be acquired from the stores on my account by your personal application or they may be sent to your Honor if you wish to receive them. But there will be no need of money from the office in Irkutsk or Okhotsk, if you wish to order articles from there; you may have open access to my account in such cases as well. For the rewarding of pupils with outstanding aptitude the agent Vasilii Ivanovich Malakhov will place at your disposal from the store an assignation for one hundred rubles. In the meantime I remain with due respect

Your Honor's humble servant
Aleksandr Baranov

23rd April
1807
Kadiak. Pavlovsk Harbor

REPLY OF HIEROMONK GIDEON TO ALEXANDER BARANOV 12 MAY 1807

Your Excellency!
Dear Sir!

For my own purposes I find it necessary to set out for Okhotsk on the vessel *Sitkha* so I humbly ask you, my dear sir, to order a berth to be made ready for me, to supply me with provisions for the said journey and for my other needs and those of the two grown-up pupils who will be with me, Prokopii Lavrov and Paramon Chumovitskii, and the minor Aleksei Kotel'nikov; of which there is here attached a list. As far as religious matters here are concerned I shall soon be contacting Your Excellency again. I remain with complete respect, etc . . .

LETTER OF CATHEDRAL HIEROMONK GIDEON TO ALEXANDER BARANOV, 26 MAY 1807

Your Honor,
My dear sir!

By the will of His Imperial Majesty, which has been, in the words of His Excellency, vested in both him and me, the great work your honor knows of and its championing by me in my position as delegate, I am compelled to remind you, my dear sir, of the way of thinking of the most solicitous founder about methods of best implementing His Majesty's will: namely, that the organization of this region has taken all his spiritual and physical strength (a fact to which I myself can bear witness), and the many areas of activities so diverted his efforts that sometimes he himself did not have enough strength to go round. "The attitude of the Russians living here," he declared in one of his letters to me, "has up to now been based on rules incompatible with humanity." "Their depraved minds," he continued in another letter, "result from their having gone to America to grow rich and only then on their return to fritter away in a few days what they have earned from many years of other people's sweat, and toil. Are such low people going to respect their neighbors? They have given up family life forever, and have no good examples to follow. Therefore the poor Americans are, to the shame of the Russians, sacrificed to their immorality. The hunters are such people that the majority of them up to now have posed, it could be said, more of a threat to the Fatherland and to America." For this reason His Excellency asked me sincerely in his absence to harness their minds in all cases to the three principles which he had established: (1) agriculture, (2) enlightenment and (3) increasing the population, by which means he thought to bring as quickly as possible the maximum benefit to this area.

And, although I am his delegate, I am inspired by the same ideas, both by the will of our Monarch with his love for humanity and even more by the laws of the King of Kings and His strong truth, dedicated to a love of mankind. I have tried to the best of my ability in all this arduous undertaking to be of aid; however, His Excellency, giving even greater emphasis to works for the common good, did not neglect in one of his letters to me to ask all of the members of the clergy here to exert all their efforts to make this great undertaking successful; and indeed, he also said this personally, and he asked especially before his departure for your honor's island, that the worthy Father Herman should in accordance with the Emperor's will have special care for this region.

I have already had the honor to inform you, my dear sir, that on my departure the affairs of the Religious Mission here will be handed over to this industrious elder: and now, by way of fulfilling that same Imperial behest and the Solicitous Founder's ardent desire for the benefit of these regions, I have prescribed for his consideration the three guiding principles outlined above, the basis of which had already been laid under the watchful oversight of Father Herman with the desired success before His Excellency arrived on Kadiak. (1) With regard to agriculture, various experiments had been conducted for several years with different kinds of seeds in different plots. (2) With regard to enlightenment, His Excellency thought that at least some families should be settled in order to act as good examples of moral probity and husbandry and in that way to soften the savagery of the native people, and this would be the first step towards enlightenment. Also Father Herman's kind behavior, his duties as preacher amongst these savage people have turned some of them to industry, to friendly contacts and to a life of good husbandry, and for their obedience in this matter they have been rewarded by our Plenipotentiary. Looking on all this with great attention and a favorable gaze, the Solicitous Founder was so good not only as to respect the unexpected beginnings so well made, but he also asked me to provide him with reports on the experiments, the successes, and other notes so that in his most humble submission to His Most Imperial Majesty about these matters which are so vital to America he might give due credit to the Fathers of the Religious Mission, and their leader for their excellent efforts and labors in agriculture.

To the second principle there also belongs the Russian-American school which I have established. I believe that Your Honor is aware of the fact that it came into being, on my arrival on Kadiak in 1805, on 20th March, from the virtually defunct former Kadiak school. On 15th August of the same year it had grown to contain fifty pupils—and with such a complement it had the pleasure of showing the fruits of its labors at a public examination honored by the presence of the Gracious Organizer of the Russian-American territories, Nikolai Petrovich Rezanov, and kind visitors such as the senior naval officers, an official representative of the clergy, and worthy representatives of the Kadiak citizenry. Those pupils who had distinguished themselves by their application and their successes in learning and good behavior were given their rewards personally from the generous hands of His Excellency. Soon after the departure of His Excellency for the port of Novo-Arkhangel'sk on Your Honor's island of residence—it increased in size to 80 pupils from various tribes, with a practical agriculture section. On the occasion of your arrival on Kadiak in 1806, from October on under your system of beneficial care for orphans there were 100 pupils—amongst whom there were even hostages from the Koliuzh people, who had eagerly and voluntarily accepted our Greek-Russian Orthodox faith on 26th November 1806. The names of these hostages are: (1) Nikostrat L'Kaina, 25 years of age, (2) Niktopolion Tygika, 19 years of age, (3) Nirs Shukka, 19, (4) Narkis El'k, 18, (5) Neon Kashk'inat, 17. With the above-mentioned number of pupils in the Russian-American School I had the pleasant opportunity on 21st April, 1807 of conducting a second public examination, in the presence both of your Honor and the chief Benefactor of the institutions in America, as also your colleague the worthy Father Herman and other people from the clergy. In addition there were present foreign sea-captains and citizens from the newly-established Kadiak society. I had ample proof, both from your favorable communication of 23rd April of the great emotion with which you were filled and with which your soul was filled when you saw the fruits of our efforts and also by the noble reflection by the shareholder Vasilii Ivanovich Malakhov of your great example of devotion to the good of the area. Now (I can tell you frankly) it would be balm to the tender heart of our Solicitous Founder to receive the sweet news that some of the pupils of the Russian-American school had already taken teaching posts. Also at the special injunction of His Excellency, there has begun to be compiled a dictionary of the Aleut language under the guidance of a senior pupil, Paramon Chumovitskii, and the basic work has already been done towards a grammar of the same language. The pupil who is most capable at this kind of work at the advice of your honor I shall leave under the special supervision of the leader of the local clergy, Father Herman. You, my dear sir, for your part, I would most humbly beg you, should leave him attached to the Russian-American School. In the autumn because of the shortage of food stocks here, he could spend the whole winter working for the common good with a special detachment of pupils at the Alitat artel, where he would be with his Godfather and benefactor, the worthy baidarshchik Timofei Leont'evich Chumovitskii, and in the spring, on 1st May, he should present his detachment for the public examination and then continue with his activities until the autumn at the port of Pavlovsk—i.e. correcting the dictionary, translating under the guidance of the leader of the Religious Mission, Father Herman, whatever the latter sees fit in the light of circumstances. This also goes for the younger pupil of grammar—Aleksei Kotel'nikov—he should stay here with his teacher Ivan Kadiakskii and his colleague Khristofor Prianishnikov. These people have all been placed by me directly into the hands of the man so richly endowed with honor of God, Father Herman. He will teach them the fear of God and the basis of true wisdom. (3) As regards the third principle, the multiplication of the population in accordance with the Imperial will, the solicitous founder advised the clergy to co-operate with the company's Kadiak administration in caring for the people.

As a conclusion I would ask you most humbly as an especial lover of the local area to offer all possible aid to the leader of the Mission, Father Herman, in the carrying out of the two aims outlined above, for the common good. And as far as the third aim is concerned, perhaps you would be so good, in your absence, to let me know who is in charge of secular affairs so that in necessary circumstances the co-operation mentioned above by the founder may not be denied.

I have the honor to be
with absolute respect etc.

May 26th
1807

LETTERS FROM CATHEDRAL HIEROMONK GIDEON TO THE MONK HERMAN, 1 JUNE 1807, 11 JUNE 1807

Worthy Father Herman!

In his generous communication to me of 23rd April His Honor, Aleksandr Andreevich Baranov gave me leave to present you with the enclosed sum of 300 rubles. This is to reward those pupils of the Russian-American school who distinguish themselves both by their exemplary successes in learning and by showing sufficient success in training other pupils at the examination held on the 21st of that month. The sum is to be shared out as follows: Ivan Kadiakskii—ninety rubles; Paramon Chumovitskii—ninety rubles; Khristofor Prianishnikov—eighty rubles; and Aleksei Kotel'nikov—forty rubles.

With sincere respect I
have the honor to be etc.

1st June, 1807

Most Worthy Father Herman!

As I set off now for St. Petersburg I consider it an essential duty to hand over to you the direction of the American-Kadiak Religious Mission. I have already informed His Honor Collegiate Counsellor and Chief Manager of the region Aleksandr Andreevich Baranov. But I also consider it necessary, in addition to my personal explanation, to make certain points to you about the improvement in organization:

(1) Paying due respect to your virtues and to your ardent solicitude for the good of the region, I cherish the fond hope that you will not neglect, by dint of your experienced teaching, to instill into the hearts of both Russians and Americans the rules of a true knowledge of God, a love of their country, and friendly relations between both peoples. You are well aware that it is the first duty of a priest to set an example of Christian piety in his own life; and so I have no doubt that you will exercise your leadership to this end. It should be one of your first tasks, as it is of everyone, whatever their calling, to dispense authority, purely, honorably and nobly.

(2) The whole church building here leaks terribly, and I have told the Kadiak office about it, and so I make it a task of yours to see that it is mended. The vestments, utensils and books for the services should be placed by you into the keeping of either Hieromonk Afanasii or the monk Ioasaf—and you are to take special care that it is all kept in good order.

(3) On my arrival from St. Petersburg I noticed with pleasure in your accounting a rare sense of moderation and exemplary husbandry—in your reliable ways of preserving grain in which even His Excellency gave you sincere praise, being indebted by forty sums for the upkeep of his journey. Thus I consider it unnecessary to remind you of the need to maintain a similar economy with the grain which remains, and with other possessions, since I am completely sure that you will not neglect to do everything in these matters that results from your ardor.

(4) His Excellency informed me that "in future, in accordance with the will of His Imperial Majesty, marriages should only be solemnized between those wishing to remain here, and to accept from them in such cases written undertakings, witnessed by the Manager and three persons claiming to be permanent residents". Please continue this practice which is already established at the office. As regards providing the office every year with a list of births, marriages and deaths, this is not possible because the company disperses people of both sexes to various distant points without informing

the Religious Mission in any way, and also because the Religious Mission has only one Hieromonk who cannot move far away from the church or the harbor; the population remaining in their villages are under the jurisdiction of the company baidarshchiks and the clergy receive no information regarding births and deaths from these people either. And since the Religious Mission has no clerk attached to it it has to ask for help from the office in cases of registering christenings and marriages. I have already informed His Honor the local administrator about this.

(5) On my arrival on the *Neva* in this savage and distant region my first sight of both the severity of the climate and the naked savagery of nature made all my feelings shake with terror. But when I saw the fruits of your ardent efforts at kind treatment of the Americans and in the husbandry and agricultural achievements produced by this, this unexpected pleasure filled my spirit with sweet contentment. His Excellency, when he arrived, viewed your achievements in this wild country with similar pleasure, and as an encouragement to greater efforts personally rewarded those Americans trained by you for their devotion to you and their industry. Then, for the further development of this region, he thought it best to establish three principles: (1) agriculture, (2) education and (3) increasing the population and he asked me to turn toward these ends all minds, so that the area might benefit as quickly as possible. Thus, before my departure, I charge you, as someone who has already helped to establish these principles, with the further managing of these tasks, though I consider it unnecessary to explain this to you in detail as you already have sufficient experience in these matters. You will receive help in this from the company. His Excellency has already written to the office about this, and I have informed His Honor Aleksandr Andreevich Baranov.

(6) It is with especial pleasure that I place in your keeping, Your Worthiness, the Russian-American school which I established. The order established there should be maintained in the future. I have left instructions in the school. Ivan Kadiakskii is appointed teacher with his colleague Khristofor Prianishnikov and with Aleksei Kotel'nikov as assistant. Paramon Chumovitskii, with the help of others, will be responsible for compiling a dictionary of the Aleut language and a brief sketch of the grammar of the same language. He will also act as your interpreter. Give due attention to the special group of students of agriculture. The company will supply you with the funds needed for this. Above all else strive to instil in their young hearts the rules of the Faith, a fear of God and a sense of morality and punish them for transgressions. Your love towards all that is good gives me no reason to doubt that you will carry all this out in the best possible order.

(7) His Excellency assured me that your keep (as you are aware) will be paid by the local Manager. I have also addressed a request to him on this

subject. For better ease of organization the needs of the whole mission should be presented by you alone.

(8) More than anything else try to maintain peace and harmony among your fellow brothers. I for my part shall pray and beseech the Almighty Giver of all Gifts that he should send you strength and fortitude so that you may do good works in praise of His name.—The Cathedral Monk of the Aleksandr-Nevskii Monastery, Hieromonk Gideon, 11th June, 1807. On Kadiak. Pavlovsk Harbor.

LETTER FROM REV. PRIEST JOHN VENIAMINOV TO ARCHBISHOP MICHAEL OF IRKUTSK, 5 NOVEMBER 1829

[*Translated by Lydia Black. In "Ivan Pankor Architect of Aleut Literacy,"* Orthodox Alaska *8 (1978).*]

By nature and upbringing I am very far from believing various superstitions and still less inclined to invent false miracles. Yet, I have no wish to hide from Your Grace anything, including my weaknesses, and therefore I want to apprise Your Grace of the following occurrence, which is not impossible, as the ways of the Lord are unfathomable and the strength of His mercy does not diminish, but nevertheless an event most rare and unheard of in these our times.

During my stay in April of 1828 on the island of Akun and the other three islands belonging to the former, I learned through the interpreter Ivan Pan'kov that the resident of the village Recheshnoye on the island of Akun, on its SE side, about 10 *versts* [a *verst* is equal to 1.0068 km. or 0.6629 miles. 500 *sazhen'* make up one *verst.* (*Sovetskaia Entsiklopediia,* 3rd ed.) L.B.] from the main settlement on the island, Ivan Smirennikov, an old man of about 60 years of age, is regarded by the local inhabitants and by many others as well, as a shaman, not an ordinary person, at least.

1) The wife of the Toion of the village Artelnovskoye, one Fedor Zhirov, on October of 1825 was caught in a fox trap, and her leg was badly hurt. There were no means to help her, and she was expected to die momentarily. The trap hit her at the kneecap by all three iron teeth, about two *vershok* [a *vershok* is equal to 44.45 mm. or approximately 1.75 inches (*loc. cit.*) L.B.] in length. Her kinsmen secretly asked the said old man Smirennikov to cure her. After thinking the matter over, he said that the patient will be well by morning. And, indeed, the woman rose in the morning from her deathbed, and is even now entirely well, not suffering any pain;

2) In the winter of the same year, 1825, the inhabitants of Akun suffered great lack of food, and some of them asked Smirennikov to pray for

a whale to be washed ashore. After a short time the old man instructed the people to go to a certain place, where they indeed found a fresh whale carcass—precisely in the spot designated;

3) Last fall I planned to visit Akun, but because of the arrival of state ships from Russia, I had to postpone the trip. Yet, the Akun people sent an escort and all expected my arrival. Only Smirennikov boldly asserted that I would not come that fall, but should be expected next spring. And so it happened, contrary winds did not permit my departure, then the cold weather set in, and I was forced to delay my visit until spring.

There are many additional instances which prove his gift of clairvoyance, but I shall omit them here.

Such tales, confirmed by trustworthy informants, convinced me that I should meet Smirennikov in person and personally inquire how it is that he knows the future and what means does he employ to learn it? He thanked me for my interest and told me the following:

Soon after being baptized by Hieromonk Makarii there appeared to him first one, then two spirits, not to be seen by any other man. The spirits had the appearance of humans, light of face, dressed in white robes and, according to his description, these robes resembled church vestments and were trimmed with rose bands. 1) They told him they were sent to him by God to instruct, teach, and preserve him, and they continued to appear to him for thirty years almost daily. The spirits instructed him in Christian teaching. 2) They granted his requests, and through him requests of others (though pretty seldom); they repeated to him my own teachings and told him not to confess his sins to anyone, listen to my teachings and not to listen to *promishlenniki,* that is the Russians. Even this very day, as he was *en route,* they appeared and told him that I am calling him and for what reason, and instructed him to tell me all, not to be afraid, that no evil shall befall him.

I asked him, what did he feel when the spirits appeared—sorrow or joy? He said that only if he was conscious of having done something bad did he feel a twinge of conscience, but otherwise he did not experience any fear. Moreover, as the people regard him as shaman, and he does not want to be a shaman, he asked the spirits to leave him alone; the spirits replied that they are not demons and cannot leave him. To his question, why they do not appear to others, the spirits replied that they were so ordered.

It is possible to suppose that this man has heard from me or from somebody else the teaching of our faith he recounted and only for effect or out of vanity invented the appearance of the spirits. Yet, I must state that Aleuts do not fall prey to pride, vanity and empty bragging. Moreover 1) I, when preaching, for the sake of brevity and in order to avoid complications, omitted the story of creation, the fall of angels, of the tree of knowledge of good and evil, of the first murderer, of Noah, Abraham and John the Baptist and usually also the story of the Annunciation of the Birth of Christ. But he, Smirennikov, told me these stories in detail. When I preached, he was the first to confirm the truth of my words in the tone of a person conversant with the Holy Writ; 2) Aleuts who live here, all except the interpreter Pan'kov and very few others, even though they had Faith and prayed prior to my arrival, had little knowledge to whom they pray. Hieromonk Makarii, my predecessor here in 1794 and 1795 did not instruct the people here for lack of any kind of interpreter. It is only very recently that interpreters are on hand and among them Pan'kov is the best and most intelligent. But he, Pan'kov, afraid to fall into error, and having firm faith in the One God, never entered into any conversations with the old man and he also protested and tried to restrain others when they called on the help of Smirennikov. This fact was attested by many Aleuts, and therefore there was no one from whom Smirennikov could have learned in the matters of Church teaching; 3) He himself is illiterate and does not know any Russian; therefore, he could not have read about it and finally, 4) I asked him if I could meet with his protectors—the spirits. He replied that he does not know, but that he will ask. Shortly thereafter, in about an hour, he came and told me their answer: What does he want? Does he consider us demons? If he insists, he can see and converse with us. And then they said something very flattering to me, which I omit here. But I refused the meeting with the spirits. One could ask why did I do so? My answer is that there was no need for me to meet them. Why should I want to see them personally when their teaching is Christian teaching? Out of curiosity, to learn who they are? For this I should ask the blessing of my Archbishop, to avoid the pitfall of error, should I meet those spirits.

All of the above is attested to by Smirennikov under oath, and transmitted by me not word for word but true to the meaning, without additions or omissions. Moreover, the freedom, fearlessness and even pleasure of his discourse, and above all his clean manner of life, convinced me and confirmed me in the conviction that the spirits which appear to this old man (if they appear) are not demons. Demons may sometimes assume the image of Angels of Light, but never for the purpose of instruction, teaching and salvation of human beings, but always for their perdition. As the tree of evil cannot bear the fruit of good, these spirits must be the servants sent to those who seek salvation. Therefore, in order not to weaken (among the people) the faith and hope in the One Omniscient God, I, until I receive instruction from Your Grace, determined to render the following decision: "I see that the spirits which appear to thee are not demons and therefore I instruct thee to listen to their teachings and instructions, as long as these do not contradict the teachings I deliver in the assembly; just tell those who ask your advice about the future and request your help to address themselves directly to God, as He is common Father to all. I do not forbid thee to cure the sick, but ask thee to tell those thou curest that thou doest so not by thy own powers, but by the power of God and to instruct them to pray diligently and thank the Sole God. I do not forbid thee to teach either, but only instruct thee to confine this teaching to the minors.'' I told the other Aleuts who were present not to call him a Shaman, not to ask him for favors, but to ask God.

In reporting to you, Your Grace, I deemed it necessary to ask Ivan Pan'kov who translated my words and those of the Old Man Smirennikov, to sign this statement, in witness of the truth of my story and the correctness of his translation. I also requested him to keep this matter secret for the time being. I beg Your Grace to let me know if my decision was right and if there is any need for me to meet with the spirits which appear to the old man, and if so, what precautions I should take. If I erred, forgive me.

Signed: Your Grace's Priest John Veniaminov, of the Church of Ascension in Unalashka, June 1828;

Signed: below by interpreter Pan'kov as follows:
To the truth of the words of Priest John Veniaminov and the accuracy of translation of the words of the old man Ivan Smirennikov attests Tigal'da Toion Ivan Pan'kov.

True copy of the original, Tobol'sk, 5 November, 1829.

LETTER FROM NEWLY CONSECRATED BISHOP INNOCENT VENIAMINOV TO METROPOLITAN FILARET OF MOSCOW, 30 APRIL 1842

Translated by Serge Bouteneff
[*The following text was originally published in* Orthodox Alaska, *July 1970.*]

Your Eminence, Merciful
Archpastor and Father:[1]

At last, glory be to God, through His mercy, and the intercessions of the Most Holy Virgin, and the prayers of the Saints, as well as Yours, I am in America! I will tell you of the journey and our arrival, etc., in America on the 20th of August in the year 1841. On one of the best days, in the most pleasant of circumstances, we left the mouth of the Ohotsk River on the brig *Ohota,* and directed our journey towards one of the islands of the Kurils

1. To the Metropolitan of Moscow, Filaret. Page 73 in Barsukov's Letters.

Archipelago—Samsirou. We approached the Samsirou Island on the 2nd of September and I sent a priest ashore, for the edification of the Russians and Aleuts living there (indigenous peoples do not live on this island; they all live on Shoumshou, another island) and for the serving of their pastoral needs. That same evening we departed from the island and made straight for Sitka. For nearly 20 consecutive days there were favorable winds. It was warm and clear and our ship sailed so quickly that on the 21st of September we were only 750 versts[2] from Sitka, having sailed from Ohotsk some 6,250 versts. The weather was so good that we celebrated each feast day on deck, rather than in the cabin as is usually done. You can imagine what a fine sight this was: a ship in the middle of a boundless ocean under full sail, sailing full speed ahead; it is peaceful; on the deck—people, and there a service is conducted! This is a unique picture in its own right! The 25th of September, on the feast of St. Sergius, at 4 o'clock in the afternoon (in Moscow it is approximately 4 o'clock in the morning), through His prayers and ours, we saw Mt. Edgecumbe, which is near New Archangel.[3] On the following day, the 26th of September, on the feast of the beloved disciple of Christ,[4] to whom the Church prays—for the dispersing of the infidels, we entered the harbor of Sitka and at 10 o'clock dropped anchor. On the 27th of September, on Saturday, I went ashore where I was met by the head governor, all the functionaries and all the Orthodox.[5] In small omophor and mantia I went to Church where I greeted my flock with a short speech and celebrated a thanksgiving Moliebin to our Lord God. On the 28th of September I celebrated the Divine Liturgy for the first time. The Church in New Archangel was in rather good repair; but it is fast aging and in 4 or 5 years there will be need for a new one. But it was above my expectations, decorated as though they were really awaiting the arrival of a Bishop. This is all due to the efforts of the chief governor, Mr. Etolin, who asked that the Church be repaired upon his arrival.

Our activities, since our arrival in Sitka, are not really great. They are: 1) A mission was sent to the Nushagak, which will arrive at its appointed place no earlier than the middle of June this year. The priest is trustworthy, even if he is not one of the scholars. He is supplied with detailed directions and all articles from us. 2) On the 17th of December a Pastoral School was opened, consisting to date of 23 persons—creole and native. The supervisor

2. One verst—3,500 feet.

3. New Archangel was the capital of Russian America; it is now called Sitka. Very early in the history of Russian-America, Sitka and new-Archangel were used interchangeably. Thus whenever New Archangel is mentioned it refers to the capital but when Sitka is mentioned, it could refer to either the capital or to the island which is now known as Baranov.

4. St. John the Theologian.

5. Included in this group were some baptized Kolosh, who stood among those ennumerated. The Russians referred to members of the Tlingit tribe as Kolosh.

is the priestmonk M.,[6] a student of the Moscow Theological Academy. 3) The student I. T. was sent to Kodiak to learn the language, and within a four-month period showed remarkable success. He is a man with abilities. 4) Priestmonk M. is zealously speaking to the Kolosh, and, it seems, not without some success—I do not dare to say with success. Some 80 persons are ready to be baptized and ask to be. I do not think to rush: the more and better they get to know, the more dependable. 5) In the spring, I was in Kodiak to survey the Church there, and was consoled by it above any expected hopes. The Kodiak people now became completely different than before. The rumors of my arrival in America, the zeal and piety of the local priest who arrived in Kodiak in the latter part of 1840, as well as the Christian assistance by word, deed and action, of the local supervisor, Mr. Kostrometnov, worked quite a lot on the Kodiak people. However, they, poor ones, had not heard any good word from anyone until now, and, as they said to me, *"They are beginning to come out of the darkness into the light."* Before, barely a hundredth of them were ever in Church and they know nothing of fasting and attending services before confession and communion. Today the Church is full at every feast day, and during one Great Lent there were more than 400 fasters—and they came for this even from faroff places. Unlawful cohabitation (common-law marriages, of which there were many) ceased. To such an extent was the Kodiak Church neglected that of 3,700 souls ennumerated by the register in the year 1841, there were more than 1,000 unbaptized. And many died thusly, especially during smallpox, which took some 2,000 persons from the Kodiak area! As proof of the good change of the Kodiak people and of the actions of the local priest I recount several of his accounts which were sent to me. A) "The Great Lent of this year, 1842, on the first week, approximately 40 Aleuts came to the Pavelsky harbor from the Three Saints area[7] to observe the fast. For three days these Aleuts were exhorted by me in the Christian faith and when and how a Christian can worthily partake of the Body and Blood of Christ. Among the group was a toyone.[8] During the time of the second talk with them—during which we spoke of confession and of the Eucharist, when it was said that if each sinner repented before God and in the presence of a priest, without any outside witness, then God, for the sake of the intercessions of His beloved Son, Jesus Christ, will forgive all the sins and will not even remember them through the ages, if only the penitent would not again repeat them—the fore-mentioned toyone said in the presence of all that he will publicly tell all his sins, and no one should be ashamed, and he will conceal nothing. When I began to oppose his desire and said that he should

6. Misael: vide infra, Letter 34, note 15.
7. Now called Old Harbor.
8. Leader of a tribe or clan.

not do that, he answered: 'If I did not feel shame in sinning, why then should I feel shame in confessing my sins, even if it be before all?' The fervent faith of this man moved my soul. Despite the fact that I spoke with them a lot and for periods of time, he would not leave and afterwards would constantly come to my quarters and subsequently came to study. Once I asked him in my quarters why he was more diligent than others, and more frank than his brothers? He answered, 'because I am worse than they: and in Church, when you looked at me (which, incidentally, I do not remember) within me an idea was born—to come straight to you and to study under you.' This toyone repented and partook of Holy Communion. It was noticed that for the whole first week, during which he fasted, he ate almost nothing, from which his face became gaunt and pale; his voice changed and often incomprehensible sighs were heard. The talks with these Aleuts were conducted in the presence of the governor of this colony. B) On the fourth week of Great Lent, again from the Three Saints area, there came some Aleuts to fast. Among their number was a shaman. After the talk with them in the Church, the shaman came to me in my quarters and announced the following: 'Five years ago the local priest, Father A, saw me, looked at me and said to me: 'You will burn.' Well, a lot of time has passed and I cannot forget his words. I feel that I fear something and in spite of the fact that I am a toyone—a leader—I think the last of my underlings is better than I. Tell me, is it true that I shall be burned?' The mercy of God, which brings sinners to salvation, brought this shaman to a contrite repentance, and he vouchsafed to partake of the spiritual food—the Body of Christ, and to drink of Eternal Life. Leaving the harbor on the sixth week, he came to my quarters with two other toyones to thank me. This, word for word, is what he said: 'os *'Thank you very, very much,* and never will I forget you until the day I die.' '' The last incident is proof positive that we all, even from the peal of the bell, serve as the arm of the mercy of God. C) The opening of the divinity school (14th of October)—the first one in America and, amazingly, before any secular school. In two days I leave on a trip to survey my Diocese, a trip which will last 16 months. First I intend to go to the Islands, then to Petropavelsk and from there, having travelled all of Kamchatka, in March to Ohotsk, where I must live until the middle of July or longer.

Commending myself to the prayers of Your Eminence, I have the honor, with filial devotion and love to Your Eminence, Merciful Archpastor and Father, to be Your humble servant.

Innocent Bishop of Kamchatka

New Archangel
30 April, 1842

MISSIONARY OATH

[*Reprinted from* Orthodox Alaska.]

Each missionary who came to Alaska from Russia was required to take an Oath before leaving Russia for his new assignment. He signed it and it was witnessed by the priest who gave the Oath. The following was the Oath used when Bishop Innocent Veniaminov was the Bishop of Kamchatka, with jurisdiction in Alaska and the Aleutians.

"I, the undersigned, in front of this Holy Bible, promise and swear by Almighty God that I am obligated by my position and am earnestly willing, in the work of Christianization assigned to me, to think, to teach and to act as is maintained and taught by our Orthodox Church and as is prescribed and ordered by the instructions of my Archpastor, The Right Reverend Innocent, Bishop of Kamchatka, in accordance with the decrees of His Imperial Majesty.

"I swear by the Living God that, ever keeping in my mind His awful words, 'damned is he who preaches God's word carelessly,' I will earnestly perform the work of God which has been assigned to me to my utmost mental and physical strength, without hypocrisy and avarice, avoiding all threats, deceit, extortion and other unlawful acts, and without any force or violence; but sincerely, disinterestedly, kindly, considerately with true meekness and Christian love, keeping in mind the glory of God and the salvation of people's souls as the final aim of all my thoughts, words and acts, seeking not my own, but that which is of Our Lord Jesus.

"I furthermore swear by Almighty God that I am obligated and am willing at all times to be the loyal, good and obedient subject of His Imperial Majesty, the All-Merciful Emperor, and of the lawful heir of the Russian Throne in carrying out the work entrusted to me; and I will preserve and defend the interests of His Imperial Majesty to the utmost of my understanding and ability, being ready to sacrifice my life if necessary.

"I furthermore swear by Almighty God that I do not entertain any mental reservation, equivocation or misinterpretation of the promises pronounced by my tongue: Should it be otherwise, God, He to whom all hearts are open, be my Righteous Avenger.

"I seal my oath by kissing the words and the cross of my Savior. Amen."

ADDRESS OF METROPOLITAN INNOCENT VENIAMINOV AT HIS INSTALLATION AS METROPOLITAN OF MOSCOW, 1868

[*The following text was originally published in* St. Innocent, Apostle to America, *St. Vladimir's Press, 1979. Translated by Paul Garrett.*]

Who am I to dare take up the word and authority of my predecessors? A mere student from bygone days and far-off places, who spent over half his life in a country still farther off; no more than a humble worker in one of Christ's small fields, a teacher of children and babes in the faith—how can *I*, the least of all workers, work in this great and glorious and ancient vineyard of Christ? How can a teacher such as I instruct a flock from whose midst teachers and guides—indeed, teachers of teachers—have gone out to all parts of Russia? True, I could say these things, almost anywhere I might be sent, but *here* there is something quite particular. Look at whom I must follow. Who was my predecessor, then who am I? There can be no comparison (or rather, any comparison which might be drawn would be far from favorable to me, and would in fact be rather against me). I understood the full difficulty, the bitterness of such comparisons—comparisons wholly natural, unavoidable and just (and not at all of the same nature as gossip); I understood too how fully sublime and difficult it would be to minister here, and I ought to have (or at least *could* have) shirked it, having indeed reasons for doing so. But who am I to oppose God, the Heavenly King without Whose will not a hair falls from our heads? Or who am I to contradict our earthly king whose heart is in the hand of God? "No," I said to myself. "Let it be with me as the Lord wills. I will go wherever I am told!" And so, I have come. O Lord, bless me to begin my work. O Lord, I am Yours, and I wish to be Yours, everywhere and always. Do with me as You wish in this life and in the life to come. May I be here just a tool in Your hands!

O Most Holy Lady, Theotokos, my Surety! Do not take from me here your aid, your help, your intercessions, your prayers! O Hierarchs of Christ: Peter, Alexis, Jonah and Philip—and all of you who lie at rest here—accept in your prayers me, your most unworthy heir. Brothers and fathers—especially you learned instructors and fathers—you do not deserve an illiterate hierarch like me, but bear with me for the love of Christ, and accept me in your daily prayers. Pray even more that false doctrine and human philosophizing may not creep into Orthodoxy by means of my illiteracy. I ask all of you, my brethren and my children, to pray for me, a sinner.

"Grace and peace to you, from God the Father and from our Lord Jesus Christ!"

ADDRESS OF METROPOLITAN INNOCENT VENIAMINOV TO THE ORGANIZATIONAL MEETING OF THE ORTHODOX MISSIONARY SOCIETY, 1868

[*The following text was originally published in* St. Innocent, Apostle to America, *St. Vladimir's Press, 1979. Translated by Paul Garrett.*]

Brethren, you have heard that the goal of our Society is to advance the conversion of those who do not yet believe in Christ our Savior. That is, we accept, each according to his abilities and the measure of his zeal, to further the conversion to the Orthodox Faith and the Truth of those among our fellow countrymen who still wander in the darkness of unbelief. As you can see, the work we hope to advance is great and holy and truly apostolic.

In order to obtain the success one desires, even in ordinary tasks and undertakings, it is necessary to muster (independently of financial means) intelligence, knowledge, experience, ability, activity and energy. When with all of this the circumstances are *just* right, one has reason to hope for success.

Now, in the work which *we* wish to advance, this does not in the main apply. To be sure, we too will need (in addition to financial means) intelligence, knowledge, experience, ability and so on, but we cannot—and must not, even under the best of circumstances—count upon these factors as a sure means to attaining our goal. And why not? Because man's conversion to the path of faith and truth depends entirely upon God. "No one can come to Me," said the Savior, "unless the Father Who sent Me draws him to Me" [Jn 6:44]. Therefore if, according to His inscrutable judgments, the Lord does not wish for a given person or nation to be converted to Jesus Christ, even the most capable, most gifted, most zealous of workers will not succeed in his task. We need not offer even the Apostles as examples here. We can point directly to Jesus Christ Himself Who, being Himself the Word and Love Itself, was (and is) better able than anyone else to proclaim the Truth and convince people to accept it. Yet how many of those who heard and listened to Him remained unconverted?

What then shall we do? How ought we to proceed when, in the words of the Gospel, the harvest is great in our country (*i.e.*, many remain unconverted to Jesus Christ)? "Pray to the Lord of the harvest," Jesus Himself teaches us [Mt 9:38]. Thus, first and foremost, *we must pray*. If even in everyday matters people fall back upon prayer, asking God's blessing at the beginning of some task and then throughout asking for renewal and strength (where prayer means nothing more than *help*), here, in the matter of conversion, prayer becomes the *means* itself—and a most effectual of means, for without prayer one cannot expect success even under the most perfect of circumstances. Thus it is not our missionaries alone who must pray. No, we their brethren must further their work by our own prayers. And what ought we to pray for? First, that the Lord will send workers into His harvest; second, that He will open the hearts of those who listen to the Word of the Gospel; third, that He will increase our Society's numbers more and more; and finally, that He will strengthen and confirm in us the desire we all now feel to further this work to the attaining of our goal.

Let us further it also by our good desire, our good word, and whatsoever sacrifices of which we may be capable. And these—no matter how small—will be, we can state, acceptable to Him Who has said, "Truly, I say to you, whoever gives a drink of cold water to one of the least of my followers because he *is* My follower, will certainly receive a reward" [Mt 10:42]. (Here we can understand as the "follower" our present missionaries.)

EXTRACTS FROM THE JOURNALS OF REV. PRIEST IAKOV (JACOB/JAMES) NETSVETOV, 1828–1842, ATKA DISTRICT

[*The following text is taken from* Iakov Netsvetov, The Atka Years, 1828–1844, *Kingston, Ontario, Limestone Press, 1980. Translated by Lydia T. Black, University of Alaska, Fairbanks.*]

1828

May 15:

In the morning we reached Kirinsk, about 950 versts from Irkutsk. Here we made a short stop, necessary in order to validate the passports of the *promyshlennye* who were travelling with us. I had the honor to visit the local Protohierei Ioann Shistin. By noon we went on.

May 17:

At midnight we sailed past the Vitim station [*Vitimskaia distantsiia*], which is about 416 versts from Kirinsk. From there on we encountered an obstacle to further progress: the Vitim River has just opened up and in front of us ice floes were yet tossed about, so that we managed to make only about 27 versts from the Vitim, to the first settlement, the Peleduisk village [*Peleduiskoe selenie*]. Here we put to shore and remained for 48 hours [*dvoe sutok*].

May 19:

We set out in the morning and sailed, without stopping anywhere, by day and by night.

May 22:

About noon, we passed the Olekmenskoe settlement, about 600 versts from the Vitim station.

May 25:

About four o'clock in the afternoon, about 30 versts from Iakutsk, the two barges carrying the *promyshlennye* were directed to the right bank of the river, to the place called Iarmanka whence [travellers] depart for Okhotsk by horseback. The third barge continued directly toward the town, along the left bank, and by one o'clock after midnight we were approaching Iakutsk, which is calculated to be about 2500 versts from Irkutsk.

May 26:

In the morning I visited the Commissioner [*Komissioner*] of the American Company, Mr. Shergin, who assigned me together with the physician Ermolaev, living quarters in a wing of the American [Company] office. Here we remained for two days.

May 28:

We crossed the Lena River to Iarmanka. Mr. Shergin accompanied us, to see us off. We remained here for three days, because our horses were not ready. Toward evening I went on horseback to a Iakut *ulus,* about 12 versts distant, to administer last rites to a sick Iakut.

May 31:

About ten o'clock in the morning I and my family set out on horseback, and so did also physician Ermolaev and his wife. Later on, the same day, the 43 *promyshlennye* started out also, all on horseback. With them was office clerk, Mr. Rikhter. They overtook us toward the evening, and went on. We, travelling with families, could not proceed at such speed. Often we had to stop during the day having travelled only a few hours.

June 7:

Past midday, about eight o'clock, we reached the station [*stantsiia*] Amga, which is about 253 versts from Iakutsk. Here is the *Amga* River, which we were unable to cross this day, because of the lateness of the hour. Besides, the *prikazchik* and his cargo and the *promyshlennye,* who had arrived earlier, were being ferried across just then.

June 8:

In the morning, I baptized a son born to the Iakut Login Zakharov on the 6th of January. The infant was named Ioann. Later on, having crossed the river, we continued on our way.

June 9:

About three o'clock in the afternoon we reached the *Nokha* River which we forded on horseback. When the water stands high and the river overflows, a ferry is used here.

June 10:

About three o'clock in the afternoon, we reached the *Aldan* River, at a place about 330 versts from Iakutsk. On this side of the river there is a postal station and station master in charge, on the other bank there is a government commissary [*komissionerstvo*] under a supervisor and several cossacks [stationed there]. I remained overnight at the postal station and, on the request of the local postal supervisor, celebrated a prayer service with consecration of the waters. Afterwards, having received news of a sick person, the physician [Ermolaev] and I went to the other bank of the Aldan River. There I confessed the *promyshlennyi* Ioakim Parokhin, left behind here because of illness. We then returned to the postal station. Parokhin died during the following night.

June 11:

In the morning, having crossed the river, I stopped here for the day in order to perform various requisite ministrations requested by the local inhabitants. I was busy performing the mystery of baptism for the following [individuals]:

1. Nikolai, son of the cossack Nikolai Bol'shev, born 6 December 1827;

2. Elena, daughter of the cossack Prokopii Malyshev, born 13 May of this year;

3. Nikolai, an illegitimate child of a Iakut woman, born 6 December 1827;

4. A Iakut girl, Akulina, 13 years of age. Afterwards I sang the funeral rites and buried the newly dead Ioakim Parokhin. Because of the lateness of the hours, I remained here overnight.

June 12:

We set out on our way in the morning and by evening reached the Belaia River, which we crossed by boats [*lodki*].

June 14:

We reached the station Chernoles, which is about 105 versts distant from Aldan. Here I baptized the son of a Iakut, born in September of 1827. The infant was named Ioann.

June 18:

We reached the station Alakh'iun' which is about 129 versts distant from Chernoles and stopped here for the night.

June 19:

In the morning I performed the mystery of baptism over the following [persons]:

1. Vasilii, son of the cossack Petr Iakushkov, born 31 December 1827;
2. Agrippina, a Iakut [woman] 40 years of age;

After [I finished] we proceeded forward.

June 20:

We reached the *Anzha* River, which we forded on horseback. When the water is high, occasionally a ferry is used here.

June 25:

In the afternoon, about two o'clock, we reached the Iudoma River, which we crossed by boats, and stopped for the night at the station called *Iudomskii Krest*. I had to stay here in order to perform various ministrations on request of the local inhabitants. This very day I performed the mystery of baptism for the following [persons]:

1. Anna, daughter of Iakov Kirenskov, the Commissioner in charge of the food provision store [*magazin*], born 22 April of this year;
2. Aleksandr, son of the cossack Aleksandr Alekseev, born in the month of October of 1826;
3. Anna, daughter of the cossack Dmitrii Komarov, born in the month of November of 1827;
4. The Iakut Pavel, aged 77 years. This mystery was performed in the local chapel which is dedicated to the True and Life Giving Cross of Our Lord.

June 26:

On request of the local inhabitants, I celebrated a Te Deum [*moleben*] and then we continued on our journey, travelling without interruption and without encountering any obstacles, every day until we reached the Port of Okhotsk.

July 3:

This day of our arrival at Okhotsk through the grace of God, we have safely completed our journey on land. The distance from Iakutsk to Okhotsk, along the route we traversed, is calculated to be about 1014 versts. We arrived not at the port [harbor] itself, but reached a location at the new river mouth, about 7 versts from the port itself. Here we stopped, as we were to continue to the harbor by boat, but the boatmen were absent and we had to stay until the next day.

July 4:

About one o'clock in the afternoon we arrived at the port. I was assigned quarters at the Russian-American Company's factory [*faktoriia*] which is situated somewhat apart from the town of Okhotsk toward the very mouth of the river. The Manager of the American Office, Anisim Lenfe assigned me quarters in the wing of the company building. The *promyshlennye* arrived here three days prior to our arrival.

July 5:

Next morning I considered it my duty to pay a visit to the local Protohierei Petr Bagriantsev. On this day the brig *Okhotsk,* sailing from Novoarkhangel'sk harbor [port] on Sitka, arrived here in Okhotsk harbor, under the command of the Fleet Lieutenant Dionisii Zaremba. The brig entered the river mouth safely and dropped anchor directly opposite the company building. It is on this vessel that I shall continue toward my destination on the next lap of my journey, this time by sea.

July 8:

This Sunday I had the pleasure of celebrating the Divine Liturgy in the Okhotsk Church, the temple of the Transfiguration of Our Lord, Jesus Christ.

July 13:

This day the brig *Nikolai* (a government vessel) put out to sea, sailing to Gizhiga.

July 22:

On this day of the Feast of the patron saint [the name day] of the Benevolent Lady Empress Maria Fedorovna, the princesses [*velikie kniazhny*] Maria Nikolaevna and Maria Pavlovna, and the good Lady and Grand Duchess [*velikaia kniaginia*] Maria Pavlovna, the entire Okhotsk clergy, the Protohierei and the priest, held a divine service and then a Te Deum, which I had the honor to attend. Afterwards, the clergy, along with Okhotsk officials and notables, attended a reception at the house of the Port Commander, Captain of the First Rank and Cavalier, Aleksandr Stepanovich Vilront. I also attended.

July 23:

The brig *Elizaveta* (a government vessel) arrived at the Okhotsk port from Kamchatka.

July 29:

The brig *Okhotsk* (a company vessel) was ready for departure for Novoarkhangel'sk Port; therefore, on this day, at about 12 noon, there was held on board a full-dress parade [inspection, *deputatskii smotr*] in the presence of the Okhotsk Port Commander, Mr. Vilront, all chief officials, and the Manager of the American Office, Mr. Lenfe. All who were to sail aboard this vessel were on board, and the Okhotsk clergy and I concelebrated a Te Deum for the voyage. Toward the evening, I transferred my family to the vessel. The physician Ermolaev and his wife, the clerk Rikhter, as well as the promyshlennye proceeding to Sitkha came on board also, but not all 42 promyshlennye, as some have been assigned to company service here in Okhotsk.

1829

February 19:

A three masted American vessel arrived at the Novoarkhangel'sk Port.

February 28:

A second three masted American vessel [the barque *Volunteer,* Capt. Charles Taylor] entered the local port. On board was a pastor [Rev. Jonathan S. Green] of the Reformed [church] who had been in the Sandwich Islands for the purposes of conversion of the local population to the Christian faith, an endeavor in which he was, according to his own statement, successful. He came to Sitkhan shores with the same aim, to convert the inhabitants of this coast, the *Koliuzhi* [Tlingit] as up to this time they have not accepted Christian faith and remain in [the state of] heathenism. His [projected] undertaking did not take place, as conversion of the Koliuzhi to any kind of [Christian] faith is not an easy business. This nation's heathenism in itself is rough, they are accustomed much more to battles and bloodshed. Being nourished by the spirit of brutality [*zverstva*] and daring and bravery, which is in opposition to [concepts of] love of mankind and meekness, they are not easily approached in matters of religion, one may safely say. Besides, in this enterprise [of conversion] it is essential to have the command and thorough knowledge and understanding of their language.

March 10:

The two above mentioned American vessels left the Port of Novoarkhangel'sk.

March 11:

The sloop *Baikal* returned from California with a cargo of salt.

March 12:

The bot *Bobr,* Ensign Chernov of the Fleet Navigators' Corps commanding, left the Port of Novoarkhangel'sk for the island of Kadiak. On board this vessel was the expedition dispatched to describe the coasts, under the command of the above mentioned Ensign Mr. Vasil'ev.

March 25:

On the Feast Day of Annunciation of the All Holy Theotokos, I, together with Father Aleksei [Sokolov] concelebrated the Liturgy. During this 5th week of Lent I performed services for those people who were observing the fast.

March 29:

On Friday I confessed several persons who had fasted and on the following day they joined in the Holy Mysteries. During the Passion Week we concelebrated the services jointly with the priest, Father Aleksei [Sokolov].

April 8:

The brig *Rurik* returned from Kadiak, under the command of the above mentioned Mr. Teben'kov. He had wintered there in order to see to the reorganization of various administrative matters in the Port of Kadiak.

April 14:

On the Day of the Bright and Glorious Resurrection of Our Lord Jesus Christ we concelebrated the Liturgy jointly with Father Aleksei [Sokolov]; the next two days I celebrated the services by myself.

April 24:

The bot *Sivuch,* under the command of the same Ingstrom, which came here from Atka last year, left the Port of Novoarkhangel'sk for Atka. This was an occasion for me to proceed to my assigned destination, but since this vessel is very small and was crowded, and another large vessel was being readied for departure for Atka also, we did not take passage [on the *Sivuch*].

May 9:

Two vessels left the Port of Novoarkhangel'sk, the brig *Okhotsk,* Fleet Lieutenant Zaremba commanding, destination Okhotsk, and brig *Chichagov,* Fleet Lieutenant Lenenskov commanding, destination the Kuriles, Urup Island, where a settlement of the Russian-American Company is located.

May 14:

The bot *Bobr* left the Port of Novoarkhangel'sk for the island of Kadiak, under the command of the Ensign Chernov.

May 19:

The sloop *Baikal* was ready for departure from Novoarkhangel'sk for Atka and therefore to-day I transferred my party on board, including my wife and parent [father], but my sister was married here to the Company *prikazchik* Grigorii Klimovich Terent'ev.

May 20:

In the morning we moved out of the harbor into the roadstead and dropped anchor, waiting for a favorable wind [in order to exit, and gain the open sea].

May 21:

At 8 o'clock in the afternoon our vessel, the sloop *Baikal,* hoisted anchor and sailed out into the open sea, under the command of the warrant officer Adolf Etulin. In the course of this voyage we encountered no difficulties of any kind but enjoyed frequent favorable and light winds until we were approaching the Islands adjacent to Atka on the east side.

June 7:

We neared the above mentioned islands and hove to in the [Pass] between them, that is between Seguam and Amukhta because of heavy overcast. We remained hove-to, not being able to see the shore, for four twenty-four hour periods. By the 11th [of June], on the basis of [nautical] observation it became clear that the currents carried us out of the Passes and toward the Atka shore, which we still were not able to see because of the overcast.

June 12:

About three o'clock in the afternoon, the Atka shore became visible, and we approached it from the N side; rounding the mountain headland holding the course for Korovin Cape in order to gain entry into the [Korovin] Bay. However, toward the evening, the strong wind, blowing directly off the Bay, not only did not permit us to enter the Bay, but made it impossible to carry proper canvas. Thus we remained for three twenty-four hour periods at sea, under storm sails only, in view of the Atka shore.

June 15:

In the morning, with the change of wind, we entered the Bay which is called Korovinskii [Korovin Bay] or Atkhinskii [Atka Bay]. Here is located the Port of Atka and the settlement. About 12 noon, we dropped anchor directly opposite from the settlement, about half a mile from shore. This very day I moved ashore, where I was assigned a smallish Company-owned house, which was built and prepared for my use.

Thus my voyage, which passed with the aid of God safely, has been concluded and I have arrived at my destination.

Remarks Relative to the Atka District

1) The Atka District constitutes one of the [administrative] districts of the Russian-American Company, under the authority of the Chief Manager of the Russian colonies in America and accountable to the Novoarkhangel'sk [company] office.

The district is comprised of the following islands (not counting the numerous islands which are uninhabited): Atka, Amlia, Amchitka, Attu, Mednoi and Bering, all of them settled. The government within the district is constituted by the [local] office of the above mentioned company. The office is headed by the manager and the clerk [*kontorshchik*]. This office is responsible for and has the authority over the above mentioned islands; on each of these islands there is a resident local manager called a *baidarshchik*. The *baidarshchiks* are accountable to the Atka Office. The number of inhabitants in the entire district, of all social statuses and of both sexes, according to the latest information, is about 800 persons, Russians, creoles, and Aleuts. The Russian-American Company employs all the Russians (of various social statuses), all the creoles, and some Aleuts, who are on salary. All other Aleuts are independent, that is they are not employed by the company. The majority of the [independent Aleuts] reside on the island of Amlia, governed by their own leader called a *toion*. He is also the paramount toion for the entire Andreanov Chain, that is for all islands ennumerated above, and has authority in all matters pertaining to the Aleuts. The district government, that is the [company] office, is located on the Island of Atka. Here, too, is located the main [company] settlement or Port. [The settlement] is called the Port because here is the permanent station of the vessel assigned to cruise through the district annually. This vessel is under the jurisdiction of the local office. In the main settlement there are 7 dwellings, of which 4 are main houses, the rest are barracks [*kazarmy*] or yurty communally inhabited in compartments by Russians, creoles and Aleuts. Utility structures are 1) storage magazine for goods and peltries and this magazine is under direct management and responsibility of the office manager; 2) Trade store which goods are sold in free trade to individuals in accordance with the established price schedule; [the same structure] houses housekeeping supplies storage, the communal supplies storage, and the equipment storage. All of these stores are managed by a *prikazchik* accountable to the local office; 3) a structure called *kormovaia barabora* [food provisions cellar] where all food supplies and locally obtained provisions are stored; 4) a cattle barn, as there is cattle here. There are also other [subsidiary] structures, needed for the maintenance of the community's housekeeping: though the latter are not perfect, they are, nevertheless, on hand. At present the management of the Atka Office consists of the manager Ivan Ivanovich Sizykh, a townsman of Irkutsk, and the clerk, Petr Grigor'evich Karsakovskii [*sic*], a townsman of Kaluga. The chief Aleut toion is the Aleut Nikolai Vasil'evich Dediukhin, who has his residence among his Aleuts on the island of Amlia.

2) The aboriginal inhabitants of the Atka District are the creoles and the Aleuts, called commonly Andreanovites or Atkans. Under this name one usually includes the inhabitants of the Rat Islands and of the Near Islands, because all are under the same district office jurisdiction, and all speak almost the same language, with some variations in lexicon, dialect and pronunciation. They have accepted the Christian faith of the Greek-Russian confession approximately at the same time as did the other Aleuts, that is the Kadiak and Fox Islanders, about 1790, but it must be noted that the Andreanov Aleuts received their faith through Russian [laymen] as no one of priestly status, nor a member of the mission which used to be on the island of Kadiak and which brought the enlightenment of the Christian baptism to the Kadiak and Unalashka Aleuts, ever visited the Andreanov Islands. Thus, all the local Aleuts, without exception, were baptized by laymen, except possibly very few [persons] who had an occasion to visit places where there was a priest. Consequently, I found here upon my arrival the entire aboriginal population baptized, and not a single adult among them remained for me to christen: my duty was, thus, to confirm them in their faith by celebrating the Mystery of Annointing with the Holy Myrrh, and thus complete the sacrament of baptism.

3) The Church, projected to be built at Atka, to be dedicated to Saint Nicholas of Myra-Lycia, the Miracleworker, I found in the process of construction. The cornerstone was laid and construction commenced in the past year of 1828, on November 13, the building being built in accordance with the plan provided by the Chief Manager of the colonies. It cannot be expected that the temple will be completed soon, because of the shortage of lumber and other [building] materials and also because of the lack of necessary church utensils, which had not been delivered [as expected]. There is no other prayer house on hand here, as the prayer chapel, which formerly existed in the [old] Atka settlement has been wrecked and destroyed when the settlement was moved to the new location. In this extremity, in order to perform the necessary church services and ministrations, I constructed a prayer tent which we erected when needed and as the circumstances permitted. This same tent later served me during my travels through the district, when I performed services and rites in [various] communities of the Atka Parish, until such time when on all the islands special prayer houses were constructed.

4) In the Atka Parish of St. Nicholas I was the sole cleric, without any celebrants or servitors, not even a sub-deacon or a reader, though in a communication from the Main Office of the Company dispatched yet to Irkutsk it was stated that readers for the Atka Church will be assigned at Novoarkhangel'sk from among the young boys who had been trained at the Church there. When I was there, however, I was not able to find anyone suitable [for the office] and noted that the Novoarkhangel'sk Church itself stood in need of [lower clergy]: the Church there had only one reader. Thus, I had to sail [from there] without assistants. Upon my arrival in my Parish, my first care was to find a young boy whom I could train for that office. I selected one from among the creoles, Vasilii Shishkin, who later, when the Atka school was organized, was enrolled therein. In the meantime, at the beginning of my service here, when it was necessary to perform various ministrations and services I had to utilize, as far as it was possible, the assistance of some pious parishioners.

Sojourn on the Island of Atka

June 1829

June 16:

The Amlia toion Nikolai Dediukhin, having been notified of our arrival here, came hither with [a fleet of] *baidarkas*. As the island of Amlia is only about 29 versts distant from the Atka settlement, communication is maintained throughout the year, and at all seasons; the travel is by means of baidarkas as there are no major obstacles en route.

As this toion is the head and representative of all Aleuts, it is with him that I commenced my first instruction in the Evangelical [Gospel] message and the teachings of the Orthodox Christian faith and its dogmas. I was greatly aided in this task by the fact that the toion was literate, could read and write. This is most fortuitous and beneficial, in general, for the Aleuts themselves, and for my intercourse with them.

1831

March 1:

On Cheesefare Sunday [*Nedel'ia syropustnaia*] performed the regular Divine Service, during the next week, the First Week of the Great Fast, on Wednesday and Friday performed the Liturgy of the Presanctified Gifts.

March 6:

On Friday confessed the faithful, who had fasted, of whom there were 39 persons of both sexes.

March 7:

On this Sabbath day (Saturday), admitted to the Holy Mysteries 39 confessed persons.

March 8:

The next week, the 2d of the Great Fast, I did not perform services here, as I was preparing to go to the island of Amlia, in order to provide the inhabitants there an opportunity to perform their holy Christian duties. For this reason, on this day I sent to the Atka Office all correspondence to be delivered to the vessel [bot] *Sivuch*. The *Sivuch,* which was supposed to sail for Novoarkhangel'sk last fall, did not do so and her commander, Mr. Ingstrom, as if in justification, began preparations for the voyage earlier than is customary [when sailing to that port]. The vessel is ready to sail any day now. I dispatched the following papers: 13 reports to the Irkutsk Consistory, responding to directives received from that office September 26 of the previous year; 1 report, with appended vital statistics record book for the year 1830; 1 report on the consecration of the Church on the island of Atka with appended explanation why this report on the consecration of the Church is directed to the Consistory and not, as per order, to His Grace the Archhierei of Irkutsk.

2d Trip to the Island of Amlia

Remarks:

On the occasion of my first trip to the island of Amlia I noted the route from the Atka settlement to the Amlia settlement, and it is apparent [from my description] that the island of Amlia is separated from the island of Atka by a narrow pass and that the two settlements are located not too far from each other; also, [I noted] that communication is maintained between [those two settlements] throughout the year, at all seasons; however, it is also noted that the journey requires variable means of travel and, largely due to the peculiarities of the Amlia Pass, is not free of effort and inconveniences. It is obvious, then, that communication is maintained in case of necessity and, especially in winter, is dependent on winds, weather etc. For these reasons, it is clear that it is not possible for the inhabitants of the island of Amlia with their families to come to the Church at Atka for performance of the needed ministration; such trips would be very difficult and accompanied by danger, especially at the time of Lent, should they [attempt the trip in order] to perform their Christian duties. It was obvious to me, that it would be much more convenient and less difficult for me to undertake frequent trips [to Amlia] to accomplish such purposes, and thus I determined to do so, even at the time of Lent, yearly, as I knew that my absence from the church would not deter the inhabitants of the Atka settlement from performance of the duties required of them. The [Amlia] toion, whom I informed of my resolve beforehand, took it upon himself as his duty to provide me with the means necessary to undertake such trips, and avoid burdening the Atka Office in this matter. For this purpose, he dispatched from the island of Amlia the necessary number of baidarkas to fetch me. This he has done in the present instance, and the baidarkas sent for me were already here.

March 11:

In the morning [the weather] was absolutely calm and we began preparations for departure. The bot *Sivuch* was also getting ready to leave the harbor and move out into the roadstead. We loaded the baidarkas with all the necessary equipment and church utensils. A sub-deacon accompanied me. We started out about 7 o'clock in the morning in three-hatch baidarkas. By noon, we were already on the other side of the isthmus [portage] but here the wind freshened gradually and became contrary, but in spite of it I continued toward the [Amlia] strait [Pass]. However, the wind grew ever stronger and we were able, and then only with difficulty, just to reach the [group of] small islets located above the strait. Here we were forced to go on shore and spend the night, though I had nothing with me which could provide us with shelter: I had hoped to reach my destination this very same day and did not take along the tent, nor even necessary provisions, except some bread and tea. It was imperative, though, to find shelter, as the wind blew ferociously and was accompanied by thick snowfall. In such an extremity, left to myself, I would have been totally helpless, but the Aleuts, experienced in facing such hardships and coping under adverse circumstances, found the means to construct a lean-to out of the baidarka mats. We had difficulty erecting [the supports] and [fastening] the covers. We covered this lean-to with grass, which it was also very difficult to locate underneath the snow, and then piled up on top the snow. Here we sheltered, myself and my companions, 8 persons in all. Towards the evening, the wind shifted to NW and began to blow even with greater strength, with thick snow falling. This continued through the night.

March 12:

The wind continued unabated, from the same direction, the snow continued thick. It was impossible to step outside, into the open, and I was forced to sit the entire day in the above mentioned lean-to. There was no conceivable way to heat the kettle and have some tea, but the Aleuts found means to do even this. With great difficulty, they located water, not anywhere close, and under snow; for fuel—the stems of *puchka* [*Heracleum lanatum*] which protruded above the snow. We broke these stems off, made fire with them, and cooked upon it. It was not thinkable to attempt to make the cooking fire in the open so we made it inside the same lean-to, and though we had to sit amidst smoke, we drank our fill of tea with bread. The Aleuts, in addition to this nourishment, also had some shore molluscs. Toward the evening, the wind began to slacken, but the snow continued. However, I was not able to bear my confinement any longer, and emerged to walk along the shore.

March 13:

By morning, it was calm and clear and I immediately set out for the Strait [Pass], but very soon we had to go on shore again and await the change of the current in the Strait [Pass]. A veritable *solui* was ripping through the Strait, a result of strong [gale force] wind which created heavy seas. Finally, we [were able to] set out, crossed the Strait safely, and by noon approached the Amlia settlement. This very day I began the necessary preparations for the performance of churchly activities, that is arrangement of the prayer tent, which for this occasion was but newly sewn and refurbished, bigger in size than the one used formerly. The old tent, due to frequent usage became tattered; besides, I intend to conduct services in the new tent differently than had been done in the old one.

March 14:

The prayer tent was secured with a view to a prolonged stay. I have arranged the interior, as far as it was possible to do so and on this same night held the evening service.

March 15:

On the second Sunday of Lent I celebrated in the tent the Divine Liturgy and joined in the Holy Mysteries 10 infants. I continued to celebrate Divine services throughout the following week. In the interim, I offered instruction to the Aleuts in the necessary Christian concepts through the intermediary of their toion. At this time I could not yet engage them in lengthy explanations, but related to them only through the Mysteries of religion.

March 19:

Through the entire Thursday I confessed those who have fasted. Of these there were 22 persons of both sexes.

March 20:

Also was busy confessing those who fasted; of these there were 27 persons of both sexes.

Remark:

The above mentioned persons who fasted were divided by me into two groups for confession, as they were preparing for the first time, after performance of this duty, to receive the Holy Communion. They required, therefore, detailed and prolonged explanation, which was not easy to give, and thus I spent these two days with them, [assisting them in] cleansing their consciences.

March 21:

This day, the Sabbath [Saturday], at the Liturgy, joined in the Holy Mysteries 47 persons who had made confession.

March 22:

On the 3d Sunday of Lent, in the morning, annointed with the Holy Myrrh 5 infants of both sexes, born in the course of the past year, and who were baptized by laymen. Later on, at the Liturgy, joined in the Holy Mysteries up to 30 infants. Throughout the next week, continued to celebrate the Divine Services, in the same order and manner as in the preceding week.

March 24:

Throughout the entire day instructed and confessed the minors, of whom there were 71 persons, of both sexes. I was preparing them for the forthcoming Feast and also because there were so many [people] who fasted this week.

March 25:

On the Feast of the Annunciation of The All Holy Theotokos joined in the Holy Mysteries 71 persons who have made confession.

March 26:

Throughout Thursday, I was engaged confessing those who were fasting, of whom there were this day 40 persons of both sexes.

March 27:

Through Friday also I was engaged confessing those who were fasting, and on this day there were 42 persons of both sexes.

March 28:

On this Sabbath day [Saturday], at the Liturgy, united in the Holy Mysteries 74 persons who made confession. Thus, having served in this locality for two weeks of Lent, and having provided the local inhabitants with the opportunity to fulfill their Christian obligations, I determined to return to Atka, which was really necessary.

March 29:

During my sojourn here the following persons died and I sang the funeral services for them:

1. (Agrippina), Anna [*sic*], daughter of the Aleut woman Fedos'ia Startseva, who died 27 March;

2. Ol'ga, daughter of the Aleut woman Natalia Lazarev, who died also 27 March; and

3. Aleksandra, daughter of the Aleut woman Fekla Stepanov, who died yesterday;

[all] were buried in the Amlia cemetery, presently in use. After this action [burial], I dismantled the prayer tent and immediately set out on the return journey, which passed safely, and I arrived at the Atka settlement about 11 o'clock after midday.

Sojourn on the Island of Atka

Remarks:

Upon my return from the island of Amlia and the arrival at the Atka Port, I was apprised of the disaster which overtook the *Sivuch:* something that could have been foretold. I described earlier the difficulties I encountered on the 11th of this month while crossing to the island of Amlia, due to the sudden shift of wind and weather. Though I was travelling at the very shore, I found myself in a difficult situation. It will be remembered that the *Sivuch* was getting ready to sail on the same day, the 11th. And so she did sail, moving into the roadstead, but not stopping there in order to utilize the favorable wind which blew in the morning. The wind, however shifted, as described above before the vessel, having entered the open sea, had a chance to move away from shore. By evening, the weather and the force of wind brought the vessel into a critical situation, as by nightfall, the wind having shifted to NW, that is to starboard, reached such force that she was deprived of the use of her sails, while downwind she had the shore, which stretches here far to the west. In this extremity, they surrendered to the will of fate, and during the night were driven by wind and wave downwind, directly toward the shore. Next day (the 12th), while the wind and conditions continued the same, the vessel found itself just off shore, and as soon as proper depth was reached, dropped anchor. The anchor held for some time, but finally, the force and pressure of the wind overcame the vessel's resistance. The anchor cable, their sole hope, as they had only one anchor on board, parted. Their last hope betrayed, the vessel was immediately and irresistibly driven on shore, by wind, by seas, and finally, the breakers, which cast her onto the sandy beach of the Il'inskaia Bukhta which lies about ____versts from Atka settlement [figure missing in the original]. The kind of wreck which had occurred might be considered a fortunate one for the crew. The vessel itself sustained heavy damage, but, being cast on shore in a sandy place, all aboard were able to save themselves. Had the case been opposite, and had they been cast ashore at a rocky coast, there would have been no hope of safety. The vessel's master dispatched a yawl to notify the Atka Office in which my brother Osip returned to Port. Thus, when I returned here from the island of Amlia, I found him, to my great surprise, in residence here. The vessel's master and the entire crew were still at the site of the wreck, as was the vessel's entire cargo.

During my absence here and sojourn on the island of Amlia, the creole Moisei Kipriianov died in the local settlement on the 22d of this month and was buried in the cemetery, presently in use, by laymen.

April 2:

Having received word of the wreck of the *Sivuch,* the manager of the local office, Mr. Sizykh, accompanied by my brother Osip, left for the site of the disaster, travelling in 3-hatch baidarkas, in order to inspect the wreck and take any measures necessary in this matter. A baidara was also dispatched to the site of the wreck.

April 5:

On the 5th Sunday of Lent, I celebrated the Liturgy, and held services throughout the following week.

April 8:

Manager Sizykh and the shipbuilder Netsvetov returned in the baidarkas from the site of the wreck. The baidara has returned also [carrying] Mr. Ingstrom, master of the vessel, the crew, and all [other] personnel, as well as the cargo and all necessary [salvaged] things. The vessel itself was abandoned on shore, as she was completely wrecked, and was judged unfit for [further] navigation.

April 10:

On Friday, confessed those who fasted, of whom there were 32 persons of both sexes.

April 11:

On the Saturday of Lazar [St. Lazarus] during the Liturgy united in the Holy Mysteries 32 confessed persons.

April 12:

On Palm Sunday [vayi] celebrated the Liturgy and throughout the following Passion week celebrated all proper services.

April 15:

This day confessed those faithful who fasted, of whom there were 22 persons of both sexes.

April 16:

On the Great Thursday, celebrating the proper Liturgy, united in the Holy Mysteries the 22 confessed persons.

April 19:

On the day of the Bright [and Shining] Resurrection of Our Lord Jesus Christ, after performance of the proper Divine services, there was a celebration. The wind blew from the north, with snowfall, but there was intermittent sunshine. The cold by the thermometer was 2° [−2°R]. On the following days Divine services were performed also.

April 26:

On the feast day of the St. Apostle Thomas [Foma] celebrated the Divine service. The baidara left the Port of Atka for the site of the wreck of the vessel *Sivuch*. On it travelled Mr. Shipbuilder Netsvetov, engaged by the Atka office to salvage and haul ashore the wreck and take charge of all necessary matters in this affair.

1836

Remarks:

This same day, May 29th, I received the news of the death of my wife on March 19 of this year in Sitkha. She did not obtain the restoration of her bodily health, but she was cured spiritually, and, by the Will of God, entered eternity. On this occasion, to give me solace, my two brothers Osip and Anton, came here aboard the above mentioned transport vessel. Osip had leave to visit his kin. Anton had the opportunity to do so as he was aboard in the line of duty, serving as First Office on the brig. He, after completion of his education in St. Petersburg, [entered] into the employ of the Russian-American Company and proceeded to the colonies, arriving at Novoarkhangel'sk Port aboard the [globe] circumnavigating vessel. [The latter] arrived at Novoarkhangel'sk in April of this year and my brother was given a transfer to the Okhotsk transport vessel in order [to enable him] to visit me. This day, then for me, was marked by various events [in my life] which were met unexpectedly.

May 31:

On Sunday, while all of the requisite Divine services had been performed, I also celebrated a thanksgiving Te Deum and read the Manifesto relating to the birth and baptism of the Grand Duchess Anna Mikhailovna, as instructed by the directive from the Consistory, of which [special service] I informed the Atka Office in writing.

June 30:

By morning the wind shifted, became favorable so that the vessel could leave the bay.

July 1:

We crossed the mountains along the shore to the south side where we met the hunters of the said party; our baidarkas were portaged. Moving from one place to another along this shore, we spent here three nights, but no sea otters were hunted because of bad winds and improper time. Therefore, Mr. Volkov and I very soon returned [home]. On the return trip, we also portaged, but from another cove [on the south shore] to the north side, to the bay called Sarana Bay, which is situated along the shore directly across from the Atka settlement. From here we travelled directly to the settlement.

July 6:

On the night of July 7th the will of the One Whose Providence and [decisions on] Fate are unfathomable and Whose deeds are not to be grasped by Man, my house, where once I, within the circle of my family, was content and at times found happiness, in spite of all the lack, poverty and meagerness met in this desert which is Atka, went up into the air in flames. Thus, at two o'clock past midnight while there was no [light or] fire anywhere in the house at all, and everyone was asleep, it ignited. The fire started in the top story and spread to the foundation. Through the night, and while the wind was light, the fire burned so hot that one could not approach it to put it out. We salvaged very few belongings, as much as we could, just from the lower apartments, the rest, and all that was on the second story, burned just as the entire house structure did, which by daybreak was completely consumed. On the spot where the house used to be there is now but bare earth.

July 7:

This day I moved to a small house where [I now make] my quarters.

July 12:

Baptized the newborn infant Prokopii, son of the widow of the Aleut Feodor Saposhnikov, who was born on the 6th of this month.

August 1:

On the Feast Day of the Exaltation of the True and Lifegiving Cross, with the observance of all requisite Divine services, [the service] of the Consecration of the Water was held and then I baptized the newborn infant Apolinarii, son of the Aleut Filimon Galkin, born on the 23rd of the past year.

August 6, 15 and 22:

On these Feast Days, with the observance of all appropriate Divine services there were celebrations, on the last [occasion] accompanied by the celebration of a Te Deum and the ringing of church bells.

August 23:

I baptized the newborn infant Diomid, son of Diomid Grigor'ev, a Russian, born on the 17th of this month.

August 29 and 30:

On these Feast Days there was a celebration and Divine services were held.

September 8 and 14:

On the Feast Days, services were held, and there was a celebration.

September 23:

I baptized the newborn infant Nadezhda, daughter of the Russian, Semen Dobrovol'skii, born on the 17th.

Remark:

By this time, the school students, who have been on leave for the purpose of putting in needed provisions, were transported to the Port. This summer they have put up 30 bags of sarana, 2 bladders of *nura,* and 5 casks of potatoes harvested from the vegetable garden.

October 1:

On the Feast of the Protection of All Holy Theotokos [Pokrova] performed the requisite churchly Divine services.

October 11:

The galiot *Morekhod,* returning from Okhotsk, entered Korovin Bay. The vessel was under the command of the independent navigator Anton Netsvetov (my above mentioned brother) who assumed the command of this vessel following the death by drowning in the mouth of the Okhotsk harbor of the former master Ensign Fedor Afans'ev. On the return voyage from Okhotsk, the *Morekhod* had put in at the islands of Bering and Attu.

October 15:

The galiot *Morekhod* entered the inner bay, the harbor, where the vessel was moored for wintering.

1837

January 1:

On New Year's, the Feast Day of the Circumcision of Our Lord Jesus Christ, I held the church services, then there was a celebration. The day was clear with sunshine.

January 3:

Sang the funeral services for the infant Apolinarii, son of the Aleut Filimon Galkin, who died on the 1st of this month. Buried in the cemetery.

January 6:

On the Feast Day of the Epiphany of Our Lord Jesus Christ, after the celebration of the appropriate Divine services, [held] the Church procession with the Cross for the Consecration of the Water. The day was clear but snow fell intermittently. The temperature was down to 7° Reaumur below zero.

January 7:

Married two Aleuts, not in the service of the [company] who came for this purpose here from Amlia Island.

January 10:

Married one Russian and two Aleuts, [all] company employees, upon the testimony of the Atka Office.

January 13:

Married two Aleuts, not in service, who came here for this purpose from Amlia Island.

January 28:

This day I administered the last rites to my father, who had long suffered illness and was approaching the end of his life. The cold was up to 9°.

January 29:

Administered the last rites to a sick woman.

Remark:

According to information transmitted from the island of Amlia in regard to vital statistics, there were born in the course of this month two males and one female.

February 5:

By five o'clock in the morning, my parent, Egor Vasil'evich Netsvetov, died a natural death following suffering from illnesses.

February 7:

I sang the funeral services for the said dead [who was] buried under the *papert'* [front porch] of the church, inside the church palisade. These days and the following, the cold continued and it snowed.

February 12:

About eleven o'clock after noon [p.m.], there was an earthquake which lasted about five minutes. The earth tremors were rather strong, so that the bells began ringing in the church belfry.

The 5th Voyage to the Islands of the Atka District and 2nd to the Kurile Islands

1838

Remarks:

Following my communication with the Chief Manager of the colonies, both in writing and personally, he issued instructions that the Atka vessel should proceed yearly to the Kuriles. . . . The master of the galiot *Morekhod* received specific orders to carry me to the Kuriles, the island of Shumshu. Therefore, I began to prepare for the voyage and thus informed the Atka Office by memo No. 23 of May 30, in which I requested that I be provided with opportunities and assistance, wherever possible, in performance of my business. The [administration of] the Atka school was entrusted by me, during my absence, in a memo No. 24, of May 31, to the Atka [Company] Office.

May 31:

By evening, I boarded the vessel (galiot *Morekhod*) carrying with me the prayer tent and all church utensils needed in the field church. [I was accompanied] by the co-servitors: sub-deacon and one student in the capacity of the sacristan.

June 1:

In the morning, with a light and favorable wind, we hoisted anchor and sailed out to sea, the Ensign of the Fleet Navigators' Corps Khalizov commanding. Mr. Volkov, Manager of the Atka Office, was aboard this same vessel, intending to inspect the Atka sub-districts and to audit the affairs of the local managers there, the latter being his subordinates. Also aboard was the physician's apprentice Ivan Galaktionov to perform his duties, as necessary.

Having set course for the Kurile Islands, as the most distant point [on our route], we sailed under various winds, rarely favorable, mostly contrary, without sighting any coast until the 20th [of June]. On that day we neared the Kurile Chain, but the contrary winds prevented us from reaching the desired destination.

June 22:

We passed either the Third or Fourth Kurile Strait, sailing between the large islands Paramushir and Anekatan [*sic*] and the small ones Shirinki and Makanrushi [*sic*] and continued along the western coast of Paramushir Island to the First Island, Shumshu, which took us three 24-hour periods because of strong and contrary winds.

2. In matters of religion, I found the Kuriles to be devout or, as one may say, ready to be devout. However, presumably because of very rare approaches to them on behalf of the Christian Religion, they have no proper understanding either of the Christian faith or of their obligations as Christians. For this reason I observed among them several heathen customs and superstitions and attempted to eradicate these by all means [at my disposal]. In [the behavior], the character and morals of the Kuriles, I noted an inclination to obedience and conformity *[poslushanie i povinovenie]* and even timidity. This, as I noted, of course, stems from fear: not the dread which is generated by knowledge of God and which in turn leads to still greater understanding of God, and love for Him, but the slavish fear, with which they became imbued through the treatment meted out by persons in superior and dominant positions. This fear, since they came under the authority of the Russian-American Company, has eased somewhat, of course, but even nowadays there are still persons around who exploit this trepidation and obedience at every possible occasion.* The [general] condition of the Kuriles has much improved since they came under the authority of the said Company, especially so because the peltries which they deliver are exchanged at a very favorable price in goods, and the latter bring them many benefits, a situation which did not exist previously, when they delivered their catch to various hands and in effect almost lost their property.

3. At the time in question, the local manager on Shumshu Island was the *baidarshchik,* Sergei Moskvitinov, a townsman of Kaluga, appointed by the colonial government. His duties consisted of receiving from the Kuriles their catch, paying them in goods and equipment provided by the Company in accordance with the proper price rate, and delivering the peltries to

---

*Here is one instance, among many, which came to my notice: During my stay on Shumshu as described, a Kurile lodged with me a complaint against the master, Ensign Orlov, of the bot *Aleut,* which is assigned to the Kurile sub-district on patrol. The said Orlov, when wintering on Shumshu, took into his house the ten year old daughter of this Kurile, while the latter was absent, without permission, and for unknown purposes: even, had it been claimed, that the girl was taken for education, it would have been inconsistent with Orlov's family status to have a person of this sex either as a ward or as a servant. [This act] served solely as sore temptation [for him] and injury to the parents. The father, no matter how insulted he felt and how unhappy he was with Mr. Orlov's action, did not even dare to bring the matter up with Orlov, not to speak of removing the girl from [his keeping]. Even their toion, out of fear, was not able to speak up or take any action against the perpetrator, expecting to be punished had he done so. I have determined to bring this action by Mr. Orlov to the attention of the Chief Manager of the colonies, in order to prevent similar occurrences in the future, which acts are contrary to the Christian religion.

the proper [depot] destination. For this purpose a special transport vessel is stationed in the Kuriles. This vessel delivers the collected peltries to Okhotsk. Beyond those duties, the local manager has almost no influence on Kurile affairs, perhaps only occasionally, when obtaining some provisions, or in rare instances, assistance from the Kuriles; but in these circumstances the Kuriles look out for their own interests and benefit: either they get paid or whatever has been obtained [provisions] is properly apportioned to them also. I instructed the said manager in writing that it is imperative to keep in this sub-district vital statistics records, annually and in sufficient detail, in accordance with the standard form that I was given, and that these statistics are to be sent as occasion permits to the parish church, as it is being done by managers in other sub-districts and islands in my parish.

4. The Kurile sub-district contains within it the entire Kurile Chain, that is beginning with the First Island, the Shumshu, to (and including) the eighteenth island, Urup. On this last island is located the main Company settlement and the chief manager of the sub-district to whom the local manager on Shumshu is immediately responsible. There are no Kuriles on Urup Island, but it has been settled by the Kadiak Island Aleuts for the purposes of the sea otter hunt. This island [Urup] or the above mentioned [Kadiak] Aleuts are nowhere mentioned in the [various] directives regarding the inclusion of the Kurile Islands within the Atka Church Parish. Moreover, the orders issued by the Chief Manager of the colonies to the ship's commander instruct him to proceed to the island of Shumshu, that is to the territory of the Kuriles, and do not mention Urup. Thus, though I know that the Aleuts [Koniag] residing on the island of Urup are not visited by any other priest, I cannot extend my activity to them unless I meet one of them here, on Shumshu. Then, of course, I shan't leave their needs unattended. This neglect of the above mentioned settlers in matters of religion is inconsistent with the [general] measures and care taken by the Company in the matters of salvation, which in this particular instance, the Company evidenced in attending to the needs of the Kurile [population]. The work of salvation should proceed without any kind of limitations or worldly aims and be extended to all [peoples] in general without any exceptions whatsoever, so that [all] may be led to the way of salvation and follow that way to the end. Much more this applies to those who have had once partaken of the gift of grace of Jesus Christ. Those should under no circumstances be neglected and forgotten, and the Aleuts [Koniag] and in general all inhabitants of this region fall into the latter category: in respect to their Spiritual rebirth, they are still in infancy and have not yet reached that age in which men are ready to strive for perfection and be prepared for every godly deed. They are still not firm in the Christian piety. For this reason, as has been observed, at the slightest slackening [of effort] and neglect they are prone to fall, and may easily be-

come through their acts, once again heathen. The above statement is made not in order to extend the visitation originating at the Atka Church to Urup Island (which, of course, would be very difficult for the Atka vessel) and not out of any wish to extend my own activities to the above mentioned Aleuts [Koniag], who are Kadiaks, who are in moral and spiritual matters very different from the Unalaskha and Atka Aleuts. With sorrow in my heart, should I be ordered to, would I extend my activities to those people, because their language, which has no resemblance in vocabulary with the [languages] of other above mentioned Aleuts is totally unknown to me. I am noting [the situation] because, in the first place, these Aleuts [Koniag] are resident within the district which is now in certain respects within my parish and I do not wish their neglect to be attributed at some future date to me. In the second place, as they are Christians, they should not be neglected under any circumstances, because, in the words of the Apostle, [often] where spiritual neglect begins, the flesh perishes. Thus, the work of leading the Christians along the road to salvation must be extended to all, to everyone everywhere: here, there, yonder and yon, lest some fear greatly [*da vel'ko nekieopasiutsia*].

30th Trip to the Island of Amlia

1841

February 18:

Having loaded onto the baidarkas all the equipment necessary for the performance of churchly activities, I set out in the morning along the well known route. Having completed our trek safely, by evening we reached Amlia Island, the [main] settlement. Here I encountered [news of] the death of the infant Natal'ia, daughter of the Aleut Vasilii Nevzorov. [She] died on the 16th of this month. Also [the news] that 1 male infant was born in the course of the past month and was baptized by a layman.

February 19:

This day I commenced to hold in the local prayer house the Lenten services; all the minors began preparing for communion and cleansing of their consciences. In between, I sang the funeral services for the above mentioned infant, who died, and buried [her] in the local settlement's cemetery. This day I was engaged in the investigation of the teachings which are contrary to the Gospels which appeared among the local inhabitants. [This matter] will be discussed in a [separate] remark [following the account] of this trip.

February 22:

Confessed the Faithful who have fasted, who numbered 44 persons of both sexes. In between, I annointed with the Holy Myrrh the male infant, previously baptized by laymen.

February 23:

On the 2nd Sunday of Lent at the Liturgy joined in the Holy Mysteries 44 persons who had made confession. The following 3rd week of Lent, I continued holding the requisite church services, at which those Christians who were preparing to cleanse their consciences, made preparations for communion.

February 28:

I confessed the Faithful who were fasting, who numbered 31 persons of both sexes.

March 1:

On this day of Saturday, at the Liturgy, 30 persons who had made confession, joined in the Holy Mysteries. Afterwards, I confessed the remaining [persons] who were fasting, 21 in all, of both sexes.

March 2:

On the 3rd Sunday of the Great Fast, 19 persons who had made confession joined in the Holy Mysteries. The following 4th Week of the Fast, I continued to hold all appropriate church services at which those who were getting ready for confession, prepared themselves for communion.

March 6:

I confessed the Faithful who were fasting, of whom there were 31 persons of both sexes. I confessed them on Thursday, because of the large number of those who were keeping the fast during this week—and all of these were adults, requiring much of [my] time.

March 8:

On this day of Saturday, at the Liturgy, 65 persons who had made confession in the past two days were joined in the Holy Mysteries. Later on, I confessed the rest of those who fasted this week, numbering 28 persons.

March 9:

On the 4th Sunday of Lent, at the Liturgy, 29 persons joined in the

Holy Mysteries, among them were two women who had made confession on the 2nd of March. Thus my activities here were concluded.

Remarks:

During my current visit to Amlia the following occurrence took place: Upon my arrival on the island of Amlia, the toion of this island, Nikolai Dediukhin reported to me that actions were discovered [among the populace] which were contrary to the Gospels and to the True Christian teaching. [These actions] took the following form [which was discovered] through the exposure of a local Aleut woman: She perverted the Evangelical faith and true teaching of the church, turning it into schism and superstition, and into blasphemous use of the name of Jesus Christ. She, being tempted herself by the spirit of malice [evil] and base flattery, by the adversary of Jesus Christ—the devil, led astray others of her sex, [causing them] to desert Christ's flock, and has already succeeded in causing 6 women to leave the true path. These have left the right and true way and the true teaching, and easily accepted the false one. But this [false] teaching could not remain hidden among them for long, but became apparent in its true form, through the grace and compassion of God, who does not desire the death of sinners.

These [events] were discovered shortly before my arrival here. The toion, through the above mentioned women, called the [originator] to account. She was at the time ill, and apparently as if unconscious, and, when confronted publicly, [her behavior] evidenced how much within her was active the spirit of evil. When her own blasphemous words were [quoted to her], she could not stand it, and after strong jerking movements of her body and screeching in [her] voice, she fell down unconscious and then [entered] into a state of weakness, in which condition she remained and was at the time of my arrival, and thus I found her.

This frightening and strange wandering [off the path] by a ewe brought me into a state of shuddering trepidation. This [event] occurred, of course, only because this woman spent most of her time and lived away from the Amlia settlement. [Were it otherwise], she would not have been able to keep her activities secret from others, especially so since the settlement toion, upon my urging, is vigilant in these matters, and would have intervened. She, being away, and unobserved by others, was able to expand her activities. Acting secretly and stealthily, she began to teach [others] and perform various blasphemous acts, and through these bent [other] hearts to follow her. I must remark, that though my communication with [these people] is sporadic and rare, there were occasions when this very woman and all those who followed her, have, almost yearly, performed their Christian duties and followed the Christian church rituals punctiliously, without giving me the slightest occasion to notice that the enemy of Christ had led her astray from the path of truth and kidnapped her from the flock of Jesus Christ. What internal suffering for one who proclaims the truth of the Gospel, [to know] that a false teaching led away some who were among those who listened to his words! What blindness on the part of the one who acts as a guide along the road to the Leader of Pastors, God, to Jesus Christ, to have failed to discern and see among his charges the spirit of evil and flattery who leads along the false path! How was the pastor, who failed to guard his flock, lulled to sleep and thus failed to notice the kidnapping of ewes from his flock! . . . These are the circumstances, and when confronted with this unexpected event, I blamed myself.

On the next day [after being informed] (on the 19th of this month), in between other church activities, I investigated and ascertained in most minute detail the circumstances surrounding these events. The women, the very ones who had been tempted by the false teaching, were brought one by one into the prayer house, where I questioned them and tried to persuade them to disclose the true form of those teachings and acts which tempted them to deviate from the true teaching. Having listened to all, and having tested their feeling of inner contrition and return to the path of truth, I assembled them in the prayer house, and to all of them collectively declared clearly their error in [following] the false teachings, and showed them the right way, along the true Evangelical teaching, which they left so lightly. Then, severely exposing their error, having presented the evidence, I gave them the proper teaching; they, with contrition of the heart and tears, proclaimed their return and submission to truth. In conclusion, I imposed upon them an epitimia, consisting of strict fast and prayers, for which reason they were to attend every service during my stay here.

Afterwards, before evening, I visited the very woman who was exposed [as the leader] and saw her, lying helpless and indisposed, almost unconscious, unable to talk. Thus, until this time, I was not able to do anything for her. As she was at that time in the large dwelling—the barracks [*kazarma*] among a large number of people and noise, I ordered that she be transferred into another house and kept apart from communication with others. Having thus brought her to a separate place, I began to visit her and observe her movements and states. At times she was totally unconscious, so that it seemed she ceased to breathe; she was totally unable to talk. She continued in this state the next day (the 20th) also. Having seen her thus possessed and tortured by the evil spirits, finally, toward evening, I performed the first exorcism of the spirits and left her for the night, but left orders that she be watched and that I be informed of any change. Thus, when during the night she began in delirium to talk in words that were not coherent, I was notified. I came to her at the very hour of midnight and performed the second exorcism over her, against the evil spirits. It should be noted at this point, that while I was preparing for the action, having burned the incense in the censor and begun to read the exorcism prayer, this woman, who heretofore lay [immobile], made a sign of the cross, hurriedly and seemingly without effort rose, climbed down from the *urun* [bed] to the floor, and placing herself next to me, began to pray to God, accompanying her prayers with bows to the ground. When [the prayers] were finished, I sprinkled her with the Holy Water. Thus the ailing one regained consciousness, a state of health and true reason, began to answer questions and to talk. I told her to sit down and asked her what did she know, remember and feel of what had happened in recent days and just now? She responded that she did not know or remember anything at all, what happened to her, where she was and when, until the moment when she regained consciousness during the prayer just said, when she saw me and all the people surrounding her.* Further, from her answers it was evident that she had been without consciousness and suffered a total loss of memory, so that, as if reborn, she had no idea about where she was, what her surroundings were, which house she was in, who was with her, and she did not know anybody by name. She looked at all with curiosity and wonder, did not volunteer any remarks, but only answered when asked. Finally I asked her if she wanted [something] to eat or to go to sleep. She said that she did not want to do [either]. Thus I left her, giving instructions that she be watched, but that she was not to be questioned or engaged in conversation, only be answered, should she ask any questions herself.

In the morning of the 21st, I visited her (she spent the time since regaining consciousness, [remaining] in one place and mostly in silence, until morning) and learned [from her] in greater detail what she remembered, her thoughts, understanding and present feelings; then ordered that after she was fixed up [dressed] she be brought to the prayer house and this was done before the Hours. Here I asked her, if she knew what [building] she entered, where she was and before whom she was standing? She answered that she did not know anything and did not understand anything. My further investigation here revealed that she lacked any kind of concept of God, religion, and Christian duties. She was like an infant who lacks all understanding and judgment, and her face mirrored simplicity, innocence, meekness, humility, complete submission and obedience. Thus having understood her present state and seeing her feelings, I called on the aid of God and His Grace, through which he leads, teaches and heals the ailing, and began to nourish her with the milk of words, like a newborn infant, of the very beginning and fundamentals of the Christian teaching to confirm her within the Chris-

*Though this action took place at midnight, many people, including the toion himself, were not asleep and witnessed the events, as they were possessed by fear as well as curiosity, observed both all her actions and my activity over this woman; in the latter, they were struck by the power of God in the conversion of sinfulness.

tian flock, like a ewe lost in the wilderness and regained. I also instructed her to observe fast and prayer, with proper limits according to circumstances, instructing that she attend every service in the prayer house until her case was properly disposed of. As far as the deeds, teachings, and actions perpetrated by this woman which were against God and Church, through which not only she herself but others were led from the true path, she could not, through this entire time, remember or cognize any of her deeds, nor any circumstances or teachings involving anybody else. However, in order to make her feel properly her perilous unreason and how far she strayed from God, and also in order to give her the opportunity to express the contrition of the heart, her feeling of being sorry for her own sake and her repentance, I presented to her in the prayer house all those women for whom she performed her activities and each woman was permitted by me in person to disclose all her acts, deeds and teachings; in such manner her former state was disclosed and evidenced to her. She listened without giving answer, in silence. Though she herself was not able to recall anything, she accepted the accounts offered with gentleness and meekness. The meekness was attested to when, at the conclusion of this personal testimony, she begged forgiveness from all those [women] whom she had seduced. The latter, with sincere acknowledgement of their own error and blindness, with hearts devoid of anger, with tears, forgave her and in turn wished and asked forgiveness from God whom they offended. Through this staggering event, I was able to demonstrate to them how true and powerful is the Divine teaching in comparison to personal teachings, which stem from the Devil, and [I was able] to disclose to them the horrible consequences to which they exposed themselves when they listened to the Devil's teachings . . . Tender emotion, contrition of the heart and tears of repentance accompanied my arguments, words and conversations . . . What a spiritual joy to see the hearts touched by God's Love and shedding tears of repentance! What an inner triumph to see vanquished the enemy, who thought himself victorious! Glory to God and Gratitude to Him who gave us victory through Jesus Christ Our Lord.

Throughout the 3rd week of Lent which I spent conducting daily church services, the converted woman constantly attended every service in the prayer house, as well as all services following, observing the fast and prayers. Between services, she attended the lessons which I gave for all the Faithful who were fasting, as well as lessons and instruction I gave her personally, which I held at an appointed time. At the end of the 3rd week, as my service here was coming to an end, I absolved all the other women involved in the error, in view of their sincere repentance and conversion, and following the cleansing of their consciences, joined them to the Holy Mysteries. However, I did not lift from them the [imposed by me] fast nor excused them from the prayers [they were instructed to observe] until the appointed time. The very woman [the cause of it all] whose state, her outward activities, mental set and inner feelings, by now were known to me, I did not dare to absolve here on my own. I decided to have her accompany me to the Atka settlement, the place of my permanent residence, where I could continue to work with her and test her. It was imperative that she receive long-term constant attention, following her conversion, that she lead a totally new life, a life totally different from her former lifestyle and, in general, apart from the mundane every-day vanities and bustle. She evidenced in her intercourse with people and also in her words an inner innocence, simplicity [of spirit], unangered heart, meekness, gentleness, and unquestioning obedience to all demanded of her. She remained for the most time silent, answered or spoke only when addressed. She did not recognize people's names, not only strangers, though with them she had lived previously, but even her husband and children she did not recognize, nor the persons with whom she was involved in her reprehensible activity, nor did she remember any communication with them or what influence she had exercised upon them—until the very time when I let her meet them in person and when they disclosed to her her deeds. Being in such a state, she did not attempt any kind of activity and would not even talk about it. The activity of other people she observed with indifference, and at times with wonder, especially the churchly activities which took place during the Divine services, she looked upon them with great curiosity and wonder. She said repeatedly, that she could not remember ever having seen these (though she had previously, in fact) while now she saw and understood everything clearly. Because of her state, I tried very hard to imbue her heart with the sense of the Divine Beginning, that is with the concept of God, religion, and of Christian duties. On each occasion, I observed and tested her [reactions], her inner state, feelings, and state of mind. I have strictly forbidden that she be bothered with idle questions and conversations [about her experience] or that anything be said in her presence that would be harmful or tempting, and even more any acts which could serve as indecent examples. I also gave instructions that all her activity, acts, deeds, and even words, be unobtrusively observed and reported to me. This was done [now] as well as later in the Atka settlement. Other persons involved in this matter, who remained in the Amlia settlement, though absolved by me, were entrusted to the responsibility of the toion, who, after my departure was to keep an eye on their life, activity and various acts, and upon occasion not only let me know about their behavior but, in general, bring to my attention any similar occurrences for which he was to look out with utmost strictness.

1842

July 14:

The brig *Baikal,* Fleet Lt. Vilichkovskii commanding, entered Korovin Bay and about 8 o'clock in the morning dropped anchor. Aboard this vessel arrived safely His Grace Innokentii, Bishop of Kamchatka, the Kuriles and the Aleutians, expected by us. The entry of this Archpastor into Atka Bay was met, first of all, by bell ringing; then, about 10 o'clock in the morning, His Grace disembarked and came ashore where he was met by a Church Procession with the Cross and the icons; and thus, with these churchly ceremonies, escorted by the entire population of this settlement, he entered the local temple of St. Nicholas. Here he was greeted with a speech by me and he, in turn, made a speech of greeting and blessing, with a prayer for the gift of Grace and Peace from Our God the Father and Our Lord Jesus Christ, addressed to all those present. Then His Grace, the Lord [*Vladyko*], held a thanksgiving Te Deum, offering prayers for the Tsar and all the people; after [the service] was finished, having given all the people his blessing, he took up quarters in the house of the local priest.

Remark:

His Grace's retinue consisted of the steward, hierodeacon Nikolai, *keleinik* hypodeacon Lev, a singer [*psalomshchik*] and 3 boys, choir singers. Also with the arrival of the ship I received a directive from the Novoarkhangel'sk Consistory, notifying [me] of the confirmation, in the office of the Dean of Clergy for the American churches, of the Hieromonk Misail and that in the absence of His Grace, he will act as the Head of the clergy at the Novoarkhangel'sk Cathedral.

July 15:

Beginning this day, His Grace busied himself with the inspection of the Atka Church, including the written business matters, the administration of the church and its servitors. For this reason, I submitted to him the following reports: 1) on the state of the Atka Church and on the number of people within this parish; 2) about the receipt of his instructions issued from Novoarkhangel'sk; 3) about the co-servitors, with the appended roster of clergy and their service records; 4) accounts for the Atka Church and Amlia chapel for the year 1841; 5) a petition for needed equipment both for the Atka Church and for all the chapels attached to this church; 6) petition to return to the Atka Church a sum due for the Poterion and Paten and belonging to this Church but through error shipped to the Unalashka Church; 7) report on the collection of funds for Destitute clergy throughout this parish, with appended lists and monies in the sum of 1168 rubles 95 kopeks; 8) petition to invest (consecrate) to the sticharion my nephew, Mikhailo Terent'ev as one who has already been admitted to the clerical status.

In the following days, while His Grace was ordering, organizing and confirming various administrative matters pertaining to the local Church, the following persons entered [formally] the clerical status: 1) the creole *Lavrentii Salamatov,* acting sub-deacon and 2) the creole *Ivan Ladygin,* acting sacristan, who entered upon their own wish, and as His Grace found them able to [perform the duties of these offices] He admitted them to the clerical status. The third person admitted to the clerical status was my nephew *Mikhailo Terent'ev,* who entered upon the wish of his parents, and being found able, was so admitted by His Grace. He has been studying with me since 1837. As a new bishopric has been constituted for the American Churches, all churches and chapels in the colonies of the Russian-American Company, without exception, are now under exclusive jurisdiction of the Eparchical Clerical Superiors. Therefore, all priests and church servitors, previously supported by the above mentioned Company, are now to receive support from the Novoarkhangel'sk Consistory, which office is to assign and pay them a salary. The Atka clergy were assigned the following salaries by His Grace (while their old salaries, paid by the Company ceased on the 1st of January 1842): priest, base salary 560.—rubles and per diem [living expenses] 1540—rubles, for a total of 2,100.—rubles; sub-deacon, 400.—rubles; sacristan, 150.—rubles, baker of communion bread 90.—rubles. The salaries were paid to the clergy according to this schedule for the year 1842.

July 19:

On the day of Sunday, His Grace celebrated the Divine Liturgy and through this act made all of us happy, [honoring] the local temple and all parishioners who were spectators at the Arch-hierarchical service. The Arch-pastor made a speech, addressed to all those present, on firmness in faith and in Christian devout life, and even more he stressed the teaching of children and their education in Christian piety. In the course of the Liturgy, His Grace invested those who were accepted into the clerical status, Lavrentii Salamatov with the sticharion with the orarion and Ivan Ladygin with the sticharion and both were confirmed in their offices. With them my nephew, Mikhail Terent'ev was also invested with the sticharion. During the same service, His Grace rewarded me with the thigh shield and gave me a certificate to that effect. He also issued a certificate of merit [*gramota*] to both the sub-deacon and to the sacristan.

8th Voyage Through the Islands of the Atka District

Prior to the constitution of the Kamchatka-Aleutian bishopric, the priests were given the opportunities to visit their parishes, spread over various islands, aboard the Company vessels which cruise through the Districts. Nowadays, after the institution of the Bishopric, the priests continue to be given opportunities to voyage through their parishes. Thus, this summer, though the vessel on station here, the galiot *Morekhod,* had been ordered as a primary assignment to proceed to Kamchatka to carry thither His Grace, she was, for convenience in navigation and because of other considerations to call at Bering Island and elsewhere, as possible. Thus, I had no obstacles to my voyage. Besides, it was His Grace's will that I accompany him, as a member of his retinue, to Kamchatka. I, therefore, prepared to sail aboard the galiot *Morekhod* and accordingly notified the Atka Office by a memo, No. 46, of 18 July 1842. I took with me, from among the local clergy, the sub-deacon and my nephew, in the capacity of the sacristan. I also assembled the field church and all pertinent equipment. We were ready, waiting only to board the vessel and enter upon our sea voyage.

July 24:

In the morning, having been apprised that the wind was favorable for hoisting anchor, His Grace, who has blessed these shores by his footsteps, left the same. He gave his Arch-pastoral blessing and wished peace to all who saw him off at the wharf and boarded the vessel, in our company, that is of those who were to follow him. [His departure] was accompanied by the ringing of bells. At this time the vessel hoisted anchor and raised the sails. We sailed onward under various winds that favored little our progress. At the *traverse* [*sic*] of the islands Attu, Mednoi and Bering the wind was favorable for a sail to Kamchatka and we decided to press onward, without putting in anywhere.

August 8:

On this date, having passed Bering Island but while yet about 150 miles distant from the Kamchatka coast, the wind shifted, became contrary and we decided to turn toward Bering Island. This day, utilizing the favorable wind, we sailed toward that island. Enroute, toward evening, we met a whaling vessel, a three-masted ship, Danish. The master of this ship visited us briefly on the galiot, during which time both vessels were hove-to. We parted in the evening, and continued on our route.

August 9:

By evening we approached Bering Island.

August 10:

By noon we entered the bay where the settlement is located and dropped anchor. At this time, I immediately went ashore and busied myself with the performance of churchly ministrations. Later on, His Grace also came ashore and we remained on shore until my business here was finished. His Grace willed that the business here be finished quickly and that we continue on our voyage without delay. Therefore, I commenced the necessary activity this very day, and first of all, annointed with the Holy Myrrh 4 infants, previously baptized by laymen, then confessed the minors, the adolescents, of both sexes, who numbered 40 persons and prepared them for communion on the morrow and then I held the All-Night Vigil in the local prayer house.

August 11:

In the morning, prior to the Liturgy, I annointed 4 more infants and then held lessons for the local inhabitants, both for those who were preparing for communion and cleansing of their consciences and for those partaking in the Holy Mysteries. Later on, at the Liturgy, joined in the Holy Mysteries 40 persons who had made confession, as well as all the infants. The Liturgy, as all other services, I conducted in the presence of His Grace. Afterwards, I confessed 47 persons of both sexes and then celebrated the All-Night Vigil.

August 12:

In the morning, prior to the Liturgy, I confessed the remaining [persons] who had fasted, 15 persons total. At the Liturgy, I joined in the Holy Mysteries 62 persons who had made confession. After the Liturgy, His Grace celebrated a Te Deum for the sea voyage; then he made an address to the local inhabitants on the topic of Christian life, on reverence for the Grace of Our Lord Jesus Christ, and the love of God the Father, in communion with the Holy Spirit, and thus the service ended. After this, I married 2 men, one creole, one Aleut, and thus my activities here were concluded. His Grace went aboard the vessel in the afternoon and we all followed, so that about 3 o'clock in the afternoon we hoisted anchor and safely sailed out into the [open] sea.

Sojourn on the Island of Atka

September 25:

Beginning this date and until October 4th, I resided at the vegetable gardens, harvesting the vegetables.

October 11:

On the day of Sunday, prior to the Liturgy, annointed with Myrrh 1 infant of the male sex, born and baptized by laymen during my absence.

October 18:

On this day of Sunday, after the Liturgy, I performed the marriage ceremony for the creole Stepan Goloi with his common-law wife the Aleut woman Feodora. They have remained to this day unmarried because of the degree of kinship between them, but now, with the permission of the Ecclesiastical Superiors, they were able to be wed.

October 20:

I travelled in a baidarka to the isthmus, to the grist mill hamlet, where I baptized the son of a Russian, [named] Kiriak, born on the 29th of September and annointed with Myrrh a son of another Russian, named Mikhii, born and baptized by laymen during my absence.

October 23:

This day I performed the marriage of the toion's son, the Aleut Fedor Dediukhin, a company employee, with the spinster creole Pelageia Danilova.

October 25:

It is the will and the wish of His Grace that the children of both sexes from infancy be carefully educated in Christian piety and taught their duties, in accordance with their age, that their hearts and minds be trained as demanded by the Truth of Christianity. He personally proposed to me that this wish of his be carried out in this parish also. Desiring as far as it was possible to comply with His Grace's wishes I had announced on the previous Sunday after the Liturgy that forthwith I intend to call the children into the Temple on Sundays and Feast Days, either prior to the midday service or at some other time. The signal that the children are called to the church would be a special ringing of the church bells and when such ringing is heard the parents ought to send their children to church and the children themselves should hurry there. After this announcement had been made, I this date commenced to call the children to church before the Liturgy on Sunday. Then I held a Te Deum [for them] and prayed with them calling on God's aid in the learning and study which we commenced. Then I began to talk about the prayer, how the prayer is needed in asking God's help and all good things and how, therefore, it is necessary to pray to God before commencing any kind of activity etc. etc. After the midday service I performed the marriage ceremony for a creole, a company employee, who married an Aleut woman.

October 26:

Today the instruction at the Parish School commenced, and twenty boys, children of creoles and Aleuts, were enrolled. I appointed the parish sacristan Ivan Ladygin to teach literacy and elementary reading, and the sub-deacon Lavrentii Salamatov on a regular schedule to conduct the instruction of children at a more advanced level.

October 28:

This day at the above mentioned Parish School we opened a class in singing, and the boys selected for this class are to assemble for instruction 3 to 4 times a week. Ten boys were selected, and 5 more boys joined on their own. The preceptor of this choir is the clerk Petr Vykhodtsev and he was given the authority to organize this choir and teach singing.

November 1:

On the day of Sunday, prior to the Liturgy, I assembled the children in the Church and talked to them about God, that is at the level that the children can understand the [concept] of God and demonstrated his quality of omnipresence and omniscience etc. Today I administered the last rites to an ailing woman, that is confessed and joined her in the Holy Mysteries.

November 5:

Baptized the newborn infant Nastasia, born on the 29th of last month to the Aleut spinster Dar'ia Galkin.

November 8:

On the day of Sunday and the Feast Day of St. Archangel Michael the children were assembled in the church prior to the midday service, and I talked with them about God's love, and demonstrated to them that God loves all people, but especially the children, and therefore the children in turn ought to love God and come to Him, and how they can [show] their love of God, through what kind of acts etc. etc.

34th Trip to the Island of Amlia

1842

Remark:

As I was supposed to go to Amlia Island during the advent fast, both to give the people who had not made confession and had not partaken of communion during Lent, an opportunity to do so, and also to perform the necessary church rites and ministrations, I waited in readiness for baidarkas from that island which were delayed by strong winds and stormy weather until the 19th of this month.

November 20:

Today the weather grew calm, and after the church service I set out in a baidarka carrying with me all the equipment needed for the performance of Divine services and was accompanied by the sub-deacon and 2 boys from among the choristers. On this occasion the company clerk, M. Vykhodtsev, came with me. After a safe journey, we arrived at the settlement and I immediately commenced preparation for the approaching Feast Day services which I held in the chapel. The people present in the settlement began to prepare for communion.

November 21:

Prior to the Liturgy I annointed with Myrrh three infants, of the female sex, previously baptized by laymen. Then I celebrated the Liturgy, at which the singing was partly in the Aleut language, specifically *Lord, Have Mercy, To Thee, Grant It, O Lord, And to Thy Spirit, Father, Son and Holy Spirit,* the *Symbol of Faith, I Believe in One God,* the *Lord's Prayer: Our Father.* The gospels were also read in the Aleutian language. At this service I delivered the address given by His Grace, Innokentii, Bishop of Kamchatka, the Kuriles and the Aleutians, at his visit to the Atka Church in the temple of St. Nicholas in 1842 on July 19, which was translated into the Aleutian language, the local dialect.

Remark:

From this day on in this chapel the readings of the Gospel and singing, as required, continue in the Aleut language.

November 22:

On the day of Sunday all Aleut children of both sexes from the local settlement were assembled at the chapel prior to the Liturgy and I conversed with them and taught them about God, about prayer and how they must understand the quality of omnipresence and omniscience and that it is necessary to pray to God.

November 22:

Afterwards, I celebrated the Liturgy at which the infants were joined to the Holy Mysteries, and after the Liturgy I read a translation into the Aleut language of the address made by His Grace to the inhabitants of the island of Bering in the local chapel, during his visit there on August 12, 1842.

Remark:

The two [copies of] the above mentioned address by His Grace, already translated into the local Aleut language, were left here by me for frequent readings in this chapel.

November 23:

Today, in between the Divine services, I talked with the Faithful who were keeping the fast, about the meaning of fasting, how those, who are contrite about their transgressions should fast and pray and how one should prepare oneself for the cleansing of the conscience. (As the local inhabitants are all Aleuts, all lessons, of course, as always, are delivered in their own language.)

November 24:

Today, in between Divine services I told those Faithful who were fasting about the Law of God, that is I explained to them what God prescribes and proscribes in the ten commandments, and also cited for them several places from the Gospels, which are conducive to self-knowledge and contrition of sinners.

November 25:

Today I confessed those who were fasting, of whom there were 54 persons of both sexes.

November 26:

On the occasion of the Feast of St. Innocent, I held the vigil. In the morning prior to the Liturgy, I baptized an infant, born to a local Aleut on the 19th of this month. Then all children of both sexes were gathered in the chapel and I talked with them about God's Love for men and especially for children and that they too, must love God and what they ought to do out of this love for Him. Afterwards, I celebrated the Divine Liturgy, at which 50 persons who had made confession joined in the Holy Mysteries. Later on I visited the cemetery and sang the Requiem for [all] those who died [here] since my last visit. The rest of my time today was spent in performing marriages. I celebrated 8 weddings, of which 6 were first marriages and two were second marriages. After the ceremonies, I gave a lesson to the newlyweds on the meaning of marriage and on the duties of husband and wife respectively. Thus I concluded my activities here.

EXTRACTS FROM THE JOURNALS OF REV. PRIEST IAKOV (JACOB/JAMES) NETSVETOV, 1845–63, YUKON DISTRICT

[*The following text is taken from Iakov Netsvetov,* The Yukon Years 1845–1863. *Kingston, Ontario, Limestone Press, 1984. Translated by Lydia T. Black, University of Alaska, Fairbanks.*]

1845

July 14th:

On this day we set out from the Mikhailovskii redoubt in baidarkas, on our first trip [into the interior]. We traveled along Pastol' Bay to the Pastol' River, or rather to the village located on that river. The Missionary remained in this locality from the 15th through the 22nd of July, as at this time many of the savage tribes were congregated there.

The Missionary preached the Word of God, both to those who had been christened in the past (in the years 1843 and 1844) and to the heathen. As a consequence 13 Malemiut, 14 Chniagmiut and 9 Kvikhpagmiut, a total of 36 souls of both sexes, having accepted the Word of God and belief in Jesus Christ, and having stated their desire [to become Christians], received the Holy Baptism.*

July 23rd:

Returning from the trip, arrived this day at the Mikhailovskii redoubt.

July 24th:

This day, at the redoubt, an Inkalit [Ingalik] boy of adolescent age was baptized. An infant, born to a Russian father, was also baptized.

August 2nd:

This day dispatches were sent to the ecclesiastical superiors with the brig *Okhotsk* which was returning to Novoarkhangel'sk. Dispatch No. 15 was addressed to His Eminence, dispatches Nos. 12, 13 and 14, with appendices, to the Consistory.

August 15th:

On this day the mission left the Mikhailovskii redoubt for Ikogmiut on

*On this occasion the creole Grigorii Kurochkin, a company employee stationed at the Mikhailovskii redoubt and assigned to us as a guide, acted as interpreter.

the Kvikhpak River, where we planned to winter at the Russian odinochka. The mission traveled in three-hatch baidarkas.

Though according to the instruction from the Consistory, cited earlier on page one of this journal, the Mission were to locate initially at the redoubt, the Missionary was moved by various considerations set forth in a separate note** to relocate.

The creole Kurochkin, mentioned previously, was assigned to the Mission as an interpreter, because he was to join the crew at the odinochka at Ikogmiut anyway.

August 19th:

We reached the Pastol' River, but there was no activity to report.

August 28th:

We reached the first settlement located at the mouth of the Kvikhpak River, at the place where the stream divides itself into several channels. Here begins the territory of the tribe [*plemia*] Kvikhpagmiut. The village is named Kagliugvagmiut. Here two of the inhabitants, adult men, were baptized.

August 30th:

We arrived at the next, the second, settlement, called Kanigmiut. Here 3 local persons, adult men, were baptized.

September 1st:

We reached the next, the third, settlement, called Ankakhchagmiut. Here in the course of two days 11 persons of both sexes, adults and minors, were baptized, among them one of our oarsmen, a Chnigmiut.

**Considerations which moved the Missionary to decide to travel to Kvikhpak already in 1845 were as follows: 1) it was evident from observation as well as from information received that, in terms of supplies, it would be inconvenient for the Mission to winter over at the redoubt. Perhaps only the living quarters might have been better there; 2) it was evident that little activity in regard to the natives could take place at the redoubt during winter, especially since the Mission lacked an interpreter; 3) prolonged uncertainty in regard to the [permanent] location of the Mission would have interfered with the [flow of information] desired by the Consistory; 4) our desire to settle as soon as possible in a permanent location; 5) as the Ikogmiut odinochka was scheduled for relocation in 1846, we wished to use the opportunity [while the odinochka personnel were still there] to learn [from them] about local conditions and possible subsistence means; 6) we also hoped that the trip along the Kvikhpak River to Ikogmiut would afford an opportunity to get acquainted with the natives in their settlements and also, as possible, to preach to the natives the Word of God; 7) I am also hoping that during the winter season it will be possible at an early opportunity to travel to the Kuskokwim River and to the Kalmakovskii redoubt, to fetch the creole Konstantin Lukin, who has been assigned to the mission as a sacristan and to serve as an interpreter; and finally, 8) wintering over at Ikogmiut would enable the Missionary to communicate with Ecclesiastical Superiors via Kalmakovskii redoubt and Nushagak.

September 3rd:

We reached the next, the fourth, settlement, called Takchagmiut. Here seven persons, local inhabitants, adult men, were baptized.

September 4th:

We reached the next settlement, called Ingigagmiut, but the inhabitants on this occasion were absent.

September 5th:

En route we met some of the inhabitants of the Ingigagmiut village. We camped with them. This day, 6 persons of both sexes were baptized, also 3 of our oarsmen, Mallegmiuts, a total of nine persons.

September 7th:

We passed two empty villages, Chukagmiut and Ikuagmiut, and reached the village Kakagmiut. Here in two days (September 8th and 9th) 41 persons of both sexes, minors and adults, were baptized.

September 9th:

This day we safely reached the village Ikogmiut, where the Russian Company odinochka is located and where the mission is planning to winter. For this reason members of the mission occupied themselves for the next few days with various practical tasks associated with the establishment of the Church and also with the matters of housekeeping and subsistence.

September 13th:

The church tent has been erected (the field church), properly arranged and the tent secured appropriately.

September 14th:

This day the first Divine Liturgy was celebrated in the said Church. Only Christians who reside in the odinochka attended. None of the natives were in attendance as the people hereabouts have not yet been enlightened through Holy Baptism.

September 15th:

This day the missionary began to preach God's Word, addressing himself specifically to the Ikogmiut inhabitants, the wild ones, as all of them have gathered at this time in the village. As a consequence of this address, 30 adult men received Holy Baptism on the same day.

September 16th:

40 persons of both sexes were baptized. They were members of the families of the ones baptized yesterday.

September 17th:

Today 9 persons were baptized, among them a blind, paralyzed old man and a woman, sick, bedridden and also paralyzed.

September 19th:

Today 8 persons of both sexes were baptized. Two marriages for native couples were performed. Within four days, as indicated above, a total of 87 inhabitants of Ikogmiut village have accepted Holy Baptism. Only a very few remain unbaptized.*

September 23rd:

On this day I performed marriages for three native couples. The newly baptized were asked to come into the Church tent during the Divine Services, and when they did so, they were offered appropriate and much needed instruction.

September 24th:

On this day the missionary traveled in a baidarka upstream along the Kvikhpak to the next village, called Ikalivagmiut, in order to inspect the locality and [assess] its potentialities, as well as to visit with the local inhabitants and engage them in instruction. However, all of the local villagers were absent. For this reason the missionary returned home by evening.

September 26th:

This day the missionary and the deacon went in a baidarka upstream for timber and towed back several logs.

September 27th:

We sang the service for the dead for a newly baptized infant who died, a child of newly baptized natives. We buried [the body] at the old cemetery at the Ikogmiut odinochka.

October 1845:

In the month of October it became difficult to perform Divine Services

---

*Creole Andrei Glazunov, baidarshchik of the local odinochka, translated for the Missionary when the latter preached. The conversion of the savages to Christianity was also aided in not inconsiderable measure by cooperation of the Ikogmiut toion, Iakov Angiliq, who was baptized on July 20th of this year at Pastol', when the missionary visited there.

because of the cold and frost. Even though the field church—the tent—remained secure, it was not always possible to hold services there. The matins and vespers were held then in the small yurta, where the missionary lives, and the Liturgy and the hours in the field church, as far as it was possible to do so.

There was also little activity as far as the natives were concerned because the latter dispersed soon after receiving the Holy Baptism in September, leaving Ikogmiut to hunt various game. A few remained at Ikogmiut, but because of the difficult conditions, lessons were given very seldom. The natives were instructed only occasionally, when they attended the Divine Services in the Church tent or when they visited the Missionary in his house.

October 28th:

On this day, finally, the ice on the Kvikhpak River firmed up. This year the ice has not stabilized for a long time due to unstable weather. For this reason, [we] suffered a food scarcity.

November 11th:

This day the Missionary, accompanied by the deacon, set out on the winter track on a trip to the Kuskokwim River and to the Kalmakovskii redoubt. We traveled by means of a single sled with a three-dog team. The sled carried baggage, both church and personal.

November 13th:

This day the Kuskokwim River was reached and the party arrived at the village Kal'kagmiut. Here we met the creole Konstantin Lukin.* He was dispatched by his father from the Kalmakovskii redoubt for Ikogmiut to join the Mission and to assume his office as sacristan, in accordance with the order of the Consistory. He joined the Missionary's party as they continued upstream along the Kuskokwim. By evening the party reached the village Ukhagmiut where they stayed the night in the native kazhim (a large yurta). On this occasion the Missionary preached the Word of God to the local inhabitants, the Kuskokwim people, through his interpreter, the above mentioned Konstantin Lukin.

November 14th:

We reached the village called Tuliukagnagmiut, but continued on our

*Semen Lukin, father of the said Konstantin Lukin, was notified in writing in September that his son had been appointed by the order of the Consistory to serve as sacristan to the Kvikhpak Mission. The dispatch was sent from Ikogmiut, upon the Missionary's arrival there. It was requested that Konstantin Lukin be sent to Ikogmiut at the first possible opportunity. He set out [on this journey] in the beginning of November and this is how he came to meet the Missionary en route.

way without stopping, as it was early yet, just about mid-day. By evening we found an abandoned barabara and spent the night there.

November 15th:

Arrived safely at the Kolmakovskii redoubt, reaching it about noon. On this date creole Konstantin Lukin officially assumed his office as sacristan and interpreter for the Missionary.

November 16th:

This day the church services commenced and were held in the prayer house, [which is] small and simple, and serves here (at the Kalmakovskii redoubt) as the chapel named for the Transfiguration. The Faithful, the local inhabitants, commenced preparation for communion (*govenie*) and between services, instruction [lessons] was given to them as needed. In between, on this same day I annointed with Holy Myrrh [chrismated] 7 infants (2 of the male, 5 of the female sex), all, except one, born of Christians and baptized by laymen, after the visit here by the Nushagak Missionary in 1843.*

November 17:

This day, between the Divine Services, those Christians who prepared for communion, creoles and natives with their families, a total of 31 persons, made confession.

November 18:

On this day of Sunday, at the Liturgy, the 31 persons who made confession joined in the Holy Mysteries. All infants were also joined in the Holy Mysteries.

November 19:

This day, upon invitation by the natives from the nearest village who came here,** the Missionary preached the Word of God, both to those baptized and unbaptized. Subsequently, those who were baptized were instructed to prepare for participation in the Holy Mysteries through fast and prayer. The unbaptized who had accepted the Word of God were instructed to prepare for Holy Baptism on the morrow.

---

*In the Kalmakovskii redoubt a small and very simple house has been transformed into a prayer house and since the year 1843 has served as a chapel named for the Transfiguration, as the local inhabitants constantly hold communal prayers therein, and in 1843 the Nushagak missionary held churchly rites and the Divine service there.

**This settlement is called Kvigimpainagmiut. It is located on the opposite bank of the Kuskokwim River, above the redoubt, about one verst distant.

November 20:

This day I spoke the Word of God to the natives who came from the same settlement as did those who participated yesterday; I preached to them as well as to the newcomers. Thus, in the afternoon 15 persons were newly baptized and 10 annointed with Holy Myrrh, the ones who had been joined to the Christian faith by the laymen,*** a total of 25 persons (13 of the male, 12 of the female sex). All were preparing for joining in the Holy Mysteries on the next day, and with them another 17 persons from among baptized natives did the same.

November 21:

On this Feast day of the All-Holy Theotokos at the Liturgy, 47 persons who had prepared themselves were joined in the Holy Mysteries.

November 22:

This day I performed 3 marriages for the natives who are at the redoubt in company service.

November 23:

This day I taught the Word of God to the natives who came from the self-same settlement [Kvigimpainagmiut], both to baptized and unbaptized ones. Subsequently, the baptized ones were instructed to commence preparation by fast and prayer for the Mysteries of contrition and communion. Those unbaptized, but who accepted the Word and believe in Jesus Christ were instructed to prepare to receive Holy Baptism on the following day.

November 24:

In the morning I preached the Word of God to the visiting natives, and to another group but newly come [to the redoubt]. In the afternoon, ten of those, after being properly instructed and having prepared themselves, were baptized and 26 persons, newly converted heathen, were annointed with the Holy Myrrh. [These were] from among those who were joined to the Christian faith and baptized by laymen, a total of 36 souls (25 males and 11 of the female sex). All of them prepared themselves to receive the Holy Mysteries on the morrow.

***Here on the Kuskokwim River in some villages there are, since times long past, baptized Kuskokwimtsy. [They were] baptized by laymen, to wit by the Russian Fedor Kalmakov and the creole Semen Lukin, in 1832. Some of them had the opportunity to attend the preaching of the Word of God and other lessons, and receive the anointment with the Holy Myrrh as the sign of joining the Christian faith during the current visit of the Kvikhpak Missionary to the Kalmakovskii redoubt, as already noted.

November 25:

On this day of Sunday, at the Liturgy, 38 persons, exclusive of infants, partook in the Holy Mysteries. The infants, as many as there were, also were joined [in the Holy Mysteries]. Afterwards, I performed 1 marriage for a native [couple].

November 26:

This day the Missionary was in the settlement of Kvigimpainagmiut, visiting with the natives. Having performed in the kazhim the consecration of the waters, I consecrated their settlement and houses (the yurtas) [parenthesis in original]. Later on, also in the kazhim, I offered to all those inhabitants who are Christians a lesson on Christian duties and also about how the newly-baptized ought to live. Thence I returned to the redoubt.

November 28:

On this date the Mission started out on the return trip from the Kalmakovskii redoubt to Ikogmiut. The Mission was now accompanied by the newly installed sacristan and interpreter, Konstantin Lukin. The return was along the same route we had taken earlier.

November 29:

We stopped en route for the night at an empty odinochka and this day, in the morning, about 9 o'clock, reached the settlement *Tuliukagnagmiut* [emphasis in original]. Here we stopped, specifically in order to preach the Word of God to the inhabitants, who this time were all at home. Consequently, the Missionary taught long to all, men, women, and children, assembled in the kazhim, the Word of Salvation as a result of which almost all accepted the Word and manifested faith without doubt. Later on, as there were, among the local inhabitants a number formerly baptized by laymen, as already noted above by Fedor Kalmakov and Semen Lukin, 16 persons were confirmed in the Christian faith through the Mystery of anointment with the Holy Myrrh, among those were the toions and zakashchiks from the local settlement.

November 30:

We started early in the morning, and about 9 o'clock arrived at the next village, Ukhagmiut. As we had spent a night here en route [to the redoubt], the Missionary had already preached the Word of God to local inhabitants, but by no means to all. After we settled here for the time being, all inhabitants assembled in the kazhim and the Missionary preached the Word of God until midday [noon]. As a result, here, too, [the people] accepted the Word and came to believe in the Savior Jesus Christ. Afterwards, about one o'clock we set out on our way. By evening, about 7 o'clock, we came to the next village, Kalikagmiut [Kal'kagmiut], where we stopped for the night, lodging in the kazhim. To the inhabitants who were present on this occasion, the Missionary preached the Word of God, but here the preaching encountered more resistance and opposing views, because the local toion was also the chief shaman. Answering for all, he contradicted and at first resisted with exceptional strength, but later on, through clear logical arguments and disproof of his false opinions, he became convinced. He fell silent, then agreed in all things, accepted the Word and came to believe. After him, many expressed their faith without doubt. Thus, my lengthy preaching ended about midnight.

December 1:

In the morning, about 7 o'clock, we left the village Kal'kagmiut and the river Kuskokwim, following the same portage route we used going in the opposite direction, toward the river Kvikhpak. On this trek we spent a night in an abandoned hut [*baraborka*].

December 2:

We started out very early, by moonlight. Continuing our march throughout the entire day without stopping, at about 5 o'clock in the afternoon we reached the Kvikhpak and the Ikogmiut odinochka. Thus, the Mission returned from the journey safely.

1846

January 6:

This day the church service was performed in the field church and the visiting natives were taught, but [everything] was very difficult because of severe cold. Beginning with this day the Missionary began to call in the children of the newly baptized natives for lessons, assembling them in his own small house. Records were kept [of attendance] on subject matter taught, and all other pertinent circumstances. Related notes were also kept.

January 7:

This day the Missionary taught the Word of God in the kazhim, addressing all newly baptized natives who had assembled.

January 8:

This day, as the occasion was propitious, the Missionary preached the Word of God, again in the kazhim, to all, in general.

January 12:

On this day of Sunday the clerics and others attended lessons. The topic was the tenth article of the Creed of Faith, also the Mystery of the Holy Baptism was explained on the basis of the expanded catechism and the Orthodox confession.

January 19:

This day, Sunday, the clerics and all other students attended lessons. They were addressed about the mysteries of baptism and chrismation [explained] on the basis of the Orthodox confession and expanded catechism.

January 26:

On this day of Sunday the clerics and other students attended lessons and were addressed on the topic of the Mysteries of Communion on the basis of the expanded catechism and the Orthodox confession.

On this date I performed two marriage ceremonies for inhabitants of the Ikogmiut settlement.

February 9:

On this day of Sunday the clerics and other students attended instruction, and the topic was the remaining four mysteries: of contrition, priesthood, marriage and blessing of the oil [*eleosviashchenie* or extreme unction] taught on the basis of the expanded catechism and the Orthodox confession.

February 16:

On this day, Sunday, the clerics and other students attended instruction and were told about the eleventh and twelfth articles of the Creed of Faith [taught] on the basis of the expanded catechism and the Orthodox confession.

February 23:

On this day, Sunday, the clerics and other students attended instruction, and were addressed on the topic of *hope* [emphasis in original] and discussed what the content of hope was and the means of salvation [to fulfill this] hope, as for example, prayer; also [talked] about the state of bliss [*blazhenstvo,* state of felicity], all on the basis of the expanded catechism and the Orthodox confession.

March 9:

On this day of Sunday the clerics and other students attended instruction and were offered an explanation of the Lord's Prayer, also invocation, petition and praise, on the basis of the expanded catechism and the Orthodox confession.

This same day the Missionary held a conversation [discourse] with a native who came here from the village of Ingigagmiut. This same native had been baptized on the 13th day of August of the past year during Missionary's visit to the settlement Chukagmiut, following his [the native's] recovery from insanity. We talked about his subsequent life, and it was made known to him that no curse hangs over him, now that he has been baptized, as was the case prior to the Holy Baptism, which had resulted in insanity and ravings.*

March 16:

On this day of Sunday the clerics and others attended instruction and were taught about the state of bliss, specifically about the original sin [*o pervom grekhe*] on the basis of the expanded catechism and the Orthodox confession.

March 18:

Today one newly baptized native was anointed with the Holy Myrrh.

March 22:

This day (Great Saturday) the clerics attended instruction and the 4th and 5th states of bliss were explained to them on the basis of the expanded catechism and Orthodox confession. Also this day they went to confession, together with others, a total [who made confession] of 5 persons.

March 30:

On this day, Sunday, the clerics and others attended instruction, and the remaining 4 states of bliss were explained to them on the basis of the expanded catechism and the Orthodox confession. Other instruction was given them for future guidance this day also.

April 6:

The clerics and others attended instruction and were taught about the union of faith and love [charity], about the Law of God and the Commandments, on the basis of the expanded catechism and the Orthodox confession.

---

*The exactness of wording is important here, as the process and means of conversion to Christianity, the motivation for conversion is evidenced. [Alternate rendering: "It was made known to him that the curse to which he was subject prior to the baptism, which resulted in insanity and ravings, was no more, following the Holy Baptism".] Apparently, it was believed that this person was under a curse, possibly by a shaman. Tr.

April 13:

On this day, Sunday, the clerics and others attended instruction, and the Christian virtues were discussed on the basis of Orthodox confession.

April 20:

On this day, Sunday, the clerics and others attended instruction and were taught about sins, that is about the concept and the categories [of sins] etc. on the basis of the Orthodox confession.

April 27:

On this day, Sunday, the clerics and others attended instruction. The previous topic, i.e. discussion of sins, was continued.

May 4:

On this day, Sunday, the clerics and others attended instruction, and were taught about the Law of God, the Commandments, their division [parts] and then the First Commandment was explained to them.

This same day sang the funeral services for a native woman, who was then buried in the cemetery of the native settlement.

*May 18:**

On this day, Sunday, the clerics and others attended instruction, and were taught the second and third Commandments on the basis of expanded catechism and the Orthodox confession.

Remarks:

Today the local natives held the ceremonial commemoration of the dead. Those who held the memorial ceremonies [*pominki*] for their deceased kinsmen had been during the past days feasting visitors and distributing various items. Today, about noon, all of them, men and their wives, dressed in their best garments which were prepared beforehand especially for this occasion. They repaired to the kazhim, and a lot of people progressed thither. After awhile, they began to emerge from the kazhim. In front went one [man] with a drum who sang; he was followed by men dressed in their best outfits (offerers of the memorial feast). They went slowly and carried nothing in their hands; behind them came their wives, also decked out in their best garments, carrying in their hands thin rods, painted and decorated with feathers. They [the women] swayed to both sides in time to the song and the drum beat. Behind them came once again a solitary man with a drum. He was followed finally by the multitude of

*Today the ice broke up and began to move along the entire river Kvikhpak (Yukon).

people, everyone except the spectators. They all had by now emerged from the kazhim into the open [lit. street, *na ulitsu*] and sat around, some on top of houses [baraboras] others on [illegible word—possibly squatting on the ground, Tr.], watching the action. Having emerged from the kazhim, the procession went around the cemeteries [*po kladbishcham krugom*], where the bodies are buried and the grave markers stand. They marched solemnly, in front and in the back the drums were beaten, as already stated. They marched in silence [*bezmolvno*]. In this manner they went over the entire (and each) cemetery. Afterwards, they visited the cemetery again, but this time individually, each person going to the place where the kinsmen's bodies were buried, husbands accompanied by their wives, and started to lament [*plakat'*—cry] at the grave markers, both husband and wife, while the singing and drum beating continued without stopping. When all the burial places had been visited, they re-assembled and in procession returned to the kazhim, where the ceremony, which lasted more than an hour, ended.

Afterwards, they began to make, in the kazhim, a fire [*zhar*—reading doubtful, Tr.] and in the evening the entire festival ended with entertainment [*igrushka*] and a dance [*pliaska*]. This custom is, of course, contrary to Christianity, as it is based on superstition and it ought to be abandoned, however there are still many heathen here and very few Christians. In a great assembly, as is here now, the latter humor the former, willy-nilly, and observe what is demanded of them as of old. I, however, note this, and talk to them about it, and at present even speak strictly, almost forbidding their old customs, addressing everyone in general but the Christians in particular, our own Ikogmiut inhabitants; later on one must take strict measures against such superstition on their part, as just reasoning and my words have little effect. Though they at times listen and agree and promise to fulfill what is demanded [by the faith, Tr.], later on, at a meeting or other occasions they change [their intent] and do the contrary and even persuade others. Inconstant is this folk!

1848

January 18:

On this day of Sunday, I, sinner and unworthy one, performed the Liturgy in the local chapel safely and peacefully [*blagopoluchno i bezmiatezhno*], though the cold was severe to the utmost [atrocious]. All those confessed, 35 persons, in addition to infants, were joined to the Holy Mysteries. Afterwards, I performed two marriages for the natives in the service [of the company, Tr.], who were among those who received the Mysteries on the Sunday past.

Remarks:

It is very difficult, almost impossible, to stay in the local prayer house which serves as the chapel, while such cold as is occuring now lasts, because [the prayer house] lacks either a stove or fireplace. Therefore, all other activities, even the baptisms, instruction and other church services, I conduct in the house where I am quartered. Only the Liturgy I performed in the chapel, which on the previous day is heated by hot stones, that is the stones are heated red-hot outside, then carried into the chapel and placed in the corner on a special [platform] prepared beforehand. This makes the cold somewhat bearable enabling [me] to act the necessary span of time.

Difficult and burdensome circumstances [conditions] exist in this region everywhere, but especially so in winter. Many improvements and means for necessary action need to be instituted in order to spread and confirm the Christian faith among the peoples inhabiting these regions!

January 19:

Today I was busy at home, that is with written matters.

January 20:

Today I was engaged with one newly converted heathen (a Kuskokwim person from the Ukhagmiut settlement) who arrived here specifically to receive baptism. When he declared his intention to me, I asked him what had moved him to become baptized. "Because now I firmly believe, without doubt," he replied. "I heard the preaching about God at Nushagak, but remained in unbelief and doubt; then here I heard the preaching more than once, and now I believe without doubt, and wish to convert and be baptized." Following these words of his, I began to preach for him, demonstrating that these matters are not the province of Man, but are of the Word of God [*logos,* Tr.], and cannot be anything else but the truth, that such is being preached into all corners of the world, as it has been [from of old] without change, and so on. Then I preached to him about the turning [*obrashchenie*] of Man to God which is possible only through faith in the Savior of humanity, and then continued to preach about Him. I taught him about faith, Christian Law, the mysteries, and so on. He listened to everything with great attention, and as was evident, with unquestioning faith, which he expressed following each verity communicated to him; he did not offer arguments to the contrary at any point. Finally, having obtained from him the appropriate assurances and promise, I performed over him today the mystery of the Holy Baptism. Besides that, I baptized today an infant, born to Christian parents in November of the previous year, and brought here yesterday from the Ukhagmiut settlement by its parents specifically for baptism. Glory and Thanks to God in these matters.

February 14:

I left in the morning, rather early, and toward 10 o'clock came to the next settlement, Ukhagmiut. Here I stopped for a short while, as it was necessary for me to talk with one old man, unbaptized, about whom I learned that he argues against the Christians, and dissuades the young folk from [Christianity]. I told him that he will be subject to strict action, because if only he himself does not wish to convert or has no inclination to accept Christianity, it is his own business, and no one would compel him or even bother him with talk about it; it behooves him then, in turn, to leave his brethren who have turned to the Christian faith in peace, and so on. He listened to all, and remained almost totally silent, not offering me any argument. Then, having chatted with the toion Petr and others, about necessary matters, about 12 o'clock, I continued forward. In the evening, about 7 o'clock, I came to the next settlement, the Kal'kagmiut, and stopped overnight in the kazhim. As there was a sufficient number of local inhabitants in assembly, I talked with them, about whatever was necessary, as most of the locals are as yet unbaptized. Only a few are baptized.

February 15:

I set out in the morning at 6 o'clock, and traveled through the day, which was calm and clear, except that the cold was strong throughout the entire day. I covered more than halfway along the portage from the Kuskokwim to the Kvikhpak. Stopped for the night at an open uninhabited place, but I must confess it was very cold. The frost, and the wind which came up about midnight, interfered. Especially it was hard for me because of my illness. Therefore, about 2 o'clock after midnight, we arose and

February 16:

continued onward. We covered the second half of the way along the portage to the Kvikhpak and about 3 o'clock in the afternoon reached home. Thanks be to Lord God, I completed my journey, though ailing and with difficulty, but I safely returned home.

Sojourn at Ikogmiut

February 23:

In the following days I continued to perform services at home, conducting all Lenten services with the exception of the Liturgy of pre-sanctified gifts. I, together with all members of my household, prepared for communion. Also some local natives prepared themselves for communion and attended the services daily, doing so exclusively on their own initiative. I made it known to them that I shall conduct services, and what kind, and told them that anyone who wished may come. It is not appropriate at this time to tell them to come imperatively, because of the cold and continuing frosts. To my great pleasure, they, however, came to the services, adults of both sexes, and almost half of the children. Even two very old women came. In the course of the following week I offered them instruction, in accordance with age and circumstances.

February 28:

On Saturday I confessed those who had fasted, my own folk [household—*svoikh*] as well as the natives and was preparing to celebrate the Liturgy tomorrow in the field church. Though the cold is so severe that it is impossible to hold services there I cannot leave this matter, as the natives have prepared themselves. Whatever the Lord will send!

February 29:

On the First Sunday of the Great Lent the Missionary, through God's grace, celebrated the Liturgy, at which 20 persons who have prepared themselves safely joined in the Holy Mysteries. Of these, 5 were members of our house, 15 were natives. I must confess, though, that it was very difficult to serve due to cold, as the Lamb on the discos and sacred [illegible word] in the chalice froze, but with available means we managed everything safely. I was again bothered in increased degree by my illness in this cold. If it had not been for the natives, I probably would not have dared to celebrate. It is for them that it was necessary to make the decision to celebrate, as they prepared themselves for communion through the whole week and were ready for the event. The rest of this day I spent in pleasant conversations both with the native-communicants who did not leave my house almost the entire day, and also with my co-servitors. We spent the time singing church songs and in spiritual inner enjoyments.

March 2:

Beginning this date and through the days following I was totally incapacitated, was unable to do anything at all, and did not even leave my bed, applying all possible remedies remaining from my pharmacy stores.

March 5:

Today, while I myself was severely ill, we received the unpleasant news from the winter camp, Nukhliuagmiut, that it had been struck by an alleged epidemic, that several people are so ill that they cannot even stand [keep their feet]. Having considered the situation, I decided to dispatch my sacristan [to help]. I collected all the medicines I had for treatment of illnesses, instructed him in the curing of sickness and what to say [to the people] and sent him off in the afternoon. I myself (this I can say) being in fear of my own illness and besides not knowing what else will transpire, I remained hoping and relying not so much on medicines and cures as on faith, even if it is not their faith. I prayed to God that He should grant them according to their faith, healing. Therefore I instructed the sacristan whom I was sending out that he tell them that they were to take the medicines without any doubts whatsoever but largely relying on God and that they were to pray to Him and so on. Thus I dispatched him, ordering him to return by tomorrow evening.

March 6:

Today the sacristan dispatched by me returned in the evening. He reported that the medicines I sent almost all had beneficial effect. Almost every person given medicine in accordance with [my] prescription was better. The sacristan himself expressed amazement as he related [to me] how those to whom he gave medicine yesterday, some of whom were almost totally immobile, in the morning were observed moving about, against all expectations, on crutches, and some felt very much better. Having received this news upon his return, I thanked God. Only my illness remains.

In the further course of this day my illness continued in an increased degree, and I suffered various pains. Not only was I unable to do anything, but even in leaving my bed I could only with great effort and then for a brief while only, move around the room. This condition lasted for 20 days. Only these days I am able to walk around the room.

Remarks:

Being in this state of illness I even began to think that the Lord is angry with me and that the end of my being in this world approaches. Consequently, I began to issue the necessary instructions.

March 21:

On this day of Sunday, though with difficulty, I celebrated a household Divine service. Natives came to attend the Hours. I addressed the Faithful briefly, in what was necessary, to wit: as it is my desire to do so and if the Lord lets me, I intend on the 25th of this month to perform services and celebrate the Liturgy. I suggested to them that if anyone wished to prepare themselves through fast and prayers, I would conduct for them services in my house, at home, as far as I was able. They expressed their desire to do so, among them the toion Iakov Angiliqin, who only these days arrived here from Nukhkuagmiut.

March 22:

I commenced to hold services in the house for those who were preparing themselves for communion, though it is difficult for me to do so. Especially difficult is it to stand for any length of time. However, as there are those who wish to prepare themselves for communion, I decided to perform services in the hope that God will permit me to perform the Liturgy on the Feasts in the field church.

March 24:

This day I confessed those who were preparing for communion. It is our misfortune that these days the cold increased, the frost is harder than it was during the first week of Lent. I do not know what shall happen but I am getting ready to serve and am preparing for tomorrow those who are fasting.

Remark:

Today the baidarshchik of the Andreevskaia odinochka, Ivan Zakharov, arrived here to attend a sale as part of the trade relations with the natives. On this occasion I received the necessary intelligence from the Mikhailovskii redoubt in respect to vital statistics as well as about the construction of the chapel of the Protection of the Theotokos.

March 25:

It is not possible at all to hold services in the tent. The cold is great. Besides, my health is yet weak and I cannot persevere for the duration of the lengthy service in this cold. Even when I am at home, I am barely able to continue standing throughout the service. Therefore, I decided not to serve Liturgy [in the church tent, Tr.], but instead held in the house the morning service and all other services, as is prescribed in the rules, except the Liturgy. Those who have prepared for communion, I joined to the Holy Mysteries by means of pre-sanctified [reserve, literally, *zapasnymi*] gifts. They were 22 persons of both sexes.

Remarks:

The fact that we have no church makes for difficulties and is to be regretted. This is especially true these days, when the newly baptized Christians could properly prepare themselves for communion, as far as it is in their powers and the conditions permit, through fast and prayer and thus little by little become more accustomed [to churchly ways, Tr.]. Of course, they pray in my house, but that is not enough. [The house] is cramped, I myself am inconvenienced and they [the Faithful, Tr.] do not experience the proper setting as they would in the temple. Besides I am grieved very much indeed that I am unable to conduct a proper Divine service, and there is not even a proper place for it. Though the field church stands [the tent], how is one to serve therein in such cold, which until present continues to hold here? One ought to wonder that at this calendar date the temperature stood at minus 10 degrees and even lower. The snow does not melt in the shade at all, and even in the full sunshine just a bit, and then only at midday. I experienced this [dilemma] more than once, and more than once resolved not to perform services there during such cold, especially the Liturgy which is open to certain dangers [during the service, i.e., the communion liquid etc. may freeze, Ed.]. What is one to do? It must be celebrated, for the sake of the newly baptized, as this time is better for them, they are more free, even though in the daytime they leave to fish or [seek] other game. But such absences are brief, they miss perhaps one service only and when it is time for them to confess and join in communion no one goes anywhere. At other seasons, beginning in May or even earlier, during the entire summer and fall they are completely occupied and do not remain in one place but are in dispersal.

March 26:

Today and in the following days I did not hold any services, as there is no hope that I shall be able to celebrate services next Sunday in the tent. The cold continues to hold as great as in the middle of winter and the snow shows no signs of melting.

March 28:

On this day of Sunday held services at home. There were few native faithful in attendance, as nowadays not many remain in the settlement. Some went to the tundra for the black fish. The toion Iakov Angiliqin himself, having performed his sacred obligations (for which reason he brought his family here), left again for his winter camp [*zimnik*] Nukhliuagmiut.

Remark:

For some time now some of the natives have been suffering scarcity of food, as this winter the ice fishing is bringing in very little fish. Even we ourselves are not as well off as last year, but Thanks be to God we have some fish stored. We use these and also share with others, helping the poor among the natives. The local inhabitants, on the other hand, during the festivity held here, that is the general assembly, used up their winter stores. Nowadays the lack is beginning to be felt keenly. Their only hope is the small black fish [Alaskan blackfish] which during winter can be caught in considerable quantities on the tundra, in swampy places and in the lakes, under ice. They leave now to catch this fish and will continue to live there until the river opens up, that is, until summer.

March 29:

This day and in the days following I did hardly anything, except some writing, because of the continued weakened state of my health. I cannot even sit for any length of time, as well as stand or walk. Besides, it is not yet possible to hold services in the tent, and only house services [can be conducted], as the frosts continue, especially mornings and evenings.

April 4:

On Sunday held all services at home, except the Liturgy, as I am still unable to hold services in the field church, in the tent. The cold continues, and the frosts are severe especially in the mornings. Had I been well, I would have dared to [hold services] but my weak health barely permits me to stand at service in my house. The natives came to the morning service, men, though they are few and attended also the Hours. I spoke a sermon about this Feast Day and the approaching Passion week.

April 5:

In the course of the following Passion week, I held all services, up to the Great Thursday, at home, as I could not bring myself to hold services in the tent as my health continues to be poor and even at home I am able to continue to serve only with difficulty. The last [few] days, however, I began to perform the appropriate Divine services in the field church. This week there were plenty of Christians who were preparing themselves for communion, contrary to my expectations. They were creoles and natives, as the baidarshchik of the Andreevskaia odinochka, Ivan Zakharov, and his assistant Ivan Serebriannikov, accompanied by some of their people were here for the preparation and communion. Also, some people from the Kalmakovskii redoubt, who did not communicate during my sojourn there in January because they were absent from the redoubt, came here for this purpose. Besides, the considerable number of local inhabitants, who are now in the settlement, also prepared for communion this week. To my great pleasure they attended the services very well and stood without expressions of boredom, in spite of the fact that the service was long. At the same time some were preparing for baptism: one family from the Ikalivagmiut settlement, also some local inhabitants, women, and visitors from downstream, from the Andreevskaia odinochka. I left this for Saturday.

April 9:

On the Great Friday, in between the Divine services, I was busy confessing those who were preparing for communion and with instruction of those who were preparing for baptism.

April 10:

On the Great Saturday, prior to the Liturgy, I performed baptism over 8 persons (4 of the male, 4 of the female sex) and joined to Christianity two women through the mystery of the annointment with myrrh. [These women] were among those who came here from the Kalmakovskii redoubt to fulfill their sacred Christian obligations and [participate] in rites. Afterwards, at the Liturgy performed in the field church, joined in the Holy Mysteries a total of 45 persons, of both sexes, adults. Among them were also the newly baptized [persons]. Thanks be to God for this! He gave the grace to me, sinful and unworthy one, to live out this week safely, and in spite of bodily infirmities with inner satisfaction.

April 11:

The day of the Glorious, Bright and Shining Resurrection of Christ I spent, I am able to say, in inner satisfaction and joy. The reason for this is a coincidence of various favorable circumstances. For the before-morning service [*zautrenia*] which customarily begins at midnight, the entire native population of this settlement came, and the better half did not leave but repaired to the church tent where the Deeds of the Apostles were being read. In addition, there were the visitors from the Andreevskaia odinochka, from the Kalmakovskii redoubt, and Christians from the upstream settlements, so that there assembled a multitude of people, and some could not be accommodated in the tent and stood outside, and the weather cooperated. The night was calm and warm, it was possible to stand and without any difficulty we even carried the small candles during the procession with the cross around the tent. This multitude of people, with burning candles, made the Christian Celebration very impressive. [This celebration] was observed by many natives for the first time with wonder and [illegible word] the resurrected Christ, they stood on both sides of the tent and in a circle behind me, praying piously [*blagogoveino*], all observing my actions. And I, seeing them standing there and praying, experienced such great joy within me and in my heart. Thus it continued throughout the morning service. And then, when the time came for the Christian mutual greeting and the kiss of greeting, all they, natives, and I among them, and they between themselves, greeted each other and kissed each other and some said in Russian "Christ is Risen!" [*Khristos Voskres!*]. Of course they understood the meaning of these words in their own language[s] only pronounced them in the Russian tongue. All of this was very pleasing for me to see. They continued [to act] this way even after the morning service, even with those [people] who did not attend the service. Later on, the same multitude of people were present at the Liturgy, and I spoke a sermon on this great Christian Feast of Feasts [Celebration, *torzhestvo*] and told them what we human beings were given through the suffering, death and resurrection of Jesus Christ and why for the Christians this feast day is the most glorious one and so on.

May 3:

Today my co-servitors again left to hunt geese in the islets.

May 6:

Today they returned with a bag of 36 geese. The ice on the Kvikhpak remains immobile, only at the edge one may break a bit with one's feet. There is still a great lot of ice, especially below [underneath the surface]. Though the days are warm now and on the surface the ice melts rapidly, there is still a lot of it.

May 9:

On the Sunday of the Samaritan performed the Divine service in the field church. In the evening the ice on the Kvikhpak began to break up, separating through large [fissures] but accumulating again at the shallows [on the spits—*na bankakh*]. The water has begun to rise, but there is still much snow along the banks [shores].

May 11:

Today in the afternoon the ice on the Kvikhpak really began to move along the entire river.

May 12:

Today the ice moved without stopping and the water in the river rose considerably. We are ready for the trip having repaired whatever was necessary.

May 13:

Today the ice moved without break and rapidly along the entire river.

May 14:

Today again the ice moved without stopping along the river.

May 15:

The ice on the river Kvikhpak today moved only in a narrow band along the middle of the river and by evening even that thinned out.

May 16:

On Sunday (the Sunday of the Blind Man) performed the Divine service in the field church. I was barely able to serve because of illness, as these few days my health took a turn for the worse. I am barely able to do a few tasks at home preparing for the journey.

As today the ice on the Kvikhpak is very thin, navigation on the river commenced, maneuvering between the ice floes. Thus the local toion Iakov Angiliqin arrived here for the sole purpose of seeing me, as he knows that I am about to depart. He brought me news and informed me of the death of a boy from among the local residents. Starshiny [leaders, elders] from the upstream settlement also came to see me and informed me about the state of affairs in their village. I held with them several conversations on various subjects. I also investigated the situation concerning one marriage and performed the ceremony this very day for the local resident a Kvikhpak man.

May 17:

Today there is practically no ice on the Kvikhpak, only occasionally chunks are carried by. By this day I am ready for departure, that is the water craft are ready: the baidara and two 3-hatch baidarkas. This time I intend to travel with the baidara accompanied by the baidarkas. In this way I decided, all of us will be able to go: myself, my two co-servitors, the subdeacon and the sacristan, my nephew who as it is known lives with me, and the two creole boys in my care. Consequently, we are leaving our house and the habitation unattended [empty].

May 24:

The absent persons, [company] employees of this odinochka, returned by evening. Besides, to my great pleasure, a family of Kvikhpak people arrived from the Kvikhliuiq [spelling uncertain, Tr.] (an arm of the Kvikhpak), travelling in a single baidara. It is the same family which was baptized on the Kvikhliuiq last year. They came because they figured that at this season I shall be travelling downstream and will stop here. They were planning to receive whatever is due according to Christian faith [i.e., sacraments, Tr.] and to fulfill their sacred Christian obligations. I was overjoyed, seeing such effort and firm faith and noting how well they remember everything they heard in the course of instruction last year and that they came here in order to fulfill all. I received from them needed information.

Remark:

Since yesterday I am very ill. Am barely able to stand up or walk. I suffer internal pain, my bones feel like breaking, I cough and I have a pain in my throat. All this is a complication of the cold suffered from exposure to the wind.

May 25:

Today, in spite of severe illness, I commenced to hold in the field church simple Divine services for those who were preparing for communion, both Russian and natives, for whom I ordered a fast. I also today gave instruction separately for Russians and then for the natives.

May 26:

Today I also held services, instructed those who were preparing for communion and in between baptized 3 infants (1 of the male, 2 of the female sex). The first was born to Christian parents in January of this year, into the family mentioned above who arrived here on the 24th, the other two are daughters of a heathen from the Kagliugvagmiut settlement who is preparing, together with his wife, to accept the Holy Baptism.

May 27:

I continued to hold services and instruct those who were preparing for communion and gave special instruction to those who were preparing for acceptance of the Holy Baptism.

Remark:

The baidarshchik of the local odinochka, Ivan Zakharov, arrived here in the evening, travelling in a 3-hatch baidarka.

May 28:

Today I also held services and gave instruction to those who were preparing for communion and in the meantime I baptized 7 heathen persons (5 of the male, 2 of the female sex). Among them the above mentioned heathen, whose daughters were baptized on the 26th, and his wife were baptized.

May 29:

Held services today and confessed the Russians and natives who were preparing themselves for communion, and in the evening performed the services in preparation for the approaching Feast Day.

May 30:

On the Sunday of the Pentecost, through the grace and good will of God, I performed the Liturgy and all other appropriate services and those who have prepared themselves, total of 23 persons of both sexes, joined in the Holy Mysteries, exclusive of infants. After this, I performed three marriages for the natives and their wives, who have fulfilled their sacred Christian obligations. Toward evening I dismantled the field church, as my activity here ended. The visiting natives left this same day, also toward evening, and some locals are scheduled to depart from this odinochka. I, too, plan to leave presently.

Remark:

Though I performed services and rites in the course of the past few days, I must say I did so only out of sheer necessity. I am very ill, weak in my entire body, but the most difficulty is caused by a strong cough, which gives me no peace during the night. I am thanking God that I was able, in spite of all, to perform the services and complete all [necessary] action safely.

May 31:

We departed Andreevskaia odinochka about 5 o'clock in the morning, travelling as before in one baidara accompanied by two three-hatch baidarkas.

St. Michael's Redoubt, June 16, 1848

The epidemic of the cough is widespread here and all of us, that is I and my co-servitors and other members of my household are coughing. The cough gives us no peace, and all feel poorly [two illegible words inserted above the line] and I am acting now only out of necessity.

July 19:

In the morning, at 10 o'clock, the Pre-eminent sanctified Lord [Bishop] came ashore and was met with appropriate honors. Proceeding to the chapel, the Archpastor gave his blessing to all and asked for the Grace of God and Peace to all. He then took up residence ashore for awhile. All appropriate matters and papers were presented to him in person.

Further, on orders of His Eminence, this very day the sacristan Konstantin Lukin and my nephew Vasilii Netsvetov were confirmed in the clerical estate. Consequently the very same day I submitted to His Eminence a petition, under no. 115, for consecration and wearing of the sticharion. In the evening, the all-night vigil was held in the local chapel.

July 20:

On the Feast Day of the Prophet St. Elias His Eminence performed the Liturgy in the course of which he consecrated to the wearing of the sticharion Konstantin Lukin and Vasilii Netsvetov. The Archpastor's well-wishing extended also to me, unworthy one, when he elevated me to [the rank of] Proto-presbyter. In conclusion, the Archpastor addressed the newly baptized savages [the wild ones] and their toions, to confirm them in their faith and Christian piety and so on. Afterwards, at his house, the Archpastor conversed with the toions and starshiny and to some of them, upon my presentation, he gave awards, red shirts: to Iakov of Ikogmiut, and Iuda of Ankakhchagmiut. Moreover, all were given silver [body] crosses. They were feasted together with their retinue and others.

July 21:

This day His Eminence was busy with me attending to matters of the Kvikhpak Mission. [We considered] what is necessary for the Mission's improvement and [the needs] of the clergy [*pricht*]. As a consequence a proposal for changes in the clerical personnel was addressed to me; specifically that the former sub-deacon Innokentii Shaiashnikov will presently proceed to Unalashka; that in his place the former sacristan Konstantin Lukin be appointed as sub-deacon, while the seminary student Nikolai Gol'tsyn be appointed as Lukin's replacement to the position of sacristan. [We also] discussed related matters, salaries of the clergy and other expenditures of the Mission.

July 22:

Today I was again busy with correspondence.

July 23:

Today again I was busy with correspondence.

July 24:

Today I was also busy with written matters and presented to His Eminence a full report on the state of the Kvikhpak Mission for the period from 1845 to 20 July 1848. In the evening a vigil was performed in preparation for tomorrow.

July 25:

On this day of Sunday His Eminence concelebrated the Liturgy.

July 26:

Today I was finishing all the papers to be dispatched to N.[ovoarkhangel'sk, Tr.] Consistory.

July 27:

This day I finished up all correspondence and all other business.

July 28:

Today I surrendered all records and papers for dispatch in a single common packet. Toward evening, the Pre-eminent and Sanctified Lord, whose Archpastoral footsteps [on these shores] and blessing brought us happiness, transferred to the vessel.

July 29:

Today and the days following I remained in residence here attending to the issue of supplies for the Kvikhpak Mission and settling accounts with the manager. This same day, in the afternoon, the ship hoisted anchor and sailed away.

1849

March 25:

On the Feast Day of the All Holy Theotokos through God's Grace we celebrated the divine services, as is proper, and I performed the Liturgy in the field church, in the tent. In the course of the Liturgy the 54 persons who have made confession partook of the Holy Mysteries, and in addition a considerable number of infants. The warm weather permitted me to hold services in the tent without hindrance, but wet snow continued to fall throughout the day, the same as yesterday. At the evening service, I offered the final instruction to the communicants, and then I released them [from further obligations] so that they are free to depart from home as needed.

Remark:

I am able to say that I finished this engagement with these [people] who fasted with a deep sense of Spiritual joy. First of all, they came in response to my first invitation to prepare themselves for communion, agreed willingly, and commenced to pray, not as it was in the years past. And this, in spite of the fact that nowadays they are especially pressed by their own affairs, that is, the need for daily excursions to forage for subsistence because of the shortage of food. Secondly, in the course of each service they came diligently, in spite of the bad weather, slush, and wetness, which was especially bad on the days of confession and communion. During the services they stood, without any sign of boredom, and listened attentively to the sermon. Throughout the entire morning service [*utrenia*] and the Liturgy, which were performed in strict observance of the [church] rule.

The Liturgy, consequently, was rather prolonged; they stood in the tent, which due to the heavy wet snow was leaking, and in spite of being dripped on, they remained through the entire service and came to the Holy Mysteries in good order, as is proper, decorously, carrying their infants. One may say they came with zeal, and accepted everything with understanding which was expressed in their faces. This, this is what makes me joyous! Glory to God for this!

April 2:

On Great Saturday celebrated divine services in the tent, also the Liturgy, at which the 7 persons who have prepared themselves partook of the Holy Mysteries. Thanks be to God that though it was difficult to serve and even stand in the tent while there was a 13 degree cold, all went well to the end.

Remark:

There arrived here, from the Kalmakovskii redoubt, Semen Lukin, who travelled hither especially for the Feast Day. From the Andreevskaia odinochka came Ivan Serebrennikov replacing the manager I. Zakharov who went to the odinochka from here. From both of these men I received various necessary intelligence. Unfortunately, not all the news is pleasant. Everywhere nowadays there is a lack of food. The natives have left their settlements and scattered to various places looking for sustenance.

April 3:

On the Day of the Shining and Glorious Resurrection of Christ celebrated all the appropriate services and the Liturgy, all in the field church. Some of the local native residents and a few visitors attended. It was very difficult to stand through the service in the tent, because of the cold and the wind.

1850

April 16:

On Palm Sunday, performed the Divine services, everything as appropriate, except the Liturgy, as I celebrated the services in the house. The field church has as yet not been erected. It is impossible to do so, because the cold continues to hold, 10 degrees [below zero] and below. In addition, the foul weather continues, with wind and snow. I am at present in a very sick condition, and serve with difficulty and great effort. I cough, am totally without voice, and the internal pain makes it hard to stand. Just the same, in spite of everything, in the evening I commenced to hold services for the following week, for those who are preparing themselves for communion, my clerics, the Aleut laborers and others.

April 17:

Continued to hold church services, but with great effort due to illness.

The heavy cough and pain interfered with my effort to stand properly, even though I held services in the house. These days the wind freshened even more and the cold increased (below 10 degrees). It is as yet impossible to put up the church tent. The same situation prevailed on the 18th, 19th and the 20th.

April 21:

As the church tent was erected yesterday, the entire morning service was celebrated as is appropriate, in the field church. As of today I continue to hold church services in accordance with the Rule [in the field church]. In between services, I prepare those who are readying themselves for communion.

April 22:

On this Great Saturday, performed the Divine service and at the Liturgy joined to the Holy Mysteries 17 persons who have prepared themselves for it. Glory and thanks to the Lord God, who granted us to fulfill all without mishap or hindrance, except for my bodily ailments. This past week I was very ill, and just barely was able to force myself to celebrate the services. I had no hope that I would be able to bring the services to conclusion or that I should live to see this day. However, God has come to my aid.

April 23:

On the day of the Bright and Shining [Glorious] Resurrection of Christ, the Divine services were performed as they ought to be, and, I may say, with my heart being consoled [with my heart's consolation], with joyous feelings, as if in recompense for my bodily weakness, God granted me to partake of this day. The faithful gathered in considerable numbers, even from among the natives, who returned here unexpectedly yesterday from their sojourn elsewhere [absence], with the sole purpose of meeting this joyous day here, which significance they already know and fully understand. Thus, to my intense joy and consolation, all of them, as many as are residents here, assembled for the *zautrenia* [midnight Easter service, Tr.] the old and the young, and even the most ancient oldsters came and eagerly stood throughout the entire morning service and even through the Liturgy [which followed]. The day and the night were clement; clear and calm, especially so in the night, which made it possible to complete the procession with the Cross around the church tent.

1851

February 21:

I continued to be busy as yesterday, but in addition I was engaged in instruction of newly-converting Heathen, who made known last Sunday their desire to be christened. These are a man, a local resident, and his family. He remained so far [unbaptized] mostly because of the lack of firm belief and the presence of doubts, as he himself confessed to me now openly, saying: ''I heard this preaching long since (during my travel downstream along the Kvikhpak in the year 1846, in the summer camp Kakagmiut, which is recorded in the journal under the appropriate date). I did not reject it outright, but I believed that all this was an invention and I left it alone. But presently I became convinced that Christianity is not an idle invention, but God's work''. With him, too, were two very old women, local residents, who up until this time evaded baptism, remaining in doubt. I grieved greatly about these old women, grieved that they remain unbaptized, and was afraid that they might pass into eternity in this state, but the Lord heard my prayer, uttered by a sinner, and converted them. They were joined by some persons from other settlements and one man from the Kuskokwim, of the Kal'kagmiut settlement, who happened to be here on his own business.

February 22:

Continued with the usual activities, that is church services; again I was engaged with those but newly converting, explaining to them the essential meaning of the conversion and taught them about the Christian faith, the Law, the mysteries and so on. Then I performed over them, a total of 9 souls (5 of the male, 4 of the female sex) the Holy Baptism; to wit, one entire family mentioned earlier [of whom only the man's wife postponed baptism to another time due to feminine infirmity), 2 old women, of whom one is blind, 2 from downstream village and one Kuskokwim man.

Remark:

I cannot express the spiritual joy I experienced when I christened the above named people, in spite of all my infirmities and ailments. This joy is given me from above, and is the greater because now in the local settlement all residents (except one woman who is to be baptized later) are now Christened and none remain heathen. I, as I said earlier, grieved especially for the two old women who remained in the state of heathenism, to the peril of their souls, but now even they are Christians, joined their brethren, the Christians [here] and are so strong in their faith that they desire, together with all the rest of the newly converted, to prepare themselves for partaking in the Holy Mysteries. Glory and Thanks be to Lord God in this!

February 23:

Performed the church services and was engaged in instruction of those who were preparing for communion, confessed them and prepared them for communion tomorrow, if God be willing. The laborers continued to work at their tasks, insofar as it was possible, without my supervision. These days the weather is poor and snowy. Most [of the laborers] are busy clearing snow around the dwellings and at the construction site.

February 24:

Saturday. Performed the appropriate Divine services. At the Hours [*obednitsa*], held in the house, joined all those who prepared themselves to the Holy Mysteries, a total of 60 persons of both sexes, and thanks be to God all went well and I completed the action without any [spiritual] care. I cannot remain silent and not mention the eagerness and diligence of those who have prepared themselves for communion. Willingly, diligently, they came to every service (the morning service, the Hours and the evening service), in spite of the foul weather which continued throughout the last few days, and listened to the sermons without being bored, patiently bore the necessity to stand during a long period of time, which earlier they could not endure. Now they are used to it, stand quietly, with proper comportment, without making any noise. God, grant that they evidence the same piety in the church [when it is built, Tr.]!

At the evening service I offered a special instructional word to the communicants, speaking about Christian piety and various Christian rites.

Remark:

I think it appropriate to mention here that this winter season I have been treating the sick in very considerable numbers, mostly in the local settlement where I reside permanently. Rarely a day passes when no one calls on me to treat the sick. There are plenty of those sick hereabouts, with various illnesses. The same occurred during my entire sojourn at the K[almakovskii] redoubt, where I had to treat plenty of the employees residing there. Moreover, there is now hereabouts, as it happens every year when spring approaches, sickness resembling somewhat an epidemic. The sickness is manifested in a cough, headache, throatache, and severe nasal cold and congestion. I myself did not escape this sickness, neither did all who live with me, but it is passing, without endangering [us] further, through God's grace, and we give our thanks to God for it. But the natives, seeing that medicines which I give do help, ceaselessly come running to me asking for aid and treatment. I respond diligently, wherever possible. Thus, I, myself, plagued by illness, am constrained to treat the illnesses of others.

March 18:

Sunday. Held, insofar as I was able, the Divine service in the house. [At the service] I gave a sermon addressed to the Faithful and the natives, that is I explained to them the Gospels [text] read today, on the topic of [Divine] joy [*blazhenstvo*].

March 19:

Everyone worked. Two were sawing, two clerics continued on their task of inserting the window frame logs [*kolody*], while I, together with the rest [of the workers] began shingling [*obshivat'*] the octagon. The snow and wind interfered with our work, but what is one to do? The work needs to be done!

March 20:

Because of foul weather, with snow and wind, there was no work outside. All worked in the shed, cutting and planing the roofing boards [shingles].

March 21:

Today, too, it was impossible to work outdoors, a strong wind with snow and rain hinders the work, though everyone did work in the shed.

March 22:

The weather was clear and everyone worked outside. Two clerics continued with their task, while I and the rest worked on the top, shingling the octagon.

NB.:

With the arrival here of I. Serebrennikov from the A[andreevskaia] odinochka, we received news from the Mikh[ailovskii] redoubt that all is well there, and the same at the Andreevsk[aia] odinochka. However, unpleasant rumors are flying about the attack by the savages [*dikie*] on the Nulato odinochka, already mentioned. [The rumors are disturbing] the more so, as the savages intend to spread [their attack] further, along the Unalaklit trail, or along the Kvikhpak, with the same evil intent. Therefore the manager of the redoubt, as he informs me, has sent new people to the Nulato odinochka in order to learn how the attack ended, and what are the consequences, and if the employees there are alive and so on, but he has not as yet heard from them. He is apprehensive that in the summer season, after the Kvikhpak River opens up, the savages might proceed downstream along the Kvikhpak which might reach the local settlement and my habitation and presence here. However, all is as God wills!

April 8:

On the Bright and Shining Resurrection of Christ I performed the appropriate services in the field church. There was a great assembly of people, as all the local residents who were in dispersal, came [home] for this Feast. However, I must say that it was only with great difficulty that I was able to celebrate the services, because of very severe cold and hard frost. It is so cold that not only I, the sinner, was barely able to stand through the morning service (I am completely exhausted by suffering from a cold) but it was very difficult for all. All Faithful, however, ignored the difficulty, praying eagerly, with diligence, as I could see this. We were aided in [our prayers] by the night, which was still, so that even the smallest candles did not go out in the course of the procession with the Cross and the meeting of the Resurrected Christ. Seeing all this, I, too stopped feeling [the cold] and together with the Faithful, rejoiced in my spirit, and prayed with them, and spent the entire day holding the services at which there was a great multitude of people. Glory to God in this!

April 9:

On the following two days, I also performed the appropriate Divine services in the field church, but then I stopped to hold services, as my health does not permit me to serve. Besides there are urgent tasks [requiring my attention].

April 11:

We began to work on the construction. The laborers prepared the lumber [shingles] while the clerics worked on the door frame logs.

Today, toward evening, the natives invited me to visit them at their kazhim, specifically to hold instructional conversation [*dlia nazidatel'noi besedy*]. I spent considerable time there with them, in pleasant conversation. I spoke about the commemoration of the event of the Resurrection of our Savior, J[esus] Christ, recounting everything in proper sequence, then talked about the Lord's Ascension, and the Shining Appearance of the Holy Spirit over the Apostles [descent of the Holy Spirit onto the Apostles], the spread of the Christian faith throughout the world and to all peoples, and so on.

March 18:

All, except one laborer who is sick, were working. Two were sawing, the rest together with the clerics worked around the church, laying the pavement.

March 19:

All, except the one who is sick, worked the same as before. I am very ill these days, so that I spent the entire day at home, in bed. I am not able even to sit up.

March 21:

Today I baptized an infant, born to a local resident, a native on the 8th of this month. At the same time, I baptized 3 minors, one boy and two girls, of whom two were brought for baptism by their brothers, while the second girl was brought by her own father, a Kuskokwim man, as I have mentioned on the 24th of February, the one who resettled here together with his entire family. Now only his wife remains unbaptized.

The laborers were hewing all the timbers felled yesterday in the forest, though they were hindered by snowy, raw weather.

1852

March 24:

I continued to hold appropriate Divine services in the church, and all the remaining residents commenced preparation for communion. This very day I sang the funeral service for the infant, baptized on the 21st, who died on the 22nd.

March 25:

On the Feast Day of the Annunciation of the All Holy Theotokos, performed the Divine services [as they ought to be performed], and [I] was deeply touched spiritually, as there were Faithful in attendance both at the early morning service [*zautrenia*] and at the noon service [*obednia*]. As the services were not long, the native Faithful stood throughout very well, with great eagerness and goodwill. I offered them a sermon on the subject of this Feast and the Great Festive days which are now with us [Passion Week].

March 28:

On Great Friday, at the services confessed those who were preparing for communion, a total of 30 persons of both sexes. Besides, I was also preparing for baptism tomorrow those who were converting out of Heathenism to Christianity and intended to be christened and were preparing themselves for baptism for a long time.

March 29:

On Great Saturday I performed the services in the proper manner, and prior to the Liturgy (before noon) I performed the Holy Baptism over 6 persons from various settlements who have assembled here: 3 of the male and 3 of the female sex. [NB. They came with S. Lukin for the holidays.]

March 30:

The day of the Bright and Shining Resurrection of Christ, who rose from the dead through God's Grace and benevolent will, was for the first time here celebrated as it really ought to be, in the Church and with such masses of people congregated that the Church was full. The Faithful were at the morning [midnight] service and also at the Liturgy, and the evening service. I conducted the service without any obstacles from the cold, celebrated freely, with soul's content and joy. I was touched to the heart seeing the Faithful who were praying, they who but a short while ago were heathen.

I cannot help but mention with what diligence, good will and eagerness the Faithful, both the local residents and the visitors, were coming to church, to every service throughout Passion Week, and praying, not only those who partook of communion, but all, including those who have already communicated earlier continued to come to church up to the Paschal days. Then on the Day of Pascha, so many people congregated here! Yesterday many came from the Kuskokwim, and from K. redoubt with S. Lukin, the manager. The celebration of the service in the church apparently attracts the natives. Attendance at the services convinces them, through the beauty and order of the services. This for them constitutes an object of curiosity. Glory and Thanks be to God for everything!

September 9:

In the morning I dispatched all my people, the workmen to tow driftwood, the sub-deacon K. Lukin to shoot caribou. However, in the afternoon I received news that the ship came to the Mikhailovskii redoubt, arriving on the 14th of August and leaving on the 22nd. I also received a packet from the Novoarkhangel'sk consistory, forwarded to me by the manager of the Mikhailovskii redoubt, containing 8 orders [ukazy] regarding various matters—and that is all. I received nothing else. I am sorry that I left without waiting for the ship to arrive, but what to do now? The news I received presently, puts me into great difficulty. First of all, I must fetch from the Mikhailovskii redoubt items which were brought there for the Church and secondly, goods for the mission should be brought here, but how? The season is late; to fetch the things in winter, we lack the means, especially from Mikhailovskii redoubt, though even to do so from Andreevskaia odinochka is somewhat difficult. Therefore, I have decided to send the baidara to Mikhailovskii redoubt to fetch the cargo and bring as much as possible at least up to the Andreevskaia odinochka. But the people are not at home; I must re-assemble them. In the evening I sent off natives to notify my workmen and the sub-deacon K. Lukin to return here. I have decided to send the baidara under sub-deacon K. Lukin and my nephew Vasia and with my workmen, should I fail to find volunteers among the natives. In the meantime, I began to prepare dispatches to the manager of the Mikhailovskii redoubt.

September 10:

My workmen returned from the forest in the morning, but the sub-deacon failed to return during the entire day. The time, however, is so precious that not a minute can be lost. Therefore, I changed my plans and determined to leave myself immediately with my workmen. Repaired whatever was necessary on the baidara and made fully ready to leave, deciding to leave the sub-deacon here at the homestead together with my nephew and one workman. I left for them instructions what to do during my absence and what to attend to.

Departure from Ikogmiut and the Journey to St. Michael's Redoubt

September 11:

In the morning, after prayer to God, I departed in company with 5 of my workmen and the sacristan Gol'tsyn. I am leaving, as mentioned already, the sub-deacon K. Lukin at home (though he has not yet returned) and with him my nephew Vasia and one of the Aleut workmen.

We continued on our voyage throughout the day, passing the settlements, except that we took on 2 natives as oarsmen to fill out the complement [crew] of the baidara. We did not stop in the evening either, continuing on through the night. Thus,

September 12:

In the morning we arrived at the Andreevskaia odinochka. The day was spent here, the people resting and doing necessary repairs. However, during the night a fresh E wind began to blow, accompanied by rain.

September 13:

Though the wind continued fresh, the weather was a bit clearer and I decided to press on. Continued travelling through the day, with fair wind, along the arm of the Kvikhpak. During the night we entered the

September 14:

Apkhun and stopped until morning. We went on in the morning and safely traversed the entire length of the Apkhun and passed the mouth of the Pastol' River. In the evening, we stopped for the night on the other side of the river mouth.

Remark:

A pious and God fearing person will understand and know perhaps what were my inner feelings and what pain of the heart I suffered this day. How sorry [I felt] that the circumstances forced me to be on this day away from my church and the pleasure of celebrating the Divine service in the Temple of the Feast [v Prestol'nom Khrame]. What can one do? In accordance with my sins and my unworthiness, the Lord so ruled. Work Thy Will, Oh Lord! [Note: This is the date of the Feast of the Exaltation of the Holy Cross, and the Feast Day of the church Netsvetov built at Ikogmiut, Tr.].

September 15:

Though the wind blew contrary, it was light and I started out, under oars, along Pastol' Bay. About midway along the bay, the wind freshened and the seas began to run high. It became impossible to row. We turned directly to shore and landed. Here we unloaded the baidara and dragged her up the shore, as the breakers [*burun*] and shallow water did not allow that she be left afloat in the water.

September 16:

We went on in the morning, under a light breeze, but all the time under oars. We passed the cape Aziachiak and continued along the second half of the bay, also under a light breeze, under oars. By nightfall we entered the Kanava. We continued along the Kanava without stopping through the night. Having traversed the entire length of the Kanava

September 17:

We arrived safely at about 7 o'clock at the Mikhailovskii redoubt. Having unloaded the baidara and dragged her out on shore, my people and I spent the day resting after the arduous journey.

September 18:

I spent the entire day receiving cargo for the Mission from the store [*lavka*]: whatever is assigned for the church and provisions and goods for [my] people, all in sufficient quantity.

September 19:

This day I celebrated the Liturgy on request of the residents in order to admit to communion of the Holy Mysteries all the infants. I also celebrated one marriage, for a Kad'iak Aleut just arrived and in residence now here. The rest of the day I was engaged on business matters with the manager.

September 20:

Today I was busy settling the final accounts with [the manager] as I am by now completely ready for the return trip.

September 21:

In the morning we loaded the baidara and departed close to noon. The manager of Mikhailovskii redoubt assigned to me passengers, to be transported to the Andreevskaia odinochka, a total of 5 souls. He asked me to take them there. We did not travel far during the day, and by nightfall I stopped about halfway along the Kanava.

September 22:

We went on in the morning, left the Kanava and continued along Pastol' Bay under adverse winds. For this reason I put in at the Pitmikhtalik River and spent the night here.

September 23:

We went on in the morning, under a light and favorable wind. En route, we met the boat [lodka] which was safely returning from the Nulato odinochka. I took the opportunity to inquire about the well being of all at the Nulato odinochka as well as at my habitation, Ikogmiut. Having rounded Aziachiak Cape, I continued along the other half of the Pastol' Bay. Though the wind turned contrary, I continued on, without stopping, until nightfall. Having reached the river Pastol'iak, I stopped until the following morning.

September 24:

We continued on in the morning, again under an adverse wind. Having crossed the mouth of the Pastol', we stopped on the other side because of low water.

September 25:

Though we made a start in the morning, the fresh contrary wind and low water kept me back. Having travelled but a short distance, we stopped for the night.

September 26:

We went on in the morning, continuing under a light breeze and by nightfall, near the end of the Apkhun, were forced to stop rather early because of low water, to await the tide. But during the night it became cruelly cold, there was frost, and the water froze fast along the shores.

September 27:

In the morning, with the rising tide, we continued on and by noon reached the mouth of the Apkhun, i.e., we reached the arm of the Kvikhpak. We again stopped early because the fresh contrary wind did not permit us to continue.

September 28:

Because it was impossible to continue, I spent the day here in camp. Snow fell to the depth of 1/4 of an arshin and the cold continues.

September 29:

We set out in the morning, and travelled all day under oars. Stopped by nightfall for the night.

September 30:

Setting out in the morning, we continued to travel through the day, at times under oars, at times under sail. Toward evening, the wind turned fresh but was favorable. Therefore, I continued through the night without stopping. But the night was dark, and as it was not possible to distinguish objects or even river banks, it was dangerous travel. I put into the shore to await the morning.

October 1:

At dawn, I went on, passed the channel [protoka] and the cape [mys] where the Kvikhpak divides itself into [several] arms. However, thick slush and the cold did not permit me to reach the Andreevskaia odinochka during the night. I stopped, not far from it.

October 2:

We went on in the morning and arrived at the Andreevskaia odinochka by noon. We immediately unloaded the baidara and dragged her out on shore for drying out and repairs.*

October 3:

On this date, during the night a most severe frost occurred, so that the entire river iced over [*zastoiala*]. I, however, refloated the baidara in the morning, loaded her immediately and left at once. The wind blew contrary. The baidara moved [sluggishly] against the current; however, there was no time to await a fair wind as all signs indicated that soon I would encounter *shuga.* Therefore we moved on, by tow where possible, otherwise under oars, as I was trying at least to reach a settlement from where the cargo could be transported in winter. I was unable to reach a village today and about

*The passengers I have taken on I brought here safely and delivered them to the baidarshchik.

half way through the night stopped at an uninhabited place. The frost continues, so that through the day, moving without stopping, we had continuously to chip ice off the oars.

October 4:

This day, during the night, the *shuga* appeared and my baidara was stuck in it. What are we to do now? It is impossible to return to the odinochka, it is still a long way to the settlement. We decided, however, that it is better to continue. Thus, having prepared poles and rods with which to break up the *shuga* or to divert ice [floes], we set out. At first, it was difficult as we had to pass through the thickest *shuga;* afterwards, choosing [less congested] places, we travelled all day in this manner and by evening safely reached the village Kanigmiut. The residents have already left, as they winter downstream, along the river Kizhunak [modern Kashunuk River]. And thus I stopped at this empty village. We selected the kazhim as our quarters and settled down to await the [winter] trail.

October 5:

Since morning I was busy with the cargo which we stowed in a summer dwelling. The baidara was dragged out and put up on sawhorses [*na kozly*]. The *shuga* this day became even thicker, covering the entire river. Thus I lived here, from this day on through the 14th. It was no particular hardship to stay here, as far as provisions or bread are concerned: we found means to make bread here: we made in the kazhim a fireplace out of rocks. We started it going often warming ourselves, and baked excellent bread. The rest of the provisions were plentiful, too.

There was one thing, though: the boredom of waiting and worry about our habitation and those resident therein. This caused me to feel sad and sorrowful. But the *shuga* continues to move and there is as yet no trail. My impatience with waiting compelled me to decide to send two men on foot along the shore—that is along the river but beyond the immediate river bank—to the next settlement Ankakhchagmiut. I asked that at first opportunity a sled and dog team be sent to me from there.

October 10:

Today I dispatched one of my workmen, in company with a native who knows the passable trails. However, I instructed them that should the way be impassable, they were not to try to continue but were to return.

Following this, two days passed and the weather turned warm. The *shuga* thinned out. I was awaiting the return of my messengers either along the shore or by the river.

October 13:

Quite unexpectedly, a baidara from the village Ankakhchagmiut arrived here. The starshina Iuda himself accompanied by 7 men came and with them came my messengers. The starshina and all the natives counselled me to go upstream in the baidara to their village, saying that it is quite possible to pass safely between the ice-floes. As far as refloating [my] baidara and loading it with cargo was concerned, they volunteered immediately to attend to it themselves right away. Thus, this very same evening we lowered the baidara to a place where it was easiest to drag her along the ice to open water and then moved the entire cargo and left everything there until morning.

October 14:

Early in the morning we started the process of refloating the baidara and though it was difficult work, we managed everything safely, including loading the baidara. Then we started out. The natives' baidara led the way, I followed behind her: the ice and the *shuga* moved in places along one side of the river [or the other] so that it was necessary to cut across the *shuga* and cross to the other side of the river. We continued in this manner throughout the entire day.

Finally, about midnight, I safely arrived at the settlement. The natives' baidara arrived here earlier. The cruel cold which began yesterday and continued through the day as well as the following night was such that we constantly had to chip off the ice of the oars. The ice formed very rapidly in this frost and very thickly and even the sides of the baidara were iced over. Having reached the settlement, we left the baidara until morning while all of us settled down in the native yurtas.

October 15:

We unloaded the baidara, stowed the cargo in a native yurta and then hauled out the baidara. Then we commenced to await the time and means to go ahead, but the river continued to flow though filled with moving ice. Consequently, it was not possible to travel along the river or even along the shore close to the river. I was told of an alternate route, along the tundra, by which it is possible to reach the next settlement. Unfortunately, the local residents were not able to transport [our] cargo [along this route] for lack of sleds and dogs. I decided to proceed by myself, with a single sled, leaving the cargo behind and in charge N. Bel'kov with two workmen. The rest were to accompany me to look for rentals of sleds and dogs or otherwise to go on to Ikogmiut and to send sleds and dogs from there.

October 18:

In the morning I set out as I planned with a single sled, in the company of a guide who showed us the way. We proceeded just fine, mostly along the lakes, and toward evening came to the village Takchagmiut. Here I was told that it is not possible to go on—the trail has not set yet—and thus it is necessary to stay here awaiting the trail. The local residents, however, agreed to transport here our cargo from Ankakhchagmiut, as they have plenty of sleds that are ready, and plenty of dogs.

October 19:

In the morning I dispatched 8 sleds which I had mustered, and my people and natives. I stayed, in the company of one workman.

October 20:

Toward evening, the sleds I had dispatched returned with the loads. In spite of the fact that the sleds were fully loaded, there still remains cargo to be transported, about 5 sled loads full. For this reason, N. Bel'kov has remained yet with the rest of the cargo. The cargo transported here I stowed in a summer dwelling where we all were quartered.

October 21:

I did not dispatch the sleds for the rest of the cargo today as the sleds were being repaired. Because of overload, many sleds were damaged. The natives were repairing them.

October 22:

In the morning I dispatched 5 sleds for the rest of the cargo, with the natives and two of my own men. They reached their destination early, immediately loaded the sleds and set out on the return trip right away. Thus, they arrived here by midnight. N. Bel'kov came with them also bringing the rest of the cargo. The entire cargo is now unpacked here, while the baidara was left for the winter at Ankakhchagmiut.

October 23:

I issued instructions and made arrangements in respect of the cargo and, leaving here the same N. Bel'kov with 2 workmen, I myself and the rest of my people got ready to go on by means of two sleds, though the river directly opposite the settlement is not yet stationary. It is assumed that upstream it is by now fast. Having decided [on this course of action], we left about 10 o'clock in the morning. I travelled well and safely, though at times it was difficult to follow along the trails [*torizi,* archaic, plural—cut trails]. Already late in the evening, I reached the settlement Ingigagmiut and stopped here until morning. There were but few of the inhabitants on hand.

October 24:

I set out in the morning, going forward, as from here on the way is clear: as I am told, the river already has been stationary for a long time. I continued travelling all day long and by evening came to the winter village Niukhliuagmiut where we stayed overnight. Here are some of the Ikogmiut residents and with them toion Iakov. All is well here.

October 25:

In the morning I went on, but the warm weather which set in already yesterday ate through the snow and today it rained. Everywhere, water stood over the ice and I was able to reach home only with great difficulty. I was wet through and this caused me to catch a cold: I proceeded on foot [I walked] and got very tired, reaching home I felt almost sick. At home I found everyone safe and well and my Vasia [nephew Vasilii Netsvetov] presented me his daily notes which he kept while I was away. I did not find the sub-deacon, K. Lukin at home: he went off, with one sled, downstream in order to find out news about me or where I was. [However, I missed him en route.] It is to be supposed that he passed over along the channel downstream past the village Takchagmiut, and that when he reaches the villages of Ankakhchagmiut or Kanigmiut and receives news about me he will return.

Remark:

From the notes of my nephew Vasilii it is learned that when the natives' assembly took place during my absence, some wild ones once approached our buildings at night, coming out of the woods. Having discerned this by the behavior of the dogs, they scared them off by gunshots (discharged, of course, into the air). Nothing more was heard about them. Of course, the savages [*dikie*], knowing that I am absent, were either trying to scare [my people] or even had it in mind to attack and rob them. But, God save us, so far all is safe and sound.

Sojourn at Ikogmiut

October 26:

Though it was Sunday, I was not able to perform the Divine service in the church. I only held a thanksgiving prayer, offering thanks to Lord God who aided me in completing this arduous trek, or better to say, this journey. Afterwards, I commenced to ready the sleds and dogs to be dispatched for the cargo. It is not possible as yet to send them off, because warm weather, with rain, continues. All stood idle the following two days also.

October 29:

This morning I sent off 8 sleds, as many as I could muster in this village. The frost set in. I sent off all my people and in addition some natives. After I dispatched them, I became ill and was sick the following days, unable to work myself at anything.

November 1:

To this day no one has yet come [returned] and I continue to feel ill. Sub-deacon K. Lukin arrived here during the night and reported to me the following morning.

November 2:

He came with two loaded sleds. His party travelled as far as Kanigmiut and, having learned there that I have passed on my way upstream, returned through the villages. Having reached Takchagmiut, they took on some cargo and proceeded hither.

November 3:

No business was attended to today, as there are on hand only the subdeacon and the workman who came with him, and they both rested.

November 4:

The sleds which I have dispatched returned safely, bringing considerable cargo, though some sleds suffered damage. Not everything has been brought here, cargo for two sleds still remain and for this reason N. Bel'kov stayed behind.

November 5:

I sent three of my workmen and the sacristan with two sleds to fetch the remaining cargo.

November 6:

Sub-deacon K. Lukin set out for the Kalmakovskii redoubt, as I have no one else to send, while it is necessary to deliver there for use in the local chapel, candles and everything else which they need. Besides, I need some information from the manager S. Lukin. In short, our economic needs compelled me to send someone thither. He [sub-deacon Konstantin Lukin] will inform them that I safely reached home. I know that they worry about me.

November 7:

Little by little I am feeling better and today I was busy writing, but even that only a bit. Three of the workmen were sawing firewood.

November 8:

On the Royal Festival Day, I was barely able to perform the Divine service and the Te Deum, and then only with the aid of the heated fireplace [*s pomoshch'iu kamina*]. The natives have all dispersed, to fish for lampreys. Lamprey fishing began on November 5.

November 9:

On this day of Sunday held a simple Divine service, but there were few Faithful in attendance, as the natives are not at home.

The following few days I was busy exclusively with writing, and the three workmen were putting up firewood. The rest, dispatched for the cargo, have not yet returned.

November 11:

The weather turned warm, but the same day the wind blew fresh, accompanied with snow.

November 12:

This day, towards evening, the two sleds dispatched for cargo returned safely. N. Bel'kov came with them, bringing the last of the load. Now, Glory be to God! Everything is at our place, and though with great difficulty and large expenditures on my part the entire cargo has been brought here. Still, thanks be to God, all ended safely and everyone is well. Now we can attend to other business.

1853

Remark:

Today the Chag'liuk toion Aleksandr Kantil'nuk arrived here in a baidara. He is travelling to the Andreevskaia odinochka on his own business. [He] asked when I intend to come to him this season or to travel along the Chag'liuk River in order to reach the Kol'chane who inhabit the upper reaches of this river, that is, to the villages whose inhabitants have come down along the Chag'liuk River and were waiting me in the settlement of the Toion Kantil'nuk. A number of them have visited here in the previous year, in the last days of May, and have accepted baptism. As this season the inhabitants are making use of the early clearing of the Kvikhpak River, I decided to travel thither on the 15th. When I made my decision known to him [Chief Kantil'nuk] and asked if I might proceed without him and count on locally available aid for travel to the settlements along the upper Chag'liuk, he said that I can count on his son travelling with me to the Kol'chane territory. I shall have need of him as a second [second language] interpreter. He helped me proceed thither, saying further that the local inhabitants in all probability will assemble in one settlement or another to await my arrival, which I have promised the visitors from there to do last year. After our conversation, this very same evening he went on downstream toward his destination. I commenced preparations for departure.

May 14:

The workmen continued the usual tasks at the construction and sawing. I completed today all preparations for departure. I am taking along from among the clerics the sub-deacon K. Lukin and my nephew Vasia. I am leaving the sacristan Gol'tsyn at the church here. All the workmen remain here in charge of creole N. Bel'kov. Only the adolescent Silitr [?] Zakharov is coming with me, the rest of my companions are local natives.

Departure from Ikogmiut and the Journey

May 15:

Having prayed to Lord God asking for His aid and blessing, we left Ikogmiut about noon, travelling in two three-hatch baidarkas going upstream along the Kvikhpak River. I was accompanied by the Ikogmiut zakazchik Pavel Kintil'nuk [Kantil'nuk] who travelled in his own three-hatch baidarka and by natives in their own baidara. Thus, our party consisted of 4 oar-propelled vessels. The only obstacle, of no great significance, was the driftwood and debris carried by the current which we encountered in the stream. About 4 o'clock in the afternoon we passed the settlement Ikalivagmiut where there were but a few people on hand. Going on a not very great distance, I stopped for the night at an uninhabited place.

May 16:

We went on at 5 o'clock in the morning and continued travelling through the day, meeting nothing and no one—just the driftwood and debris. By evening, having reached the summer location belonging to the Paimiut village, we stopped for the night. There were residents here.

May 17:

In the morning at 6 o'clock we went on and continued travelling through the day. About noon we entered the channel of the Chag'liuk River [Shagaluk Slough], that is, travelled through the islands, at the mouth of the said river. In the evening we entered the real river Chag'liuk [var. Chalgliuk] where, beginning at the river's mouth, I began meeting the nomadizing residents of the village Anilukhtakhpak who have begun the spring fish catch of the fish sigi [plural, whitefish]. I stopped for the night when I reached the summer camp [*stanov'e*] of their toion Konstantin Napugak. I received from him various necessary intelligence about their well being and so on.

May 18:

I went on at 7 o'clock, travelling along the river Chag'liuk. The above mentioned toion left with me, as he wanted to accompany me and, should the need arise, be of help. We continued travelling throughout the entire day and about 5 o'clock, going on evening, came to the place of residence of the toion of Chag'liuk, Aleksandr Kantil'nuk. Here we stopped for the night. As stated earlier, the toion himself is not in residence. His son, Nikolai Knikhtaiuli, is here, with two families. The rest of the people are all in dispersal along this river.

May 19:

I set out at 6 o'clock in the morning. On my invitation, the said toion's son Nikolai accompanied me: I need him as a second [second language?] interpreter, for [communication with] Ingalit [Ingalik] and with the Kol'chane [Kolchan]. My interpreter, sub-deacon K. Lukin, does not know this language. We continued to travel through the day, without stopping, meeting up at various places the local inhabitants who are nomadizing, and are busy with fishing. About 4 o'clock in the afternoon I arrived at the [permanent] Chag'liuk settlement. Here I met three Kol'chane men, who travelled hither from upstream and were awaiting my arrival in order to notify their compatriots. Immediately upon my arrival, two of them set out up the river, the third stayed.

May 20:

Though it was my intent to travel through [all] the Kol'chane settlements, I have learned that on their own initiative the Kol'chane [Kolchan] gathered in the lowest village Kholiachagmiut in order to come to this settlement upon my arrival here. Thus, I settled down to await them here. In the meantime, I was busy with those who were newly converting whom I met in the course of my first visit here in the year 1851, but who remained [unbaptized] because they went off [in dispersal on hunting and fishing]. In the morning I preached the Word of God and then, according to their faith and express desire I performed over them the christening, a total of 15 persons (9 of the male and 6 of the female sex). Among those who became christened was the Kol'chane who stayed behind yesterday. Besides these, I christened an infant, born in the past year to Christians. Then I waited for the arrival from upstream. They came by evening, in birchbark boats [canoes] and in baty [wooden large canoes] and one baidara. I counted up to a hundred of such canoes and boats [*baty*], as they came all together, at once, so that the river Chag'liuk was covered in its entire width with the canoes and boats.

After the Kol'chane have arrived, the starshina of the Nagistuligmiut settlement, Ivan Nikunitsagi, who became christened at Ikogmiut last year, came to me with a visit and declared that all the Kol'chane from the lowest villages have come, and also part of those living along the river Tlachina, together with their families and that they have been joined by a number of Ingalit [Ingalik] from the river Kvikhpak who reside near Nulato in various localities, also accompanied by their families, who came to them, at the time they were leaving hither, via the channel [*protoka*—slough] and who are called Tseiaki [plural?]. I questioned the starshina about whatever was necessary and left the rest for tomorrow.

Remark:

Action taken in respect to these people is described in special extracts.

May 21:

Beginning in the morning, upon my invitation, all the Kol'chane and the Ingalit [Ingalik] from the Kvikhpak and the local ones gathered at my place and I preached the Word of God, continuing beyond the noon hour. Everyone listened to the preaching with attention and apparent [inserted above the line, next word illegible] . . . without the least statement to the contrary or argument and in the end they all expressed faith without doubt and their wish to accept the Holy Baptism, both the Kol'chane [Kolchan] and the Ingalit [Ingalik]. I made a census, by families and kin groups, and then in the afternoon began the act of baptism. First of all, I baptized 50 adult persons of the male sex, Kol'chane and Ingalit, the latter from Kvikhpak and Chag'liuk. This act was finished already when it was evening.

May 22:

I began the act of baptism in the morning and prior to noon baptized 72 persons, adults of the female sex; in the afternoon I baptized the older children, of those who were newly christened, 54 persons. The act was finished by evening. A total of 126 persons were baptized today (33 of the male, 93 of the female sex). From this activity [adjective, illegible] I became dreadfully tired and by evening felt [middle] pains from prolonged standing.

Besides the days at this season are clear and hot and this is very tiring. However, the Spiritual joy at the sight of so many souls joined to the flock of the Christian Church made up for everything and the bodily weaknesses became unfelt, and [two words illegible] when in the night I made the written record of the action taken.

May 23:

Prior to noon I again performed baptisms, christening the smaller children and the infants whom the newly christened parents willingly brought forth to be christened. I also anointed with myrrh [chrismated] the family of a Kol'chane, a wife and daughter, who were baptized in 1846 by Semen Lukin. The total of souls who joined the Church of Christ today is 36 (17 males and 19 females). Besides them, I baptized an infant, born to Christians during the past year. This concluded the act of baptism, everyone became christened, with the exception of two women whom it was impossible to baptize [in all probability, the women were menstruating at the time, Tr.]. Afterwards I started on written business and continued to be busy with it the entire day.

May 24:

Since morning I was again busy with written matters, as it was necessary, besides this record, to write out many certificates for all those but newly christened. As it was Sunday, I then held a service to God, in the open field. All those newly christened, all that are here present, attended and prayed. One must imagine the joy in my heart at the sight of so many souls gathered in one place (there were more than 300), praying to God, people of various nations [*raznoplemennye narody*], formerly living in strife with each other, enemies, now united as Christ's Church's flock, offering prayers to the true God. After the service I offered them a sermon, as to the reborn children, first declaring why I held such a communal prayer, that is explaining that today is Sunday. Then I taught them the Christian law, taught about prayer, Christian love and virtues, but most of all about human kindness [love of Man—*chelovekoliubie*], about peaceful and cordial coexistence of all peoples and so on. Afterwards, and when I finished writing, on my invitation once again everyone gathered before me and I gave out the certificates [of baptism]. Then I gave a final sermon for their instruction. Thus I finished my activity with them at 4 o'clock in the afternoon and then commenced preparations for my departure. They, too, began to disperse, but all of them first came to me for my blessing. I left at 5 o'clock on my return trip along the [river] Chag'liuk. All my companions came along with me. Travelling with the current, we moved very fast and by 10 o'clock at night we arrived in the village of the toion A. Kantil'nuk. He has not yet returned. Here I stopped until morning. His son, Nikolai Knikhtaiuli remained here. He helped me very much yesterday during all my engagements with those who were newly converting, translating whatever I said for the Ingalit and for the Kol'chane and for this I remain grateful, very much so.

1860

April 2:

The same on the Great Saturday, performed the services.

April 3:

On the day of Bright and Shining Christ's Resurrection performed the Divine services as they ought to be held. The day was warm, but it snowed the entire day, with wet snow.

I continued to hold services in the Church the following three days, then stopped because of illness, mostly because of the cough which plagued me, the entire Passion week and these [Feast] days. I sent my clerics out to hunt caribou.

April 9:

Today I received news from the manager of the Kalmakovskii redoubt, I. Lukin, that during his absence from the redoubt, the crew [command] there mutinied. The company employees Ivan Andreianov and Neofit Riazantsev aroused the entire command against the manager [blaming him for] the scarcity of food that they are suffering. Manager I. Lukin asked my help in liquidating the mutiny. It was absolutely impossible for me to go there in person and quiet the [company] employees and other residents of the redoubt. However, I wrote a letter addressed to all residents of the redoubt, reasoning and persuading them. The very next day, on the 10th, I sent the letter there, dispatching with it my sub-deacon K. Lukin who was charged to read the letter in my name, to be heard by all residents of the redoubt.

Thus, my entire clergy being away, I was not able to perform appropriate Divine services on the Sunday of St. Thomas.

April 15:

Today, with the return of my sub-deacon K. Lukin, I received from the entire command of the Kalmakovskii redoubt a petition addressed to me. They acknowledged their transgression against the superior authority, the grumbling and dissatisfaction which they demonstrated, and stated that they took to heart my admonitions and in the future will be obedient in respect to higher authority.

1861

April 16:

On Palm Sunday I performed the Divine service. The Te Deum, which ought to be celebrated tomorrow, I held today. I served but with great difficulty and yet I must continue to hold services in this last Lenten Passion Week. Such is the need, but I do not know how the Lord will let me complete [the service cycle]. My eye affliction is worse, I cannot see with one eye at all.

The following days I continued to hold services.

Remark:

I find it necessary to state here the following: since the month of January of this year I have begun to suffer with an eye ailment, both eyes were painful. In the beginning this was bearable and I supposed that it was a temporary condition, that my eyes would get better. I treated myself with eye compresses with solutions I have on hand in my pharmacy. However, in the end it happened that I could not see anything at all with one eye and this constitutes a great obstacle in reading or writing; what will happen with the second eye in the future, I do not know. Please God, may I not become totally blind.

April 19:

This day I confessed those who were preparing themselves for communion, a total of 20 persons, among them all the clerics.

April 20:

This day, Great Thursday, performed the appropriate Divine service and joined in the Holy Mysteries the 20 persons who have prepared themselves and all the infants. Then I continued to hold appropriate services.

April 23:

On the Bright and Shining Day of Christ's Resurrection, I held all the appropriate Divine services and also the Te Deum which ought to have been celebrated on the 21st of this month on the Royal and Most Solemn Festival Day. Thanks be to God, all was completed well. The day was cold, though clear.

The following two days, I was able to continue services, but then had to stop because of severe eye pain. I suffer very much from the eye affliction, and can barely see with one eye only.

The days continue to be clear, but cold in the mornings.

In the next days I was absolutely unwell, in my entire body, but especially with my eyes. I sent out my clerics to hunt caribou and geese. The latter appeared here on the 18th of this month.

Being very ill, I was unable to celebrate the services on the 30th, the Feast Day of the Apostle Thomas. These days the weather continues poor, it snows and is wet.

May 1:

The same weather prevailed, it snowed, and it was wet. Along the Kvikhpak, leads are beginning to open near the banks, but few, so that it is yet safe to walk on the ice.

In the following days, the Mission's ekonom [household manager] N. Bel'kov and the workmen were building a new three-hatch baidarka. The rest are all away, hunting.

May 7:

Sunday. Performed the services, such as my strength permitted.

May 9:

(marginal comment by Bishop Petr: ''What happened to May 8th?'') On the Feast Day of the Church Teacher Nicholas the Miracleworker, I performed the Divine service, as my strength permitted, and a Te Deum.

In the following days I had to take to my bed, as I began to suffer very much from internal pain so that I was unable to sit up to write. I am forced to keep to my bed. For this reason I was unable also to hold services on the following Sunday (the week of the Paralytic).

The river is still yet, the leads are forming slowly, because the temperature is not high yet. The cool weather, with overcast skies, continues. I am still very sick.

At St. Michael's

1863

March 24:

On Palm Sunday, celebrated the Divine service in the chapel, as is proper.

March 25:

Also on this Feast Day of the All Holy Theotokos, celebrated the Divine service by the rule [*po ustavu*], in accordance with the church regulations. The day was again cold, with wind and snow.

These days of the Passion week I continued to hold services but with great difficulty because of the very high wind and cold. Especially on the

26th, the wind increased. One was barely able to go outside. Besides, there was a snow storm.

March 27:

This day I confessed those who were preparing themselves for communion, a total of 15 persons, and celebrated the Divine service as it ought to be.

March 28:

On the Great [Holy] Thursday, celebrated the appropriate Divine service and at the Liturgy joined in the Holy Mysteries all those who have prepared themselves.

NB.:

Today the weather continued very stormy; fresh wind with snow, so that it is difficult to walk down street to the chapel. Being unwell, I fulfilled my duty but with great effort, continuing the churchly services.

Continued to hold Divine services, as is proper, all the days following, though with difficulty, one might say because of illness but also because of severe strong winds and stormy weather.

March 31:

On the Day of the Bright and Shining Resurrection of Christ celebrated the appropriate Divine services, but the weather continued to be as stormy as in the preceeding days with wind, snow and cold up to 17 degrees. It was difficult to walk about outside.

April 1:

This day and the next, the 3rd day of the Paskha [Pachalia] I performed the Divine services, but then was unable to continue to do so, because ill health and general weakness of my body do not permit me to do so. The weather cleared but the cold increased to above 20 degrees.

April 5:

Beginning this date, the weather turned warm again, and it snowed again. In the mornings the cold is up to 10 degrees.

April 7:

On the Sunday of the Holy Apostle Thomas, celebrated the Divine service. The weather was snowy, the cold 12 degrees.

The bad weather continued in the next days. Incessant snow and cold.

These days I suffer greatly in my legs, very painful in the bones [joints] and greatly swollen. I am able to walk only with difficulty.

The following week the weather was snowy, the cold up to 10 degrees. I am busy with written matters, but am unable to sit up for any length of time because of illness.

April 14:

On the Sunday of the Women bearing Myrrh I performed the Divine service. The day was bright, but the cold in the morning was 13 degrees. My leg ailment continues. I can walk or even stand only with great effort.

The following days the weather continued clear, with cold in the mornings from 10 to 12 degrees. I am suffering from my leg ailment, pain and swelling and cannot even get up. The paramedic [*fel'dsher*] Panshin, who examined me, says that this illness is something in the nature of scurvy, which often strikes [people] here at the Mikhailovskii redoubt in the spring. On his advice, I am not supposed to sit at home over my work, but constantly walk about and exercise. Though it is difficult, I walk with effort, until I am unable to continue, and am exhausted to the limit of my strength. For this reason, I stopped work on written matters.

April 17:

On this Most Solemn and High Royal Festival Day, I celebrated the Divine service and the Te Deum. It was very difficult for me to stand though because of my leg ailment. The cold this day and the days following continues to be from 5 to 8 degrees, with clear weather.

On the following, the 18th and 19th of the month, the days continued clear, the cold in the mornings was above 5 degrees. I am plagued by the leg ailment, and am barely able to go on walking, against my will.

April 21:

On the Sunday of the Paralytic, celebrated the Divine service, but with difficulty, because of my leg ailment. The day was bright but cold; in the morning the cold was 5 degrees.

The clear weather continued through the days following, but with increased cold in the mornings, from 15 to 18 degrees. I am in serious condition, unable to attend to any business. I am not able even to sit up. The legs ache so that I am unable even to put down my left foot.

April 24:

Today the cleric [reader] from the Ikogmiut Mission [Zakharii Bel'kov] arrived here. He was sent by the Missionary, Father Ilarion, to fetch the needed provisions, obtaining them from the local manager. He informed me that they attempted a journey hither in the month of March, intending to proceed from here to the Nushagak odinochka. They had to turn back from the trail because of insufficient means and lack of dogs. For the rest, they are well, except that food supplies are scarce and they subsist on the local produce. This lack is aggravated by the fact that under-the-ice fishing along the Kvikhpak is, this season, almost nil.

April 28:

On the Sunday of the Samaritan I was already unable to perform the Divine service, as with my leg ailment I could not stand through the service. I am only able to move about a little at home. The paramedic who is resident in this redoubt is employing every possible means to help me, but I am getting no better. I get up with great effort and move with difficulty.

The weather in the next few days continued cold (from 5 to 12 degrees in the morning) and not completely clear. At times it would clear and then grow overcast again. There was also rain mixed with snow.

May 5:

On the Sunday of the Blind Man I was also unable to celebrate the Divine service, as I am still unable to stand in one spot for any length of time. I can move about a bit, forced against my will, with great effort. I am also unable to sit up and, according to the medic, I ought not to either. The pain in my legs is severe, and it, together with the swelling, exhausts me. No remedy is effective. I am nowadays unable to do anything, not even attend to writing.

The following days the weather was clear, but cold, in the mornings the cold is more than 5 degrees by thermometer. Even at midday it does not turn warm. For this reason there is even at this time no real hunting for any kind of fowl or geese. Though they have come, they appear but seldom and then only a few of them.

May 9:

On the Feast Day of the Lord's Ascension and the Church Teacher, St. Nicholas the Miracleworker, I celebrated the Divine service and Te Deum. My ailments, however, do not lessen, and I am unable either to stand, walk or sit. Consequently, I served only with difficulty. For this reason I could not bring myself to celebrate the Divine service on the following Sunday.

Remark:

During my illness, while unable to celebrate the church services, I instructed the creole Egor Shushakov and my sacristan Dionisii [Denis]

Bel'kov to perform the simple laymen's services in the chapel in order to give the local residents the opportunity to participate in common prayer.

May 10:

This day and the days following I suffered terribly with my leg ailment. Not to speak of walking, I was unable even to sit and attend to work while sitting. It is necessary for me to walk and exercise, and I try—with great difficulty—to do so a little. The days are overcast and cold; from time to time it snows.

May 12:

Sunday. I was unable to celebrate the Divine service because of my leg ailment. Almost all the local employees have left to hunt geese for their own benefit.

The following days I was unable to do anything, not even to sit over my written work. My legs ache so, that walking is barely possible, even at night I have no peace. The days continue overcast, cold, mornings the temperature is from 3 to 6 degrees below zero.

May 15:

This day and the next one the weather was warm and clear. I am unwell.

May 17:

The weather again turned grey, with rain and cold. I continue unwell.

May 19:

On the Feast Day of the Pentecost I was barely able to perform the Divine service, as my leg ailment continues. I stand and walk with great effort, but am unable at all to sit and attend to my work. The medic is in difficulty and unable to help, though he treats me daily with hot compresses and various salves, and does not permit me to sit still and even less to lie down. My only occupation, consequently, is to get up at 2 in the morning, go outside and try to stroll around. Today was overcast and cold.

May 20:

I again celebrated the Divine service and Te Deum on occasion of the Royal Festival Day. The weather through the day shifted from clear to overcast, it was cold. I continued to suffer with my legs very much, unable to stand or sit and work.

In the next few days my state of health grew worse, only with difficulty could I get to my feet. Am absolutely unable to sit and work. Days continue to be clear.

It is cold, though: mornings the temperature is from 3 to 6 degrees below zero.

May 26:

On the Sunday of All Saints I celebrated the Divine service, though my leg ailment continues. For this reason I am unable to sit and work. The day is overcast, with a cold wind. In the morning the cold was 2 degrees. The ice in the bay at the Mikhailovskii redoubt is still firm.

In the following days the weather continued to be cold, overcast, and at times it snowed. The ice in the bay stands immobile. I am still suffering greatly with the leg ailment, unable to sit and work, but force myself, on the fel'dsher's advice, to get up to exercise my legs.

June 2:

Sunday. I did not celebrate the Divine service, first of all because of my leg ailment, and secondly because almost everyone has left the redoubt, going out on their own business to hunt and fish [*na promysly*]. The weather is cold.

INSTRUCTIONS FROM BISHOP INNOCENT VENIAMINOV TO HIEROMONK THEOPHAN, 1853

To leave one's native country and seek places remote, wild, devoid of many of the comforts of life, for the sake of turning to the path of truth men who are still wandering in the darkness of ignorance, and of illuming with the light of the Gospel them that have not yet beheld this saving light.—this is an act truly holy and apostolic. Blessed he whom the Lord selects and appoints to such a ministry! But doubly blessed he who labors with undivided zeal, sincerity and love in the work of conversion and enlightenment, enduring the hardships and sufferings which he encounters in the course of his ministry, for "his reward is great in heaven!" But woe unto him who is called and appointed to tell the good news, and who does not tell it! and woe still more unto him who, after travelling over land and seas to convert men, makes them he has converted into sons of Gehenna, worse than himself!

And so thou, O priest art now appointed to a work for which thou shalt *either* "enter into the joy of the Lord," as a good and faithful servant, *or* receive condemnation, as a false, wicked, and slothful servant. And may the Lord preserve thee from the latter fate and grant thee the will and the strength to compass the former! When thou findest thyself in the place of thy ministry, thy duties shall be many and peculiar:—1-st spiritual, as celebrant at the altar and preacher of the word of God; 2-d temporal, as a member of a well-ordered community's government, and therefore do I here offer thee, for thy guidance, a few instructions bearing on both classes of duties.

Part First
Most Essential Instructions concerning a Missionary's spiritual duties.

The instructions bearing on this subject are very clearly set forth in the *Ukaz* of 1777, in which it is said "that he should not regard as his duty the hasty administration of baptism (to converts), but should do his best to instil into them the force of Christian teaching, and to guide them towards all manner of good morals, without which baptism administered to savages can hardly be called anything but an abuse of one of the greatest Sacraments of the Christian religion."

I.
Preparation to Missionary Work.

1) The first and most efficient preparation is *prayer,* which alone can open the spring of highest teaching and bring down a blessing upon every good beginning and work. Therefore always, and especially before addressing those whom thou wishest to illumine with the light of truth, turn towards God in ardent prayer.

2) Cultivate always a modest and lowly spirit, and do not presumptuously promise thyself extraordinary or certain success in thy labors. Such expectations proceed from pride, and grace is not granted unto the proud. Remember always that the conversion of a sinner or a heathen to the right path cometh not from us or from our skill, but directly and solely from God. If it be His pleasure to convert anybody, then the simplest words (so they be full of the truth), from the lips of a simple reader will touch the hearer's heart and sink deep into it, and bear fruit in due time. If it be not His pleasure,—the most convincing words from the lips of the greatest orator will have no saving effect. For we all, from the first to the last, are nothing but tools in the hands of God.

3) Every time that thou addressest thyself to thy work, strive to be calm and to have full control of thy faculties, else canst thou not put into words what thou knowest most thoroughly.

4) Do not begin any work without previous thought, and do not perform it in a careless and absent-minded way, for thy work is God's work, and he is accursed that does it negligently.

5) Remember always that if the preacher has not within himself *love* to his work and to them to whom he is preaching, the very best and most eloquent expounding of the doctrine may remain absolutely without effect, for love alone creates,—therefore do thou strive to cultivate within thyself the spirit of holy love.

6) Make it a rule, when thou visitest remote localities (where the foundations of Christianity have already been laid), not to begin any service, nor to administer any Sacrament without first giving to them thou visitest if only some brief instruction.

7) Thou shouldst naturally begin to preach the word of God there where thou hast thy permanent residence. Bnt should circumstances compel thee or opportunity induce thee to visit remoter places, then, even though thou shouldst not as yet have accomplished much among those who live in thy own vicinity, do not miss a chance of going anywhere, and be ready to teach in any place and anybody, according to age, condition and time.

8) Choose for thy teaching and for talks with the natives preferably such times when they are all assembled together. For this purpose thou mayest either go to them, or, if feasible, invite them to come where thou shalt be thyself.

9) At first, while still ignorant of the natives' language, thou shouldst employ an interpreter, to translate thy words for them. Take care to select for the post a man from among the most pious and well-intentioned, and instruct him in good time in the Catechism. It will be best to employ always the same interpreter.

II.
The Order of Preaching.

10) Christianity is a need, and a comfort which appeals principally to the heart, not to the mind alone, and therefore, when instructing in the faith, the teacher should aim at acting more on the heart than on the mind. The mind's curiosity is insatiable; but he who feels in his heart the craving for faith, who tastes of its comfort,—he will receive it quickly and with ease, and it shall not remain within him barren of fruits. But in order to act on other men's hearts, a man must speak from his own heart. "From out of the abundance of the heart the mouth speaketh". Hence his lips and wisdom only shall prove irresistible to the hearts of his hearers, whose own heart overflows with faith, and he alone shall know without fail how and when to speak, and what to say. Do thou therefore note and take advantage of such moments when the hearts of them that listen to thee are well disposed. That is the favorable time for the sowing of the Word.

11) Methods of instruction vary according to the state of mind, age,

and faculties of him who is to be instructed. Bear in mind, with regard to this, that those with whom thou shalt have to deal, are, in manners and ideas, heathens and erring, and in grade of culture—children. To these facts should be adapted the method and order of instruction in the saving truths.

12) The order of instruction should be made to conform to that which Providence itself points out to us.

The law of Moses was given earlier than the law of the Gospel; and even before the written law of Moses, the unwritten natural law was known and the author of it—God Almighty, the Creator. Just before the law of Moses solemn signs were manifested of God's power, almightiness and glory.

Keeping in view this great and universal model, do thou order thy small and individual work as follows:

a.) Starting from the existence and harmony of visible things, demonstrate the existence (whiich, however, none of those people appear to doubt), the almightiness, power and glory of the Creator of the Universe, His goodness, knowledge of all things, etc. At the same time with this, tell them the story of the creation of the first man, and of his being the progenitor of all men and peoples, who, in this respect, are living monuments and visible proofs of the Creator's supreme power and wisdom. Then explain how man consists of soul and body, in what he differs from other animate beings, how he is possessed of an immortal spirit, and indicate the intent of God in creating man *i.e.*—blessedness.

b) Further, show them the moral law of Moses, as being the divinely written natural law, the means towards achieving blessedness; all this do simply and concisely.

> *Note.* When speaking of the law, thou shalt surely hear from the crudest savages things confirming that law, which is graven indelibly upon the tablets of every human heart. Thus, for instance, who does not know that a man should honor his parents, that he should not steal, kill, etc.?! Try to arouse this feeling in them, and make use of it for thy purpose.

c.) When thy hearers shall have become convinced of the existence of God and the law, then (but not before), show them the necessity of observing the law, as being the will of God, and the visible consequences of not observing and of breaking it. Illustrate this with a brief narrative of the Deluge—(the tradition of it, though confused, exists among savage races)—as being the consequence of not keeping the law of God; tell them of the blessing bestowed by God upon the Patriarchs after the Deluge, and especially upon Abraham (whose descendants exist to this day)—as being the consequence of keeping the law.

d.) Only now begin the Evangelical instruction proper, in the way that

Jesus Christ Himself began it *i.e.* by announcing repentance and consolation, and the approach of the Kingdom of Heaven. Try to lead them to a feeling of repentance or of something nearly akin to it. This can be accomplished by convincing them that they will inevitably be punished for disregarding the law written within their hearts, in this life and the next, or if not in this life, so much more heavily, and for all eternity, in the next; that no one can, of his own power, escape these punishments, etc.

Here thou shouldst shape thy speech so as to arouse in them a certain dread of the future; and when thou shalt have brought them into this frame of mind, then do thou announce to them Jesus Christ, the Savior, Redeemer and Hope of all men, to give them comfort.

> *Note.* To bring souls to a state of repentance and contrition is one of the preacher's most difficult tasks. But this condition is one of the most important factors in the work of conversion; it is as the ploughed up soil, ready to receive the seed of Christianity, which then can sink into the very depth of the heart, and, with the later assistance of grace, can bear abundant fruit.
>
> When thou announcest the Savior to a sinner who feels guilty before the law, thou dost suddenly and without any persuasion thereto implant in him the love of this Savior, Whom as yet he does not know. And one who has in this manner learned to love Christ, will love Him all the more when he does know Him, and will believe all that He said and all that thou shalt say about Him. It will then be easy for thee to preach to unfold all the mysteries of our salvation, and for those who listen to thee in such a disposition of mind to receive them.

e) Having demonstrated the necessity of the redemption of the human race and shown the greatness of God's love towards men, thou shalt tell of the coming into the world of the promised Redeemer,—of His birth before the ages from the Father (this will be the time and place to touch on the mystery of the Holy Trinity),—of the incarnation, nativity, and earthly life of Jesus Christ, of His teaching, sufferings, and death, of the resurrection of the dead (in which all American savages believe in their own peculiar way),—of the future life, and the retribution to be dealt to the good and the wicked, according to their deeds.

f.) Lastly shalt thou tell them that Jesus Christ, during His life on earth, had many disciples, out of whom He chose twelve, imparting to them a special grace and power, and whom he sent forth into the world, to preach the Gospel unto all creation;—tell them how all that these chosen ones taught, and all that Jesus commanded is recorded iu their writings, which have come down to us, and which are known to nearly all the nations of the earth,—and how all good and simple-minded men to whom it has been given to hear their teachings, have received them with joy and have followed, and are following, in His steps. Tell them that such men are usually called Christians, and that those among them who have strictly kept the commandments of Jesus Christ have become Saints, and the bodies of many among them have reposed these many centuries exempt from corruption etc.

After this (on no account before), thou mayest make them an offer, and ask them whether they should like to join those who believe in Jesus Christ and hope to obtain through Him eternal salvation, blessedness, etc, etc. This instruction will be sufficient at first for such as have not before heard the word of saving truth.

13) In expounding matters concerning the faith, thou shouldst express thyself with deliberation, clearness, precision, and, as far as possible, concisely; otherwise thy preaching will have but poor success. In imparting the teaching of Jesus Christ it is not necessary to expatiate too much; *i.e.* thou shouldst not repeat all that He said, but only say that the entire doctrine of Christ is comprised in this: *that we repent, believe in Him, and have towards Him and all men a feeling of pure, disinterested love.* In confirmation of His teaching, thou mayest briefly mention His miracles.

14.) When thou shalt see that thy hearers have understood thee, and when they express a wish to be counted among the flock of Christ, then tell them: a) of *the conditions* upon which they may be admitted among the faithful; b) of *Holy Baptism,* as the mystic means of regeneration through water and the Spirit, which opens the new Christian life, and of the other Sacraments as the means of receiving the grace of Jesus Christ; and, c) of the manner after which he should live, who aims at being a true Christian and, consequently, at obtaining all the fruits of salvation.

a) *The conditions* upon which one who wishes to become a disciple of Jesus Christ may be admitted are the following: 1).—he must renounce his former creed, give up Shamanism and not listen to the Shamans; 2).—he must not observe any customs contrary to Christianity; 3).—he must agree to perform all things that shall be demanded of him by the new law and the Church; 4).—he must confess his sins.

b) Those who are willing and desirous to fulfil all the above named conditions must be told that entering the Christian fold is a great and important act, which must be performed solemnly, the neophyte renouncing in the presence of witnesses all that is opposed to Christianity, pledging himself to be a disciple of Christ and confirming all this by receiving holy Baptism, which is at once the visible *token* of having entered the community of Christians, the *means* of purifying the soul from sins, and the *door* for the reception of the other gifts, or means for imparting the grace of God in other words—the Sacraments of Holy Church, which should here be explained.

This also is the time for explaining the importance and dignity of the holy Cross and the virtue of the sign of the cross; also the reason for the reverence which the Church pays to the holy ikons, and her beneficent intent in so doing.

Note. In speaking of ikons, it might be advisable to mention, among other things, that, for the unlettered, they supply the place of books, etc.

c) As regards the *instruction* about *how a Christian should conduct himself,* it is best not to go into too much detail at first, but merely say that *whoever wants to be a true Christian i.e.* a disciple of Jesus Christ, and to profit by all the gifts which the Redemption has brought to man, should, 1), with faith, hope and love, give himself up to Jesus Christ; and, 2), imitate him in all things, *i.e.* try, as far as possible, always to act as He acted. Here Christ's virtues as described in the Gospel should be briefly touched upon, so that the neophyte may understand exactly how he ought to act.

Note. For instance: Jesus Christ forgave His enemies, and we should do likewise.

15) Lastly it should be shown that no one, especially if he rely on himself and his own strength alone, can, without divine assistance, be a true disciple of Christ, and that if Jesus Christ, out of His great love towards men, had not granted us His help, no one ever could become a true follower of His; but that now every one who wishes for it may receive assistance from Him. This assistance is the Holy Spirit, Which is given for the asking, and is obtained chiefly through prayer. And prayer is a turning of the heart towards God with submission, faith and hope. We can pray at all times and in all places; but divine grace and help are especially near when we ask for them in the prayers of the Church.

16) Such a course of instruction is sufficient for new converts. Further Christian instruction—as an extensive and more spiritual interpretation of the ten commandments, etc., expounding the words of Christ written down in the Gospel, the teachings of the Apostles, and (in part), the traditions of the Holy Fathers—such instruction cannot be called elementary and offers spiritual nourishment not fit for infants in the faith, but for the maturer, or at least for those who are growing up in Christianity.

Part Second.

Special Directions concerning instruction, public worship, the Treatment of Natives, etc.

III.

17.) The dogmas of the faith and the substance of actual doctrine should be kept to so strictly as not to allow anything contrary to them in word or deed, though in the face of death itself. But some allowance should be made for new converts, as regards certain imperfections in the rites, partly in consideration of local conditions, partly in expectation of their growing firmer in the faith and the new mode of life.

18.) The nature of those countries makes it almost impossible for the inhabitants to observe the fasts after the usual manner, *i.e.* by changing animal flesh diet to a wholly vegetable diet, and *their fasting can more conveniently modify not so much the quality as the quantity of the food and the time of taking it*. Therefore they should not be compelled to observe the fasts by change of diet; but, in the first place, the object of the institution of fasts should be explained to them, and the good of it; then, as their conviction and zeal increase, they should be led to observe the fasts on certain days in this manner: that they should, according to circumstances, diminish the quantity of the food they take, and not take that in the early hours of the day. As regards the Holy Week, and especially the last days before Easter Sunday, all converts should be urged to spend them in the utmost self-mortification, bodily and spiritual, in memory of the passion suffered by Jesus Christ for our salvation.

19.) Attendance at ordinary services, with the exception of the Liturgy, should not be made an absolute duty. Hence, in the course of thy travels in the remoter localities, when those whom thou dost visit are bound to confess and receive the Sacrament, thou must not make it absolutely incumbent on them to go to church during a whole week, as is customary with us, but only so much as circumstances will permit, and thou must be content with reminding and advising them that they should, during this time, pray to God as frequently as possible in their hearts for forgiveness of their sins, and also observe as strict a fast as they can. For such converts, instruction in the Word of God is always a better preparation for partaking of the Sacrament than reciting the usual Psalms and prayers, because none of them will, for a very long time yet, understand what is read and recited in church.

20.) With regard to the celebration of marriages, departures from the strictness of existing rules can be permitted only for the most cogent reasons and in cases of extreme necessity; and in what these departures may consist, that shall be specified in special instructions which shall be given thee. In view of the scantiness of local populations, recalling the patriarchal times, it will not be advisable to extend overmuch the forbidden degrees of relationship. Still, the prohibitions recorded in this matter in Leviticus (ch. XVIII), should be unswervingly kept in view.

21.) Ancient customs, so long as they are not contrary to Christianity, need not be too abruptly broken up; but it should be explained to converts that they are merely tolerated.

22.) Natives who have not received holy baptism, if only there is no reason to fear that they may in any way commit sacrilege or violate decorum, should not only not be forbidden from being present at our services,—such as vespers, matins, or Te Deums,—if they so wish, but should be invited to attend. As regards the Liturgy, it is against church rules to allow their presence at *the Liturgy of the Faithful.* Still, as the envoys of St. Vladimir in Constantinople were permitted, though they were heathens, to remain during the entire Liturgy, to the unspeakable benefit of all Russia,—thou also mayest grant the same favor, in the hope that the sacred act may have a salutary effect on hearts as yet unenlightened.

23.) No matrimonial unions or contracts entered into before baptism must be considered as hindrances to the administration of the Sacrament; and no marriages contracted before baptism, (with the exception of such incestuous ones as can scarcely occur at all), must be annulled, nor must such marriages be inquired into.

24.) Neophytes must be given no presents, either before, or at, or soon after baptism, nor must the sponsors be allowed to give them any, in order that the expectation of gifts may not serve as an inducement or suggest various cunning devices; therefore nothing must be given at baptism, neither shirts nor anything else, except the small crosses they are to wear.

25.) Upon the holy Antimins given to thee thou art empowered to celebrate the Liturgy in any place whatever—in a clean dwelling or under the open sky. But for many reasons, it is preferable to have for the purpose a special tent, which should be pitched in places as clean as possible; and on such places the natives should be persuaded to erect crosses, which may later on serve as landmarks, to show where the Bloodless Sacrifice has been offered, and also be a consecration to the place, so the people may assemble there for common prayer in thy absence.

26.) Thou art to take up thy residence more or less permanently where thou shalt judge thy presence to be most needed and useful. Happy indeed is the preacher, whose presence among them the natives regard as a privilege!

27.) While shaping thy course of instruction after the order indicated above, be careful not to proceed to a new subject before the hearers—all or at least the majority—have well grasped the preceding ones, even though this may delay the baptism of many. The more firmly the foundation is laid, the more durable will be the building and the easier to erect it.

28.) Thou shalt not bring in support of instruction in the faith and the Christian law any proofs not confirmed by Holy Writ, nor, still less, false miracles and invented revelations, under penalty of the severest censure. But, should the Lord in any place manifest His power, either by some miraculous cure or by some extraordinary revelation, thou shalt not conceal such divine manifestations, but, after instituting a proper and most impartial investigation, with all possible proofs, report the matter to us.

29.) Thou shalt on no account attempt to increase the number of those who are to receive holy baptism by any measures or means inconsistent with the evangelical spirit and unbecoming a preacher,—such as compulsion, threats, bribes or promises (of exemption from taxes and the like), nor by any vain allurements; but thou shalt always act with apostolic sincerity.

30.) Thou shalt not proceed to administer holy baptism to natives before they have been thoroughly instructed by thee in the above-named matters, nor then, unless they shall have expressed the wish to receive it.

31.) On arriving in some settlement of savages, thou shalt on no account say that thou art sent by any government, or give thyself out for some kind of official functionary, but appear in the guise of a poor wanderer, a sincere well-wisher to his fellow-men, who has come for the single purpose of showing them the means to attain prosperity and, as far as possible, guiding them in their quest.

32.) From the moment when thou first enterest on thy duties, do thou strive, by conduct and by virtues becoming thy dignity, to win the good opinion and respect not alone of the natives, but of the civilized residents as well. Good opinion breeds respect, and one who is not respected will not be listened to.

33.) On no account show open contempt for their manner of living, customs, etc., however these may appear deserving of it, for nothing insults and irritates savages so much as showing them open contempt and making fun of them and anything belonging to them.

34.) From thy first interview with natives, do thy best to win their confidence and friendly regard, not by gifts or flattery, but by wise kindliness, by constant readiness to help in every way, by good and sensible advice and sincerity. For who will open his heart to thee, unless he trust thee?

35.) In giving instruction and talking with natives generally, be gentle, pleasant, simple, and in no way assume an overbearing, didactic manner, for by so doing thou canst seriously jeopardize the success of thy labors.

36.) When a native speaks to thee, hear him out attentively, courteously, and patiently, and answer questions convincingly, carefully and kindly; for any question asked by a native on spiritual subjects is a matter of great importance to the preacher, since it may be an indication both of the state of the questioner's soul and of his capacity, as well as of his desire, to learn. But by not answering him even only once, or answering in a way at which he can take offence, he may be silenced forever.

37.) Those who show no wish to receive holy baptism, even after repeated persuasion, should not in any way be vexed, nor, especially, coerced. And although justice demands that converts and such as are ready to become converts should be treated with greater kindness and consideration, still thou, as preacher of the Gospel, shouldst not be insulting in thy treatment of such as show no disposition to listen to instruction, but shouldst be friendly in thy intercourse with them. This will be to them the best proof that thou dost really and truly wish them well.

38.) Among some savage tribes in those parts polygamy is to be met with, but only among the rich and powerful. Therefore, while striving to incline them to monogamy, do thou proceed with caution and tact, never in a masterful spirit, but so as not to anger and embitter them.

39.) From new converts or neophytes thou shalt not on any account whatsoever demand contributions or donations for the church or for any good work; yet shalt thou not refuse, but kindly accept gifts from such persens as may voluntarily offer anything,—taking care however, to explain on each separate occasion the object of the gift and the use it will be put to, in order that they may not get the idea that God, like their own spirits, demands offerings, or that such gifts are expiatory or propitiatory sacrifices, and the like.

40.) Henceforth, unless a special instruction be given thee, thou shalt take laborers or guides in thy travels from among the new converts or the natives of the places thou visitest. In this matter thou shouldst act in such a manner as not to lead them to fancy that, in becoming Christians, they at the same time become in some sort the slaves or bound laborers of their teachers. Hence, whenever such an occasion arises, thou shouldst request the natives' assistance in a friendly manner, and thou shouldst pay guides and all other help for their services.

41.) On no account shalt thou require of new converts or any natives presents or contributions; *nor art thou to enter into any commercial transactions with them, either personally or through third parties,* under penalty of severest censure. Even what is needed for food thou shalt receive only in case of absolute necessity and against payment, or else what is offered spontaneously at the hospitable board.

42.) Journeys are to be undertaken at seasonable times, *i.e.* when the inhabitants are comparatively at leisure from hunting and fishing, so that, by undertaking a journey at an unseasonable time, thou mayest not interfere with the earnings of either the natives or the Company. But, shouldst thou find it impossible to visit some locality to the greatest possible advantage at any other time than the working season, thou shalt report the matter in good time to us, explaining all the reasons for and possible consequences of the one or the other course.

43.) In order to be of the greatest possible service to thy parishioners, thou shouldst quickly learn at least so much of their language as will enable thee to understand them. But the acolyte who is with thee as thy assistant must regard it as his bounden duty to study the language thoroughly, and thou art to see that he does.

44.) Make it thy business to find out all about the religion, rites, customs, tastes, disposition, and all that makes up the life of thy parishioners, more especially in order to be able the more surely and easily to influence them.

Note. It imports not a little for thy success that thou shouldst do justice to any good customs they may have.

45.) During thy visits and residence in that or the other locality, give the natives, as far as time will permit, advice and directions for the improvement of their manner of living, avoiding, however, anything like coercion, and taking care not to give offence in any way, all in a friendly, openhearted spirit; and the advice and directions should be adapted to the local conditions and the simplicity of their manners.

46.) Do not meddle with any temporal affairs, and do not, either openly or by secret insinuation, discredit in their eyes any of the authorities placed over them either by the government or by their own choice; for Jesus Christ Himself, while He dwelt on earth, insulted no existing powers and touched nobody's rights of property. But should the actions of an official and his treatment of the natives be too cruel and unbearable, exhort him at first in all gentleness and friendliness; then, should this prove inefficient, report the matter confidentially to us, with every detail and in all fairness or, in case of our absence, to the dean of the district, who will bring it before the higher authority.

47.) In all matters exceeding thy powers, thou shalt apply to us, and of any scruples or misunderstandings that may arise, thou shalt write to us, officially or confidentially, according to circumstances.

48.) Judging from the gentle temper of many of the natives of the American coastland, it would seem that, if thy conduct be peaceable and such as beseems a preacher of the Gospel, no attacks or attempts against life are to be expected. Yet, should thy life, against all expectation, be in any way endangered, thou shouldst have recourse to the last and decisive measures for thy defence only in a case of absolute extremity. But a hundred times blessed shalt thou be if thou be found worthy to suffer for the name of Jesus Christ.

49.) That thy labors, acts, and progress in the work entrusted to thee may be the better seen and thy services the more correctly appreciated, thou shalt keep a diary, in which thou shalt set down all thy acts, all the principal thoughts and words that shall have occurred in thy talks with the savages, and everything noteworthy generally. This diary thou shalt submit to us each year, together with thy other reports.

50.) Concerning the order in which the church matters are to be held, such as the keeping of the books, of various registers, and the forms to be observed in both, special instructions shall be given thee.

51.) Wherever possible or convenient, try to start a primary school for the instruction of children in the Catechism, reading, etc., after the model of those which are ordered by imperial decree to be organized in monasteries and in connection with churches. Should it not be possible to organize schools on these principles, then at least assemble in thy own dwelling or in the chapel, once or twice a week, the children of both sexes, first those of resident Russians and half-breeds, then those of new converts; instruct them in their duties to God, their parents, the authorities, to each other and to their neighbors. Thou mayest employ thy acolytes to assist thee in teaching the children to read and write.

52.) It goes without saying that thou art, in addition to all the above rules, to fulfil strictly and faithfully the general and particular rules concerning churches and the persons attached to them conformably to local conditions and institutions, and all such directions as shall be given thee from time to time, and also all the regulations and ordinances of any kind whatever, issued by the local authorities for the general community,—and, by thus fulfilling them, thou shalt give a good example.

Bear in mind that thou art in a position where it is possible for thee to receive greater rewards, and more promptly, than do many others,—rewards both heavenly, in the future, and temporal, in the present. The heavenly rewards are in the hands of the Great Distributor of needs, Who will constantly behold thee and thy actions, thy intentions, and the spirit in which thou wilt act. As regards temporal rewards, of this earth notice shall be taken of the number of converts thou shalt have made; but still more of the zeal and ardor thou shalt bring to thy labors,—of any translation thou mayest make of portions from books of the Scriptures into the language of thy parishioners,—of thy efforts to teach them to read the portions thus translated; and if thou succeedest with at least fifty pupils, this shall be considered as sufficient proof of thy zeal, and as a merit deserving of the highest rewards open to the clergy.

Do thou strive to stand before God, a laborer unashamed, righteously administering the Word of Truth. Devote thyself to thy teaching and abide therein,—and by thus doing, shalt thou save both thyself and them that listen to thee.

The grace of our Lord Jesus Christ be with thy spirit.

Signed on the original:
Innocentius, Archbishop of Kamtchatka,
of the Kuril and Aleutian Islands.

LETTER FROM ARCHBISHOP INNOCENT VENIAMINOV TO THE OBER-PROCURATOR OF THE HOLY SYNOD, 1868

[*Reprinted from* St. Innocent, Apostle to America, *St. Vladimir's Seminary, Crestwood, NY, 1979. Translated by Paul Garrett.*]

Archbishop Veniaminov and the Sale of Alaska

A few months after Alaska had been transferred to American rule, Archbishop Innokentii wrote from Siberia to the Ober-Procurator of the Holy Synod:

"Rumor reaching me from Moscow purports that I wrote to someone of my great unhappiness about the sale of our colonies to the Americans. This is utterly false. To the contrary, I see in this event one of the ways of Providence by which Orthodoxy will penetrate the United States, (where even now people have begun to pay serious attention to it). Were I to be asked about this, I would reply:

A. Do not close the American diocese—even though the number of churches and missions there has been reduced by half (i.e. five).
B. Designate San Francisco rather than New Archangel the residence of the vicar (bishop). The climate is incomparably better there, and communications with the colonial churches are just as convenient from there as from New Archangel, if not more so.
C. Subordinate the diocese to the Bishop of St. Petersburg or some other Baltic diocese, for once the colonies have been sold to the American Government, communications between the Amur and the colonies will end completely and all communications between the headquarters of the Diocese of Kamchatka and Alaska will be through St. Petersburg—which is completely unnatural.
D. Return to Russia the present bishop and all the clergy at Sitka (except readers and wardens) and appoint a new bishop from among those who know the English language. Likewise, his retinue ought to be composed of those who know English.
E. Allow the bishop to augment his staff, transfer its members, and ordain to the priesthood for our churches converts to Orthodoxy from among American citizens who accept all its institutions and customs.

F. Allow the vicar bishop and all the clergy of the Orthodox Church in America to celebrate the Liturgy and other services in English (for which purpose, obviously, the service books must be translated into English).
G. To use English rather than Russian (which must sooner or later be replaced by English) in all instruction in the schools to be established in San Francisco and elsewhere to prepare people for ordination and missionary work."

REPORT: "EDUCATION IN ALASKA," BY ARCHIMANDRITE ANATOLII, 1900

[*The following text was originally published in* American Orthodox Messenger *nos. 7 and 8 (1900).*]

Education in Alaska.

The lately published second volume of the Report of the Commission of Education for 1898–99 contains, among other things, the report of the Superintendent or General Agent of Education in the District of Alaska, Dr. Sheldon Jackson.

This document begins with brief reports from the teachers, male and female, of the public government schools, supplemented by short statistical tables, showing the number of school days or months in the different schools, and the number of attending scholars in individual months and for the whole year. The minimum number of school months given is 7, the maximum—9; the general attendance in the 28 schools is computed at 1,369. The government appropriation for the support of the schools and teachers remains the same as in the preceding year—$30,000. This sum the Superintendent considers wholy inadequate.

"By strict economy, he writes in his report, it has been possible with these amounts to support the present school system. Within the past three years thousands of white men have settled in Alaska, many of them taking their families with them. The population of the older settlements has largely increased and several new towns have sprung up, which are clamoring for school facilities. If Congress regards it as the duty of the Secretary of the Interior to continue to provide schools for the white population of Alaska, I cannot state too emphatically that it is absolutely necessary that the appropriation for education in Alaska be largely increased. In order to provide school facilities which shall approximate the present needs of the increasing population of Alaska an annual appropriation of at least $60,000 is an imperative necessity. This is the amount which has been urgently recommended by the governor of Alaska''.

The report includes, as an integral part of it, information on the work of the various missions and the schools connected therewith, which have multiplied so notably of late years. This information is given in the form of reports from the heads of the missions. The first place, of course, is given to the Presbyterian Mission; then follow: 1) the *Congregational* Mission, whose sphere of action is the extreme north of Alaska; 2) the *Methodist* Mission, with its ''Jesse Lee Home'' at Unalaska; 3) the *Baptist* Mission, with its headquarter on the Island of Lesnoy, the Home founded by the ''Woman's American Baptist Home Mission Society''; 4) the *Moravian Brothers'* Mission whose work extends over the Nushagak region; 5) the *Episcopal Church's* Mission, 6) the *Friend's* Mission, and 7) the *Swedish Evangelical* Mission.

Of the Greek-Orthodox as well as of the Roman Catholic Missions—not a word, beyond the names of the missionaries and teachers. This silence may be attributed to one of two reasons: either Dr. Jackson supposes the educational labors of these missions to be too generally known to require a special mention; or—he considers them too unimportant to deserve being mentioned at all. In either case the silence is significant.

We might pass over the fact of the Superintendent's general report including the reports of individual missions, were it not that the latter contain certain details which convincingly demonstrate that the said Superintendent, in direct violation of the law on confessional liberty, makes use of his position and of the government money to assist one mission to the detriment of the others, and to hunt down Orthodoxy in Alaska, by fair means or foul, forgetful of its services in the past and unmindful of its present services. The prophecy which Dr. Sh. Jackson once uttered in a fit of anger provoked by Bishop Nicholas' farewell message to the President—namely, that ''the days of the Orthodox Church in Alaska were numbered'', and that ''twenty-five years from now there would not be one Orthodox Christian left there''—really expresses the aim which he is pursuing not openly indeed, yet systematically, by the present educational system, at the rudder of which he stands on his unrelieved watch as guardian of Alaska.

In submitting his report to public attention—(it would be interesting, by the way, to get a glimpse of his unpublished statements, the intimate ones, where facts are not glossed over)—this report which is devoted not so much to public as to sectarian and personal interests, the author must have exulted in his heart. With every year the number of American missions increases in Alaska. They spring up, not among savage tribes, not in remote corners of the country, but in the midst of the Orthodox population so obnoxious to Jackson. In the year now reported on he had the pleasure of recording the statements of such prominent missions and missionaries as the Episcopal Mission and its representatives in Alaska. True, the presence of statements on the work of the Episcopal Church in a report on the Alaska schools, does not necessarily imply that Jackson controls the actions of its missionaries after his own pleasure, making their labors subservient to his own plans,—but can the same be said of all the other missions, the reports of which are published in the superintendent's general report?

In order that Orthodox readers may clearly understand the policy pursued by Alaska's permanent guardian with regard to the Orthodox Church, we will borrow a few details out of this same report. In so doing we must call the readers' particular attention to the distribution of all missions over Alaska. Any one in the least familiar with the early history of the evangelization of the country and with the location of the Orthodox parishes at the present time, will at once realize that the distribution of the non-orthodox missions *is not due to change,* and that public schools are opened not *in accordance with the needs of the local population,* but solely with a view to the interests of the missions themselves. The substance of the entire educational scheme in Alaska may be reduced to a propaganda carried on among the Orthodox natives by the different Protestant denominations, the government schools being used as tools in this campaign work. For greater convenience, and in order that the Protestant missions may not clash amongst themselves, Jackson has divided the Orthodox districts as follows:

The entire south-eastern portion of Alaska, settled by Indians, with a white population at Sitka, Juneau and other towns, is appropriated by the Presbyterians, with "the chief Presbyterian of Alaska," Jackson himself, at their head. True to his time honored system, of supporting the anti-Orthodox missions, the superintendent of the district has secured *government salaries* to nearly all the employes of the Presbyterian Mission. There is a law which entitles every benevolent society or institution to a teacher paid by the federal government provided such society or institution has about 150 children of school age. Armed with this law, Dr. Sheldon Jackson arbitrarily distributes government teachers to the missions which please him (that is the first condition), and which declare a contingent of over 40 children of school age. And thus it comes to pass that the Presbyterian Mission in Alaska has the free services of over ten men provided for by government salaries. The most zealous among them are: the superintendent of public schools in the south-eastern portion of Alaska, W. A. Kelly, who has his residence in the Presbyterian mission at Sitka; his assistants, G. C. Beck, M. A. Carty, Miss Olga Hilton, Mrs. M. A. Saxman, Mrs. E. C. Heizer, Miss A. R. Kilsey, Miss F. L. Campbell, and others; in Khuna—Mrs. J. W. Mc.Farland, who, it is remarked in the report, continues, after her husband, Rev. J. W. Mc.Farland, the missionary labors among people of

Khuna which were begun by him in 1881;—at Juneau and Douglas—Miss E. Saxman and G. H. Spiers, etc.—With the help of these so-called government teachers, and several more whose names are not given, the Presbyterian Mission has been carrying on its work for over a quarter of a century. Formerly, Dr. Jackson used to contrive to get from the government enormous subsidies for his mission, but of late they have grown rather stingy at Washington.

What then are the results of all the Presbyterians' efforts?

They are very poor. Mr. W. A. Kelley's report on the industrial schools at Sitka is as inflated as the famous frog who would be as big as the ox. No figures, no facts; nothing new. And yet this is the centre of the Presbyterian Mission, its very heart. Possibly the influence of this centre may be credited with the fact that great revival of the winter of 1899–1900 brought into the churches nearly 100 native souls as is remarked in the report. Those who have been able to observe on the spot the Presbyterians methods of computation know what these "nearly" and "about" really mean. Hence one finds it difficult to believe both this comparatively definite statement and another according to which the Juneau Mission, in the report year, was in a very satisfactory condition, having effected about 100 conversions in the course of the year, although this statement is immediately followed by the remark, that the industrial work which was carried on for several years, having served its purpose, was closed in 1898, and the pupils were transferred to Sitka.

It would be interesting to hear what the Orthodox priest, Father Yaroshevitch, will say when he reads of the very satisfactory condition of the Presbyterian Mission at Juneau, of the hundred conversious and of Mrs. Mc.Farland's estimating the attendance at her school not at 80, which he thinks an exaggerated figure but at 126,—and of the mission at Hoonah working successfully and of the people there making "more than rapid progress" in Christian life, and proving their faith by works.

Of the other Presbyterian missions the report merely says that they are *in good condition.*

The following missionary advanced post, next to the Presbyterian Mission in Southern Alaska, is the Baptist Mission on the Island Lessnoy.

In the western part of the Gulf of Alaska is a cluster of islands known as the Kodiak group. These islands are in the center of the district assigned to the Baptist denomination which extends from Mount St. Elias around the Gulf of Alaska to the Shumagin Islands, a distance of 1,100 miles.

As to *who* assigned this region to the Baptists, the report wisely keeps silence. But whoever did, one thing is certain—that Dr. Jackson took the Baptist home on the Island Lessnoy under his paternal protection, as one of the very bitterest pills ever administered to hated Orthodoxy. Kadyak, with its environs settled by Aleuts and half-breeds, always was and now is one of the finest spiritual vineyards ever owned by the Orthodox Church in Alaska. There have long been no traces here of paganism. And lo! here, in this stronghold of Orthodoxy, inaccessible to Jackson, there appears a wolf in sheep's clothing who, in something like five or six years, steals over fifty sheep from the fold. During the report year there were said to be about 28 children in the Baptist home. The propaganda was carried on among the natives, under the show of sewing classes, conducted by the manager's wife, Mrs. Coe. Could such zeal and such success go unrewarded? So Dr. Jackson gives Mr. Coe a government teacher as assistant. "The government" we read in the report, "has, for last two years, sustained a teacher at this place and the school is taught in the mission building".

This government teacher was a certain Mr. Slifer, whose name deserves to be remembered, if only because of his report on the work of the school and home, which reads as follows:

"The work here is worthy of the attention it is receiving. It is doing a vast amount of good. It has never been my lot to meet a people who were so degraded, and in many ways so hard to work with, as the creoles of this section. The creole children are in most cases the very worst that could be found to deal with when they come into the mission; in a short time they are better than the rest of the outsiders".

Such sweeping condemnation of the Lessnoy creoles and their children strikes one as rather strange coming from Mr. Slifer, in view of the opinion expressed by the teacher of the public school at Kadyak, Miss A. Fullomer, about the children who attend her school. She came, if I mistake not, at the same time as Slifer, if not even on the same steamer, and although the children in her charge in no way differ from the Lessnoy children, any more than their fathers and mothers differ from the Lessnoy parents, she cannot say enough in praise of her pupils and declares that she never met anywhere with such enthusiasm as they evince for learning. The question involuntarily obtrudes itself: what made Mr. Slifer so anxious to depreciate the creoles and their children and to extol Mr. Coe and his Home? And one as involuntarily remembers a line from our great fabulist Krilof: "What makes the Cuckoo praise the Rooster so? Why, the Rooster praised the Cuckoo first, you know".

The third so-called stronghold of education in Unalashka, the "Jesse Lee Home", was quite lately connected with the government school, until it was strong enough to stand by itself, when it openly began that iniquitous war of which our readers know from Father Kedrofsky's communication. The region assigned to this home and the Baptist Mission includes all the Aleutian Islands, together with the adjoining Pribylof group and other, smaller islands, and a portion of the neighboring continent.

The fourth missionary district, commissioned to extirpate Orthodoxy, belongs to the Moravian Brothers and covers the whole Nushagak region. This is one of the oldest missions in Alaska, The Moravian Brothers came here even earlier than Jackson. They worked much and persistently against Orthodoxy, sometimes seizing by force the children of Orthodox Nushagak natives, and transferring them to their own schools and homes. Yet their mission cannot, any more than the others, boast of great success. At Bethel, the central station of their mission, they had to close their school, from lack of means and teachers. At the present time their missionary efforts are confined to visiting the native villages and preaching. They no longer display their former fanaticism and boastfulness.

It is hardly necessary to speak of the other missions, in view of the fact that their work lies outside of the Orthodox parishes. One circumstance, however, should not be passed over unnoticed: it is the space occupied by the Episcopal bishop's report on his own mission: it takes up a larger portion of the general report than any other. It is curious enough anyhow that reports from missions in Alaska should find a place in the reports of the Educational Department of Washington, seeing that it is contrary to the law. But then, in these same reports are printed extensive accounts from Dr. Jackson on the purchase of Siberian reindeer, their feeding and distribution in Alaska! . . .

It is scarcely needful to add anything to these few items taken from the Superintendent's report in order to grasp the spirit and drift of his educational efforts. All that he tells in his report, all that he presents as "progress of civilization", he of course ascribes solely to himself and to his long experience in Alaska. But even in his own report he could not quite conceal a number of facts which, in our opinion, repeatedly expressed, show that Dr. Jackson's educational system is not absolutely successful on all points. One such fact is, that all the Protestant missions in Alaska, without exception, succeed with the native population only during the first years of their existence, until the natives come to know them better. Just now, the Mission of the Moravian Brothers, the Presbyterian Mission, and others, are examples in point. The excitement to which these missions rouse the natives during the first two–three years is generally followed by utter indifference, sometimes even positive hostility to the missionaries, and by the disorganization of the missions. We can observe this curious reaction now at Unalashka and on the Lessnoy Islands. What is the reason? The reason—or indeed reasons, for there are several—have been more than once pointed out by the Orthodox missionaries in Alaska. The fallacy of the religious doctrines taught by the Protestant missionaries cannot but be felt even by the natives, who, if uncultured, are very sensitive to truth. Then they are repulsed by the "civilizing" methods practised by the missionaries in their dealings with the savages,—sometimes involving regular child-hunts with forcible abduction and, in extreme cases, actual purchase of children, in the expectation that the investment will be made good by the government subsidy, be it in the form of a government teacher, or possibly the entire support of the school. But the chief reason lies in the wrong system created by Dr. Jackson—a system which does not educate, but corrupts the whole Alaskan people. Nothing can be more to the point than the opinion expressed on the Jacksonian system by a thoroughly competent judge in the matter, the Rev. William Duncan. This venerable, aged missionary has spent very nearly half a century working here among the Indians. Formerly he and his flock used to live in the British dominions, but absurd laws and the barbarous treatment of the natives by the British officials drove them to betake themselves to one of the small islands subject to the United States, where they formed the settlement of Metlacatla. Many were the hardships and difficulties encountered by the missionary in his undertaking of settling his flock in the new place and of giving them some kind of organization, as well spiritual as material, but he succeeded and, at the present day, Metlacatla is one of the best and most prosperous settlements in south-eastern Alaska. It numbers about 1,000 souls—Indians of the Tsimsian tribe. Duncan is now a reverend old gentleman, near on seventy, an autocrat in his own parish, respected and beloved of all. And this man, an undisputed authority on Indian life, a witness of all Jackson's experiments on poor Alaska, (but a sharer in none), gave voice a few days ago to the following opinion on the educational methods in force in the country, denouncing the present system of "civilizing" by means of missionary homes and industrial schools as a positive harm to the natives.

"Not long ago", he said, "the United States Marshal told me that, of twenty Indian criminals then kept by him in jail, nineteen had been pupils of the training schools. The young men come out of these schools disgusted with work and gradually sink into sloughs of vice. The girls, on leaving the schools, take to a dissolute life". . . . The old gentlemen thinks, from his own experience, that the parents ought to be cared for as well as the children; that the latter should not be taken away from their parents, under pretence of educating them, because the only result of such a course is that they, in time, are ashamed to return into their own proper sphere. He is of opinion that in each community a school should be opened, where they should be taught in their own language, while an eye should be kept on the community generally. . . . On the whole, his standards in the educational question are precisely the same as those which the Russians pursued when they owned Alaska and when, seeking the good of the natives and aiming at their true enlightenment, they gathered them into communities, built churches, organized parishes, etc. etc.,—in short did all those things which Dr. Jackson and his assistants now so strenuously oppose.

Time will show, let us hope, in how far Alaska is benefited by Dr. Jackson's civilizing methods, and what kind of a worker he is himself: *By their fruits ye shall know them.*

Archimandrite Anatolius.

REPORT: "SCHOOL WORK OF THE RUSSIAN ORTHODOX CHURCH IN ALASKA," BY HIEROMONK ANTONIUS, 1900

[*The following text was originally published in* American Orthodox Messenger *nos. 6, 7, and 8 (1900).*]

Report for the School Year 1899–1900.

The report for the last school year on the schools controlled by the Orthodox Church in Alaska was an attempt at making clear the type of these schools, at showing the necessity of continuing the conditions which had given them birth, and the character of the work they are doing. To these topics the entire preamble of the report was exclusively devoted.

In the present school year we hold it our duty to continue our review of the work in connection with new facts in the Orthodox Church's life and activity, and with that generally progressive movement to which, by the law of evolution, all the creations of the living human spirit are subject. The brief period of one year gives no chance for an exhaustive presentation of a subject which has many essential phases of it own, besides being co-ordinate with a number of individual facts that have come in contact with it during that period. Add to this that the type of the Orthodox parochial school is a great novelty on American soil, vastly different from that of the educational institutions prevalent in the country, and therefore stands in still greater need of frequent presentation in the proper light. It is only under this condition that it can appear a good and desirable beginning in American eyes.

It was our present incumbent, Bishop Tikhon's excellent idea to make regular publicity one of the bases of the work—a publicity meek in spirit, serene, truthful, as remote from morbid self-scourging as from violent denunciation of the ways of our neighbor's schools, but convincingly revealing all our hopes for a bright future in our own work of religious education. It is therefore necessary to state frankly what, in our own existing conditions, promises well for the progress of Orthodoxy in Alaska, and what is likely to hinder it.

To begin with—it would be wrong to cast the blame for every failure on the other creeds. The latter are confronted by the same condition as ourselves, and their interference serves to test our patience and tact. Holding fast to our own faith in God's help and mercy and to our love for our work, let us leave them in peace and hope for mutual fraternal comprehension and harmony in the future. The Russian cause has to face another and harder trial, galling as undeserved wrong. It is the hostile attack of foes of the Russian nationality, not so much convinced as embittered: mostly, in the first place Russia's own apostate sons, then literary men wielding a dishonest pen, having nothing in common with the serious press, men like Geo. Kennan, the literary crowd of Franklin Square Library, poster artists, whose productions serve as an excuse for an inflammatory text, representing life in Russia in slavish imitation of the illustrations of Butes's "Darkest England"; to this same category belong also the so-called "Polish lectures" on Siberia, and the musketry sharpshooting kept up by Russian-Jew nihilists, who dig up all the filth they can, in the way of slander, insinuation, defamation, etc. and strive to pull Russia from her eminence among nations.

But all such malignant and furibond attacks miss their mark. For some time past Russia and the rest of the world have been trying hard to become mutually acquainted, with the result that there is a constant increase of hearty sympathy and serious respect in the universal attitude towards the great empire. In a deep-going, exhaustive study of any one subject, it is always more profitable to turn one's attention to the conditions of one's own existence than to find fault with circumstances outside one's sphere of action. Such is the by no means easy task we are undertaking, keeping before us as a leading standard the brilliant conclusion of the manly and patriotic speech delivered by the High Procurator of the Holy Synod on occasion of the opening of a school-board in connection with the Synod: "Of outside foes", he said with much animation, "we need have no fear. It is the internal foes that are dangerous, and especially that pernicious system of reports announcing that 'all is well' in everything and everywhere". Just about the time of the present report on the Alaska schools, a very interesting book appeared in Russia, excellently well translated, beautifully, artistically made up and commented on most ably in a few well-hit strokes. The interest of the book lies as much in the information it conveys as in the conclusion it draws from it. The title is: "The New School". The author, Democlin, is a Parisian. The book is dated 1897. The Russian edition was published at the expense of C. P. Pobiedonostsef. Consistently with his title, Democlin examines into the condition of existing schools, and gives the final preference to that of Abbotsholme, with the founder of which he became acquainted in Edinburgh, at a summer meeting of the University Extension.

The author analyzes the French school system, and finds it meagre, deficient in nourishment. The German system he disapproves of, because of the excess of material forced upon the pupils, and the unproductive results of the system, which makes of a young head a cemetery of old things. The English system he praises for its practical tendency, and lingers long on the merits of this moderately positivist school, more particularly as represented by that of the Abbotsholme type. While he praises the school of Dr. Cecil Reddy, who takes it into the shrine of his heart and indeed into that of his own family, Democlin does not advise a general imitation of Dr. Reddy's somewhat special methods, as was the case at one time with immoderate classics and realists, but merely holds it up as a bright example, the personal achievement of a noble sower, worthy of an abundant harvest. The author admits of no compromises in education, and therefore rightly admires Dr. Reddy, who gives the school a place in his own family, has made its interests a subject of profound study, has devoted all his own labor to it, and has begun, with the most moderate expectations, to reap the fruits of his sowing. Yet Democlin ends with the following remark: "Fathers of families who undertake this great task trusting to their own strength alone, we commend to the grace of God. We pray Him that He may support us, for we labor for the good of our children, because we are men of good will, because it is said '*Aide toi, le Ciel t'aidera*' ('Help thyself, and Heaven shall help thee'). . . ."

Thus Democlin's "New School" is merely a school of hope, of promise, a bright beacon light. Of a certainty, all beginning based on the hope for better things is a good beginning. Our eyes too turn the way of hope and light. But if the avowedly best type of modern school does not make labor light, what then shall we say of the most arduous of all—the missionary school?

Just at present the school work which the Orthodox Church is doing in Alaska is no easy work. Its object is to save children from crushing egotism and coarse materialism, to keep them from falling victims to a hypocritical age which ruthlessly deceives by giving stones for bread, serpents and scorpions for fishes. Such signs of the times are hard to fight. The fight requires men of firmness, and genuine, self-denying, god-fearing workers, not curious seafarers, roaming the oceans for the sake of their own trading ends. The future of the school in America as everywhere else is undoubtedly this: the triumph of faith and its spiritual ideals. Without the corner-stone of Eternal Truth, no walls of any "new school", will be built up. The truth of this is clearly visible, only one must not look through a dim glass but penetrate with understanding eye into the interior of what L. Kellner calls, "the colossal cathedral, with its stained glass windows, wherein dwelleth Christian Faith. Those who stand outside do not see the splendor, but to those within each sunbeam reveals glory unspeakable". "The sun is not as universal and patent to all as is the teaching of Christ", says Erasmus of Rotterdam.

But mankind, rebellious and stubborn-necked, will strive a long time yet over the work of evolving the right principles of education before coarse realism is beaten off the field, and the unprofitableness of moderate positiveness is found out, and decrepit classicism finally perishes from unskilful, unwilling handling, and men turn to the eternal truths of the Gospel.

The Russian has already turned to these truths. But, to organize a school on such a basis, we repeat, men are wanted—many willing workers and much labor. Let us hear what the well known Russian pedagogue Ratchinsky has to say on the subject:

"The school can bring living fruit only if supported, in word and *in deed,* by the community, and more especially by those members of it who, from their culture, fortune, position, are in full view of all, objects of unconscious comparison and imitation. It is not enough to build schoolhouses, to fill them with aids to learning, to place them in charge of patented teachers. We must ourselves live the moral and spiritual life which we wish to inculcate into the learners in our schools. A hard word, but a true one. For our lives are better seen from the schoolhouse than from the village; for the impressions received at the school age exert a profound and powerful influence; for all shams in school matters are not only useless, but criminal; for upon us are turned the eyes of the yearly increasing mass of the scholars of our rural schools; for it is not merely our manner of speaking and dressing they appropriate—they try to imitate all the details of our mode of life, which is to them the fruition of the knowledge they seek, the sum total of our culture. What if this fruition, this sum total, on examination proves to be the utter repudiation of those devout habits of mind which are instilled into them at school, a constant trampling under foot of those ten Commandments which they memorize there, an absolute negation of those divine truths which constitute the only essential substance of school learning? What if observation proves to them that these cultivated men need neither prayer, nor church worship, nor the sacraments of the Church? Children's eyes are keen; the examples of moral looseness are alluring. If, in planning our school work, we wish to pass out of the realm of phantoms and unrealities into that of real things,—if we mean to produce something more valuable than material for school statistics,—if we have in us but a drop of love and pity for those children on whom we perform our pedagogical experiments, we are in duty bound to turn our attention to this aspect of the school problem".

In this clear and convincing plea Ratchinsky, one of the greatest workers in the field, places himself on the highest standpoint bearing on the education and self-culture to be obtained from the school, taking in both teachers and learners. In so important a matter, he will not allow the light that is in man to become darkness, Reviewing all known horizons of knowledge and history, he arrives at the inspiriting idea of the necessity of a union between the Church, keeper of divine light and grace, and the school, which is to develop in man the highest spiritual organs.

"The union between the Church and church life and the school" is indeed a great idea, capable of inspiring a noble soul; an idea which warms the heart more than arid arguments in favor of separating that which God united. No one will seriously deny that the union of these agencies for strength and love must bring incomparably greater blessing to mankind than the persistent effort to separate them. We live in an age of union, an age when all tends to unity, and each individual wants to feel himself part of a whole; and yet many insist on separating the school from the church! Were it not better, instead, to think how best to establish a permanent connection between them through bonds of love, conviction, and mutual trust, and how to free those bonds, by mutual affectionate devotion, from all trace of compulsion? Men would see again paradise on earth, if Church and school, realizing that self-love, coarse sensuality, bold contempt of law, and modern unbelief are their common enemies, to be fought and repulsed, should declare to these enemies, with the help of the State, an eternal war.

A teacher who is estranged from his church will be estranged also from the hearts of his people, for whom it is his duty to live, and from his work itself. Our national school would fall into an error pregnant with dangers if, under the influence of an excessive self-reliance, it should seek in itself alone its own centre of gravity, and look at itself and prize itself as the principal agency in national education, and thus gradually become detached from the only living source of all education,—the Christian family and community. At the same time it would renounce its own noblest mission and forget that only that education which proceeds with the external and internal help of God, has a permanent value and holds a promise of present and future life"*. "A school with enlightened ideals, tending towards true culture, must be the vestibule of Heaven"**, says one of the men most versed in the philosophical bases of education, a man of noblest heart-gifts. "The Christian religion's fundamental meaning", he goes on, "demands that the spiritual pastor shall be not alone a minister at the altar, not alone a preacher of the Word of God, but a teacher and instructor. Upon him lies the duty

---

*L. Kellner.

**K. Ushinsky.

not merely of admitting into the Church new members by means of the Sacrament of Baptism,—but also of initiating into the meaning of Christian truths, of introducing into the inner temple of Christianity''.

From the point of view of the principles we have just laid bare, the Orthodox Church in America cannot complain of being misjudged. There is much interest in her, even if there is little knowledge. We have repeatedly heard American Protestants declare that their grudge is against Roman Catholicism, with which alone they have had dealings—never with the East, the spiritual wealth of which attracts their gaze as the light of the rising sun.

A certain Dr. D. was recently sent by an American community to the East, with the object of studying the forms of Church life amidst the Greeks and Arabs, in connection with the history of Christianity. Finding himself there on the spot, he could only exclaim, rather helplessly but joyfully and with faith in Revelation, that everything there was so old as to be contemporaneous with Christ, and at the same time so fresh as to preserve the complete image of His holy undivided Church, firmly established upon the Rock of the Apostle's profession of faith.

The present spiritual condition of the Americans shows them to be ready for some great and inevitable crises. The Anglican Episcopalians are on the road to a fundamental renovation by a return to the luminous fountainhead of the apostolic spirit, and are not at all averse in their ideal aspirations, from alliance with the East; the Presbyterians are hopelessly tangled up in the contradictions of their by no means strong doctrine; the lesser denominations, at times and in places, reach the line beyond which lies nothing but sheer despair. Millions of human beings vegetate along without any hope, without any church. The efforts of individuals and communities to find some point of support in ecclesiastical and ethical questions are nothing more than pious exercises which do not reach far and give scarcely any results. The Salvationists sing in the streets, the Masons hold their secret conferences, the ministers of a variety of sects dispute openly behind their pulpits; temperance societies pull hard on the reins,—but in all this striving and laboring there is no element of unity, no wholesome and universally acknowledged common goal, there is not the animation and depth of true religious feeling, hence it all amounts to little in the end.

Eternal truth finds no favorable soil where one encounters at every turn the sceptical, sarcastic query ''*What* is truth?'' where life insurance takes the place of eternal hope.

What does such a picture reveal? What sort of harvest yields such a field? An answer to these questions can be found only in words of prayer, uttered with the firm hope that God's active grace may touch these immobilized masses with its miraculous virtue and gently force them on to the new path of spiritual renovation and union in peace.

Can it not be that Orthodox Christianity answers this crying need by the principles on which it bases its school?

The year which forms the subject of the present report, far removed as it still is from world-wide problems, may yet be pointed to with a certain satisfaction, as having succeeded in establishing good relations between our diocesan authorities and the American Department of Public Instruction.

In September 1899 our Bishop sent instructions to the Dean of Sitka, to the effect that he should prepare a report on the Orthodox parochial schools in Alaska, with a view to making them better known to the Department. Later on the Bishop and the Superintendent of Education in Alaska exchanged their ideas in the most Christian spirit of tolerance and a tone of most impersonal moderation. The Superintendent, on one hand, requested the Bishop to cooperate in the school work in Alaska by giving greater room to the English language in his own schools, and, on the other hand, begged him to give no credence or attention to printed rumors, malignantly directed against events and persons unconnected with the work, but privately implicated through circumstances of a purely personal nature.

The tone of this request showed it not to be entirely free from just a grain of misunderstanding and distrust, which found expression in the reason adduced for the request concerning the language, the instruction in which was said to be limited, *"except by private tuition"*. Now the Orthodox Church never and nowhere subjects the Engl. language to any limitations in her schools, but, on the contrary, gives her best care to its propagation and to proper instruction in it; and, if some think differently, it is only owing to mistakes which will soon be cleared up. Publicity alone, without special efforts, is quite able to dispose of so simple a matter.

At the same time, the very fact of such intercourse should be greeted as one good omen, betokening a mutual willingness to actively combine and join forces in the interest of public education through the agency of schools, both parochial and secular. On the recommendation of the Governor of Alaska, the Superintendent further invited the Dean of the District of Sitka to become a member of the U.S. Schoolboard in Alaska, to represent the interests of the Orthodox Church and mediate between that Church and the Department. The Dean was authorized by the Bishop to accept the invitation. This fact also should be duly valued as a token of the confidence and international courtesy which are taking the place of the former irritability and neglect, and we feel bound to emphasize it as a favorable and hopeful sign of the better times that are coming.

"Spreading knowledge and proficiency in the three R's", is a task demanding profound concentration in thinking out the methods and aims of educational work,—a task which can be compassed only by peaceful, honest, humane, enlightened, and kindly means—*viribus unitis* ("by united efforts'') as the ancients have it, or, to use America's motto, *ex pluribus unum*.

In God we trust!

District of Sitka.

Ordinary times, when things in general are peaceful, with nothing to put any great strain on conscience, honor, and duty, are usually called ''prosperous''. But with such a work in hand as the religious and moral education of a people in the spirit of the true Orthodox Church, such humdrum ''prosperity'' is insufficient, for we are impelled to strive for the greatest possible enlargement of her moral sphere, for the victory of the cause of light and the triumph of good.

Let us attempt to survey with unprejudiced eyes the condition of the Orthodox school in Alaska for the report year.

Sitka.

This place is just at present in a fairly favorable condition for the advance of the Orthodox school. With a population of less than a thousand souls, the town has six schools of different denominations and types. The success of any prosperous school is visibly tested by the number of the learners in it and the quality of the teachers. While tending towards a desirable standard in these respects, the condition of Sitka for the present year may be described as one of transition (*mutatis mutandis*), as regards programmes, branches of study, text books, methods, number of pupils; some sides of the town's external life and environing social sphere have also been touched. It may be said, therefore, that the school, without blackening in the matter of instruction has been moving cautiously and with thoughtful deliberation, as though in accordance with J. J. Rousseau's philosophical aphorism, that ''the education of children is a pursuit in which it is necessary to know how to waste time, in order to win in the end''.

The Right Rev. Bishop's idea is to enlarge considerably the Innocentian Missionary school of Sitka. In its present condition it does not by any means cover the needs of the diocese or even of its own immediate district. The admission and dismissal of the children after the ''rapid ringing'' system must result only in sterile blossoms, which will prove of as little use in life as to the Church. The simultaneous operation of three missionary school of identical type can but prove burdensome to the diocese's resources and hindering to the work, which demands a compact organization and strict centralization.

Until the time when these points can be settled at headquarters, after going through all the unavoidable formalities, in accordance with the Bishop's ideas, the Sitka school has had a second teacher added to the regular staff; the Indian school has been put in such order as will enable it properly to fulfil its appointed parish work, and has been given a teacher who is also a physician, that he may watch the better over the general well-being, spiritual and bodily of these most child-like people and their youthful offspring. Another change has been made in this school beginning with this last year, by introducing the English language as a special branch of study. This innovation was absolutely necessary in order to transform an originally confessional school into an open one, of the type desired by the government; but religious instruction is imparted strictly in accordance with the dogmas of the Œcumenic doctrine. These liberal changes at once affected the school attendance: in the place of the few dull day-scholars of the Indian school, we immediately had forty two eager Indian children.

As regards the Innocentian school, it is purposed, in the near future, to substitute for the present teacher one of greater experience as an educator, versed in better methods, and, besides, an American citizen, capable of teaching geography, arithmetic and history in the English language. This teacher will also, as part of his regular duties, give instruction in English in the place of the lady teacher who is at present especially engaged for the purpose, and this also is a welcome token of the actual and desirable establishment in the Sitka school of a professorship of the national language and the branches connected with it. It may be mentioned here that, with a view to an impartial judgment on the work done in English in the last school year, the teacher of the public shool at Sitka, Miss C. Patton, and the honorary trustee S. I. Kostromitinof, were invited to be present at the examinations, with the result that a certificate was made out, awarding the Innocentian Missionary school the palm of precedence in this branch over all the other schools of the place.

The health of the children in the Innocentian school is under regular medical supervision. They are experimentally trained in apiculture, an industry undoubtedly new in Alaska, indeed probably a first attempt, but likely now to be as successful there as anywhere in Central Russia.

General hygiene is to be introduced, with rational preventive measures against the local danger from climatic influences, various inherited evil maladies, and alcoholism, which latter disease holds the lower classes at Sitka in a clutch like demoniacal possession.

Such are the modest beginnings to be recorded for the last school year. The "new school" questions, under other names—*mutato nomine*—have reached Sitka and entered into the actualities of the place's live interests.

Before the beginning of the school year which forms the subject of the present report, the Innocentian Missionary school was visited and blest by the Right Rev. Tikhon, Bishop of the Aleutian Islands and North America, who selected Sitka in preference to any locality as the place for an Orthodox school with a thorough course of instruction and for the introduction of those improvements which he has planned to have carried out at once. Towards the end of the school year the General Agent of Public Education visited the Russian Mission at Sitka. All the projects for the better organization, spiritual and secular, of the Orthodox schools in Alaska were welcomed by him with expressions of sincerest sympathy. Dr. Jackson requested that a historical sketch of the work and workers of the Orthodox Church in Alaska be prepared and sent him, to be included in his report for the current year—the first time that the school work of the Orthodox Church will take its place on the United States registers.

Altogether, it is desirable to close the record of the past school year not with conceited self-praise, nor with trite assurances of general prosperity, but with a well-grounded appreciation of where the end of the school year found us, and what is to be done next in the order of our most important brightening hopes, so that the life-giving Spirit of the Lord may rest upon our work, and the instruction we impart may at the same time educate a people in the doctrine of the one true church, "arousing in them a lively interest in the object of their labor, and training the will to conscientious work, that knowledge may not be separated from practice; because then only is knowledge enduring and efficient when it is based on practice and is spurred on by practice", as C. P. Pobiedonostsef says in his preface to Democlin's essay on the "New School".

Juneau.

The parochial school has been getting on through the last school year very succesfully. Without any particular disturbances or any gloomy symptoms in the environing conditions, apart from a slight complication caused by the serious illness of the teacher, who is also reader at the church, the school has advanced quietly towards its well-defined and conscientiously pursued aims. The success was according to the true deserts of teachers and learners.

The pupils of the Juneau school are particularly good at reading the church books, at singing from notes, at choir singing at the services, and conduct the services understandingly, with calm assurance and in perfect form. They write English remarkably well, and are also proficient in reading and arithmetic, and their progress in all branches is most satisfactory.

A novel and pleasing feature of the last school year was the interest in the school shown by the Koloshes, who are not as shy of books here as in their more unapproachable native wilds.

On the whole, judging by this earnest and sincere work done at this school, we feel bound to attest with respect and gratitude that those in charge of it have done well.

At the present moment two very important buildings are being finished at Juneau, both destined for schools—a city school and a Roman Catholic one. This somewhat belated effort to give a fresh impulse to education is evidently in accordance not so much with the actual rather depressed conditions of the place, as with the earlier, when it had the ambition to become a little capital, the centre of a permanent gold market. And the new schools are calculated with a view to such definite elements of their own, that we positively hope for a peaceable and inviolate state of general and equal satisfaction for all.

Killisnoo.

The incipient and somewhat irregular condition of the primary school here attracted the Bishop's attention last year. In the present year it was given a new teacher, who should be able to get the children of the surrounding nomadic tribes settled down to their primers, and to teach them something of reading, writing, figuring, to train them to say some prayers in their own dialect, and to sing some simple hymns. But these good intentions were not crowned with success. The Koloshes about Killisnoo are particularly slow, dull, of a sullen, materialistic bent of mind. They have not yet awakened to any consciousness of the good of learning which, indeed, is hid from them by certain oppressively sordid features of local life. The last school year at Killisnoo numbered not more than fifty days: the shortest year of any known planet, age or nation! Such a brief term is utterly insufficient to secure anything like serious progress, or even to get a timid young savage at all familiar with his school, his book, and their uses.

Nor can there be much question of discipline. The Koloshes not being citizens by right, have, so far, no idea of any kind of civic, or even social, life, preferring to form a sort of abnormal ethnological wedge in the midst of the population of the United States.

The best measure for reviving and reforming the school here is to organize a regular and most persistent Sunday school. The Koloshes' attention, and possibly even liking, may be more easily drawn to the Sunday, so universally and highly honored in America, than to a certain number of days making up a school term—all ideas utterly unintelligible to them.

Wherever spiritual virgin soil has to be broken, examples and acquired habits are always more efficient, and should be used more freely, than exhortation or persuasion, to which a hunting people seldom takes kindly. After example has done its work will be time enough for oral instruction, which will best take effect in church, and lead to book-learning, so lovingly extolled in old Russian chronicles, as follows: "The written word is from God. Without its light the eye cannot rejoice in God's creation, the soul remains mute, ignorant of the law of God. An illiterate soul is a dead weight in man. What frail childhood is taught, feeble old age abandons unreadily, for what is done frequently, as a habit formed by much length of time, becomes firmly established in the character with the force of nature. Therefore it behoves Orthodox Christians to have great care of their children, lest they, from their infancy, learn bad language and frivolous boastfulness, which are perdition to the soul, and waste in idle play the golden time of childhood, which cannot be brought back at any price; and that they may, in the springtide of their lives, till the field of their hearts by learning, and joyfully receive the seed of the Divine Word, sown by their teachers, in order, at harvest time, to gather in the soul-nourishing grain, to live on it honorably in the winter of old age here on earth, and lay it up in the heavenly granary, to feast on it through eternity". After such excellent advice, it remains to us to take up the experiment sincerely and unselfishly. "Experience", says Benjamin Franklin, "is an expensive school, but fools will learn at no other".

Nutchek.

The parochial church here is in favorable conditions of time and place. Its peaceful days have been undisturbed by any hostile aggression or wrong from without. Originally excellently well organized by the teacher A. P. Kashevarof, the present managers continue in the same spirit, with satisfactory results. A pupil of the school, A. Bolshakof, graduated this year, already himself conducts the work of enlightenment at Tatitlak, near Virgin Bay and the animated town of Valdes.

The support of the school and the Home is assured by the generous donation of the honorary trustee, Timothy V. Yuritchin, to the amount of 250 roubles yearly. The study of the English language is compulsory.

The Home is small, but so are the needs of the people, who are accustomed to provide and store only the most urgently necessary things for body and soul—as we are commanded.

After what has been said, all that is needed for the school of this place, which is at present becoming enlivened by the influence of a worldly, frivolous neighborhood, is that it should strictly preserve its Orthodox character, making its walls the abode of constant zeal and profound devotion in spirit and sincerity, to the service of God, and the work most pleasing to Him after church work—which is school work, being guided therein by the excellent rules laid down in one of the old books: "Rightly and decorously to instruct young children, as well in the words of book-lore, as in good conduct, truthfulness, the love and the fear of God which is the beginning of wisdom, in purity and lowliness of heart; and thus to instruct them not by anger, or cruelty, or furious abuse, but so as to win their cheerful respect training them by loving usage, and gentle lessons, and kind reasoning, adapted to the powers of each, and with relaxation, lest they become discouraged; and above all things always to keep before them the law of the Lord, for the good of their bodies and souls, and guard them from all foolish and unseemly words''.

Kenai.

The schoolwork here progresses hand in hand with the affairs of the parish, which are conducted with firmness, zeal and tact. The parochial school is flourishing and attractive both by its external appearance, and its internal well-ordered organization. Upon it are centered the hopes of the community, which lives on in the calm induced by religion and kindly hearts, thoroughly comprehending the socratic truth that education, in the words of Plato, is the best of the things which the best people can have.

It is a pleasure to mention in connection with this that the parish priest conducts the school with perfect comprehension of the true spirit of a missionary school. ''A good priest is the soul of the school; and the school is a saving anchor to the priest,'' says S. A. Ratchinsky, that competent and experienced laborer in the field of church education.

The progress made by the children in the branches on the programme, including the English language, is most satisfactory. Church and school have worked together lovingly and cheerfully, not discouraged by inevitable difficulties. Their beneficent, self-denying zeal finds a response in Russia, whence a lady, O. P. Petrovskaya, sends a yearly contribution of 150 roubles.

Just at present the school's chief need is a fund of good books, to start a library for the children and the people. This is an important question and well worthy of favorable consideration. ''Without books, the mind is like a bird with clipped wings. This aid is especially needed by graduates of the school, that they may not let those precious bonds be broken which unite them to their educational home, and may not be deprived of the high enjoyment derived from reading,—that true ''hygiene of the brain''.

Kodiak.

The character of this school is in accord with that of the first historical Russian settlement in North America. The Russian spirit, breathing power and health, is over all. The parochial educational work cares nothing for politics, does not proceed by leaps and starts, and never swerves from its historical field. An overwhelming majority of the local population holds fast to the Russian language and the Orthodox faith. To conclude from this to any separatistic tendencies would be an absurd anachronism, as it would be utterly illogical to think of any restraints being placed on so natural and vigorous a feeling in the land of guaranteed liberty. Therefore—let things remain as they are—*Sint, ut sunt*. . . .

"Russian education", says C. D. Ushinsky, "does not need external reforms, nor the substitution for an old worn out and antiquated costume of a new one, equally ill-fitting. Of course we can and must borrow much from the experience of foreign pedagogy, but we must not forget that only then is the infant not harmed by strange foods, when it has grown strong on its mother's milk and has acquired the power to digest those foods and by the action of its own independent vitality, to transform them into flesh and blood. Such a mother's breast to us is our nationality and our national religion, which form the bond between each of us and every other Russian, though he be hidden from our view somewhere far away in the darkest mass of the people, in some remotest nook of our immeasurable native land,—also between ourselves and generations long gone and yet to come—in a word with all those things that alone secure us an enduring historical, not an ephemeral existence. It is idle to want to *invent* an education; it has existed in the Russian people for as many centuries as the people itself, was born with it, grew up with it, reflected in itself the people's entire history, all its qualities, the best and the worst. It is the soil out of which grew successive generations of Russians. That soil can be improved, fertilized, by adapting the process to its own nature, its demands, its capabilities, its defects—but it cannot be made over. And let us thank God it cannot!"

In the Kodyak school, with all these good intents pursued with conscientious and unflagging zeal by its enlightened managers, things get on satisfactorily. The English language is a compulsory study and occupies a very prominent place.

The school is an object of envy to the Baptists. The aggressive ill-will of these sectarian politicians, however, avails them nothing, but is only irksome to themselves, and in no way diverts the concentrated attention of the Russians from their work. The fundamental rule of education should be remembered here: education, not to be inefficient, must be popular. It is at present in good hands, on the true patriotic road—there is no use in wishing for any change. Terrible is the noise made by the stonebreaking machine used in the Alaska gold mining works, but still more terrible is the machinery employed to break up a nation's individuality, for here we do not observe the effect of that optic law, in obedience to which the smallest particles of a broken mirror continue to reflect the brightness of the photosphere. This parable teaches us to keep the integrity and the unity of the Spirit in the bond of peace (Eph 4:3).

The Kodyak parochial school, named for the first American Orthodox bishop, Loasaphus and the Home of the name of Hermanus are under the care of a trustee—the priest F. Dashkevitch, who has engaged to pay to these two institutions a yearly stipend of 250 roubles.

Afognak.

This island is morally constituted exactly like Kodyak: here also the Russian spirit prevails—of course only in a national sense, with no suspicion of political feeling. The Russians here are most loyal American citizens. The possession of the precious light of spiritual truth, the treasured native language and nationality only make the local civic type stronger, firmer, and morally finer.

The Orthodox school stands very high owing to the objects it pursues and therefore demands skilful management. Not words alone, but deeds, a living example in life faith and charity are required of the priest. Although his task is not particularly hard owing to the local favorable conditions for the sowing of the religious and moral in the spirit of the Orthodox Church, still his labor, by the grace of God, will be counted to him as equally worthy of a great reward.

The success of the parochial school at Afognak has hardly been influenced in the past school year by the somewhat depressed condition of the public school, with which the Orthodox school has to share its work, taking for itself only the religious instruction, the Russian language, and church singing.

It is highly desirable that the harvest from the new seeds, tended by new sowers may prove a richer one and their labor more fruitful in the spiritual field, for the greater good of the good people of Afognak.

The Unalaska District.

The district of Unalaska is an Orthodox congregation scattered over the neighboring islands, whose shores are not always easy of access. The greatest activity is to be found in the chief station of the District, where the populace is more alive spiritually, and where there are more workers for the Church than in the other out of the way corners of the Siberian missionary region.

The general impression of our church school activities in this country is that the foundation for the education of the masses has been established, they being taught religion, reading and arithmetic. The satisfactory state of the work in the Sitka District only increases our wish, that it should be enlarged and strengthened as far as possible so as to be implanted in the very spirit of the inhabitants, who are constantly unsettled, in this far-away corner, by offers, flattery and invitations of various kind.

To reach this aim we need time, workers and means. The latter chiefly of spiritual nature, stable, well balanced, holding true in all human undertakings, the same means, which according to the wish of Christ, were employed by the first heralds of the Holy Tidings.

Unalashka.

The local school, which is in strict accordance with the spirit of the Orthodox Church, is highly to be commended. But its conditions are far from easy. The struggle with its sectarian neighbour is especially burdensome; they are ever anxious to get hold of any Orthodox child, during the school period. The struggle is only the more difficult because in far off Alaska the voice of truth does not easily reach a court of law of any kind. A man contemplating some evil deed can take his time about it in that country.

The conflict with the Methodists, known to us through the sad annals of the Parochial Herald of Alaska, is far from methodical: the irritability, inconsistency and arrogance displayed by this sect are startling.

The Methodists themselves are well aware that the abstract principle of their doctrine is not incontestable, and that their practical strivings after a wide co-operation are very naive. In fact, the possible fate of their contemporary work can be fitly expressed by the favorite Roman epigraph "dum tacet", yet nevertheless they persist in displaying their narrow intolerance and in breaking the rules of Christian neighborliness.

In the last report of the Unalashka Benjamin school and the Sergius asylum, depending on it, there are a few changes, some of the teachers having been dismissed, as not offering the qualities necessary for the difficult and serious task of missionary work.

But so far as it went, the labour of the directors of the school and the children was both satisfactory and considerable.

Besides the Benjamin District school, which has a good many pupils, there are many children who are taught in the chapel schools. These schools are certainly not brilliant, but they evidently keep up the spirit, following the wholesome traditions of the good old times.

The school on Atton Island especially deserves attention in this respect. This point is midway between America and Asia, on the way to Petropavlovsk. The "most Western church" of all America, a small Russian chapel, is to be found on this island. A photograph of it has been recently reproduced in one of the American Government publications, showing all its poverty and abandoned condition. But the disagreeable impression disappears as you think that under the decrepit exterior of the building there dwells the living and unchangeable spirit of the eternal truth of Orthodoxy. The relation between what is beheld here by the physical and the mental eye is very analogous to what a pilgrim to the Holy Land observes in Bethlehem: in the sumptuous Catholic chapel of St. Jerome and the subterranean Arab church built on Russian soil, the soil of the "Shepherds", first witnesses of the thanksgiving tendered by the heavenly powers on the memorable night.

Belkovsky.

The school of this parish is guided by the experienced guide of the local priest. The very foundation on which it rests consists in the unshaken prestige of Orthodoxy amongst the natives. It is very desirable that the local church, which is well off, should join forces with its dependent charitable institutions in directing its attention towards the maintenance of the orphans in the parish. They could be sheltered by the local Asylum, which would at once bring great relief and a greater freedom to the St. Sergius Orphan Asylum in Unalashka, where only children from distant localities and islands should go.

In the Belkovsk school there are more girls than boys. And so if the Russian church starts a separate institution for girls there, it will be rewarded by the firmer foundation of education for women, analogous to a whole network of similar institutions in the bishopric of Sitka.

St. Paul Island.

The school of this parish has not yet reached the perfection that might be desired but, as it was pronounced satisfactory by His Eminence, it may be considered so.

St. George Island.

Here the parish school is under the immediate guidance of the local priest, who had some training in pedagogy before he got his present position.

During the years under report, the school made good progress. The pupils' answers in Bible History and theology were commended as such by His Eminence.

Now that the Pribiloff Islands are free from any alien influence working against us it would be especially important to implant there the Orthodox church on a firm foundation, which certainly will earn a grateful memory for all the workers, according to their deserts.

Quichpach (Yukon).

According to the flattering testimony of His Eminence the Archbishop Tikhon, the first high church dignitary who ever visited this far off corner of Alaska, the progress of the school can be said to be very good. The labors of the local priest are evident and faithful. An increase of school children, though is desirable, so that the youth of the Russian Parish should not be broken into fractions amongst the alien element, who cast envious looks at our Orthodox field. Above all something should be done to raise the education of girls, which is so important an element in missionary pioneer work.

Fort St. Michael.

The local parish school has also received gratifying notice from His Eminence.

Needless to say, praise is dear to the work and the workers. St. Michael is a very lively place. Its importance is nowadays recognized in all the ins and outs of the American gold mining activity. In such places, a high standard in all church functions is especially important, as both chance and reason predestine such places to become centers where people may become acquainted with various questions of their exterior and interior lives, with that considerable spiritual benefit, which a man reaches, in most cases, by way of sound comparison.

Kuskoquim.

The school of this parish happens to be an exception in this, that being a point of a large territory, with, comparatively speaking, a considerable number of inhabitants it yet possesses the meagerest contingent of school children. This is explained by its difficulty of access and also by the absence of the impelling influence on the part of the administrative control. Let us hope that after the reliable information that the report gives us on the point, some measures will be taken, to spread in this locality the glory of the Lord's Word.

Nushagak.

The extent of the parish is very large. There are ten schools, with about two hundred pupils in all. The place has been established for a long time and has a good name. The Aleuts here are from of old well disposed towards church instruction. In the district of Sitka one often comes across original letters of Noushagak writers of perfectly faultless style. Some of them have such perfect command of the Russian alphabet when writing Aleut, that a man who has not the slightest idea of that tongue can still reproduce all that was written in a perfectly free and distinct manner.

It shows on what a firm foundation the beginning of the work was established, if grain like this has not lost the power for vital growth in the poor soil of Noushagak.

All that is wanted is a careful watch kept over all the amateur labours of the chapel schools.

There is no doubt, that some people, who have much education but a good deal of zeal, are possessed of such a fortunate and tactful gift of teaching the young, that one can not but admire the results of their labours. For instance, on Forest Island they well remember, with a good deal of pleasure, how the Very Reverend Nicholas came across an eight year old child, who showed himself well acquainted with our prayers, though he had never had anything to do with any regular schooling.

The short description of school activity in the Districts of Sitka and Unalashka, for 1900, may be completed by the following data:

802 children of both sexes have attended school; out of this number there were 28% of girls

and $9^1/_2$% of the total were the wards of the Charity institutions of the Russian Church.

And so, after the preface, in which I have tried to establish the impartiality of the educational report for 1900, and after I have reviewed the existing condition of the life of our church parishes the time comes for an adequate and natural conclusion.

In my concluding lines I shall try to be as brief as possible never leaving my subject out of sight. It is customary for the U.S. Department of the Interior to print its yearly reports concerning Public Instruction in two volumes in compact type. The volumes contain about two thousand five hundred pages of literary and statistical material: they offer you information on the schools of Germany, England, Switzerland, France, Cuba, Puerto Rico, the Argentine Republic, Uruguay, Brazil,—even New Zealand and Tasmania; they present the statistics of their Consuls' reports concerning education in Russia; they discuss the question of "foreign influence in American schools"; they argue about the "study of astronomy in primary schools and universities"; they make public the "anthropometrical and psycho-physical observations on children of school age"; they describe "the conditions of mental training in the United States"; they exhibit "University types and ideals"; they discuss the "system of education for the colored people"; and give you hints as to "the education of the deaf, the blind and those of unsound mind". . . .

To this many sided governmental labour which must keep its bearings amongst all these numerous vital interests, I now *add my modest authentic information on the labours of the Russian Church in the field of Public Instruction,* and this in a country, to which you could not apply the words of Californian guide books: "the land is high, dry, breezy and beautifully situated as to scenery". . . .

Without any doubt, Alaska offers a field for the labour of the Russian Church both vital and desirable, and likewise it promises bright future prospects. This is equally important for Russians and Americans: citizens of this Brotherhood of nations being enlightened by that grace and the light which cometh from the sight of Truth.

There should exist no narrow-minded interpretations where people carry on this sort of humanitarian, brotherly work, free from earthly interests of any kind. Moreover, the labours of the Russian Church were always carried on openly in broad daylight, and at no historic period was it influenced by lowering suspicions and evil speaking. Its labours were always directed by people of great self-abnegation, who had no stone walls and no great treasure to lean upon but were possessed of the gift of loving their country and the Apostolic faith, and, from the excess of this love, were ready to sacrifice themselves for the sake of the brotherhood of nations, in perfect accordance with the words of our Saviour about giving one's life for one's brothers.

They consider animosity and reproaches as mere misunderstanding and over sight, as a result of the natural entanglements of human relations, but by no means as a threat of some victorious all powerfull enemy.

Greeting all that was good, human and brotherly in the labours of last year, we keep silence as to the isolated facts of intolerance, which ought not to find room in annals of a relative order.

As I was concluding these lines, I received from the Curator of Public Instruction for the Alaska District a bunch of flowers, beautifully preserved and still keeping on the roots a little of the Russian earth, which he had gathered on the Arctic promontory called the "Heart" in East Siberia. Taking it as an omen, I make this wish in return. Let the hearty alliance of the two great neighbor nations grow in the likeness of the luxurious virgin blossom of our land.

REPORT: "THE MAIN PROBLEMS AND THE CHARACTER OF THE RUSSIAN ORTHODOX FOREIGN MISSION WORK. WESTERN NON-ORTHODOX MISSION WORK," BY HIERONMONK DIONYSIUS, 1901.

[*The following text was originally published in* American Orthodox Messenger *5, no. 6(1901).*]

If then our Orthodox Russian foreign missions are entirely *spiritual,* it follows that they are not, and cannot be, *political* in character. They never did, and do not now strive for the acquisition of power or influence in political affairs. They do not look on the propagation of Christianity as merely a means for the subjugation of heathens under the power of the Russian government. All this is the business of the State and its diplomatic missions—not of the Church and her evangelizing staff. And history shows that only those evangelizers successfully plied their task of converting heathens to Christ, who pursued purely spiritual objects, aimed only at the heathens' spiritual welfare, without admixture of any political scheming whatsoever. Accordingly, our foreign missions, at the present as in former times, serve exclusively the chief aim of the Russian Orthodox Church (Mt. 28:19–20)—the spiritual illumination of the heathens.

This fact was quite recently openly referred to by one of our missionary bishops, the Rt. Rev. Nicholas, late of Alaska and the Aleutian Islands, now of Simferopol, in his farewell message to the President of the United States: "Our Church never meddles with politics, and our clergy never, either at home or anywhere else, have busied themselves with any intrigues of this description. It would be wrong to confound us with the Jesuits. Our Church allows us only to intercede for the oppressed or them that suffer innocently—as I have sometimes done before you—but never allows us to incite citizens to revolt and treason".

Such—i.e. entirely unaffected by political tendencies—our missions have showed themselves in other countries also, for example in Japan. In that country the Rt. Rev. Bishop Nicholas has created a *national* church composed of Japanese. All natives: the priests, the preachers, etc. have all been taught in Japan, by Japanese teachers, in the Japanese spirit. This fact—that the Orthodox Church of Japan is already living its own life,—is a sure pledge of its enduring vitality. And the reason of many souls out of the dark satanic realm into the light of the knowledge of Christ our God *and preserve Christians residing or travelling there* (at Pekin), *from falling into the allurements of all kinds of idolatrous service,*—and thus could dwell near that church built unto God'' (by the Albazins), ''and minister there, so as, by their godly life, *to win unto the same sacred cause the Khan of China, and the men nearest to him, and their people generally*'' . . . To this purely spiritual programme the Pekin Mission has remained true in all its course of action. It has always kept within the bounds of the religious and moral sphere enjoined to it, never carried on any propaganda, nor interfered in politics, or in any court intrigues. Hence our Mission had no political character in the eyes of the Chinese themselves, and the Pekin government's attitude towards our missionaries always was a kindly one: it not only never persecuted or banished them, as it repeatedly did Catholic and Protestant preachers, but, on the contrary,'' showed them every favor, and never subjected them to the least restraint''.

Our foreign missions, then, are distinctly not of a political nature. But neither do they aim at a *cultural* character. They do not understand their tasks in the sense of propagating European culture and civilization among savage peoples,—in the sense of imparting to foreign races useful knowledge, handicrafts and the like, and never have set cultural problems in the place of their own proper spiritual tasks. The reason for this, of course, is that European culture and civilization are by no means, as so many fancy, wholly an outgrowth of Christianity. European culture owes to Christianity only the little that is really noble and lofty in it;—if we go into particulars, we shall find that it is in direct opposition to it. The two are frequently two contrasting realms, two wholly different worlds. The one—all love, meekness, humility, renunciation of all that is of earth, and hope of an eternal life in heaven. The other composed of self-love, sensuality, extreme egotism, complete attachment to earth, tending wholly to man's utter enslavement to earth, by the witchery of the earthly comforts it keeps inventing, aiming at making him not one having dominion over this visible world (Gn I: 28), but a servant of it, ready to sacrifice for its sake all that is most sacred. It is self-evident from this that a mixing of spiritual with cultural aims, and, still more, a substitution of the latter for the former in a mission's work, must lead to most deplorable results. Religious missions pursuing cultural aims make of native converts, at the best, sensible, thrifty people, craftsmen, tradesmen,—men, it may be, useful to the state in a certain sense, hardy and enduring in the struggle for existence—but in no way Christians, loving, suffering, contented with their lot and ready to give up even the little they have, for Christ's sake. At the worst, they turn out idlers, sharpers, while natives that have made money develop into taskmasters who grind down their own people.

But we must not give assertions without facts. The patriarch among our missionaries, the Metropolitan Innocentius, who, while a priest and missionary in America, was acquainted thoroughly and from personal experience with all the conditions of the natives, both baptized and unbaptized, was strongly opposed to the propagation among them of European culture and civilization. Those who go forth among foreign races, says this great missionary, frequently ask themselves: Should savages be enlightened? Is it for their good to be? If, under the word *enlightenment* we understand a change or passage from their former so-called savage condition to a later form of existence, more like our European conditions.—then such enlightenment, in Innocentius' opinion, is *not necessary* as being not merely not beneficial, but actually harmful. Savages, he says, will not gain much from the civilization we bring them, *if it is merely outward, worldly, or even if it consists only in the education of the mind.* For, in how far will the savages' moral condition be improved by his learning, say, that the earth revolves around the sun, and not the sun around the earth, if he does not at the same time learn anything about the purpose of the world's existence, nor of his own? Will he be happier in his daily life from exchanging his pelts for garments of woolen cloth and silk, *if he at the same time, take on all the abuses of "the producers and consumers?"*—As an instance of the evil influence on natives of such one-sided, merely cultural instruction, Innocentius points out the Aleutians. Together with civilization, says he, were carried to them habits and opinions which they formerly had looked upon as criminal and shameful; and together with some bad things, much that was good was destroyed in them. To take one illustration: the Aleutians never were very industrious,—in fact they were lazy, but they had things that roused them to activity and kept them active, such as wars and tribal quarrels. In their present condition, these things have been taken from them, as harmful; but on the other hand they have almost nothing that can at all times arouse them and keep them active; hence their natural disinclination to exertion, especially with the bad examples of the strangers that have come among them, has become sloth pure and simple.—The Aleutians did not know many of the comforts of life; in fact they were very dirty and untidy in their manner of living; but then neither did they know luxury and all that goes with it, and, not having any standards of comparison, they were content. Now they understand the difference between the several conditions of man, the advantages of wealth; but at the same time, having hardly any possibility whatever to improve their condition even as far as mediocrity, they find in this knowledge nothing but a source of torment, envy, discontent, abasement, etc.—The Aleutians formerly knew none of the arts most useful to men and most familiar to civilized peoples; but they were thoroughly skilled in arts of their own, necessary in their own condition; such as: the arts of handling their *baidarka* (the native boat), of hunting and fishing, and even of healing. Now, while they are learning new arts, which can be of very little practical use to them in their mode of life, under their conditions and with their means, they, at the same time, lose their national crafts, and the arts most useful to them.—The Aleutians, in their former condition, had some decidedly bad customs, as for instance that of killing slaves at funerals, to wait on the dead in the other world. But, on the other hand, they had some as decidedly deserving of praise and imitation, such as, for that of sharing their last crust with those in need. Now, together with the bad customs, the good ones are going also. Civilization teaches them "Remember thou art the father of a family; thy first duty is to thine own", etc.—The Aleutians formerly had many rules and principles not consistent with civilized ideas, but they were very strict in the observance of them; the general contempt, and even death were the price paid for violating them: they had almost no idea of forgiveness: their vocabulary has no word either for granting or asking forgiveness. Now they have exchanged those rules and principles for other and better ones; only, at the same time, they have learned that, while among civilized people all the rules of life are excellent, it does not matter so much about observing them, and that even open violation of them not only is not, as a rule avenged by public opinion, but is frequently excused on the plea of weakness, leniency, and so forth. Naturally, they begin to take advantage of such attractively "indulgent morals"*.—Such are the bitter fruits of introducing savage peoples to culture.—Yet it must not be inferred from this that savages are not to be taught at all, but are to be left to stagnate in their coarse manners and customs, and to go on dragging their old miserable existence in dirt and destitution. . . . No, says Innocentius; "it is only necessary, while leading savages out of their wretched condition, to observe a certain wise caution, so that we may not, instead of making them happier, deprive them of such happiness as they enjoy now. We must, for instance, strive to break the savage of his dirty habits; but we must be careful lest, in scrubbing the dirt from his body, we do not scrub away his own natural skin and spoil him altogether. While extirpating the wrong principles of their own peculiar morality, do not let us make of them beings devoid of all moral principle". . . . There is much more in the same strain.—In view of these dangers, what we must strive to propagate among natives is not the miscalled "European civilization", but the true Christian light, teaching them religious truths, and establishing them in the principles of a sound morality. Only such religious-ethical treatment can cure the natives of their coarse

---

*Memorials on the islands of the group of Unalashka, by J. Veniaminof, 1840. Part II; pp. 313–318.

ways and cruel customs, wean them from drunkenness, idleness, immoral living, lead them to care for cleanliness of the body and purity of the soul; in a word, only such treatment can lift them out of a condition like that of the beasts of the field—not that "culture" and "civilization" which frequently only intensify their worst vices and further, not the regeneration, but the extinction of the native races. "Christianity" says the never to-be-forgotten worker in this field, N. I. Ilminsky, "by enlightening, ennobling and strengthening man in heart and mind, in his ideas and inclinations, *leads natives most surely and directly to a nobler and more orderly manner of living*". The same view of Christianity as a force infinitely improving and ennobling in its action on savages,—nay, as *the only force capable of achieving this task,*—is taken by the best among our secular writers. A. S. Pushkin, in his *"Trip to Erzerum"*, after speaking of the Tcherkesses' (Circassians') savagery and the best means of taming them, says: "Lastly, there is a means more efficient, more moral, more in accordance with the enlightened spirit of the age, and that is—*to preach the Gospel to them*".

It follows that our foreign mission work stands outside of and above all political and narrowly cultural aims, and pursues the exclusive task of propagating the kingdom of God upon earth. In this lies its success, its power, the pledge of its vitality and duration. Very poor in material means, scant in numbers, inconspicuous by their humble external organization and the absence of striking effects, *our missions are strong by the divine spirit which animates them, their internal warmth of feeling,* and succeed where it is least to be expected they should, judging from merely human probabilities and calculations. We have a fine illustration of this in the following description of our Mission in Japan by one of its members: "One cannot help admiring God's goodness to our Mission. We have no schools with European programmes, no hospitals with a whole staff of Sisters, we cannot sow pecuniary aid broadcast, right and left. Aloof from all cultural and political problems, our mission pursues but one object—that of preaching to the Japanese Christ and His doctrine in all its purity, without any additions or misinterpretations. Hence the grace of God, which abideth in Christ's Church, never forsakes our mission. It is strong neither materially nor numerically, nor by any special gifts of its members, but in the direct grace of Christ, and that alone. What are the Missions' resources? Naught, compared to those of the Protestant and Catholic Missions. As against their armies of European missionaries, we have only Japanese, recent converts, with a superficial education. True, they have at their head Bishop Nicholas, who trains the preachers: but he is quite alone. It is not men that prevail here, it is truth and grace. The missions merely cast the seed, and God raises the crop. The Bishop told me of many cases in his own practice and that of his catechizers which positively demonstrate the independence of their work from all human calculations. The most eloquent, the most finished sermons are at times but sounding brass, when a most careless, not even logically constructed, altogether poor discourse will have a wonderful success. It mostly happens too, that the greatest success is obtained where absolutely no hopes, were entertained; while where everything was calculated with all but mathematical precision, nothing comes of it at all. Everything loudly proclaims that there is One in charge of the work, Who directs it according to His pleasure''.

IV

INTERCESSOR AND DEFENDER OF THE OPPRESSED

Editor's Note: Continuing the ancient tradition of interceding before the wealthy and powerful on behalf of the poor and dispossesed, Hieromonk Makarii and Archimandrite Ioasaph interceded directly not only with Shelikov but with the Holy Synod of the church for redress of wrongs committed against the Kodiak Natives. Their deaths in 1799 delivered supreme power in the colony to Alexander Baranov, whose rule continued until his retirement in 1818.

In 1805, the government sent Cathedral Hieromonk Gideon to Kodiak to assess the real condition of the mission and the native people. Because Father Gideon was the representative of the highest authorities, even Rezanov and Baranov had to defer to him, at least in public. Gideon spent only about two years in the colony, but while he was present, the situation generally improved. His stay in Alaska was so brief, however, that the company regime returned to its earlier exploitation of the Aleuts and harassment of the mission very soon after his departure. Consequently, Father Gideon's contributions have been largely overlooked.

Modern American historians have tended to accept Rezanov, a very low-ranking commoner and no "count" or aristocrat at all, and Baranov rather than the Valaam missionaries without investigating very deeply into the personal characters of these witnesses. Naval Lieutenent Davydov is often cited as another "reliable" source for information on early colonial Alaska. Actually, Davydov was something of an early juvenile delinquent who got himself entangled in some sort of scandal at the academy at Kronstadt and was quickly commissioned and shipped out—at the age of sixteen. Certainly he was an intelligent and perceptive observer of Kodiak life during his brief sojourn there, and his memoirs, published after he fell drunk into the Neva River after a night on the town in St. Petersburg, are a valuable source of information for early nineteenth-century Alaskan history. But Davydov also included accounts of people and events he himself did not witness, and one can imagine the amusement some of Baranov's old cronies derived from feeding to this arrogant adolescent their exaggerated or even imaginary accounts of their youthful exploits. Hubert Bancroft uncritically accepted "Count" Rezanov and "lieutenant" Davydov as reliable witnesses when in fact they were not, and most popular histories of the state have been echoing their fundamental errors for one hundred years now. Consequently, Archimandrite Ioasaph, Father Gideon, and even St. Herman are hardly, if ever, mentioned in the average "history of Alaska" curriculum. In this chapter, Hieromonk Gideon's reports to the Metropolitan of St. Petersburg are interspersed with some of Nicolai Rezanov's letters. Of particular interest is their conflicting analysis of the dispute over the administration of the Oath of Allegiance and of the death of Hieromonk Juvenaly. Father Gideon became an intercessor, but for his brother monks, before the church and civil authorities.

He was also an active missionary in his own right. Not only did he visit many villages in the Kodiak region, but on his return trip to Russia he visited Unalaska and in five days performed several hundred chrismations, and nearly fifty weddings. Unangan Aleut leaders traveled from neighboring islands to attend services and receive Holy Communion from the first priest to visit them since Hieromonk Makary, nearly ten years earlier.

With several monks drowned or murdered, the others decided to follow Father Gideon's example. They also returned to Russia. Only the Monk Herman remained.

Kodiak was too inhospitable for the saint, so he moved to nearby Spruce Island, where he initially lived in a dug-out pit. There, as Yanovskii and Larionoff reported, he lived out his days in prayer, fasting, and works of charity, later running the school with Sophie Vlasoff. When Baranov's temporary replacement, Simeon Yanovskii, arrived, it was Father Herman who initiated their correspondence. His plea on behalf of the Aleuts is perhaps one of the most touching documents in this book.

After Baranov's removal, conditions gradually improved for the native population, and the government required the company to subsidize the mission as one of its responsibilities under the new charter. In Veniaminov's time, the Russian American Company was not only providing the pastors' salary and travel costs, but providing the funds for building and maintaining chapels and supplying these with books, flour, wine, and candles. Choir directors, wardens, and even the prosphora (church bread) bakers received stipends from the company as well.

After the sale of Alaska, however, particularly after the appointment of Dr. Sheldon Jackson as General Agent of Education in the territory, the Orthodox mission encountered increasing hostility from federal agents. This prompted Orthodox laity and clergy alike to seek redress from American and Russian officials in Washington, D.C. The *American Orthodox Messenger* published a series of stories exposing the harassment of Orthodox Christians by civil servants and missionaries, including the correspondence between the pastor at Unalaska, Rev. Alexander Kedrofsky, and Ms. Agnes Newhall, the federally funded teacher/missionary. Conflicts of this sort arose across Alaska in this era, and were resolved only when the 1917 Revolution in Russia ended all financial support for Alaskan schools. In some communities the Aleuts maintained their own schools without any external assistance, gathering children at the Orthodox church after public "American" school classes were dismissed, to assure that Aleut and/or Slavonic language literacy would continue. In some villages, the authorities forcibly closed these schools as "detrimental" to the educational progress (assimilation) of the young. In others, Aleut schools continued well into the present century. Their spirit could not be broken.

[*REPORT from Hieromonk Makarii and REPORT from Hieromonk Gideon translated by Lydia T. Black. CORRESPONDENCE between Nicolai Rezanov and Hieromonk Gideon, LETTER to Board of Directors, LETTER from Baranov, and LETTER from Monk Herman to Ianovskii are taken from* The Russian-Orthodox Religious Mission 1794–1837, *Kingston, Ontario, Limestone Press, and are reprinted with permission from Limestone Press. All other documents are from* American Orthodox Messenger.]

REPORT FROM HIEROMONK MAKARII TO THE HOLY SYNOD, DECEMBER 20, 1797, DOCUMENT #3056 GOLDER COLLECTION, LIBRARY OF CONGRESS

Note: This report begins with a description of the persecution the hieromonk encountered at Unalaska because of his objection to the unreasonably high taxation imposed by the Shelikov-Golikov Company, which apparently demanded yasak (the old imperial fur tax) nearly two decades after the Empress Katherine the Great had abolished it. (To whom the furs went is not stated in any of the reports from Kodiak.) Threatened with bodily harm and even death, Hieromonk Makarii sought protection from a rival firm, the Kisil'ev Company, whose local foreman, Svinyin, provided three guards armed with muskets and fixed bayonets, who prevented Shelikov's men from entering his barabara ("yurt"). On one occasion, his enemies tried to break into the dwelling and were prevented by Svinyin himself, who actually punched Kachutin, Shelikov's foreman at Unalaska. (ED.)

To the Holy Ruling Synod

From the Hieromonk Makarii, member of the North American Spiritual Mission, a most respectful Report:

"One Aleut died and I did not dare to perform the funeral. I asked that he be buried without me, while I sang the funeral service in my dwelling. That Aleut died without confession because I did not dare go to his house to confess him. I married couples and baptized infants under armed guard. It became so bad that I did not dare leave my dwelling without being accompanied by an armed guard.

"The Shelikov-Golikov Company men act like barbarians toward the people. They exhibit no humanity whatsoever. They forcibly take women and children as concubines. They beat people to death. Beginning in early spring they send both the healthy and sick to hunt sea otters against their will. The sickly often die on the way. They force them to continue hunting until autumn so that they have no time to attend to their own subsistence activities, to store food for themselves, or to take animals to make winter parkas. The same company does not provide them with bird skins for parkas or any other clothing. They suffer greatly from cold. Because of the humilation of being beaten, they commit suicide. Many die of starvation. If someone fails to make his quota of foxes, that Aleut is thrown to the ground, stripped of clothing and mercilessly flogged with thick leather chords and they say, "You are too lazy to hunt sea otters and foxes for Yasak!" and they take everything for the company. They even force those whose bodies are infected, or whose legs are rotting. Those who walk with crutches and cannot walk are forced to fish for the company, to tow in drift wood or make baidarkas. Also people are deported to the uninhabited northern islands [Pribilofs] against their will to harvest seals for the company. Even those who walk on two crutches are deprived of their children, so there is no one to feed them. Sometimes they bring a baidarka to the seashore and such disabled persons are forced to fish for their own subsistence and household. If they catch nothing, they go hungry.

"The manager Maxim Kribdin kept a minor girl who had been baptized as his concubine. At one time he committed a licentious act and that same day called her to his bed. When she refused, he beat her on the back with a stick until she bled. There is no one to offer protection for anyone. The Russians do whatever they want. The Aleuts are in despair of the monarch's mercy, and they say that there is no one to whom they can go for help. I was barely able to persuade them that the Sovereign's mercy is great and they should count on it.

"One of the members of the Shelikov-Golikov Company called himself a Kodiak priest and administered "blessings" to the Russians, thus telling the Aleuts that anyone who does not allow them to keep girls is sinning. Another told the Aleuts that I am a Tatar! Another ridiculed me, asking the Aleuts, 'Did the Pope baptize you? What did he give you?' They are leading the newly baptized people into temptation and confusion with blasphemy. There is no one to prevent them from talking this way.

"During my stay in the islands, I was made privy to secret matters which concern the government and which are being forwarded in a report to His Imperial Majesty. No one but His Imperial Majesty can be trusted with this information. For this reason I asked for the foreman Svinyin's vessel which was scheduled to sail to Okhotsk. Upon arrival, we went to the commandant to complain. I was accompanied by chiefs who had been awarded state medals. More than twenty people have come to request protection from the men of the Shelikov-Golikov Company and their unbearable audacious conduct, and the extreme debauchery of the manager Vasilii Merculiev and his foreman Kachutin and their crew who are acting illegally in North America.

"The head chief Alexei Shelikov, and Petr Mukhavl'ev who signed contracts with the Shelikov-Golikov Company are kept in virtual slavery. The chiefs who were charged with the administration of the islands and have been awarded medals have petitioned the foreman Svinyin to take them under his protection. One chief from Kusikh village, Feodor Asitrov, is without feet. He walks with two crutches. He gathered all his subordinate Aleut men in his village and called Svinyin into his dwelling. There he knelt down before Svinyin and cried bitter tears, asking him to take them under his protection. Seeing this, I could not restrain my tears, and Svinyin himself began weeping, feeling so sorry about their predicament. Seldom does one find an adult who has not been beaten in this village. They asked for protection not in joy but in great sorrow.

"The island chiefs petitioned the Okhotsk administration to appoint Svinyin as its representative at Unalaska, but this was rejected, and now they are without any kind of protection. The authorities will send written instructions to the Russians, not to rob, not to insult, not to commit any evil deeds, but nobody will pay any attention to this. They will do whatever they want. They always say, "The sky is high, the Tsar is far away," and they can do whatever they want. There will be no regrets, they say, as long as there are sea otters.

"The newly-enlightened people cry not tears but blood. They hoped to have relief. They thought that Svinyin will be sent, because they like him, respect him, and are loyal to him. They love him for his kind conduct and sincere support.

"A chief Yelisei Popachev, accompanied me, and two Aleut interpreters, Nikolai Lukanin and Nikifor Svinvin. We are proceeding to His Imperial Majesty with secret reports and complaints. We left the islands June 25, 1796. We arrived in the Kurile islands on September 7, and spent the winter there. On June 30, 1797 we departed for Okhotsk, where we arrived July 28. We left Okhotsk August 8, and arrived at Yakutsk on September 12. We stopped in Yakutsk to await the [freezing of the] winter trail, and if the Lord Wills that we survive, we shall leave Yakutsk along the first passable trail.

"I, most humble and unworthy, dare to report because I myself have been in extreme danger and am in a very difficult state. In the Aleutians it was bitter. At my arrival at Okhotsk, the office of the Shelikov-Golikov Company manager, Kursk merchant Nikifor Shmatov, and Rylsk merchant Zidor Shelikov tried to keep me in Okhotsk or send me back to Kodiak. When I humbly informed the Okhotsk commandant, Prince Minitskii in writing that I am proceeding to His Imperial Majesty with secret reports, they ceased their opposition. Thus I passed Okhotsk. I fear that in Irkutsk, the administrator, at the request of Golikov and Shelikov, might detain me and the Aleuts there, and will confiscate the documents and secret reports I am carrying. Therefore I am reporting in advance to the Holy Synod, so that they will be informed about these matters."

Hieromonk Makarii

Note: The "secret reports" Hieromonk Makarii delivered to St. Petersburg are not available in any Western archive, but the originals probably survive in the Soviet Union and await discovery and translation. The accusations leveled in this document against the Shelikov-Golikov company are precisely the charges this company made against its rivals in order to secure and later justify its monopoly in the name of "law and order." ED.

REPORT FROM CATHEDRAL HIEROMONK GIDEON TO THE HOLY SYNOD, 1–2 JUNE 1805

[Working Conditions]

Of the seventy families brought over from the Fox Islands in 1786 some thirty people have remained who are employed in summer in bird hunting on the Peregrebnye Islands, and in the area from the mouth of Kenai Bay near the mainland to Voskresenskaia Harbor [Resurrection Bay], Chugach and the adjacent islands. They carry on this hunting together with the Kenais and the Chugach. They are required by the company to catch enough for ten parkas. Over and above this they must hunt for themselves, their wives and children. Anyone who does not succeed in hunting for himself is given a parka by the company but, as has been described above, as a result five foxes or fur seals are deducted from his winter catch, not counting the fact that each summer the company receives 10 parkas from each man completely free of charge, for which it receives an otter each. Anyone who catches more than the five animals mentioned is paid by the company as much as it sees fit. Their wives are also used as kaiurkas.

In 1801 the company drove out the Aleuts in the Sitkhin otter hunting party in the following manner: They prepared beforehand leg irons and neck yokes, and made ready birches for the young ones, ropes' ends for the thirty-year-olds and canes for the old men. A baidara was sent off armed with a cannon and rifles. On the western cape of Kadiak, on coming to the shore, the Russian hunters stood on guard with loaded rifles, shouting: "If you don't want to go on the expedition just say so now (cocking their guns), and we'll shoot." Under such pressure who could show displeasure? When they arrived off the island of Sitkhinak, they fired the cannon and, standing with rifles ready, spread out the iron shackles on the ground near the dwellings, together with the birch rods, canes, manacles and yokes, saying, "Anyone who doesn't want to go with us should choose one of these." At this one man began to protest. They seized him, put him in irons, and flogged him until he was hoarse from screaming and could hardly say, "I'll go!"

In the same year, at the beginning of May, one of the old men recruited for the bird-hunting party was sent out in such a state that he could hardly crawl to the night camp some hundred sazhens away, and he spent the night with his wife on the beach. In the morning he was summoned, or rather carried to the administrator's house for a medical examination. There they told him: "Even though you cannot walk you can still keep watch and stop the dogs from eating the baidara."

In 1798 some twenty men in the Sitkhin party were drowned and about the same number died in the course of the journey.

In 1799, 140 men in the same party died as a result of eating shellfish when they were starving. Some 40 more died on the journey.

In 1800 the Tugidok party was sent to sea in bad weather by the hunter Lopatin, in spite of their protests, and 32 baidarkas were lost as a result—some 64 men.

In 1805 an inhabitant of Ubaguitsk was sent out in a bird-hunting party when seriously ill, concerning which I wrote the following letter to the assistant manager, Banner:

> Dear Sir
> Ivan Ivanovich!
>
> Nikolai Chunagonak from the village of Ubaguik on the island of Sitkhinak is lame and seriously ill with a dangerous affliction of the throat. This has already caused a sore to break out on his neck. His lower lip is festering and he has sores on his legs. His chest has crepitation so that he cannot speak. Artamonov has dispatched this unfortunate sufferer on a bird-hunting expedition. Can you not judge for yourself, My dear sir, what sort of birdcatcher he would make in this sorry state and what profit he would bring to the company? Take pity, I beg you, on this feeble man and order instead that he be sent to the medical hut, i.e. to the kazhim. He is still young, and when he recovers he could be of use to the company. By such an act of compassion you would be doing a service to humanity, and I would be deeply indebted to you if you heed my request. Firm in my hope of your magnanimity, and with sincere respect I have the honor to be
>
> etc.
>
> 1805. 8th June

In the same year in the last days of October as the party was on its way back from Sitkha, some 300 men were drowned.

Because of the above-mentioned onerous company duties the Aleuts in all the villages are subjected to great hunger in the wintertime. They eat the seal bladders in which they store fat, the bitter salmon roe and laftaks, cord and other articles made from gut, because they have no shellfish and seaweed when the beaches are covered with ice. A man with any feeling can hardly keep back the tears when he sees these unfortunates in such a situation. They look more like corpses than living people. When the husbands go off on hunting parties the wives and small children, and the feeble old men and women, both because they have no baidarkas and because of the summer duties imposed upon them by the company, such as cleaning fish, digging sarana root and picking berries, are unable and have no time to lay in the necessary foodstocks for the winter: and thus it often happens that many of them starve to death. Is all this not more onerous and destructive than the payment of *iasak* or tribute which has not been collected since 1794? And is it a sign of *kind and friendly treatment?* These words always occupy pride of place on the company's lips and in its documents, but not in its deeds.

In 1805 I had the honor to send to your Holiness through the agency of Lieutenants Arbuzov and Povalishin the following report:

Most Holy Archpastor!
On my arrival on 2nd July, 1804 at the main possession of the Russian-American Company I considered it my first and most sacred duty to give thanks in the American Kadiak Church to the Source of all goodness for our safe arrival after a journey half-way round the world. My pen is too weak to convey all the outpourings of my soul when I sweetly heard that in the New World, a country so remote from easy communication with bountiful Russia, a country still savage, the name of Triapostolic God was so devoutly praised, and that pronounced more often than the name of any other mortal was the name of the most august of His Anointed—worthy and adored genius of expansive Russia—Alexander the First. Let us leave what I cannot describe, Most Holy Archpastor, and examine the following:

Of the people left here by the Bishop designate of Kadiak Ioasaf there remain four men: Hieromonk Afanasii who celebrates the services, Hierodeacon Nektarii who looks after the vestments and the monks Herman and Ioasaf who are in charge of the economy—men suited to their task. All of them have tried to the best of their ability to instruct the local people. With their own hands they have started vegetable plots from which in one year they harvested eighty chetveriks of potatoes, and there are also reasonable quantities of turnips and radishes. From the potatoes they make flour; the turnips are cut up into small pieces and pickled, the absence of salt is made up for by using sea water and the resulting vegetable pickle is used winter and summer instead of cabbage. The remaining fruits of their labors they put towards helping the poor inhabitants. Their attitude as preachers is marked by kindness and they have impressed a good opinion of themselves on the minds of the Americans. In the past year of 1804 as an experiment they sowed four pounds of barley in ground which had been manured, and had a yield of one and a half puds. The soil in these regions is fertile only in certain places, where there have been Aleut villages, and of these there are quite a few on Kadiak and the nearby islands.

On the 6th of the aforementioned month I crossed by boat to the Religious Mission's quarters and, after examining all of the church utensils, vestments, books and domestic equipment, I set off on the 26th with a company interpreter in two three-man baidarkas to preach the word of God round the whole of Kadiak and also the adjoining islands of Ugak, Shalidak, Aiakhtalik, Sitkhinok and Tugidok. When I had been to all the Aleut settlements I tried as best I was able to instill into the newly enlightened what they needed for faith, some civic virtues and skills of husbandry. I tried by all the means at my disposal to penetrate their earlier superstitions. I first revealed them through friendly counselling and then showed them the obvious stupidity of such beliefs and the evil which was rooted in them, and by such means I brought them to the rules of the true aspect of God. To judge by external appearances they seemed to listen to me willingly. It would often happen that they would sit for more than eight hours without getting up and going away, and I was everywhere received with kindness. In addition to fish I was entertained with sarana and whale fat and berries: raspberries, shiksha, cranberries and blackberries also mixed with whale fat. I made them gifts of tobacco, beads, needles, worsted, iamanina or long goat's hair.

On the 21st of August in the straits separating Aiakhtalik from Kadiak my heart was filled with sorrow. For after a calm and a mist a strong contrary wind arose—the rowers were tired—the weather grew worse—we seemed at a point of no return. But, thank God, we gradually drew nearer to a barren shore, where we spent three days and nights. We gave thanks to the Creator of all things that we were not short of food, i.e. iukola and whale meat.

During the whole course of my trip, i.e. for two months and five days, I baptized 503 souls of both sexes, between the ages of one and ten, also 22 souls aged forty, and I wed 32 couples.

On the 21st of November the Russian-American Company arranged a feast to celebrate the successful capture of the Kolosh Sitkha fort on Baranov Island and the inclusion of those areas under the scepter of Russian power: at the end of the liturgy a prayer of thanks was offered to All-generous God for the health of His Imperial Majesty and that of all his most august house. On the evening before there was a funeral service for those killed in the taking of the fort, ten men in all, i.e. three sailors from the vessel *Neva,* three Russian hunters and four Aleuts from Kadiak. Those wounded included the manager Baranov, Lieutenant Povalishin, the junior surgeon, the junior bo'sun, the quartermaster and eight sailors, one cannonneer and seven hunters.

In the remaining time at my leisure I took up composing and preaching sermons on the Lord's Day, on high days and holidays, I exercised myself by translating from French into Russian Bourdaloue and Blère [?]; I also undertook the training of Hierodeacon Nektarii as teacher in the Kadiak school. He has great willingness and aptitude for learning, especially for mechanics. Before my arrival, and without any aid from anyone else, he had been teaching Russian grammar—he had also taught himself to make wall clocks. I introduced him to the basic principles of other sciences, arithmetic, history and geography, and also taught him some French.

The Kadiak School opened in 1805, and consisted of two classes. In the first thirty pupils were taught the rudiments of reading and writing and the short catechism. In the second class twenty were taught Russian grammar, arithmetic, sacred and profane history and geography. In addition to the sciences, attention was also given to instruction husbandry. Instead of resting they were taught how to prepare the vegetable plots and plant and sow vegetables, how to cut and harvest various grasses, roots and how to fish. There was also a section for the shoemaker's and cobbler's craft.

For this small, growing Russian-American garden inspiration and precipitation from above is needed: therefore the American Kadiak Church, turning its gaze towards the Russian Zion, devoutly calls upon You, Most Holy Archpastor. Stand at north and south and blow into this place, and let your mercy flow, for the greater benefit of these newly enlightened regions.

And I throw myself on your inexhaustible mercy, I call to you and say. I call to you in my hour of need. Hear me and take heed of me; never forget me.

Your Holiness's etc. . . .

1805 1st June
Kadiak

Secret

Benevolent Metropolitan

Since the receipt of reliable information about the unfortunate wreck of the company vessel *Phoenix,* on which the Very Reverend Bishop of Kadiak, Ioasaf, had set out from Okhotsk, the following has happened to the clergy remaining here. In addition to encouraging the Aleuts to commit many stupid acts, which could have only been thought up on the company's part to besmirch the honor of the clergy, out of envy for the great love which this childlike people has for its enlighteners, the manager Baranov, thinking this to be the reason for a diminution of his authority over the Americans, worn out by their various duties and the company taxes, on 14th July, 1800, in a letter to the steward of the Religious Mission, the Monk Herman, forbade the clergy to have any contact with the Americans and ordered all those who were on close terms with the preachers to be driven off.

In accordance with the Imperial Manifesto published in the year 1796, the Kadiak people should have been brought to swear an oath of allegiance to the Russian Throne. As a result of being sent great distances by the company and lack of time this had not been done. Therefore, on 1st January 1801, Hieromonk Afanasii sought Baranov's permission to do this. In return the Hieromonk himself was shouted out and driven off with a warning not to come back. Then some twenty men from various villages gathered with their taions to ask Baranov to release them from the obligation of any further distant hunting trips by the Sitkha party, promising in return to hunt near their villages, but they were chased away and threatened with dire consequences. Then all were ordered to prepare for another spring expedition. They were then very bitter and desperate and dared inform the missionaries that they did not want to go on this expedition because many of their relatives had died [on previous ones to Sitkha] and some of their villages were deserted. And if Baranov were to have them killed as a result they had each brought a new parka along and they asked the missionaries to bury them afterwards in their new clothes, and bear witness to this killing of innocents. On hearing this the clergy and the officers who were present—navigator Talin and the Religious Mission's interpreter Prianishnikov—were horrified and tried to talk them into forbearance, assuring them that His Imperial Majesty would be favorably disposed. When the taions had calmed down a little the matter of the oath of allegiance to the Sovereign was raised. They readily agreed to this and promised to obey in all things. Thus they set off for the church, accompanied by the same two officers and the swearing of the oath was conducted by Hieromonk Afanasii. As they left the church and were only just getting into their baidarkas, Baranov's deputy, Kuskov, with his hunters, seized one of the leading taions and took him off to the company barracks. Here he was put in irons and flung into a dark cell where not only the windows but every crack had been boarded up. The hunters then set out after the others in a baidara, with their rifles, but they caught no one.

After this incident Baranov wanted to seize and imprison another taion, a godson of the Bishop, who had come to see the priests on a friendly visit. When they learned of this the priests decided to accompany him that night on his return journey. As a precaution the Hieromonk Afanasii ordered his own baidarka to be made ready first, then he walked to it and was about to enter it to travel for a short distance when suddenly some hunters, acting on Baranov's orders, stopped the baidarka and seized the Hieromonk. Then Baranov himself, in a towering range, began to curse, calling Afanasii a runaway state serf and all the priests and the two above-mentioned officers rebels.

Faced with such an unpleasant series of events, the monk Herman asked Baranov to declare in decent language the reason for his displeasure. The manager shouted: "Now you've found some kind of oath and used it to turn the Americans against us!"

The humble elder replied: "The Imperial Manifesto was made public to all; if indeed the Religious Mission has acted at all illegally then the matter should be reported to the government where everything can be examined in accordance with the law."

But Baranov paid no heed to this and continued shouting: "What manifesto? What court?" And at the height of his rage he made many threats. First he said he would have them put in irons and taken to Unalashka, then that the mission's quarters would be locked and boarded up so that no one could get to them and they could not go out. This made everyone greatly afraid and they all expected at any moment to be seized by the hunters on Baranov's orders and dragged off or beaten. They hardly dared leave the shore to return to their house, around which they could see a crowd of armed hunters. For the same reason they did not even dare go freely to the church, and consequently for more than a year they conducted all their services in the house, and they also doubted their loyalty, because the oath of allegiance had been forbidden.

When the time came round to form the otter hunting party, Kuskov armed a baidara not only with rifles but also with a cannon and set out for the village inhabited by the natives who had sworn the oath. In order to achieve a greater effect, partovshchik Kondakov was ordered to travel ahead. Arriving at the village he cursed foully, made sneering remarks about the priests, and then shouted loudly: "Come out to meet us—the priests are coming, and Osip (the interpreter) is here to get you to swear the oath!" And when the rudder was carried ashore from the baidara they all shouted: "Here's your cross! Get down and worship it!" And they went on to commit angry, violent and shameless acts against the islanders, too shameful to mention.

Baranov explained this evildoing by alleging that the Americans, at the instigation of the priests and the two above-mentioned officers, had rebelled and would have killed all the Russians, and this was why Kuskov took hostages on this expedition. After this Baranov began in every conceivable way to oppress the priests, in the preparation of winter food stocks and in other vital matters.

In 1802 in Holy Week the hunter Chernov arrived drunk and said with great coarseness that he came from Baranov with orders that Hierodeacon Nektarii should unlock the belfry. The Hierodeacon was unwilling to give him the key because the church was only secured with one lock, and the large bell was broken. The hunter then flew into a rage and brazenly threatened either to drag him there by force or to smash the windows in the bell tower. Meanwhile the interpreter Prianishnikov, who was ill, had sent a note to the Hieromonk and the Hierodeacon asking them to sanctify his house with the Holy Cross. No sooner had they gone there when Baranov came running up together with his hunters, beside himself with rage, shouting, cursing and threatening to put the Hieromonk in a baidarka and set him adrift. He grabbed the Hierodeacon violently by the chest and wanted to hang him from the bell tower. This caused the latter such fright that he was forced to yield the key to the church. During all these brazen acts the hunters would say with reference to their manager, "God is high and the Tsar is far away—all is fine as long as our boss is alive and well!"

For reasons described above, as well as the fact that the Americans no longer dared to visit the priests openly, and the priests for their part were afraid to have the relations with them that their calling demanded—when they would have been able to instill Christian teachings into them—the success of the Religious Mission did not come up to expectations. For those of our compatriots who were obliged to work for the company were of the lowest and most immoral kind, as the local manager himself testifies constantly when he calls them people from the Kama and the Volga. The Americans, on the other hand, are so burdened by endless labors and so harassed that wherever the Russians set up settlements they attract hatred. Even distant peoples on the fringes of our territories found the word 'Russian' an object of hatred. The women kill their babies in the womb and sometimes later, rather than let them be tortured by the company. In this current year in the settlements on the island of Shalitok mothers deliberately stopped feeding children aged between eight and ten, and killed five by starving them in this way so that they should not become workers for the Russians.

The Manager, growing fearful lest the oath should be confirmed and that reports of oppression of the clergy should become known to officers on visiting company ships tried to smooth over what he had done; and for this reason he found himself forced to forward the Manifesto and letters belonging to the Religious Mission which had up to then been held back, and let it be known that all should be made to swear the oath—thus the priests, no longer in doubt about loyalty, began, as from 15th September, 1802 to conduct services in the church once more. Baranov became more favorably disposed towards them: first he sent two pounds of tea and four pounds of sugar, then a barrel of whale fat, a cask of whale meat, and a barrel of shiksha berries mixed with fat, which is known in the northern area of Russia as *voronitsa,* but the people there do not eat it. A short while later he sent a paper which, in return for the conducting of the service for those killed at Sitkha, gave the bearer the right to draw any goods from the stores to the value of 500 rubles. Subsequently another note arrived from the same office, in which as a result of a collection among some hunters and the manager during their operations there was forwarded to be used as befitted more than three thousand rubles, the greater part to go to the church and a lesser portion for the brothers. Against such a sum they took what they needed from the company stores at the very highest prices as, for example, a pud of tobacco at 75 rubles, a pound of sugar at 3 rubles 60 kopeks, a pound of tea at 8 and 6 rubles, a pud of wheat biscuits at 20 rubles, a measure of vodka at 25 rubles and for domestic use hempen rope of the lowest quality at 1 ruble a pound.

The clergy all live in one house allotted them by the company, in a cramped position between the manager's house and the communal company baths. They feed themselves, by and large, on the fruits of their own labors. Apart from their vegetable crops they gather various berries and mushrooms, catch fish and receive supplementary supplies from the company. All of these tasks are carried out with the help of Americans, whom the company tries in every way to drive away.

The priests wear clothing and shoes from the stock remaining since the time of Bishop Ioasaf; they also have grain—which was originally brought here by Shelekhov—namely, 250 puds of rye, 20 puds of wheat for holy wafers and 20 puds of assorted groats. Before the departure of the Bishop, the Bishop's house on Kadiak was credited with 150 puds of rye.

Hierodeacon Nektarii is 36 and the monk Ioasaf is 32, and both wish greatly to return to Russia and with heavy hearts they beg and beseech You, Most Holy and Most Merciful Father, for your Archpastoral blessing: Let their prayers be fulfilled before you, in Christ, like holy incense. For their hearts are full of sorrow. Comfort them, blessed comforter of the Church of Russia!

The Hieromonk is 50, and the Monk Herman 48. Both are lovers of solitude and wish to remain in America. But because of the fact that the house allotted to them is right next to secular ones, making it impossible for them to escape the noise and temptations, the boundless acts of crude inhumanity committed by the Russians on each other, but mostly on the Americans under them, as well as the fact that they have far to go to fetch firewood and other things needed in the house and because of the general unsuitability and cramped conditions of the place, they are very frustrated. Their intention is to put some distance between themselves and these noisy places, to have a calm life in particular somewhere near the church, and if there is no source (i.e. either official or private) from which they can get food and the necessary supplies, then at least they can place their hopes on the fruits of their own labors. They can choose a spot which has ready supplies of wood for building, is near a stream for fishing and has suitable ground for tilling.

Most Holy Archpastor! Hear my cry! Do not turn Thy face away, most Merciful Father, from this single, humble son of Thy Holy House, for I suffer. Quickly, quickly, hear me! Lead my soul out of the darkness to confess in Thy name.

Your Holiness's etc. . . .

2nd day of June
1805
Kadiak

Your Most worthy Eminence,

Carrying the impress deep in my heart of your most holiness's Apostolic teachings I have tried in all things to act in accordance with them, but people's characters are not equal—especially those of the men with whom I was unfortunate enough to spend my time for almost a year in my journey on the vessel *Neva*—Captain Lisianskii and Midshipman Berkh were people with unruly natures and caused me much offence, against which my only cure was boundless patience, and I shall now pass over in silence the long prohibition on Sundays and the Lord's Holy Days to conduct God's services—at sea the only comfort was from them—and I am ashamed to repeat the various sneering remarks made about religion. The son of the Archpriest Lisianskii, of the town of Nezhin, although seemingly raised in the very lap of religion, was often so bold as to drink Madeira at table, addressing me with the words: "Father! To the health of the Mother of God!" During our stay on the island of St. Catherine in Brazil under the guise of being kind to me he tried by all the means at his disposal to make me quarrel with His Excellency [Rezanov]. En route from the stormy Cape Horn to Easter Island, on the 25th March, 1804, another storm from the captain was brewing up for me, humble elder that I am; he wanted to lock me in my cabin, to imprison me simply because I was sitting on the quarter-deck when he was walking on the bridge, but for love of me the other officers stepped in and protected me. On the Marquesas Islands he gave orders to the crew not to lower a boat to put me ashore because in the evening when I arrived from the *Nadezhda* I had not gone to the captain's cabin and reported my arrival to him personally, although the officer of the watch had known about it. Life would be impossible without patience. For that reason I bore all these sufferings with magnanimous forbearance: When we called at the Sandwich Islands I did not even go ashore. On Kadiak the captain could no longer commit the same insults as at first, but tried to persuade the Manager's gubernia secretary that I had been sent there as a punishment; he tried by all the means at his disposal to take away two boys who were being trained by the Religious Mission for the church, although there were many others in the Kadiak school and then he persuaded the office to send me a communication about the sending off of the two boys. As was my legal right, I refused and a copy of my refusal is enclosed. All these circumstances clearly bore witness to his hatred of religion and of the clergy. He himself offered proof of this because when he left the post here he took with him one of the best pupils, so good that his training would already have enabled him to become a deacon. There is also attached here a copy of a letter to the religion Mission, handing into my care the House of God and all religious matters—and also a copy with the papers given me by His Honor Nikolai Petrovich Rezanov. Most holy archpastor! Both bitter and sweet waters flow from one source. Firmly trusting in Thy boundless mercy I call again and again, lead my soul out of darkness to find confession in Thy name.

Your Most Holy etc. . . .

CORRESPONDENCE BETWEEN NICOLAI REZANOV AND CATHEDRAL HIEROMONK GIDEON DECEMBER 1803–AUGUST 1805

Most Worthy Father Gideon,
My Dear Sir!

Setting off from the island of St. Catherine, although I hope to have the pleasure of meeting you again on the Sandwich Islands, where, as you know, the last meeting of our ships is planned; but as it may easily happen that the stormy passage round Cape Horn could drive us so far apart that our ships will have to take such course as is dictated by the circumstances encountered—right as far as the coasts of Northwest America themselves: So I consider it my duty in addition to my personal explanations with you, and better to advance the achievement of the great design entrusted to us by the Sovereign Emperor, to explain to your worthiness my thoughts in writing as well.

I have a special respect for the cloth which you have so ardently donned and I am convinced that on your arrival in America you will in the very best fashion carry out the Most Noble will of our Most Merciful Sovereign—which seeks to encourage the spreading of the Orthodox Christian faith for the good of the American inhabitants themselves—so that their minds may be cleansed of superstition, and that you may implant in their hearts the rules of the respect for God, and so that, with all humility, driving away all prejudice which is so alien to the true Religion, you might prepare them for living together, show them their duty with relation to the Sovereign and their dependents and make them into good sons of Russia. Success in this important transformation promises you eternal fame, the grateful attention of the Sovereign, and the recognition of posterity.

On your arrival in America try to gain by persuasive behavior the favorable disposition of the local authorities and all the local inhabitants, make it your first task by every means to cement good relations between the Russians and the Americans, and make it clear to both groups that they form one Russian people, that they are both subjects of one Sovereign and that there is no better way of attracting the attention of His Most Imperial Majesty than by everywhere working for the common good by respecting humanity and obeying the authorities.

You may warn them of my impending arrival, and you can assure them that the Sovereign Emperor, as a sign of his most gracious concern for these distant parts, has most graciously endowed me with the power of honoring sons who have served their country with rewards, and that my considerations in this respect will be based upon the real experience of the industry and good works of everyone, that it is my duty to report to the Emperor on each of them, for which purpose his subjects are all equal. If it should happen that anyone, as the result of the weakness to which all men are subject, should have strayed from the true path then he will still have sufficient time before my arrival not only to put himself to rights but even to do some good.

Your worthiness is aware that in these fortunate times enlightenment in Russia is the main preoccupation of the country's ruler, lover of humanity that he is. In accordance with his noble plans I entrust to your care the running of the school on Kadiak which I hope you will transform into a properly organized institution. I have written to the authorities on Kadiak and you should receive every cooperation from them. If the young people there have already been taught reading and writing, give them a true conception of God's Laws and natural laws. Also undertake to introduce them to the rule of grammar, arithmetic and lay a firm basis for the other sciences.

Grain-growing, animal husbandry and other economic activities, although they may not fall directly into your honor's purview, would lead me to beseech you as an educated man, that if you should know anything about any of them do not fail to share your counsels with the local authorities to the general good and prosperity of the area.

In conclusion I must convey my intentions and concern for you yourself, filled as I am with sure hope that you will amply justify my choice of you in the fulfillment of these important plans. I do not find it necessary that you should return to Russia on Mr. Lisianskii's vessel. Therefore be so good as to wait for me in America and to continue your journey together with me. I have most humbly given notice to his Imperial Majesty of my intention in this respect. And now it only remains for us to await the beneficence of the All-merciful—that He should bless our good intentions with a successful outcome.

I remain with sincere respect
My Dear Sire, Your most humble
servant, Nikolai Rezanov

Brazil
St. Catherine Island
December 21st 1803/Jan. 6th 1804
No. 176

From the Company Office on Kadiak
to the Kadiak Religious Mission.

His Honor Actual Chamberlain, and Chevalier of various orders, Nikolai Petrovich Rezanov, in letter No. 175 (23rd December, 1803) to His Excellency Collegiate Counsellor and Manager of the Russian-American territories, Aleksandr Andreevich Baranov made it known that in respect to the unfortunate rumors concerning the loss of the *Phoenix,* however undesirable these may be, it must now be concluded in the absence of evidence to the contrary that they are true. In the light of this circumstance, His Honor has dispatched for the spreading of Christian Orthodoxy a clerical personage proffering this faith—Hieromonk Gideon, whose reputation as a worthy man has preceded his arrival here. If to our heartfelt and great distraction we have lost the Most Holy Ioasaf then the House of God and all religious matters are to be placed in the care of Hieromonk Gideon. Therefore this is to inform the Kadiak Religious Mission of this state of affairs and to require immediate execution of his honor's wishes. January 23rd, 1805. Signed in the capacity of Manager, Gubernia Secretary Ivan Banner. No. 99.

From the Cathedral Hieromonk Gideon
to the Company Office on Kadiak

A most important preoccupation of His Imperial Majesty is the teaching of the faith and the establishment of the Church in these parts: the company itself cannot be unaware of this. For this reason the Most Reverend Ioasaf, who was here, considered it a most important matter, and a most hard-won achievement in these far-off areas to prepare some of the children here for Sacred and Church duties, and he left written instructions on the subject.

Since the Church locally has no one to perform the duties of deacon and minister I consider it my duty, wishing the Church to be in the best possible state for the pleasure and instructions of the Christian parishioners, to state that it is necessary to have both the boys, Kulikalov and Prianishnikov, who have been illegally demanded by the office, and the others at the Religious Mission who are already trained in matters relating to Church services.

In addition, the office is well aware of the expectations of a very important person, his Imperial Majesty's Plenipotentiary and the Organizer of these lands, Actual Chamberlain and Cavalier Nikolai Petrovich Rezanov, that all spiritual and religious matters shall be left pending His Excellency's arrival.

Because of this I dare not send the above-mentioned boys to the Master of the Company vessel *Neva,* Captain Lieutenant and Cavalier Lisianskii. 11th day of March, 1805. Cathedral Hieromonk Gideon.

On the 28th day of July, 1805, Kadiak was overjoyed by the arrival of His Excellency N.P. Rezanov.

On the 7th of August His Excellency sent me a note containing the following message:

Most Worthy Father Gideon,
My Dear Sir!

As I am organizing all these areas of America I shall make it one of the first of my tasks to go into the actual state of the Religious Mission here and to take firm measures to alleviate the sufferings of those worthy men who have rejected all secular pleasures and seek in the Lord's name to enlighten and educate ignorant mankind. While with great respect doing justice to their enthusiastic achievements and expressing my sincerest gratitude to you as their main guide and mentor, I would most humbly request your honor to inform me how much is needed annually for the upkeep of the clergy and the Church buildings, and to provide me with the pleasure of adding to it the means at my disposal as a sign of that undying respect with which I am always ready to be the most humble servant of your honor and all worthy fathers.

Nikolai Rezanov

7th August [1805]
Pavlovsk Harbor

To which I immediately replied:

Your Excellency,
Dear Sir.

Noting with most warm gratitude Your Excellency's most ardent solicitude for the well-being of the Religious Mission here, I find the following absolutely necessary:
(1) The building of houses and the necessary tools and materials associated with this, e.g. saws, metal for axes, spades, mattocks and spades for digging, nails, hemp, pitch; canvas for boat sails, glass, wooden and metal vessels, saucepans, teapots, rope and cable for nets and sieves, salt, candles and writing paper.
(2) Provisions must be issued in kind as to a naval chaplain to each man, with the exception of meat and beer, but with the addition of tea and sugar.
(3) According to status of the person two changes of winter and summer clothes and footwear, and five shirts and pairs of pants each year to each man; also flannel for cowls and velveteen and chamois for ordinary dress.
(4) As a means of paying the Americans who work eagerly around the house and for other necessities such as outstanding success in education and enlightenment when they are being trained, the following are useful: tobacco, broadcloth, cotton cloth, worsted, flannel, beads, needles and crosses.

All this was angrily refused and I consequently found myself forced to answer His Excellency as follows:

Your Excellency
Dear Sir!

Noting with heartfelt gratitude Your Excellency's favorable disposition towards the problem of the annual upkeep of the clergy, the Fathers of the Religious Mission here, Hieromonk Afanasii and the monks Herman and Ioasaf have declared to me that they are most grateful for your decision to take measures to alleviate their shortages each year as concern food, clothing and other domestic necessities. As far as the upkeep of the Church buildings is concerned, I have the honor to inform you that it is entirely dependent upon the generosity of benefactors and lovers of God. The following are desperately needed for the Church: flour for breads, wine, incense, candles and wood oil—more necessary than anything else is to stop the church roof from leaking. With sincere respect for you I have the honor to be

Your Excellency's etc. . . .

Aug. 9th, 1805

LETTER FROM NICOLAI REZANOV TO THE BOARD OF DIRECTORS OF THE RUSSIAN AMERICAN COMPANY 6 NOVEMBER 1805

As for the ecclesiastical mission, they have baptized several thousands here, but only nominally. Seeing that the ways of Kadiak natives become milder I find less explanation for that in the work of the missionaries than to time and to their own aptitude. Our monks have never followed the path of the Jesuits in Paraguay by trying to develop the mentality of the savages, and have never known how to enter into the extensive plans of the Government or company. They have just been "bathing" the Americans and when, due to their ability to copy, the latter learn in half an hour how to make the sign of the cross, our missionaries return, proud of their success, thinking that their job is done. Having little to do they try to take part in the civil government of the country, calling themselves government representatives. The restless officers use them as their tools against the Manager. The result is grief and there is danger of our losing the whole country. I will give you an example. At the time of the coronation of the Emperor, the monks without a word to the manager sent out orders calling all the natives to Kadiak to take the oath of allegiance. There were no provisions at Kadiak and if the manager had not stopped the people from gathering by sending his men to their villages, several thousand of them gathering at Kadiak would have killed everybody from starvation alone.

Sometimes, unknown to the manager, they would set off uselessly to make new converts. On the Alaska peninsula trade, which promised big profits, was opened with the hill natives, on Lake Iliamna, sometimes called Lake Shelikhov. The monk Juvenal went there immediately to propagate the faith. He baptized them forcibly, married them, took girls away from some and gave them to others. The Americans endured his rough ways and even beatings for a long time, but finally held council, decided to get rid of the Reverend and killed him. He does not deserve pity, but the Iliamna natives in their exasperation killed the whole crew of Russians and Kadiak people. Since then this people think of revenge and fearing that the Russians will settle there again, show no mercy at the slightest misstep. Last year they killed Russians again. I told the holy fathers that if any of them took another step without first getting the Manager's approval, or if they meddled in civil affairs, I would order such criminals deported to Russia, where for disrupting the peace of the community such people would be defrocked and severely punished to make an example of them. They cried, rolled at my feet and told me that it was the government employees who had told them what to do. They promised me to behave, so that the Manager would have nothing but praise for them in the future. I admonished them thus privately in the presence of Father Gideon but in public I have always shown respect for their dignity.

Now that the monks understand their mistakes they do their best to help the company in agriculture and in education of the younger generation. In the field of education Father Nektarii shows talent and aptitude so I made him director of the school and have promised to intercede so that a salary will be paid to him, which he deserves for his labors. I gave Father Herman twenty boys to be trained in agriculture. They will be taken to Spruce Island to experiment with sowing wheat, planting potatoes and vegetables and to learn how to make preserves of mushrooms and berries, how to make nets and cure fish, etc. During the winter they will be returned to school where they will learn to read and write and will receive religious training. In this way I will make ready for you the first twenty families of agricultural settlers and think that after they get used to work these boys will become reliable and literate farmers.

I also explained to the monks what missionary work consists of. I shamed them for not yet knowing the American language, telling them that not only the prayers but even the sermons must be translated into the American Language. I commissioned them to make a dictionary, so as not to be at the mercy of the interpreters, who often interpret what is told to them incorrectly. Because a job of this kind looked as big and forbidding as a bear, I began to make this dictionary myself. This dictionary took quite a bit of work and enclosing it here, I beg you to publish it for the American schools and to send bound copies here. I hope that owing to its novelty there will be a demand for it in Russia also and that several percent can be deducted from the sales for the benefit of the school pupils. As far as the ecclesiastics are concerned you see that they are now living up to sound and strict rules.

LETTER FROM ALEXANDER BARANOV TO CATHEDRAL HIEROMONK GIDEON, 28 MAY 1807

A true copy of a letter written by Aleksandr Andreevich Baranov in his own hand to Hieromonk Gideon:

To the Cathedral Hieromonk of
the Aleksandr Nevskii Lavr
Father Gideon, formerly
attached to the Kadiak Mission,
from Manager Baranov:

My dear sir,

I have the honor to send you the following explanation to your letters of 27th May.

First, concerning the wreck of the company frigate *Phoenix* and the loss of the Most Holy Ioasaf who was travelling on it with all his suite, and the crew.

The said ship left Okhotsk in the autumn of 1799, and set a course straight here to Kadiak. It was sighted on the 28th day of October that year near Unalashka off the island of Umnak by the local Russians and Aleuts. Where she was wrecked is unknown, because no reliable information has been received about her since that time. The cause of the wreck is assumed to be the strong contrary wind blowing since they left Okhotsk and also the fact that there was an epidemic there of coughing blood and a fever which caused many deaths, and it may be that some of the more than 70 hunters travelling on this transport were infected by these diseases and passed them on to others. It could also be that the captain himself, Collegiate Assessor Shil'ts [Shields] died from the same illness, and that there was no one else and the boat was left without anyone in command at the mercy of the unbridled effects of the waves and winds. Though when it was sighted off Unalashka it was in full sail and with a course set for Kadiak.

The pieces of wreckage washed up first appeared in the area of Kadiak at the end of May and the beginning of June of the following year, 1800, in which months I returned from Sitkha after spending the winter there. Ship's planks were washed ashore, together with spars, the bowsprit and the windlass; on Tugidak there appeared barrels with oil, and on Shuiak and Ukamok and in various other places even as far afield as Unalashka there appeared wax candles and several beams, flagons mixed with brine which were found by partovshchiks off Cape St. Elias. On the island of Siuklia in Chugatsk Bay two leather bindings from large books were discovered and several medium and small-sized wax candles, as many of which we received we gave to the local church here. In the autumn of the same year, 1800, the rudder of the said vessel was discovered near Sitkha, and further into the bay beyond Rumiantsov Island two masts from the same vessel at about latitude 56° North. We do not know of any more wreckage and there is no reliable news of the site of the wreck. We have a report from one of the American captains, Joseph O'Cain, that he had heard from others that near Bokarelo Bay or Otter Bay where the Bering expedition under Captain Chirikov had put ashore, that there had been seen in the possession of the local natives whole suits of clothes and ragged fox furs—such as are not obtainable there either by trading or hunting, and they were therefore assumed to be Russian. But I cannot confirm the truth of this.

With regard to the second point concerning the keep of the members of the clergy remaining here attached to the Mission, during the years up to now the Fathers of the Religious Mission have never been refused anything as far as the profits and state of the company stocks allowed. I shall give orders that in future their needs shall be met when they occur and the company has a surplus. At the same time the company is itself in debt to the Religious Mission by virtue of the forty bags of rye borrowed from His Excellency and for a sizeable amount of trading goods received before that. And although at present there is not a single pound left of the former there is sufficient Sorochinsk wheat left with which we may replace it pud for pud, and as far as goods are concerned these will be issued in future in accordance with their needs, and in the meantime we must await some definitive decision by His Excellency regarding the upkeep of the Mission in its limited form. But I would most humbly ask you to decide whether issues shall be made only to the Head of the Mission, Father Herman, or to each member individually. The chief accountant and clerk need instructions on this from the Religious Mission in order to keep the accounts straight.

I remain with due Respect
Your Worthiness's Humble Servant
Aleksandr Baranov

No. 32
28th day of May
Year [1] 807
Kadiak Island

LETTER FROM THE MONK HERMAN TO SIMEON IANOVSKII (YANOVKSY), 28 DECEMBER 1818

Your Honor
Kind Sir
Semen Ivanovich!

As it is the nature of noble souls to everywhere demonstrate their virtues, so you, not having met me and not knowing me at all except from what you have heard about me, and knowing my humble self little or not at all, have not disdained in your so well-disposed letter to pay me a visit, for which I have nothing with which to repay my obligations to you, but in order to express to you the way my feelings have been struck with amazement, I shall be so bold as to say in simple words that I offer my wholehearted gratitude, and consequent with your taking up your duties I offer my most respectful congratulations, and may God speed and keep safe the ship in which you sail.

As you have been so gracious as to open to me the path of boldness and audacity to you, it is now with the hope of your favorable inclination that I shall speak.

The Creator has given to our beloved fatherland this region like a newborn babe, still without strength or knowledge of any kind, nor sense, which demands not only protection, but also, because of its weak and tender age, support. But it is still not even capable of asking anyone to do this. And as the dependence of this people is a blessing of Holy Providence, given as it is into the hands, for an unknown period of time, of the Russian authorities here, and now given into your hands, for the sake of this I, the most humble servant of the local peoples and their nursemaid, stand before you with bloody tears and write my request: be a father and protector to us! We, of course, know no eloquence, but we say, with the halting tongue of children, wipe away the tears of our defenceless orphans, soothe the sorrows of aching hearts, let us know what joy is like!

Most gracious sire, in this brief description you, with the subtlety of your intellect and your penetrating insight, may for yourself determine the full breadth and scope of the people's sorrows. We wait expectantly to see what kindness the Creator will place in your heart on behalf of the poor. But we wait more, however, in the expectation from our new master of new kindness, new joys, and new life for this area. Then sighs of gratitude and excited joyful exclamations will break through the firmanent and rise to the throne of the Almighty, wishing for you, our kind father and benefactor, all good health and a long life and happiness.

And I, the last of the last, assure you that just as in the first instance, before you had seen my humble state, you were willing to show such favorable inclination, I hope that this will continue and so remain

Your Honor's,
My dear Sir's
obedient servant
Humble Herman

dated 28th December
1818

ARTICLE: "KNOCK AND IT SHALL BE OPENED UNTO YOU" BY THE MONK ANATOLIUS, 1897

More sad tidings from Alaska, confirming again and again what we know already of the intolerance shown there by the resident Americans to the Orthodox population. New instances of most revolting acts of violence perpetrated by the Presbyterian missionaries and officials.

We have before us a communication sent to the Very Reverend Nicholas, Bishop of the Aleutian Islands, by the Orthodox missionary at Sitka Anatolius. An Orthodox Indian's wife dies. She is attended by the Orthodox priest. Her dying wish is to be buried according to the rite of the Orthodox Church, to which she has belonged all her life. Such also is the wish of the widower and the orphaned children. But might is right, and will not have it so. With no provocation, for some unknown objects of their own, the authorities seize on the body of this peacefully deceased Christian woman, and handle it as they would a beast's carcase,—take it out of the coffin supplied by the Orthodox relatives, haul it along the streets, paying no heed to the cries and lamentations of the relatives, to whom those poor remains are dear and sacred. Not content with this, they insult the priest, when, indignant at such coarse acts of violence, he protests in the name of the law and of humanity, against the arrogant desecration of the regalia of the Orthodox Church and the articles used for divine worship, throwing in his face epithets of a most offensively personal character, and hinting anything but gently that he had better take himself off from the country under their jurisdiction.

What is all this? . . . Is this the boasted religious tolerance of the Presbyterian Mission, which brags so loud and boldly of its merits and its achievements? Are these things done in the land which calls itself pre-eminently the land of liberty, where all religious creeds are equal before the law? And are they done with the connivance and approval of the authorities, who are placed at this post to see that the terms of the treaty be fulfilled? . . . Why, it looks like persecution—systematic persecution; for great indeed must have been the accumulation of grievances in the hearts of these poor Orthodox people of Alaska, if they at last found it impossible to suffer any longer in silence and poured out their sorrows in the petition addressed to the Russian Minister at Washington, entreating him to intercede for them before the Russian Government, that it may appoint a representative in Alaska, to whom Russian subjects residing there, and all Orthodox natives can have recourse whenever a violation of the treaty of 1867 occurs. Continual acts of violence both in religious and private life, endless lawsuits with Americans about lands illegally appropriated—lawsuits which never meet with a favourable decision in the local courts—such are the motives which led to this petition. Where is the validity of the "free simple title" received by the native Creoles from the Russian Government and confirmed by the treaty? Where the promised equality in the rights of whites and natives before justice? "Before us rise the images of twenty-eight of our friends and relatives, who died guiltless at the hands of white men,—and not one white murderer met with due retribution" . . .

Let us say the fault lies with the subordinates. Still, the Government must know of their blunders—why then does it ignore them? Why does it refuse all credence to the complaints of the natives, blindly accepting the testimony of its agents, who go on from year to year utterly ignorant of the actual condition of things, either because they know not how or consider it unnecessary to become aquainted with facts which, from the very nature of their functions, it is an essential part of their duty to know most thoroughly and accurately?* A certain Mr. Brady takes it on himself to destroy the Indians, buildings, appropriates lands, which have been in their possession for long periods of time and served them as cemeteries, uses a portion of their ancestors' bones to strengthen the embankment of a road he is constructing, and throws the rest into the water. In a petition presented to the Government at Washington in the course of last summer, the Indians beg that this Mr. Brady may be seriously enjoined to leave the natives alone at least in future. And now this same Brady is brought forward by the Presbyterian party as candidate for Governor and is going to Washington to work up his candidacy. Is it possible that he will be appointed? Do the rulers of Alaska want even more encouragement than they have had? And what kind of times must Orthodoxy look forward to in the territory with that man as Governor? . . .

"In the name of civilization and enlightenment! . . ." The people of Alaska have long ago been taught by grievous experience what they have to pay for these blessings, and how much evil has been brought into their midst under cover of this noble banner. And therefore they protest out of the fulness of their hearts:—"We do not want a civilization which encourages saloons and places of amusement. We do not want education which enables our daughters with greater ease and advantage to practise prostitution. Drunkenness has brought adultery into our families and adultery has broken all the ties which held family relations together."

---

*The Government Superintendent and agent Sheldon Jackson has been in charge of Alaska over sixteen years, and it is he who mainly supplies the Washington Government with information about the country. Quite recently he wrote to Bishop Nicholas, requesting the latter to give him information concerning the Orthodox Mission in Alaska, as he has, until the present time, been "unable to answer questions on the subject except only in a very general way!"

This is not a barbarian's stubborn rejection of civilization no!—it is a loud cry to Heaven against the barbarism of the civilizers.

Hearken, then, to these groans, ye who should hearken to them! Do not close your eyes to that which ye, are called upon to see.

Editor.

Very Reverend, Most Gracious Arch-Pastor,

In one of your last letters to me Your Eminence was pleased to express the wish that I should bring facts in support of my complaints of the vexatious acts to which we are subjected by the Presbyterians. I hasten to conform to Your Eminence's command. Setting aside facts which occurred in the past, I feel bound to bring to your knowledge cases of most recent date, which took place just now, on the 21-st–23-d and on the 28-th of last January.

I. On Thursday the 21-st, at 9 a. m., there came to me an Indian from the settlement and declared that the woman Catherine Kakhtutyn, the sick wife of Stepan Katlan, was very bad, indeed on the point of death, and that her relatives begged me to come and pray with her. This woman had been ill all winter. Of late three open festering sores had appeared on her neck, then gangrene of the lungs had supervened. I went and recited over her the customary prayers. She was going fast. I left her after a consultation with her family, and not more than half an hour later the same messenger came again, to tell me that she was dead, and that her people had decided to take the body to the house of Ivan Klantitch, her own brother, with whom one of her sisters, Agatha, also resided. They gave as the reason for this proceeding that Stepan Katlan's house was small and that one of the deceased's children, Alexander, was also lying sick unto death, (He lived only three days after the funeral). The family requested me to come to Ivan Klantitch's house, to perform the service for the dead. I went accordingly, about noon, taking along the Reader, A. Archangelsky. I found the body already laid in the coffin; the lid was being finished in the same room. After the service I was told that, in spite of a coffin having been made and the body having been laid in it, the two oldest sons of Katlan, (by another wife) who resided at the Presbyterian Mission, had ordered there another coffin. To this I replied that children must not oppose their father's will, and that the Presbyterian Mission had nothing to do with the deceased. Her husband and her own children, (there were four: Ananias Shakhovat, 19 years old,—Maria Kukakakh, 16—Alexander Lutaken, 8,—and Alexandra Kaskenka, 5), are all Orthodox; she herself was a most zealous Orthodox Christian, and only a few days before, when she confessed to me and received Holy Communion from my hand, her one prayer was that I should bury her with all due rites and remember her in my prayers. Having recalled all these facts, I left them.

The next day, Friday, January the 22-d, I returned, to perform the customary service: the body was lying *in two coffins!* The one in which she was laid yesterday now was inside another, the lid of which stood there too, with the words *"in her name"* inscribed on it.—"What is the meaning of this?" I asked. They replied that the two Presbyterian sons had come and made the arrangement, saying that such were the orders of the Government officials.—"And what does Katlan, the husband, think of it?" I again inquired. They said he had resisted, but at last decided to let things go until the funeral. I performed the service, and after listening to some more explanations, left the house, indignant at heart at the Presbyterians' tricks, but not suspecting that they would proceed to even greater lengths.

An hour or so later I walk into the Indian school. The deceased's eldest son Ananias comes in almost at my heels, and declares that the Presbyterians are carrying away his mother. Feeling quite at a loss to understand what is going on, I say to Archangelsky: "Come along, let us see what is up over there." We went. As we passed Taviat's house, the following picture was presented to our sight. Two Indian policemen, Bean and Jackson (Anahutz) with two other Indians, to me unknown, under the directions of the minister A. E. Austin and the assistant teacher of the Indian public school, Mrs. Campbell, were carrying away the coffin. It was followed, in line, by the Governor, James Sheakley, the Marshal, W. L. Williams, the Government interpreter Kostromitinof, and several persons belonging to the Presbyterian Mission, and after them came a vast crowd of Indians, stretching along the whole village and filling the air with loud cries and lamentations. The moment we appeared on the scene, the bearers began to hurry and haul the coffin up the high porch of Taviat's house. I let Mr. Austin pass me with the coffin, but when I found myself face to face with the officials, I could not refrain from addressing them and inquiring what it all meant. The Governor replied that they were just going to my house, to explain. Marshall Williams began at once to explain that he was acting on the complaint of Mr. Austin, whose interference had been required by the children of the deceased. They had declared that Klantitch intended to defraud them of their rights; that he had transferred the body to his house under pretence of making the coffin, but really with the intention of seizing on her property. In view of the declaration, Mr. Austin required the assistance of this Governor and Marshal and they determined to prevent the wrong.

I was profoundly indignant at all this network of lies, this assortment of artful misrepresentations. Little as I know of American law, I have a very good idea of the duties of a marshal and a governor, I understand very well that questions of property do all come within their jurisdiction, not at but only within that of the courts. And in this case there was patent perversion of facts. Therefore I tried, as far as circumstances permitted, to show to the Marshal that there were no serious reasons to accuse Klantitch of any such criminal intentions. He had taken the body into his house with the consent and at the desire of the deceased's husband and her own children; he was, after the husband, the woman's nearest relative, being her own brother. It is not easy to determine relationship among the Indians, because they do not marry after the manner of white people, but live after customs of their own. The petitioners, Katlan's two oldest sons, were in no way related to the deceased, being only her stepsons, and now were acting in direct opposition to their father's will. "In view of all these facts," I remonstrated, "I consider your actions, Mr. Marshal, as illegal. And as you took on yourself to dispose, without my leave, of priestly regalia and articles pertaining to the divine service of the Orthodox Church, which were placed on the coffin and by the side of it, such as the stole, the censer, an image of the Saviour, a candlestick, the pall—I denounce your actions as disrespect to the Orthodox religion, almost amounting to violence."

My last words to the Marshal and the Governor were:—"In the name of the law, I protest against what has been done, and find myself unable further to fulfil my duties with regard to the funeral."

Half an hour later, when the excitement had somewhat abated, I started for the Governor's office, taking A. M. Archangelsky along, as well as S. T. Kostromitinof. We were received. The conversation which ensued lasted quite some time. I made clear to the Governor the illegality of his and the Marshal's actions. It turned out that the Governor did not even know whether those two sons, Presbyterians, who had ordered the coffin at the mission, were the deceased's own children or not. Neither did he know for what reason the body had been taken to Taviat's house. When I explained to him that they were only the woman's stepsons—that they were acting in opposition to the will of their father, with whom they had not lived for a long time,—that none of the deceased's relatives were living at Taviat's house, and that the only reason why Mr. Austin caused the coffin to be placed there was that Presbyterian prayer meetings are held there, the Governor appeared partly to change his view of the case, and when I concluded with the request that the body be taken back to the husband's house, where the woman had died, he gave his consent, adding that all had been done not by him, but by the Marshal, that he was willing we should have our way, if the Marshal had no objection, and therefore suggested that we should talk the matter over with the latter.

We repaired to the Marshal's office. I at once asked his permission to take the coffin to the husband's house. He replied he had no objection to that, but he should never consent that it should be taken back to Klantitch's house. To my question "Why not?" he replied that Klantitch intended to possess himself of the deceased's property. "But" I objected, "Klantitch has said nothing about that; and since he neither did anything wrong nor expressed any intention of doing any wrong, he should not be treated as a criminal."—"He may have said nothing about it" the Marshal retorted: "but all the same he will do it, because he is a bad man". . . . "He may have shown himself to be a bad man in other cases," I insisted, "and I do not mean to defend him. But in this particular case I consider him to be in the right, for he is the dead woman's nearest relative and has taken her body into his house at the request of her husband and children." Then the Marshal in his turn referred me to the Governor, intimating that it was the Governor who had requested his interference. Kostromitinof then told him that, quite on the contrary, the Governor had referred us to him.

On hearing this, the Marshal requested us to return, with him, to the Governor's office. We were followed thither by Mrs. Campbell, who came in accompanied by one of the Presbyterian sons. A general conversation ensued, in the course of which the Governor and the Marshal heard for the first time that the deceased, whose body they had seized, was lying not in the Mission coffin, but in one of Orthodox workmanship,—or, more correctly, in two coffins. The Mission coffin, being somewhat larger and made later, served as an outer shell for the other. All this was confirmed by Mrs. Campbell. It was amusing to see how indignant both officials became. Their excitement knew no bounds. The Marshal ordered Mrs. Campbell to immediately take the body out of the Orthodox coffin and lay it into the Mission coffin, and walked out slamming the door with a bang. The governor endorsed the Marshal's order.

I was forced to protest once more, though vainly, and I tried to make them see that this new proceeding was equally illegal;—that it would place fresh obstacles in the way of my performing my priestly duties;—that, if it had been improper for me to perform them in a house belonging to the Mission, it would be far more so now, with a coffin made at the Mission and decorated with the emblems of a heretical denomination;—that it was all the same as though I were required to officiate in the vestments of a Buddhist bonze. I represented that Orthodox Christians have funeral observances of their own; that the coffins in which they lay their dead bear certain emblems and inscriptions. Lastly I proposed that, if the Governor and the Marshal absolutely objected to the woman being buried in the coffin provided by her husband and other Orthodox relations, they should allow me to have a third one made, at the expense of the Church of Sitka, which was well able to afford the outlay. But this proposition was equally rejected.

In the course of the discussion the officials did not spare me many a hit and thrust. Once the Governor said right out that it seemed I, a foreigner and a newcomer, would instruct them, instead of receiving instruction from them, and that, if American laws were not to my taste, I was free to leave Sitka, etc. etc. To these and the like remarks I replied that I had no thought of instructing them, nor of opposing American laws, but, on the contrary, was doing my best to have these laws observed especially, in this particular case; that it was not I who had raised all this disturbance; that, up to the moment when I met the procession with the coffin in the Indian settlement, it had never entered my head to visit the offices, although disrespect had been shown to my religion by the introduction of the Presbyterian coffin; for that the Orthodox people have grown used to such performances and never think of dragging the Presbyterians around the offices; but that, from the moment that the Government officials interfered, the facts assumed an official significance: clearly it was the officials themselves who were violating the liberty of worship. "I came hither to you," I concluded, "not as a foreigner, but as the representative of the local Orthodox Church, having citizens of the United States for its members, and am defending not my own individual rights, but their common rights."

At the same time that I went home from this conference, deeply pained at its results, Mrs. Campbell hurried to effect the change of coffin—an operation which she immediately accomplished.

All this was more than I could stand. I made a last attempt to bring the Governor to reason, by sending him the following note:

Sitka, Alaska.
Jan'y 22-d–1897.

Sir

If I am not authorized and permitted by you to bury the dead Indian woman, who died yesterday, in the coffin which is made according to the usage of the Greeko-Russian Church, then I will be compelled to decline to bury her.

The Russian Church has sufficient means to make a coffin, of the kind required by the said church.

Very respectfully
Rev. Anatole Kamensky
Priest of the Orthodox Church at Sitka.

Hon. James Sheakley
Governor of Alaska.

Half an hour might have elapsed after I sent the note, when I saw from my window the hearse with a pair of horses, driving fast from the Presbyterian Mission in the direction of the Kolosh settlement, Mr. Austin running behind. The thought flashed through my brain that it was for no good the reverend gentleman was running so hard, but that he most certainly was on his way to bury the unfortunate Indian woman. I thought I would go and see what would be done next. I called for Archangelsky on the way and we proceeded together at a leisurely pace. We found the hearse standing in front of the Indian public school, surrounded by an Indian crowd. I inquired where was the body, and was told that it still was where it had been placed by order of the Governor and the Marshal—it had not yet been taken back to the husband's house. "What did the hearse come for?" I asked further. They replied "For the body. Although the woman was Orthodox, Mr. Austin is going to bury her in his own cemetery. The grave was dug yesterday." This last piece of information rather staggered me, proving as it did that this ending of the business had been contemplated all along.

At the same time the two Indian policemen, Bean and Jackson, came up to me together with Judge Rogers' Indian interpreter, Peter Church, and announced that they had just been with the Judge, who had ordered them to tell the deceased's husband Katlan, that he should heed no interference, but take his wife's body to whatever house he should choose, and bury it in any coffin he pleased—a cracker box if he liked.

The policemen were on their way to give the message.

The Judge's last expression was evidently a thrust at me. Still, his interference did some good. I was told afterwards that soon after the Governor received my note, the Judge had seen him and severely reprimanded both him and the Marshal.

Now, after this talk with the policemen, I understood why the hearse had been kept waiting. Hearing that the husband was at the Governor's office at the time, I at once went there myself. As I entered, this is what met my sight: In the middle of the room the white haired old man was holding forth to an audience. Not far from him, with heads bent low, stood his oldest children—son and daughter. Near the door—a crowd of Indians with a sprinkling of Americans. Nearer to the table sat the Rev. A. E. Austin, the Governor, the Marshal, the Government interpreter, and others. The Indian Peter Church was acting as interpreter. The old man was talking with great animation. At intervals he addressed himself to Mr. Austin. I did not understand what Katlan was saying. At one time Austin interrupted him. I took the opportunity to request that Katlan's speech should be translated for my benefit. But I was asked to wait, and the entire purport of what the old man said became known to me only later. It was very nearly as follows:

"I have lived a long life, but never experienced such trouble. Two days ago my wife died, and for two days no bread has passed my lips. I am exhausted, hardly able to drag my feet along. My wife's death is a great grief to me, but this trouble is worse. And it is all *your* doing,'' the old man turned to Austin; ''we are both grey-headed men; now if in your old days you lost your wife, and your children arose to oppose your will—how would you like it?''—Mr. Austin attempted to retort, declaring that the sons had come to him in his, their father's name. But the old man vehemently denied this, asserting that he had never thought of such a thing, that they were simply lying and the minister believed them without investigating the matter. Katlan further begged that an end should be put to all this disturbance. All he asked was that he should be allowed to bury his wife after the rites of the Orthodox Church: ''Such was her own wish,'' he concluded: ''it is also that of her relatives, and mine.''

I supplemented the old man's discourse with some remarks of my own, stating that this day had indeed seen things done, such as had never been seen or heard of, and which no one could live through unmoved. ''I at least,'' I said, ''cannot look without compassion on this old man, bent with age. And, as the representative of the Russian Church here, my very soul revolts within me. Who ever saw or heard of the body of a peacefully deceased Christian woman being treated worse than an animal's, all but dragged about the streets by the feet, heedless of the cries and lamentations of relatives, to whom these remains are dear,—being taken out of one coffin and placed in another at the whim of strangers, who pursue unknown ends of their own! . . . Are these the methods of the Presbyterian propaganda, which so loudly advertises itself and its achievements here, humiliating the followers of other creeds at every step? Is violence, moral and physical, to be substituted for persuasive speech and the preaching of the Gospel? Here too, in the land of freedom, where all creeds are equal before the law!''

My discourse was interrupted by Mr. Austin, who curtly replied that Presbyterianism had nothing to do with the matter, and neither had he.

''I should be glad to believe this, Mr. Austin,'' I retorted;—''but the facts do not indorse your words. How can you explain your presence at the head of that shameful procession which I met today in the Indian settlement?''

Mr. Austin said he had been invited.

Here the Governor broke in upon the conversation in a very irritable tone, and began a series of thrusts at me, saying that I was the cause of the whole disturbance, that I incited the people,—that he, the Governor, considered me ''a bad man'', ''impudent,'' that, once I had come to America, I should learn how to behave myself, and that I had better go away from Sitka. All I could say in answer to this diatribe, was that he, the Governor, had no right to insult me so, nor had I given him cause; that he was in duty bound first to show wherein my alleged ''impudence'' consisted, and my disrespect towards American laws; that I had never uttered one disrespectful word; that I had never transgressed any American laws, and that at this very moment all I was striving for was to have those laws observed.

"Do you intend to bury the woman"? the Governor asked me,—"I know Judge Rogers' decision in the matter. I have no objection against the orders he gave to the policemen. Only let the husband make his own arrangements."

But the Marshal had something more to say:—"In what coffin will you bury her, and from whose house?"

"I shall do whatever the husband directs," I replied. "After all that has taken place here today, I should never have the heart to renew the same disturbances. Ask the husband."

The Marshal replied that he still held to his original opinion, that the remains should not be taken back to Klantitch's house. I promised to make a concession on this point, and even to influence my parishioners in this sense. As to the other questions, I once more requested that the husband should be consulted and that his wishes should be deferred to.

Katlan was told what was expected of him. He rose and replied that he had but one single wish—that all this wrangling should be stopped; therefore he proposed that the remains of his wife should be transferred to his own dwelling, where she had died; that they should be laid in the coffin which he and the other Orthodox relatives had made, and that the obsequies should take place after the rites of the Russian Orthodox Church. Regarding the other coffin, he did not wish to hurt anybody's feelings, and therefore he proposed that it should also be made use of; so his wife should rest under the earth in two coffins.

After the question had thus been settled, the Governor once more addressed me, and asked "Did I consent to perform the funeral?" I said "yes."

At 10 o'clock the next morning an extraordinary procession moved along the streets of Sitka. The body was carried by women, in its double coffin, into the Russian Church, preceded by the two coffin-lids and followed by a large crowd. On all faces could be read, if not exactly joy, still a feeling of satisfaction that the remains of the unhappy woman were to find rest at last, after all the indignities heaped upon them by the heretics.

I bring this instance of the ill usage to which Orthodox Christians are subjected in Sitka to Your Eminence's knowledge, in the hope that attention may be directed to it.

Besides myself the whole incident, from beginning to end, was witnessed by the Reader Archangelsky, who was with me all the time, and now testifies to the truth of all I have here written by affixing his signature thereto.

Of Your Eminence
the most obedient servants
the Monk Anatolius
the Reader Alexander Archangelsky.

II. The other incident occurred on the 28-th of January, the children of that same old man Katlan serving as occasion thereto.

His eldest daughter, Maria Kukakakh, came to seek me, in order to inform me that the assistant teacher of the Indian public school, Mrs. Campbell, had just come to their house, accompanied by one of the Presbyterian brothers, to take the younger children away to the Presbyterian Mission, to wit: herself, her next oldest brother, (the youngest had just died) and the little sister. I happened to have with me an interpreter, Charl. Sokolof. We went together to Katlan's house. I asked what was happening. The old man told me the same story, with the addition that Mrs. Campbell pretended to have been sent by the Governor, who, she asserted, had ordered the children to be taken to the Presbyterian Mission. Without stopping long to think, I asked the old man to dress and go with me to Judge Rogers, taking along the older children. We did not have to go as far as the court; the Judge was coming along with Kostromitinof. and we met them on the street. Katlan at once made his complaint through Kostromitinof. The Judge listened and said that no one had any more right to take a man's children than to take his head; therefore he could not believe that there was any truth in Mrs. Campbell's assertion, and advised us to go to the Governor and find out about that. We all with the exception of the Judge, proceeded to the Governor's office. He heard us, and positively denied having given any such order to Mrs. Campbell.

This settled the question.

That Mrs. Campbell did make the assertion about the Governor's alleged order, is testified to by many Indians who were present.

While reporting this additional fact to Your Eminence, my most gracious Archpastor,

I have the honor to be Your Eminence's most obedient servant,

Monk Anatolius.

Sitka
January the 21
February the 2-d 1897.
N. 10.

PETITION FROM THE ORTHODOX RESIDENTS OF SITKA TO THE IMPERIAL RUSSIAN AMBASSADOR AT WASHINGTON, DC, VON KOTZEBUE, 1897

Your Excellency.

We all, the undersigned Orthodox residents of Sitka, as well of Russian descent as of native races, take the liberty of addressing you, with the entreaty that you may extend your protection to the Russian Orthodox Church in Alaska, and defend it against oppression and violence of all sorts which it suffers at the hands of the Presbyterian missionaries and other persons, not unfrequently even at those of Government officials belonging to the Presbyterian Church.

The Orthodox natives, Indians, numbering no less than 482, are continually subjected to vexations of every description. Nor can they obtain redress in the courts and other official places, where Presbyterian influences reign supreme.

Cases are not unfrequent when Government officers, belonging to the Presbyterian denomination, themselves violate the rights of the Orthodox by their interference. Such a case occured on the 22-d of January of the current year, 1897, when, with the personal participation of the Governor Mr. James Sheakly and the Marshal, Mr. W. Williams, violence was done to an Orthodox Tayon (chief), Katlan, who was compelled to have his wife buried in two coffins, while the rector of the Orthodox church, because he protested against official interference in a purely ecclesiastical matter, was called a "bad man" by the Governor and other insulting names. This case will probably be immediately reported to your Excellency by His Eminence, the Right Reverend Nicholas, Bishop of Alaska and the Aleutian Islands.

Not a year passes but tidings of similar and even worse outrages are received from remote Alaska.

In the near future Sitka expects a new Governor in the person of the Presbyterian minister I. G. Brady and a new Marshal, in that of W. A. Kelly, former Superintendent of the Presbyterian Mission. With the entrance of these men into office, Orthodoxy expects an increase of persecution.

In view of all these facts we take the boldness to petition your Excellency:

1) To have recourse to the Government at Washington, to represent to it the condition of Orthodoxy in Alaska, and request it to impress on the officers it sends out to Alaska the duty of keeping a watchful eye on the abuses of the Presbyterian Mission, and preserving an impartial attitude

towards Orthodoxy, in strict observance of the provisions of the treaty concluded with the United States in 1867, and particularly not to allow themselves to subject the members of the Orthodox community to annoyances and vexations, which might occasion riots.

2) To intercede with His Imperial Majesty the Emperor Nicholas Alexandrovitch, Autocrat of all the Russians, that He may appoint a representative of the Russian Imperial Government in Alaska, to reside in Sitka—to whom Russian subjects residing here, as well as all Orthodox inhabitants of Alaska, may have recourse when they suffer vexations in matters pertaining to religion and in the not unfrequent cases when other provisions of the above named treaty are violated.

Whereto we affix our signatures:

A. Startsev, G. Sokoloff, I. Linguist, Stephan Chernoff, John Zearanoff, Ilia Renkin, John Miller, F. Ivanoff, Platon Larionov, Luka Petelin, Ivan Dal'strem, Kondratii Zyrianov, Matfei Shmakov, Elia Seminoff, Kharlampii S. Sokolov, Maria D. Sokolova, Petr Chernov, Vasilii Shergin, Katerina Shergin, Elicei Simonov, Nastasia Shmakova, V. Panamaroff, Jacob Panamaroff, Mrs. R. Alberstone, Mrs. M. Chichenoff, Mrs. P. Larionoff, Mrs. P. L. Hope, Mrs. L. Patelin, Mrs. N. Panamaroff, P. Romanoff, Mrs. Mary Chechenoff, Mrs. D. Chechenoff, Mrs. J. Chechenoff, Mrs. A. Chechenoff, William Hantan, Mrs. R. Patanroff, Miss A. Albertstone, Miss Z. Albertstone, Mrs. Mary Larionoff, Iulia Maret, Mrs. J. Maller, Vasilii Kashevarov, Anna Shmakova, Alexandr Shmakov, Andrei Shmakov, Ekaterina Gel'shtedt, Pelageya Ponomareva, Evgenia Malakhova, Ekaterina Trainer, Alexandr Bourdukovskii, Marfa Bourdukovskaya, Theodor Kashevarov, Ekaterina Kashevarova, E. K. Balshanin, A. Shishkin, Mrs. A. Tagg, Mrs. H. McBride, Mrs. P. Morgen, Aleck Eline, Tatiana Zyrianova, Maria Bourdukovskaya, Alexandra E. Sokolova, Elizaveta Prosheva, Anisiya Ivanova, Innokentii German, Matfei Shmakov, E. Staruyeva, Petr Staruyev, Mrs. H. U. Marshall, Fil. Gavr. Kashevarov, Iv. S. Kaznakov.

PETITION FROM TLINGIT ORTHODOX CHIEFS TO THE PRESIDENT OF THE UNITED STATES, 1897

Sir:

From the very time that the United States raised her flag here and in the whole Territory, our people represented by their chief's prominent members, have not ceased to address themselves direct to the Government at Washington, while knowing the fact that the Government is represented here by the Governor and other officials. The reason of this is following; because here we cannot get any satisfaction to our just and lawful demands. We know that the Russian Government at the time of the transfer of Alaska to the U.S. did not sell us as slaves to America, but left us some rights and privileges which were later made lawful and firm by the U.S. Congress. The Organic act, providing a civil Government for Alaska in section 8 provides that the Indians or other persons in said district shall not be disturbed in the possession of any lands actually in their use or occupation or now claimed by them. On the strength of this law we always understood that every Indian has a right to dispose of his own life and liberty and his own property whether it consists in personal possessions or real estate for instance: lands, forests, lagoons, some small bay and rivers in which we could procure for ourselves the necessary food and other things for existence.

We always thought and surmised that the civil Government sent out from Washington would punish criminals equally whether white or native, if a white man spills the blood of an Indian or an Indian spills the blood of a white man, the justice would mete out equal punishment. But in reality this equality was never practised. It is true that the first four years of the protection of the American Eagle remain in our minds clear and unsullied cloud of the misunderstanding between a white man and an Indian. It is true that, from the time of Governor Kinkaid until Governor Swineford, when the scales of justice were held by the hands of Haskett, we could sometimes receive satisfaction, but during the remaining time there never was justice and is none now, it has perished.

More so from the time the Presbyterian Mission with such workers as Mr. J. J. Brady & Co. came to Sitka, our condition became unbearable.

In our mind's eye there rise 28 souls of our friends and relatives that innocently perished from the hand of white men. Of course we always made complains to the U.S. Courts, and in Courts every where received from the Authorities only promises and never satisfaction. Not a single white murderer ending with the last Mills, by name, who killed Donald Austin, a native, ever received retaliation and now enjoys full liberty. With all this we never lost faith in the Government at Washington. This sorrowful reality only made us lose faith in persons sent out here by the Government.

From the Government we always expected and do expect to receive satisfaction to our lawful demands. We believe that the promises of the Vice President who recently visited Sitka were not empty words. And at the present moment bearing the proposition of Government Official Commisioner Geo. R. Tingle to try once more with his help, we believe that our petition will reach the desired end. We leave out the old petitions offered to the Government in former years we offer our petition which is as follow:

1) Not to allow Mr. Brady a right of way through the centre of village along the narrow beach which is situated between the water and our houses, where we keep our boats, canoes, and other things. To forbid him to destroy buildings and other property while building this road. We do not offer pretensions to the land that he now possesses, which was from time immemorial the property of our ancestors, and served us as cemetery. It is enough for him that he unlawfully took possession of this land, and with the bones of some he banked his ground and some he threw into the water. We do not wish to have such work going on, and do not wish other white men to follow Mr. Brady's example.

2) We beg to have Mr. Smith the superintendent of the Baranoff Packing Co. forbidden to take away from us our bays, streams and lagoons where we fished long before white man came. We want him to do such fishing as necessary for him with our consent. We demand that he stop throwing bars and traps across the streams, where by the fish can not enter the lakes for the purpose of spawning. His method of fishing in the last 8 years in Redout, Cross Sound, Hoonah, Whale Bay, Nika Bay, Red fish Bay, compels us to see very plainly that the places mentioned are becoming empty.

Now the Thlingits are compelled to put up their fish in distant places, which with the canoe is reached only with great deal of hard ship.

3) We do not want American saloons. We beg the Government to close them. We understand now that whiskey is poison for us. Tramps and Idle people like soldiers and sailors bring whiskey into our midst from those saloons. They give it our wives and daughters make them drunk and often seduce them in that state. We have brought such cases to the local authorities here and the result is that the white man goes free and unpunished, but the native suffers fines, imprisonment and punishment. Saloons and other places of amusement of such caliber are not necessary for the welfare of our daughters. We do not want the civilization that only does not stop saloons but encourages them. We do not want the education by which our daughters are torn from their homes and alienated, taught the English language only to give them an easier scope and advantage to practice prostitution. Drunkenness brought adultery with our families, adultery destroyed all ties by which our family relation existed. We do not want to look upon these horrible existing evils with ease and light minds and we wish that the crimes committed would be punished not by light fines, but in some way which they could do most good. We do not imagine for one moment that the dance halls and dives of Juneau and Sitka must necessarily be filled with our educated daughters.

We could go on without end to our petitions. We have shown facts and beg the Government to allow us some recognition. The answer to former petitions was never received by the Indians perhaps through the fault of the mediator, in the petition, and we beg the Government to the answer to this to Khlantich, head chief of Sitka tribe.

We have the honor to subscribe ourselves your Most Obedient Servants.

John Khlantich
Tom Katzekoni
Sergay Anlizhe
Alexander Natzlen
Paul Kattan
Oushkinakk
Nowaya
Saha
Vattaan
Quitka

LETTER FROM BISHOP NICOLAS OF ALASKA TO PRESIDENT OF THE UNITED STATES, WILLIAM MCKINLEY, 5 OCTOBER 1898

Mr. President.

Called away by the will of the highest ecclesiastical authority in Russia, I am about to leave forever America and my ministry here, and, in wishing all heavenly and earthly blessings to yourself and to the country of which you are at present the representative, I consider it my duty once more to address to you a few words on a subject not unfamiliar to you, owing to former communications from me, in the hope that these words of mine may find their way to your heart and induce you to take action in a cause dear not to me alone, but to all Russia.

Alaska stands in need of radical reform in all directions. This I wrote to you in a former memorial; this I repeat to you now. It is not enough that certain rights were secured to the country in the treaty of 1867, by which it was ceded to America by the Russian Government; those rights should be protected with firmness by the law and the authorities. A limit must be set to the abuses of the various companies, more especially those of the Alaska Commercial Co., which, for over thirty years, has had there the uncontrolled management of affairs and has reduced the country's hunting and fishing resources to absolute exhaustion, and the population to beggary and semi-starvation. A limit must be set to the abuses of officials who, as shown by the experience of many years, are sent there without any discrimination and exclusively on the recommendation of Alaska's immovable guardian, Sheldon Jackson. And lastly—Alaska must be delivered from that man. By his sectarian propaganda he has introduced dissension, enmity and iniquity where those evils did not before exist. It was the Orthodox Church which brought the light of truth to that country; why then try to drive her out of it by every means, lawful or unlawful?

In the name of humanity, of justice and freedom—of those very blessings for the sake of which you declared war against Spain—I make these requests. Will you be acting consistently, if, while waging war for the liberty of Cuba, Puerto Rico and the Philippines, for their human rights, you ignore all these things at home, in a part of your own country which has been waiting thirty years for the blessings promised to it? And are not we Russians fully entitled to demand of you for Alaska that, in the name of which you have taken up arms against Spain? I have been for seven years the head of the Orthodox Church in America,—and, Mr. President, I speak not from hearsay, but from my own observation and experience,—knowing, besides, the history of past years anything but superficially. Whatever abnormal facts were pointed out to me by Government agents—facts which were generally the product of the abnormal conditions in which our clergy are placed—I uncomplainingly corrected. Now, by the grace of God, there is nothing there, I believe, that could be laid to our charge. The only thing which may possibly be brought up against us, is that we profess the true faith, and have not yet divested ourselves of our sympathies for Russia, the land of our own faith. But is that really sufficient ground for blame and persecution? There is no danger whatever in that to American rule in Alaska, as some persons would perhaps have you believe—if only from the reason that our church never meddles with politics, and our clergy never busied itself, either at home or anywhere else, with intrigues of that sort. We should not be placed on one footing with the Jesuits. Our church allows us only to remonstrate with the highest authority on behalf of the oppressed and innocently suffering,—which I have done repeatedly in this case,—but never allows us to incite citizens to sedition or treason.

And at this moment it is exclusively from a sense of duty, not from any other feeling, that I, as the late Arch-pastor of a country subject to your jurisdiction, Mr. President, address these words to you. I should feel that I had not fulfilled my mission, my duty before God and my flock, were I to leave my post in America without unburdening my heart to you of what oppresses it at this moment.

And so, Mr. President, be indulgent and gracious to poor, hapless Alaska, and show to the Orthodox Church there the respect to which it is entitled, if not by its whole record in that country, yet at least by Art. 2 and 3 of the Declaration of 1867.

Calling down the blessing of God upon you and your country, I beg you will receive the assurance of the respect with which I always have regarded and regard your Excellency's person, and with which I sign myself,

Nicholas, *a Bishop of the Orthodox Church, late of Alaska and the Aleutian Islands.*

REPORT FROM REV PRIEST ALEXANDER KEDROVSKY OF UNALASKA, INCLUDING CORRESPONDENCE WITH MRS. AGNES NEWHALL, TO BISHOP TIKHON, 11 NOVEMBER 1900

I

The Methodist Home at Unalashka has committed a new hostile act against our holy church, which, if so your Eminence approves, should be made publicly known through the diocesan organ.

On the 17–30-th of November we went, Father Vassili and I, to the Home, to confer about certain matters with the teacher of the public school. We were met by the husband of the Matron; he seemed agitated, scared. We did not then know why the sight of us threw him into such a state; but later we learned that on that very day, while we were celebrating the divine Liturgy, they had buried Irene Titoff, a girl from St. Paul's Isle, whence the government agent is in the habit of sending children to the Home, to be educated, but with the express condition that such children shall be permitted to attend our church, and shall not be enticed into any other religion. It is clear from this that their action in the case of Irene Titoff was dishonorable.

The deceitfulness and bad faith displayed by the managers of the Home are outrageous. In September 1897—I believe that was the month—they also buried a girl without my participation, but in *our own* cemetery. Detailed reports on this case are filed in the Consistory and were, in part, published at the time in the *Orthodox American Messenger*. But there is a peculiar feature in the present case: they said that the dead girl's father, Mr. Peterson (a Protestant), gave instructions to convert all his children to Methodism (there were three of them in the Home, including Irene). We could do nothing, for their assertions were very positive, and the father, Mr. Peterson, was not at Unalashka. But he came over from Atkhe Island in 1898 (in May, I believe), when I immediately went to him, in order to tell him of what had taken place and to question him on the subject. I found that he had never said anything about having his children converted to Methodism, and he felt so outraged at the impudent lie and at the fact of his young daughter having been buried without my participation, that he at once, after his talk with me, went to the Home and took away his two remaining children—boys 9 and 12 years old. . . .

Still another case: in 1897 a boy was taken *illegally* from his Orthodox father, in the latter's absence, on the plea that the wife of the man drank and used to beat the boy. It would take too long to tell the affair in all its details. Suffice it to say that I was present in court, when I protested against the unjust order of the court, which gave that boy to the Methodist Home to be brought up *until he was 21 years of age,* while he had *a mother* at Kodyak,—and that the judge told me that, if I procured a written certificate of that mother's good behavior, he would take the boy out of the Home and make him over to her. I did get the certificate; but the matron of the Home was not ashamed to tell a downright lie, and declared that she also had received information from the judge at Kodyak, who wrote, she asserted, that the boy's mother was a drunkard and a disreputable character. This took my only weapon out of my hand at the time; but afterwards it was shown to be untrue; and when I told her of it, she *only smiled.*

This boy, whose name is Germanus Petelin, is the son of Nadejda Petelin of the Island of Kodyak. He stayed with Serapion Petelin here at Unalashka. In 1898 his mother came and took him out of the Methodist Home.

This is the way that they confuse and entice children in that home: they say to them, "you are American subjects; why then should you not, have an American religion?" In my letter, filed under No. 95, I gave them a hint "not to lead others into temptation".

A. Kedrofsky
Dean of the Unalashka District

II

Unalashka. October 16, 1900.
To the Manager of Jesse Lee Home

Dear Manager

Lately with sorrow I found out about the assumption, without necessary christian viaticum, (i.e. confession and holy communion of mysteries of the Body and Blood of Our Lord Jesus Christ) to life beyond the tomb of my spiritual daughter Irene Titoff, a resident of your home.

Your inimical action surprises me as much in respect to deceased! Admitting to your home for culture this Irene Titoff, you pledged yourself to leave her religious sentiment inviolable in regard to confession of creed which she had before entering your establishment. And this your obligation to your honor, need be noted, you fulfilled nearly to the end of her earthly life, namely: You let her come to our house of God for church services on Sundays, and she yearly (and even this ensuing year 1900) was to confession and communion of holy mysteries in our temple of God. Why did you deprive her of the latter before her end? If you fulfilled this, by inviting me—her spiritual father, you would afford her a great spiritual consolation in her last days of earthly life, once she was by this comforted her whole life! I am certain that deprivation by you of this distressed her, and she with grief in her youthful heart passed from you to life beyond the tomb! It signifies, the fulfilment of your obligation above noted in regard to now deceased Irene Titoff, was from your side purely external, and for evasion as the saying is from our eyes! Is it possible, such course of your proceedings in given case can be called by you christian actions, and is it possible, that you think they are agreeable to our Lord Jesus Christ!

If you have no possibility through some cause to notify me of such, especially ailing condition of my spiritual children found in your house, whom follows their end; then allow me, if not daily, then, at least, weekly to visit your house myself personally for this purpose. I will for granting of this my request, be very grateful to you. I think that this permission of yours from your side, concerning me and my spiritual children, will be fully judicious and Christian. I want to ask you on certain foundation the following: If there is a "Russian" or American religion I know no such religions. I only know that there is a Christian religion, to our misfortune divided in two: one orthodox; and the other unorthodox.

Therefore, if you happen sometime to address some one with a question about christian religion, them guided by the above said, it is necessary to ask by the way, this: "Do you want to be an *orthodox christian or unorthodox,*" and not thus, "Do you want to have a Russian religion or American", so as *to lead into fatal temptation*. . . .

But, it is hardly possible that such question about religion can be intelligible to children found with you, especially at their earthly end?! If even the child did answer as you wish it to, you must know that such answer will be extorted and not given voluntarily, for the sick child, seeing your attention to it for the relief of its suffering, will not want to affront you by an undesirable to you answer to your question.

Above all in given case,—besides wishing not to affront you, there is a child's fear, for an answer which may fail to satisfy you! Judge then for yourself, if this is an example of Christian actions? It seems to me, that yourself will admit unseemliness of your actions as given concerning me.

That, I observe by the way, partly from this, that you as if secretly from us, at the time of our church service, buried the deceased.

I write this to you without the ill intention to mortify or to insult you and, what more, not with—1-st that you would strengthen still more your unfounded inimical action toward me, and 2-d that between us might be animosity,—mother of every dissent and whose father is the first murderer; But this firstly to express to you my bitterness and my view of your action concerning the deceased and myself, and secondly to give feasibility to think of this and to be impressed!

May there be God's peace between us.
Yours respectfully

Rev. Father Alexander Kedrofsky.

P.S. At the time of my absence this summer, my spiritual children living with you, for a cause unknown to me, very seldom visited the God's house for prayer on Sundays, to this also I would wish to call your benevolent attention.

Rev. A. K.

III

Unalashka, Alaska,
Nov. 12, 1900.

Rev. A. Kedrofsky

Dear Sir.

In reply to your letter of Oct, 16-th, will write as follows:—

The Jesse Lee Home is an institution under the Woman's Home Missionary Society of the Methodist Episcopal church.

Its objects—the advancement of Christ's Kindgom and the uplifting of fallen humanity. Its special interest and work lies in the children of Alaska. The children placed in our care are clothed, fed, cared for, educated and their moral and spiritual welfare carefully guarded. We assume complete charge of the children while under our care. As the religious instruction is wholly under the direction of the Home management, and according to Protestant faith, your request to visit the Home for religious instruction cannot be granted. For this reason, no children are admitted to the Home with the privilege of attending the Greco-Russian Church. To be sure, four Seal Islands girls and two others are allowed to attend said church when, according to *our* judgment, the weather and their condition of health will permit.

In case of death, services and burial are conducted by the Home management except in such cases as *we* shall decide otherwise. Interference in these respects will not be tolerated. It is our aim and prayer that these children may be led to become true Christians. Is it enough to take the name of Christ upon our lips, to witness the forms and ceremonies of worship week after week, and still go on in sin and wickedness? We think not.

Is not the moral condition of the greater part of the natives in this village deplorable? Very religious as outward forms go, but intensely sinful in life. Most of their homes veritable brothels of sin.

Is not dishonesty, profanity, adultery, fornication, lasciviousness, strife and drunkenness rife? Is it not an insult to God and the cross of Christ for such workers of iniquity to call themselves Christian? We think so.

I know you realize these things and are pained by them. I know you desire to see these people true followers of God. Oh that God's Spirit may work upon their hearts! that there might be a godly sorrow for sin, a turning from their evil ways to paths of righteousness! Our hearts are made sad to think of our children going out to lead such lives. What else can be expected with such environments? Only the Power of God through the atoning and cleansing power of Jesus' Blood can change the heart and transform the life. Irene Tetoff died in this Home and by her own request you were not called. Services were conducted according to her own wishes. She was given the privilege of calling you, if she so desired. This was not a hasty decision on her part.

For more than a year Irene had been striving to lead a Christian life. As a matter of choice she attended the Greco-Russian Church, but occasionally, during that time. Irene did not attend church Easter week nor go to confession (1900). Nevertheless Irene did not depart this life without holy confession, for she made an honest confession to God, which in our faith, is more than confession to man, and realized pardon and peace from above. Hers was a triumphant death such as the children had never witnessed and can never forget. In religion we must agree to disagree and in the Spirit of Christ pursue our way. Personally, we have great respect for you and recognize the fact that *your character and daily life are an example,* such as the people *have not often had before them during the past.*

May God's blessing be with you and make you a blessing in this place,

Yours Respectfully

Agnes L. Newhall
(Matron Jesse Lee Home).

IV

To the Matron of the Methodist Home

Yours of November 12 of the present year (1900), in reply to mine of the 3–16-th of October. filed under No. 95, is on hand. The pleasing impartiality displayed therein is greatly to your credit, as well as the flattering appreciation of my unworthy pastoral efforts which you express, and for which I tender you my thanks.

This reply of yours, respected Matron, I cannot, in my turn, leave unanswered apart from my desire to express my personal thanks, as above,—for the reason that it touches on very many contestable questions, your solution of which I cannot possibly agree with; my priestly conscience will not suffer me to do so. But, at the same time that I prepare to reply to your letter, most worthy Matron, I warn you that this my reply will be far from complete, because I am just now hard pressed for time to attend even to my direct, immediate, and most pressing pastoral duties; wherefore I beg you to be content with the following for the present.

The object of your institution, the "Jesse Lee Home" (the advancement of the Kingdom of Christ and the uplifting of fallen humanity), of which you kindly inform me, is a higly commendable, noble, and lofty one; hence I thoroughly sympathize with it, and, at one time and to a certain extent, have lent it my assistance in all respects excepting the religious element—that bearing on matters of doctrine. I take it for granted, respected Matron, that you take my meaning.

It is this: Your "Jesse Lee Home" has existed at Unalashka for a comparatively long time (since the eighties, if I mistake not); but until the year 1898, it was, for some reason I cannot fathom, disguised under the name of *a home attached to the public school,* into which home children belonging to our Orthodox Catholic Apostolic Eastern Church (known to you as "Greco-Russian Church") were invited (enticed) and received (and sometimes taken by force from their parents by a government official, under breaking open of doors and beating of parents); on such occasions it was *expressly promised* that no violence, either open or secret, should be done to the children's religion. Whether this promise has been kept—let the conscience of them that gave it answer truthfully?! . . .

Now Orthodox parents, in the simplicity of their hearts, untainted by cunning or malice, believed in it implicitly, and gave their children to this *home attached to the public school;* and I did not object, not only not seeing any harm that could come to the children from entering this home, but, on the contrary, finding in it much that was good. . . . I felt assured that no violence would be done to the children's religion, since: 1) the children came to church every Sunday and on each of the twelve Great Feast-days: 2) I gave them religious instruction in the church after mass; 3) on the holy days of the Nativity, Epiphany, and Easter, I visited the Home, for the children's sake, with the cross and holy water, and, 4) all the children, without exception, came to confession and received communion once a year. In a word, there existed between me and the children the closest bond, spiritual, religious, and moral,—which it was undertaken (from the year 1897) to break most unscrupulously and persistently, in defiance of all honor and conscience, secretly at first, then openly. . . .

Can it be that Protestantism finds in our Savior's words (see Matthew, XXVIII, 19) authority for missionaries to act as your Home has acted here at Unalashka?! No! the Lord not only does not commend deceit and craftiness as methods to be used in missionary work, to propagate His teaching, but directly forbids them, for that such things are of the Devil (see John VIII, 44; Matth. X, 12–13; Luke X, 4).

Although no man—especially one that calls himself a Christian—should be mistrusted until he has shown himself dishonorable, still it appears that I ought to have been more cautious (as I resemble in this case them that are spoken of in Matth. XIII, 25).

One well known to you—the respected Mrs Baylor, said to me in your presence that "she had planted a root here" (meaning of course the Jesse Lee Home with its purely religious propaganda). But I would ask: 1) *Where* is planted this root of a tree, of which it is not known so far what sort of fruit it will bear? Sad to say—in an other's orchard! 2) *When* was it planted? By night thievishly, secretly—see (Math. XIII, 25)! 3) *How* was it planted? By deceit! 4) For what purpose? to teach a new faith of Christ—while the children already had that faith . . . (see John X, 1).

These foul spots, in my judgment, lie with all their moral ugliness on your "Jesse Lee Home", and I do not see how they can be washed away.

In one passage of your letter to me, most worthy Matron, you say: "It is our aim and prayer that these children may be led to become *true Christians*"; this must mean, of course, as regards *their life,* not *doctrine,* since our children, when they come to you, already possess *the true Orthodox doctrine*. In that case all my heart is with you, and I am ready to work with you.

You utter an absolute, indisputable truth, which is beyond all doubt (Luke 11:40), when you say that the mere external taking on our lips, the name of our most sweet Lord Jesus Christ (Philip II, 9–11) is not only not pleasing to Him, but bootless and harmful (Matth. VII, 21; XV, 8; V, 20, etc); it is necessary that external worship be the result of the worship that is within the heart (Luke VI, 45). Hence your question and answer concerning this matter strike me as strange.

You further write of the deplorable moral condition of the natives in this place, and give yourself up to the profoundest, bitterest, most inconsolable grief, on account of what appears to you an utterly cheerless prospect.

Much might be said on this head, but I will limit myself to a few remarks only.

You, respected Matron, hear of the sinning, but not of the penitent (Rom. XIV, 4); and of the sinning you hear exaggerated accounts; nay, it is possible that you exaggerate yourself, which would be to a certain extent *natural,* if I may say so, for you stand sentry, as it were, over us, and exaggerate our shortcomings (see Matth VII, 3), *striving to justify* the stand you have taken among us (by what means I have shown above). . . . A divided teaching of Christ's doctrine does not strengthen faith, but, on the contrary, enfeebles and shakes it, producing scepticism and indifferentism, more especially *where Christians deride each other's faith*—as is the case when children who live with you, after partaking of the Holy Eucharist in our church, are met on their return to the Home by such words as these: "We don't want to kiss you—your lips are sour". . . . Many sensible and impartial American citizens—Protestants, too, which makes it all the more remarkable—think and openly speak on the subject of the divided teaching of Christ's doctrine here at Unalashka, exactly in the sense that I am speaking of it here.

The natives of these parts are in some respects as much children as those in your Home, whom you, in spite of the "careful guard" and good bringing up of which you speak in your letter, are unable to establish in righteous living and to protect against temptation (witness the two girls, wards of your home, who eloped by night with young men). . . . If we are to speak of the depravity of the natives, we must not forget that the blame for it falls in great part (see Mark IX, 42) on the strangers—of course not on all—who bring here the evil example of their "beastlike" lives. "Woe unto the world because of offences!" (Matth. XVIII, 7; I Cor. XV, 33). Remove depraved persons, from their midst and the natives' life will be different! Are *they* to be blamed because their houses are invaded at night with breaking in of doors—by whom? By depraved strangers, newcomers, who bring liquor with them for vile purposes! If to the contagion of actual temptation (hard enough for infirm man to resist), we add the hereditary predisposition to evil (Rom. VII, 14–24), then it will become clear that these natives *are not* to be judged harshly (Rom. II, 1: XIV, 4; James IV, 12; Matth. VII, 1). They are not Sodomites; they are not hardened and persistent sinners; they are men with human infirmities, with "broken and contrite hearts" (Psalm 51, 17), as I, their spiritual father, very well know. I do not dare, I dread to think, let alone to say, that I am better, purer than they in the eyes of God, Who sayeth what we read in Matthew XX, 31.

You admit that they, these natives are very religious, but only "as far as outward forms go". Why, have you entered within their souls, that you feel warranted in denying the presence of religiosity within their hearts? I know that you will say "True religiosity does not go without corresponding morality" (James II, 18; II Peter 1, 5). But how then will you account for this "outward" religiosity of theirs? It is hypocrisy, habit, compulsion, or what? It is not hypocrisy, for they do not know how enough to sham. If *habit*—well, just try to get into the habit of *standing* two hours at a time and longer, without changing your place, without even shifting your position from one foot to the other, as these poor people do, so that after a service you can count by the tracks on the floor how many there were. Or else, try and make a habit of giving your last cent for a good purpose (Mark XII, 42) etc etc. As to compulsion, I can testify on my conscience as a priest that there is no such thing on any side (Luke XI, 14–20).

No; this outward religiosity of theirs is the fruit of an inward and sincere disposition of the heart. And that is why they may enter before us into the Kingdom of Heaven (Matth. XXI, 31).

Can we say, you and I, that we are holy? If so, look up Matth. XIX, 17, Mark X, 18; Luke XVIII, 19; I John I, 8–10; James III, 2—and others

And see in particular Matth. V, 20.

Again, most worthy Matron, you write: "Most of their homes are veritable brothels of sin". I don't doubt that you use these words—"*most* of their homes" not in a literal sense, but hyperbolically, *for greater effect* (I Kings XIX, 14–18). But even so you are laying on the colors too thick. This is most unfair and very insulting to us. (See Matth. VII, 1; Rom, II, 1; Luke VI, 41–42; XVIII, 9–14; John VIII, 7). In the literal sense, there are, by the mercy of God, no such houses as those you speak of,—excepting the saloons, the owners of which are "outside of our pale".

Possibly you speak thus on the ground of the "thundering" sermons which I occasionally preach in our church. If so, you make a mistake. Such sermons are indeed meant to denounce *some* individuals (not all nor the majority); but far more *to warn and prevent*.

From what do you conclude that the natives of these parts lead such *very* sinful lives? Coming to the list you give of the sins which you say prevail among the natives, I must inform you that some of those sins do not exist among them at all; others do exist, as you say, though not universally by far; and others again exist in no greater degree than, I dare say, we shall find them in ourselves, you and I—if only we take the trouble to learn impartially to "know ourselves" and if we dig, with severe self-criticism, to the bottom of our hearts. . . .

I think this a proper occasion to remark that the so-called *great* sins are really fraught with less danger to our moral self-improvement and eternal salvation in Jesus Christ than those that are termed *small* or *venial* sins, which are not so conspicuous and do not strike us at once by their hideousness or their vulgarity. The former are easy to detect, to be horrified at, and to correct with God's help, while the latter, being inconspicuous and habitual, man becomes familiar with them and ends by hardly counting them as sins at all. (Thus it is with dust and rubbish in a room: big rubbish we remove; small litter we don't notice, or don't mind: yet how much harm does not the latter do to health, in the form—say—of dust!). But these small sins take such hold on us that, in the end, they eat into our hearts like rust and then it is, more especially, that we are apt to see the mote in our neighbor's eye and not to perceive the beam in our own (Matth. VII, Luke, VI); this it is that the Lord alludes to in Matth. XXI, 31; V, 20,—and thence we are like whitened sepulchres (Mat. XXIII, 27) and shall be spued out of the mouth of the Lamb (Revel. III, 15–46).

The alleged total depravity of the natives causes you deep sorrow; yet do tell me, on your conscience, is the moral life of the people from whom you came here, any better than theirs? How will you account for what we read under the heading: "The northern region of Alaska" in the *Sun,* September 24, 1899?

Lastly you should know that, if the people here can sin, they can also repent *and that is what most imports;* (remember King David, the good thief, the sinning woman, who are spoken of in the Gospel, and pay particular attention to Rom. XIV, 4, etc.). And besides, the sins of these people are almost exclusively sins *of the flesh,* which is infirm in all of us, and they sin from insufficient moral culture,—(a shortcoming to which I, with the help of God, direct my attention, and I may say that my six years of labor among them, by prayer, exhortation, and example, have not been unblest of the Lord, but it is a terrible struggle—(Ephes. VI, 12)—and their sins are really sins of ignorance, lack of comprehension and of training, the sins for which the Lord Himself prayed (Luke XXIII, 34), and Archdeacon Stephen (Acts, VII, 60). And from such sins it is easier for them to be delivered than for us to be delivered from sins of the spirit, invisible, and accounted by us *unimportant.*

I am pleased and rejoiced that you should speak in your letter of the natives' *moral* life; but what connection, pray, do you perceive between the particular doctrine of our church and our moral life?

That the late Irene Titoff led a good Christian life under your guidance for nearly a year before her death, I am very glad to hear, and thank you on her behalf, she having been my spiritual daughter. But a moral life, such as Irene Titoff practised under your immediate guidance, is one thing, and, *doctrine* is another; now by the doctrine she professed, she belonged to our church, which commands to lead a moral life, after the ideal standard which we find in the Gospel. What need, then, had you to take from her the faith of her church, and to give her a *new* faith,—yours, as though to make her pay in this manner for that same guidance we spoke of just now? It follows, I repeat, that you see some kind of connection between the doctrine of our church and our moral life, and hence, in your letter to me, you make such a detailed statement, unprovoked by anything I may have said in my letter under No. 95, concerning the moral life of the natives, *laying the colors on thickly*.

You write: ''This letter is sufficiently plain on the subject''. Yes indeed: it is plain enough, but the argumentation is very feeble; and yet that is the most important thing in a reply, therefore I am not satisfied by it.

Once you receive children into your home on the express condition that they shall be allowed to attend our church, you have no right to turn them aside from it and into your own, merely because you feed and clothe them, and guide them in their moral life, for you are bound, as good and honorable Christians, to abide faithfully by your promises. . . . And in this case we *have* a right to interfere in your management, even though you declare that such interference ''will not be tolerated''.

The ''triumphant'' death of Irene Titoff is to me also a cause of rejoicing; but one thing troubles me and mars my joy: it is your remark that ''the children can never forget it''. You will probably make use of it in the interests of *your own propaganda*. . . .

What a pity that you are, it appears, wholly unacquainted with the tenets of our church! For, if you were acquainted with them, even but slightly, you would not write this: ''Confession to God is more than confession to man'' (See James V, 16). In saying this, you evidently intend to ''throw a stone into your neighbor's garden'', as the saying is. But you should know and not despise such other sayings as this: ''Never spit into a well: you may want a drink from it someday'', or: ''They who live in glass houses should not throw stones''. . . .

Should you wish to gain some knowledge of the tenets of our church, I will send you books—in the English language.

At all events learn this now,—that the penitent makes his confession not to the priest, but to his heavenly Father; the priest, as the person who, after confession, is to administer the Sacrament of the Eucharist, acts as witness to the penitent's sincere and profound repentance at heart (Acts, XIX, 18), in order that he may receive the Body and Blood of our Lord, administered by the priest, to the healing of body and soul, and not to his own condemnation (Corinth. XI, 27–29).

It is time to end, although this reply is far from having reached its conclusion.

My natural sincerity will not suffer me to keep silence on another view of mine concerning your home, which is—that it appears to me to be built on sand, and not on that Cornerstone, Which is spoken of in various places: I Peter II, 7; Ephes. II, 20; Matth. XXI, 42; Acts IV, 11, and others. This Cornerstone never had recourse to craft or deceit, and was always true to its promises (Matth. XII, 20).

I beg of you not to take for yourself any of the things I have here said, seeing that you do not act as you do independently, but as one under authority (Luke VII, 8). . . .

May Christ's love and peace take up their abode between us!

Alex. Kedrofsky
Rector of the Unalashka church.

November 11–24 1900.
Isle of Unalashka,
Alaska.

V

ADORNMENT OF THE ORTHODOX CHURCH IN AMERICA

Editor's Note: Saints are the glory and the verification of the Church. It is in her "holy ones" that the Church proves, even to those who reject the Gospel, that Christ is the Way, Truth, and Life, for in these men and women the full power of a Christ-like life is revealed. Alaska has witnessed the presence of four such Christians who have been officially recognized by the Church as exemplary models for all believers to emulate: the ascetic Elder, the monk Herman, glorified as "wonderworker of all America" for his miracles of healing, his words of consolation and prophecy, and his life of joyful service, humility, and love; the priest and bishop Innocent Veniaminov, canonized as "Enlightener of the Aleutians and Apostle to America" for his devotion and service to the native peoples of Alaska and Siberia; and Hieromonk Juvenaly, who died a martyr's death, probably near Quinahgak on the Bering Sea, as he attempted to proclaim the Gospel to the Eskimo people there. In addition to these known saints, there are others. Certainly if Father Juvenaly's guide also was martyred at the mouth of the Kuskokwim, he too is by virtue of his sacrifice an unnamed Tanaina Indian saint. And there is the story of St. Peter the Aleut, a young man from Kodiak Island taken prisoner by the Spanish near Fort Ross, California (where Baranov's foreman Kuskov had established an agricultural station), who died under torture for refusing to renounce his faith.

These are the four saints the details of whose heroic lives and deaths are known. But there are certainly many more. There are the laity who have maintained their faith, often with very little formal schooling, with little pastoral attention, with few material resources, who despite all odds, and sometimes enduring harassment and even persecution, have kept the faith. There are the clergy, especially after 1917, who remained at their posts, tended their flocks, supported themselves and their families, traveled, preached, translated, taught, prayed, suffered, and endured all for the sake of Christ and His Holy Church. God knows their names. And there are their wives and families who shared all this and bore this as their cross, their lot in this world, and did so with joy. God knows their names. There are the parish wardens and choir leaders, and the numerous benefactors (some of whom were not of the Orthodox Faith themselves) who encouraged, assisted, sacrificed, and lived their faith, whose examples inspired their descendants down to the present day. God knows their names too. These are Alaska's real treasure. These are the witnesses, the martyrs, the "living stones" with whom the Church is built, Christ Himself being the cornerstone. These are the adornment of the Orthodox Church in America, the fruit of two centuries of Alaskan Missionary Spirituality.

This chapter includes a biography of Innocent Veniaminov by an Aleut Orthodox priest, Father Andrew Kashevarov, who published it in *Alaska* magazine in 1927, when he was curator of the territorial museum in Juneau, together with some of the liturgical verses and hymns composed in honor of these Alaskans, and to the glory of God who is wonderful in His saints. The recently published texts of the Christmas Tropar, Kondak, Canon, Exapostilarion, together with the Tropars to Saint Herman and Saint Iakov (James the Apostle) in Yup'ik Eskimo, compiled and transcribed by Father Martin Nicolai of Kwethluk, who continues Father Netsvetov's apostolic work are also given.

"Remembering . . . all the saints, let us commend ourselves, and each other and all our life unto Christ, our God."

ARTICLE: "JOHN VENIAMINOV INNOCENT, METROPOLITAN OF MOSCOW AND KOLOMNA," BY ALEUT PRIEST, REV. ANDREW P. KASHEVAROV, FEBRUARY 1927

[*The following article was originally published in* Alaska Magazine *1, nos. 2, 3, and 4, February, March, and April, 1927.*]

Father Veniaminov's family name was Popov. He was born on the 27th of August, 1797, at Anginsk, Siberia, a small village belonging to the Irkoutsk parish. His parents were very poor; his father, Eusebius Popov, was the sexton of the church in that village and, being an invalid, could do very little toward the support of his family. When he died he left a wife and four children, of whom John was the oldest, and the boy was adopted by his uncle, Deacon Dimitrius Popov.

At his uncle's house, John learned to read and write; he was very bright and soon was able to read in church. When sufficiently prepared, he entered the seminary at Irkoutsk as a ward of the parish, and he remained for eleven years as a student in this theological school. His life there was hard and unpleasant; fellow students who came from homes better blessed with earthly goods and from more prosperous environments, made remarks about John and often by their behavior plainly showed that they considered themselves above him.

But young John paid scant attention to this, pursuing his studies with vigor and attention, thereby surpassing them all in knowledge and success. He led a very quiet and retiring life, preferring to be alone with his books, or engaged in some form of mechanical work, like carpentry, cabinet making, or watch and clock making. He was fond of reading and preferred scientific works, as history, astronomy and botany.

By his kindly disposition and lofty character, and his standards as a student, he soon gained the respect of his fellow students, and we see in his early training, the preparation for his success in later years.

A Change of Name

We know this man as Veniaminov, and the circumstances which brought about this change of name are also a tribute to the character of this unusual man. About the close of his stay in the seminary, the administration of the institution was changed. The new executive was a progressive, cultured, kindly and lofty character, and he at once reorganized the system then prevailing in studies, introduced better living conditions and made life more pleasant for the students.

This new superintendent conceived the idea of changing the surnames of the students according to their character, deportment and progress in study, and John Popov, as the most advanced and successful student, of unblemished character and excellent deportment, was selected to perpetuate the name of a highly respected and learned Bishop Veniamin, recently deceased. Thus he took the name Veniaminov, which we have learned to honor and respect in Alaska.

Father Veniaminov's early habits of mental and physical labor remained with him during his whole life. So many people marvel at his accomplishments, and so many ask, "Where did he get the time for all this?" Indeed, there is much room for wonder when we recount all the phases of the work of this wonderful man. The monuments that he left are with us now; we have only to glance casually over a bibliography of his literary work to be amazed at the variety of subjects that he covered.

Let us not overlook the immense distances that he travelled in his work in Alaska and in Siberia; let us not overlook the structural work done by him—it seems the man must have been working continuously. And so he was.

From early youth, Veniaminov could not be idle.

The Clock Maker

An illuminating incident is of record from his student days. Bishop Michael desired to build a tower clock on the Irkoutsk Cathedral, and for this purpose he imported a foreigner named Klim to construct and install the clock. The mechanic was given living quarters close to the Bishop's residence, and as the work progressed, the Bishop noticed that one of the students quite frequently visited the clock maker at his work. Thinking that this student was idling away a great deal of time, he reported the matter to the school authorities, but upon investigation it was found that the supposed idler was Veniaminov, the most earnest and serious student in the institution. It was also ascertained that Veniaminov had assisted the clock maker in filing cog wheels and generally made himself useful.

Naturally he was not forbidden to continue his visits to the tower, and later in his life we find him making use of this training for the benefit of his people and churches; today we still have the cathedral clock at Sitka, which was constructed by Veniaminov's own hands.

A year before graduation he married and was ordained a deacon, and this completely changed his plan to continue studies in the Theological Academy at Moscow. Four years later he was ordained priest.

In 1823 an order from the Holy Synod at Moscow was received at Irkoutsk in which it was required that a priest be sent to take charge of the Unalaska district. What information was at hand regarding Unalaska, came from the promyshleniki returning with furs and these men pictured it as a wild country, inhabited by savages. When the order was made public and volunteers were asked for, there was no response, for the idea of going to such a wild country deterred them all from accepting the offers held out by the ruling Bishop of Irkoutsk. Time was passing; the order remained unanswered, and the situation was fast becoming unpleasant for the Bishop when one day young Father Veniaminov offered his services.

This offer, coming from such a promising priest, puzzled the Bishop, who did not like to lose a man who stood so highly in the service. Upon interrogation, Father Veniaminov explained that he had met a man from Unalaska, who pictured the life there as less harsh than it was generally thought to be and, he said, the man from Unalaska told him many affecting stories of the Aleuts; of their kind, sympathetic and likable nature, and their eager desire to be instructed in Christianity.

For some time the Bishop withheld his decision, and seeing that the young priest was determined to go, he reluctantly gave his consent and appointed him missionary for the Unalaska district. At that time Father Veniaminov's family consisted of his wife, his mother, one brother and a very young son.

An Arduous Journey

The journey through Siberian wilds greatly distressed them, but neither their prayers nor their protestations availed to change his mind once he had resolved to go. On the 7th of May, 1823, they left Irkoutsk to go to this unknown country; the little band sailed down the Lena River, north to Yakutsk. The Lena is one of the largest rivers in Siberia; the current is sluggish, the shores are rocky and for hundreds of miles bear no human habitation until the town of Yakutsk is reached. From Yakutsk, down over tundras, mountains and forests, it is more than a thousand versts* to Okhotsk in Kamchatka, and this distance is necessarily covered on horseback.

There are no regular trails, the traveler must depend upon the best route through deep forests, boggy marshes, in which the horses sink and are extricated with difficulty, up steep mountains covered with snow, across rivers that have overflown their banks from heavy rains and melting snow. It was over such a trail that Father Veniaminov brought his family to Okhotsk.

There they boarded ship for Sitka, and from Sitka sailed to Unalaska on another ship, in which they finally reached their destination after a year and two months of constant travel, and landed in Unalaska on the 29th of July, 1824.

Beginning the Great Work

At Unalaska, the family, for want of quarters and houses, settled in a native barabara.** Father Veniaminov found a very small and dilapidated church at this place, and found the natives a kindly people, but very ignorant of Christian teachings. During the first year, his principal work was to prepare sufficient material for building the church and the dwelling house, and this is where his thorough knowledge of mechanical work proved quite useful. He instructed the natives in manual training; taught them carpentry, blacksmithing, brick-laying and masonry, and in the meantime strenuously applied himself to the study of their language, beliefs, customs and traditions. It is surprising how quickly he acquired the language, familiarized

*Verst, 1.607 kilometre; approximately 2/3 mile.

**The native underground hut.

himself so thoroughly with the character, the mental state and abilities of these natives.

And only then did he begin to apply the Christian teachings to his people. He did not try to change them too radically, or too suddenly, and that is where his wonderful talent as a teacher and a missionary shows itself.

After all the material was at hand, he began the actual building of the church; the corner stone was laid on the first of July, 1825, and history tells us that most of the actual work on the building was done by his own hands. The work of Christianizing the people then progressed successfully. Again history tells us that he made use of native ideas in propounding biblical truths. He began to travel among the many islands of the Aleutian group, going from one island to another; preaching, studying the language and the customs. One must understand that he did not have ships, launches or boats to travel in. He used the bidarki, in which he covered hundreds of miles along that treacherous and dangerous coast.

The Aleut Bible

About this time he began his monumental work of translating the gospel of St. Matthew into the Aleutian tongue. His subsequent labor, in that line was a partial translation of the gospel of St. Luke, the entire book of the Acts of the Apostles, the catechism of the church, many prayers and the inspiring pamphlet, "The Way Into the Kingdom of Heaven."

On his travels, he always carried a note book into which he recorded faithfully, the legends, stories and traditions of the people. He later compiled this into a volume that gives us the most authentic treatise on the Aleuts. During the later years of his life at Unalaska he compiled a grammar of the Aleutian language and a grammar of the Kodiak language.

His work in teaching the Aleuts to read in their own language stands out as one of the greatest monuments to his life in this district. It is recorded that not only the children but the old people as well, were reading the gospel and prayers in their own tongue.

To add to the achievements of the great missionary, it must be mentioned that he made two trips to Nushagak, in Bristol Bay. In 1829 he preached the gospel at Nushagak and baptized those who desired to become Christians, and in 1832 he had a chapel built there.

In the account of his life on the Aleutian islands a very striking incident is recorded in one of his reports to the Bishop of Irkoutsk. The original transcript in Father Veniaminov's hand writing with other manuscripts, is now at Sitka, but will be loaned to the Territorial Library at Juneau, for safekeeping. It was the privilege of the writer to read that record in the original and it is placed here for the interest it may have:

*An Aleut Prophet**

"In 1828, I made a bidarka journey to the island of Akoun, for the purpose of ministering to the natives there. On coming close to the beach, all the people of the village dressed in their best clothes were gathered on shore, evidently for my reception. On getting out of the bidarka I asked the meaning of this. They answered that they knew I was coming and came out to greet me, and welcome me to their island. I asked them why they were so 'dressed up' and they said, 'We knew that you had left Unalaska for this island and would be here today, and so to show our joy we came here to welcome you.'

" 'And who told you that I would be here today, and how did you recognize me as Father Veniaminov?'

" 'Our shaman, old man Smirennikov, told us that you had started from Unalaska and would be here today, (and he told us that)—you will teach us about God and how to pray to Him.'

"Later I met old man Smirennikov. He was about sixty years of age. He was believed to be a shaman. The reason for this was that this man performed unexplainable manifestations. One of the most striking was this: One woman, the wife of Theodore Zharov, stepped on a set Klipts trap* thereby very severely injuring her knee. The barbs on the lever of the trap, about two inches long, struck her knee cap, causing a very painful and dangerous wound. Blood poisoning set in and the woman was at death's door. In fact there did not seem to be any hope for her recovery. The relatives of the woman apealed to Smirennikov for help. He came to see the woman and after looking at her for a short time he said, 'She will be well in the morning.'

"To the surprise of all, the next morning this woman arose from her sick bed perfectly well, with no indication of wound or soreness in her knee. Another striking incident was the help in procuring food for the whole village. During the winter of 1825 the natives of Akoun island village were entirely out of food. Some of the more venturesome asked old man Smirennikov to give the people of Akoun a whale so that they would not die from starvation. He said 'I will ask for it.' Shortly afterwards he came with the information that if they would go to a certain beach on the island they would find the whale they asked for. All went to the designated spot and found a whale on the beach.

---

*[Note: Here Fr. Kashevarov includes the encounter with Smerennikov contained in Veniaminov's letter to Archbishop Michael of Irkutsk. (See Chapter 3, "Teacher and Apostle.")ED.]

*A wooden trap, powered by twisted rawhide, which caught its victim something after the manner of a single tong working against a flat board.

"This incident of his wonderful prophetic power was borne out by his knowledge of my movements at a distance so great that he could not possibly have known about me unless he possessed occult powers.

"It was my intention to visit Akoun last autumn. The people were expecting me and a bidarka was dispatched from there to bring me. Many things happened (so that I) could not visit the island; vessels came in with mail, and other things, like great storms, came. The people were expecting me. The old man forcibly maintained that I would not come that fall, but would be there next spring. The old man was correct in all his statements concerning me. There are many other events that point to his occult powers. Like narratives, confirmed by many reputable witnesses, induced me to interrogate old man Smirennikov.

"My desire was to know how he could know certain events ahead and by what means he cured sickness. Thanking me for putting these questions to him, he told me the following:

" 'Shortly after I was baptized by Father Makarius, first one and then two men appeared to me. They were not visible to others, but I could see them and talk to them and they spoke to me. They had white faces and were dressed in clothing similar to the paintings in church (representing Archangel Gabriel).'

"These spirits told the old man that they were sent there by God to teach the people and to guard them from harm. During the course of thirty years, these spirits appeared to him almost daily. They instructed him in the tenets of the Christian religion and the mysteries of the faith. It is unnecessary here to repeat all that he said on this subject, for what he said were really the teachings of Christ.

"These spirits rendered him, and through him to other people on the island, help in sickness, distress and trouble. In this connection the spirits always said that they would ask God and if He were willing to help, the help would be received. Once in so often he would acquaint the people of the events taking place in other remote parts. Seldom did he foretell coming events. In this the spirits invariably said that what they told him was not of their own power, but came from God.

"I asked him: 'How do they teach you to pray? Do they want you to bow yourself to them and to pray to them?' He answered, 'They teach me to pray to God alone. To pray in spirit and from pure heart. They often prayed with me during long periods.'

"I gave him the following instruction: 'I can plainly see that the spirits who visit you are good spirits and you must follow their teachings. To those who ask you for help you must say that they must ask God themselves; God is our Father, and He will help those who put their trust in Him. I do not forbid you to render help to those who are ill, but in helping them you must explain that it is not you who gives this help, but God by His mighty power.' ''

Father Veniaminov was very much interested in this wonderful manifestation. He wanted to meet the good spirits and talk with them, and the old man said ''I will ask them about this, and if they are willing, I shall tell you.'' The next day the old man came to him and said that the spirits would see him and let him see them. Thinking this over, Father Veniaminov concluded that he wanted to see them out of curiosity and that if he did see them, it might make him proud of this honor. He decided to report the matter to his Bishop, and ask for advice, and he rendered the report we have just read.

It was a year before he received a reply from the Bishop, who advised him to see the spirits. When Father Veniaminov reached the island again, he found that the old man had died.

Priest and Scientist

And so, while living at Unalaska and carrying on the duties of a missionary pastor, Father Veniaminov endeavored to be useful not only to the scientific world but to the industrial world as well. Having mastered the Aleutian language to a high degree of proficiency, he compiled a ''Grammar of the Aleutian-Fox Language.''

In commenting on this work he says, ''In compiling the grammar of a language like the Aleutian, at first I deemed it to be a useless undertaking; I knew it was of no use to the Aleuts, for without this grammar they can express their thoughts and converse correctly with each other; neither was it of any particular value to the foreigners. But knowing with what ardor and with what eagerness many scientists are collecting all sorts of information, and how important every little discovery was to them, I decided to compile a grammar, if not entirely complete, yet with sufficient rules governing the tongue to be of value in studying the origin of this language for historical conjectures. It cannot be possible that the Aleutian language had no other spoken tongue similar to it, but that it could show some evidence of its origin. For so far we have but meagre knowledge of it. All the information we have is a few vocabularies of the language.''

Mr. Woiyeikov, in commenting on the work of Father Veniaminov has this to say: ''This labor has opened a new field for research to the scientists who are studying languages. That great authority on the Chinese tongues, Dr. Shautt, taking advantage of the grammar compiled by Father Veniaminov, began to compare the Aleutian language with that of the

Chinese and Asiatics, and through the study of it has obtained the desired success.''*

A Versatile Character

Aside from his literary work, the indefatigable missionary, during his ten years in this district, studied the climatic conditions, the population, and the products of Unalaska district. From these scientific studies we have that authentic work, ''The Notes on the Unalaska District.'' In the matter of industries, he has also rendered unprecedented service.

Having thoroughly acquainted himself with the fauna of the islands in the adjacent waters, and having familiarized himself with the life and habits of the valuable fur animals, especially the fur seal, and knowing the mode of hunting them then in use, he offered, as a result of his extensive investigations, certain valuable suggestions to the fur company for more sensible and scientific modes of taking these animals.

The suggestions were accepted and used, and not only saved the seal herd from depletion but also from complete extermination, thereby enriching the company by many thousands of rubles in the pelts of these valuable animals.

Upon his arrival at Unalaska, Father Veniaminov lived in a barabara, but later a good wooden structure was built entirely by his own hands. The furniture of the house was also made by him, as well as the wall clock; his practical mind and mechanical ability made him capable of meeting all the varied problems of his life in the wilderness and performing all the tasks necessary for his comfort and that of his family in this pioneer country.

He spent his evenings in mechanical pursuits, making clocks, hand organs, musical instruments. He made candles for his churches. He not only taught in the boys' school which he had established at Unalaska, but also compiled the school books for use in that and other similar institutions in Alaska.

In 1834 Father Veniaminov began his work in the enlightenment of the people of southeastern Alaska and the Pacific Coast.

After ten years of active life in the Unalaska district, Father Veniaminov was transferred to Sitka. Accompanied by his family, he arrived at this historic spot on the 22nd of November, 1834. Sitka at that time was the center of commercial activities for the entire Pacific coast. It was here alone one could repair a ship; procure manufactured articles and see something

*Moscow University *Izvestia*, No. 5, 1868.

being accomplished in connection with education. Father Veniaminov found this part of Alaska like a new world. In taking up his work as a pastor of the St. Michael's Cathedral,* he found an entirely different congregation from that of the Aleutian islands. Here was a sphere new to him. He was amongst the administrative, educational and naval classes with a mixture of Kodiak and Unalaska Aleuts. The aborigines of this locality had not been Christianized. They, the Thlingits, were living in their primitive beliefs and traditions, entirely untouched by civilization. Governor Kuprianoff permitted the Thlingits to settle outside of the stockade, in the belief that having them close under the forts, they would not be apt to fall upon the Russians while their own wives and children were exposed to the fire from the forts. They were living then in complete savagery and had fierce habits.

Here, as in the Aleutian district, Father Veniaminov desired to bring these people under the influence of Christianity. He began his work carefully by studying their traditions, beliefs and customs, and at the same time determining their spiritual needs. He knew by experience and his successful work amongst the Aleuts that it was necessary for him to master their language. This work required great mental strain and much time. However, after a long and tedious study, he accomplished his purpose. Having studied their social condition and mastered their language sufficiently to be able to converse with them, he began his missionary work, but only after a series of events which in a great measure assisted him to pursue that work in safety.

His own version in his report** will tell the story in a clearer way than can be offered in other words.

"The Thlingit people being absolutely an independent race, brave and living entirely under the influence of Shamans and the sway of the old medicine women, would have continued in ignorance, superstition and obstinacy, and no outside influence or even the lure of gain would have changed their belief in Shamanism, had not God himself been instrumental in this. Moreover the example set by the lower classes of Russians and Aleuts, who lacked entirely the Christian virtues, was not envied even by the Thlingits. The Thlingits knew these people through intercourse during their work in the settlement. They saw the Aleuts living in separate quarters assigned to them and their families. They were all in the employ of the Company and received some stipulated pay, which was naturally small, but at the same time they were entirely under the control of the administration. To the Indians they were not a free people. They surmised that in their own country these people were as free and independent as themselves. And since be-

*The second church; built in 1816.

**Report on the Condition of the Orthodox Church in America, St. Petersburg, 1840.

coming Christians they had become also not far removed from slavery. This and other conditions served to check the Thlingits from embracing Christianity. The inborn savagery of the Indians, and to some extent the old, old hatred towards their conquerors were other factors preventing them from inclining their ears toward Christian teaching. These obstacles would have continued indefinitely had not Providence sent upon them an unheard of sickness, which in truth can be named the boundary line at which the harsh kingdom of ignorance ended, and that of enlightenment began.

"This sickness was the smallpox which raged among the Thlingits in the early part of 1836, in such a severe form that during the two months,—January and February, it carried off one-half of the population. Yet this epidemic, while destroying so many of them, was the means of bringing many blessings to them. Firstly it attacked the older element—those who were grossly steeped in superstititon, ignorance, obstinacy and hostility toward the Russians—those especially who had power over the opinions of the younger generation. Secondly it opened the eyes of the Indians to a realization of the benefits of vaccination and, consequently, to the fact that the Russians possessed knowledge superior to the Shamans, and, lastly it completely changed their viewpoint on the Russians and, at the same time, upset their faith in Shamans who, in spite of their own guardian spirits, perished together with the ones they were trying to save from the sickness.

"When the smallpox first appeared among them the only remedy they knew was the help of the Shaman. Every Shaman was roused up to take measures against a sickness so baneful. There was a continuous beating of drums, shouting and singing and other regular shamanistic practices but to no avail. Men, women and children died by tens and hundreds, while in the Russian settlement there was not a single case of smallpox. In spite of the frenzied efforts of the Shamans to destroy the Russians, and in spite of the rumor that smallpox virus was being put into the meat and fish sold to the town, the Russians remained unharmed. Such striking difference in the condition of the races made the wisest of them pause and consider the cause. And so the more friendly disposed among them and the most intelligent at last began to understand the reason and finally applied to the Russians for help. The Russians immediately extended all possible assistance to them.

"Dr. Bliashke, who was then in the Colonies, at once began to vaccinate all who came to him. All those who were thus treated escaped the smallpox; this had the effect of convincing those who still hesitated, to seek help from the Russians. At last even those who still believed in the Shamans came, and so the whole Indian village at Sitka was treated and the smallpox was completely arrested. Finally Indians came from other villages to be vaccinated. One must not forget that but three months previous to this, no man and no earthly power could have compelled them to take vaccination. It can honestly and truthfully be said, that were an Indian vaccinated against his will before the epidemic, he would have torn out the flesh where the vaccine was placed.

"After so memorable an event in the annals of the Thlingit history I offered my services to them for their spiritual welfare. For, after so striking and eloquent persuasion it was not so hard for me to convince them of the truth of the Gospel. At any rate I had many opportunities to talk to them. They received me, not as their enemy or as one who wished them harm, but as a man of superior knowledge. They received me with marked consideration and listened to me with patience and reverence, and in return told me of their traditions, customs and beliefs.

"Here I want to state that all good intentions of man are fulfilled in no other way than through the will of Providence, and at no other time than set by It.

"One of my main objects in coming to Sitka was to make an attempt to talk to the Thlingits about the true faith. I came here at the close of 1834 but owing to other pressing duties during that winter I had no opportunity even to get acquainted with the Indians. In summer of the following year there was no way of doing any work among them as, according to their custom they all depart from their winter quarters for their summer camps. In the fall of the same year—1835, I could not take up the work on account of other important work on hand, but I fully made up my mind, and even made a resolution, to begin this important work with the natives, during the winter. Governor Kuprianoff assured me he would render all possible help in this, and I was to begin my work on the 7th or 8th of January. Who will not marvel at the destiny of mankind? On the 3rd or 4th of January the smallpox broke out in the Indian village. Had I commenced my work a few days prior to the appearance of smallpox, it is almost certain that the full blame for this would have fallen upon me, as a Shaman brought in by the Russians who wanted to destroy them. Moreso because before my time no Russian missionary had ever set foot at their door either for preaching or in idle curiosity.

"At present the Indians are not what they were two years ago. If they are not ready to embrace Christianity in the near future, they are at least one step nearer to it. They at any rate are willing to listen to the words of salvation. Concerning the reason why so few have been baptized so far; prior to the smallpox epidemic it was impossible to convince them, and in fact, no one ever tried to do so, and after the smallpox I simply acted upon their own conviction, and had never made advances to have them take baptism, but have waited for them to ask for it of their own volition. To prove that the Thlingits have great regard and respect for religion and religious ceremonies, I cite the following instance: After the establishment of the post at

Stakhine, (Wrangell) I visited that place in 1837, where it was necessary for me to celebrate the holy liturgy. I had informed the Indians in advance that such a service was to be held and wished them to be present. As there was no chapel at this post, the place for the services was selected outside of the stockade in a building that was surmounted with a sort of a lattice fence. At my advance invitation over 1500 Indians gathered around the building, completely surrounding the clergy and all those who came to worship. Among these were some converts and newly baptized Indians of the Wrangell clans. The entire assembly of this vast number of Indians surprised me by their respectful and well-behaved bearing as they silently observed something incomprehensible to them and something entirely new. It is right and proper to comment here that not only the adults but also the children were very quiet and respectful. In return I could only respect them for their attention. The liturgy lasted over an hour. When the converts and those baptized that morning came up for the communion I thought there might be some demonstration, but they all remained just as quiet and respectful. I celebrated the liturgy on another day and followed this service with a funeral. There were just as many present and again the same respect and reverence was noticeable. Here I preached to them and they gave me marked attention. I talked to them after this when they visited me at my house. And when I returned to Sitka, I received word from them by the first ship following my visit that they wished me to come again and to preach to them."

Living at Sitka, Father Veniaminov devoted many evenings to the Indians, talking with them and teaching them. He visited them at their homes where he spent many profitable evenings, asking them about their life and getting rich material for the ethnological studies in which he was engaged. He was gladly received with all the respect due to a friend and teacher. Every family wanted to have the honor of his visit, but it was impossible to visit all of them. One evening, on his visit to a man whom he knew better than the rest, he found that the fire in the center of the room would not burn as the wood on hand was very damp. One young Indian busied himself more than others in coaxing the fire to burn. Suddenly he jumped up and brought a beautifully made cover from a box and split it up for kindling, putting the pieces into the fire. "I asked him," says Father Veniaminov, "why you destroy such a valuable piece and which takes such a long time to make?" He answered, "That's all right, I will make a new one."

Through his intensive study of the Thlingit Indians, Father Veniaminov leaves us the most authentic and comprehensive data on the legends, the beliefs, traditions, customs of the Thlingits. When the present generation of the Indians is told about the legends of the Thlingits as collected by Father Veniaminov, they are surprised at the accuracy and the spirit displayed. Father Veniaminov, in giving the ethnological notes garnered by him, says: that he did not gather them from one particular individual or in one particular place, but from many persons and at many places and then compiled them into one volume.

In the midst of his untiring labors for the propagation of Christian teachings among the Thlingits, Father Veniaminov lost no opportunity to study the native language. Whenever time permitted he devoted the whole day to the study of the Koloshan or the Kodiak tongues. This attention and the methodical care in his studies were crowned with success. Shortly after this Father Veniaminov published a book under the title: "Notes on the Koloshan and Kodiak languages and partly on other dialects in the Russian-American possessions, with an appendix of the Russo-Koloshan dictionary."* In this dictionary he had over a thousand words. During the same time he presented his grammar of the Aleutian-Fox language to the Academy of Sciences.

His study of the languages in the Russian-American colonies was a service to the scientific world beyond measure, more particularly because he was the first man to call attention to the multiplicity of tongues in Alaska.

At Sitka he reviewed and revised his notes on the Unalaska natives and his grammar on the Kodiak tongue besides working on his notes on the Thlingits.

Aside from his literary occupations Father Veniaminov found time to pursue his mechanical work. In appreciation for the many favors shown him by the Russian-American Company while on his travels in the colonies, Father Veniaminov constructed the tower clock for the Sitka Church. In a letter to a friend he says: "The clock kept on running and striking accurately, even when the belfry was leaning to one side."

In his leisure moments he made musical instruments—street organs, with two cylinders, one for sacred pieces and the other for Russian folk songs. A number of such instruments were made by him for the Jesuit missionaries at California. In one of his letters he speaks of a visit to California and recites the very pleasant and kind reception from the missionary Fathers. During his life in Sitka he was the prime instigator of the building of St. Michael's Cathedral and the Russian Mission building with its beautiful chapel, illustrated last month in this magazine. Both buildings are still in good state of preservation. At the Sitka Mission house there are pieces of furniture that are attributed to his manufacture. The furniture is perfectly preserved. Of the set one large sofa and six chairs are the work of a master. A yellow cedar writing desk is unique in construction. It has some drawers

---

*Printed for the use of the Academy of Sciences, 1841—St. Petersburg, XV and 120 pages.

with secret springs that can be released by pressing a button hidden from view. The buttons are in the main drawer which is locked with a key. The fine table clock is made so perfectly that it cannot be appreciated by any one not familiar with its construction.

Father Veniaminov had a work shop at Sitka, where he spent many afternoons in making furniture and other useful articles. Captain Belcher in his voyage on the ship *Sulphur* in 1837 speaking of his visit to Sitka, says: "I have visited the local church and was present there during the service. The interior of the church is magnificent, which could not be expected in a place like this. The priest is a manly, athletic man of about forty-five years of age, six feet three inches in height and very intelligent. He made a very favorable impression upon me. Having received his permission to examine his work shop, I saw there quite a good organ, a barometer and many other articles of his own construction. He was so kind as to offer his services to repair our two barometers, and repaired them very satisfactorily. In spite of the fact that he spoke in Russian only, we became very good friends."

His activity covered so great a variety of subjects and material that one can only wonder at his untiring energy. His first thoughts and energy was in establishing schools at Sitka. Lacking text books for the schools Father Veniaminov, with the ability to cope with all problems, at once wrote out the necessary books with his own hand. For the Indian children special books with parallel language—Russian and Indian were prepared. The Thlingits learned to love their instructor, as a friend and pastor. His untiring zeal and labors in all parts of Alaska had given Father Veniaminov first hand knowledge of the situation; he not only knew the existing conditions but was well acquainted with the wants of the people.

He fully realized the need for further education and Christian development. He saw that with only four priests working in the entire Territory the progress could not continue. More workers were needed; more schools, and more churches must be built. Realizing that through correspondence little encouragement on the part of the church authorities could be gained, he decided to present his needs to the Holy Synod of Russia in person. Above all he desired that his labors in the translations of the Gospel and the native tongues should be brought before the people. In other words he realized the great necessity of having the books printed.

He left Sitka on his way to Russia on Nov. 8, 1838. He visited Honolulu, Tahiti, and after rounding Cape Horn he stopped at Rio de Janeiro. In speaking of his trip he mentions with great appreciation the pleasure of spending the days in the warm and balmy climate of the tropical seas. Father Veniaminov arrived at Kronstadt on the 22nd day of June 1839, and after spending a few days at St. Petersburg he continued his trip to Moscow. Here he learned that the Holy Synod would not meet until autumn.

While waiting for the session of the Holy Synod he was the guest of Metropolitan Philaret, the presiding member of the Holy Synod. Father Veniaminov recounted his life and work in the American colonies and made known his problems to the Metropolitan, who later became his greatest friend and ally. Father Veniaminov's personality, and the news of a missionary from so distant a country as Alaska attracted much attention from the press and the people. Wealthy merchants of Moscow, proverbially known throughout Russia for their generosity and gifts to churches and missions, vied with each other in lavishing gifts upon Father Veniaminov for his churches in Alaska and especially supplied him with rare icons, church utensils and other rare gifts for the Sitka Cathedral. It is no wonder that now we see such rare paintings, and other artistic paraphernalia in this historic church.

Father Veniaminov spent the entire summer and part of the autumn with much profit to the Alaska churches. He had succeeded in publishing his notes on the Aleutian islands and the Thlingits. He was able to publish his grammar of the Aleutian and Kodiak languages during the same period of time.

Late in the fall he was called to the Holy Synod to make his report on the mission of Alaska. In making his report to the assembled Bishops he pictured the life on the Aleutian islands and the work among the natives of Alaska and on the southeastern shore in so vivid and interesting a way that all the members present were very greatly impressed, not only with the wonderful progress made but with the man who presented the report.

In appreciation of his great service the Holy Synod elevated him to the rank of an arch-priest. At this time Father Veniaminov received the sad news of his wife's death at Irkoutsk. Immediately he made up his mind to proceed to Irkoutsk to be with his children at this sad time and in order to place them in hands that he could trust. Metropolitan Philaret, while expressing his condolence urged him to enter the monastic orders, but considering the possibility that the family would be left without his guidance and protection, Father Veniaminov hesitated for a long time before accepting this proposal. Metropolitan Philaret obtained an order from the Tsar, which made it possible to place his two daughters in the Patriotic Institute and his two sons Gabriel and Innocent in the Ecclesiastical Seminary, both at St. Petersburg. When his family was taken care of he consented to take the monastic orders. On the 29th day of Nov. 1840 he was received into the order of monks and given the name of INNOCENT. This practice is carried out in the ritual of the church in almost all cases. The secular name is changed and a new one given to the candidate. As a rule the first letter in the name is retained.

On the 30th day of November he was elevated to the rank of Archimandrite and on the next day the Emperor Nicholas I expressed a wish to meet Archimandrite Innocent. The Tsar had heard of him and it was an honor to the Alaskan missionary to be invited to the Palace. At 11 A. M. Archimandrite Innocent arrived at the Palace and was conducted to the Emperor's apartments. The Emperor entered the room shortly after and greeted the Alaskan missionary very kindly and courteously. He expressed his appreciation in the words: "I am very grateful to you because you worked so well and so successfully in that far country and because you have decided to return there to continue your work; how many years have you lived there?"

"Fifteen years, your Imperial Majesty," answered the Archimandrite.

"How do the inhabitants of the distant country receive our faith?"

"In the place where I labored at first the people make very good Christians. Candidly speaking it is there that I have found out what true Christian consolation means."

The Tsar continued: "I have approved the project of creating a diocese at Kamchatka and Alaska, but who is to be the bishop?"

Archimandrite Innocent answered: "May the Holy Spirit guide your decision."

The Tsar then said: "I wish that you be appointed Bishop of Kamchatka and Alaska; please convey my wishes and words to the Metropolitan."

On the same day the Holy Synod of Russia passed a resolution establishing a separate diocese for Kamchatka and Russian America, with a resident Bishop, whose cathedral was to be at Sitka, Alaska. This resolution was brought to the attention of the Emperor, as in Russia all civil and religious acts were made in the name of His Imperial Majesty.

Father Veniaminov, now the Archimandrite Innocent, was chosen for this high office, with the title: "Innocent, Bishop of Kamchatka, Kurile and the Aleutian Islands."

In 1877 a bulletin was written by Rev. Karl Hale, London, entitled "Innocent, of Moscow, the Apostle of Kamchatka and Alaska," from which the following is offered: "After 16 years of missionary labors, Father Veniaminov was sent to St. Petersburg to plead assistance for his mission. The Emperor Nicholas I suggested to the Holy Synod that inasmuch as Father Veniaminov, now a widower, had proved so trustworthy as a priest, he should be sent back there with the rank of Bishop. 'Your Imperial Majesty,' observed some of the members of the Holy Synod, 'No doubt that Father Veniaminov is worthy of this high rank but there is no Cathedral there; there is no clergy or Bishop's residence.'

" 'What of it?' said the Emperor, 'Is it possible that he, being the equal of an apostle, cannot be consecrated to the rank of a Bishop?' "

On the 15th day of December 1840, Archimandrite Innocent was consecrated Bishop of Kamchatka and Alaska. The service took place in the Cathedral of Kazan with Metropolitan Seraphim as presiding Prelate. On the 10th of January, Bishop Innocent left St. Petersburg for Moscow where he gathered together the numerous gifts, presented him by merchants and others, packed them and shipped them to Alaska.

He left Moscow on the 30th of January and arrived at Irkoutsk on the 11th of March, 1841. On the following Sunday Bishop Innocent celebrated the liturgy in the church where he had been ordained a deacon and begun his ecclesiastical career. The church was filled with such a large gathering of people that the police had great difficulty in controlling the immense crowds which came to pray and to see the man who was one of their own native sons and who had risen to the rank of a Bishop from their ranks. There was quite a demonstration among his old parishoners, his fellow students and school mates who looked upon him with various degrees of feeling.

In the early part of May Bishop Innocent started on his trip to America. After a long and arduous journey covering practically the same course that he took 18 years before, he finally arrived at Sitka on the 27th of Sept. 1841. A day of significance in the history of Alaska—just a hundred years after the discovery of the country by Vitus Bering, a bishop steps on the soil of Alaska!

His work at Sitka covers a multitude of constructive ideas which he carried out. As always, his first concern was for the establishment of schools and new parishes in his great diocese.

He sent a missionary to Nushagak; he opened an ecclesiastical school and later a seminary at Sitka. He sent a young man, John Tizhneff, to Kodiak especially to study the Kodiak language for the purpose of translating the holy scriptures. He appointed a special missionary to work with the Thlingits at Sitka. This man was an earnest and conscientious man; in six months he had prepared eighty converts for baptism.

In the spring of 1842, Bishop Innocent visited Kodiak and completely reorganized this parish. From a very passive and indifferent parish, he made a living and a Christian community of the people around the island. This parish, under the right pastor, became active with devotional zeal equal to the best in Alaska.

After completing his work at Kodiak he continued his trip to Kamchatka, and on his way touched at Unalaska where, as a priest, he had done the first ten years of his missionary work.

On the 28th day of May he entered as a bishop the church which he had built with his own hands. The surprise and joy of the native Aleuts was beyond description, says Lt. Zagoskin, who was on the same ship with Veniamnov on his way to the Yukon River. Bishop Innocent spoke and preached to his former parishioners in their own tongue, filled with love and sympathy, and in commemoration of this day they presented him with an exquisitely woven grass *Orlets,* (A circular mat upon which the Bishop stands during services.)

From Unalaska Bishop Innocent sailed for Kamchatka, arriving at Petropavlosk on the 18th of August. He spent ten days here.

On the 29th of November, 1842, he began an eventful trip through Kamchatka covering many thousands of versts with dogs, on reindeer, on horse back and on foot. He suffered privations, cold and shortage of food. Many times he was compelled to spend his nights in the open when on account of terrific winds it was impossible to pitch a tent. At one spot in the road he came to a very steep cut in the mountain. The road was about a hundred feet below this elevation and it was impossible to find a foothold unless steps could be cut in the ice. He was lowered to the bottom by straps. At the bottom the road continued in a narrow cut in the mountain. This portion of the road was reached in the evening and before the party was ready to continue it was dark. Further on he lived through such terrific blizzards as are found nowhere but in the northern Siberia.

In April, 1843, Bishop Innocent reached Okhotsk, having covered more than five thousand versts in his travels. The difficulties encountered in this sort of travel are not generally understood. Often in the midst of the icy wastes the traveler is compelled to pause on account of terrific blizzards and burrow into the snow in order to find shelter, and often this condition continues for days. On this trail there are shelters every forty or fifty versts if one can reach them in time to escape the blizzard; if not, the only protection is to dig into the snow. The Bishop records instances when he was obliged to change clothes in such snowy shelters or otherwise be in danger of freezing. Aside from this hazard there are times when the traveler loses the trail, and then there is the danger of being attacked by wolves. On this trip Bishop Innocent spent sixty-eight days in actual travel.

From Okhotsk he began organizing his immense diocese in Alaska as well as in the Kamchatka districts. He sent Father Golovin from Unalaska to St. Michaels to organize a new parish in the Yukon and Kuskokwim districts. At Sitka the number of converts was now something like two hundred; at every point in Alaska the number of schools had increased. The total enrollment was then six hundred. Churches had been built at Kenai, Yukon, Kuskokwim, and Nushagak and there were chapels in all of those districts.

In 1843 he came to Sitka once more. Here he found that the building known as the Russian mission was ready for occupancy and he dedicated the house chapel in it on the 15th of December and opened a school for children in this building. At that time there were over three hundred children of school age at Sitka, one hundred of which he cared for; the rest were enrolled in the school maintained by the Russian-American Company.

He visited Petropavlosk in 1845 and in that year transferred the Ecclesiastical Seminary to Sitka.

He made his third trip to Kamchatka in 1846 and was at Sitka in 1847. It was during this year that a separate Indian church was organized. A building was begun and, strange to say, the Indians for the first time offered their labor in building the church free of charge. On April 26, 1849 the Indian church was consecrated.

The same year Bishop Innocent visited Okhotsk. In 1848 the new cathedral at Sitka was dedicated to St. Michael, the Archangel.

In 1859 Bishop Innocent was in Kamchatka again. At this time there were twenty-two parishes with resident priests; the clergy consisted of five archpriests, two hieromonks, twenty-two priests and five deacons.

On the 21st day of April, Bishop Innocent was elevated to the rank of Archbishop. During the year 1850 he had traveled in the aggregate over 19,700 versts; new missions had been established among the Tungas natives, the Koriaks, Chukchis; along the Anadir River and among the Buriats and Yakuts. It was after being elevated to the rank of Archbishop that Innocent spent many months at Yakutsk, the northernmost point of Siberia, said to be the coldest spot in the North. Here he studied the language of the Yakuts. Here also he began the translation of the Gospels into the Yakut language with the help of his priests. From here he traveled into the very heart of the Siberian wilds, preaching, establishing missions, building churches, schools and chapels. This record is offered to point out the untiring zeal of this great Apostle.

In 1857 Archbishop Innocent visited America and went over his immense diocese again. Between 1850 and 1858 he traveled over the Amur River districts establishing new parishes; building churches and schools. In this work he was assisted by his son, Father Gabriel Veniaminov. . . . In 1850 a Vicar Bishop was appointed for Alaska and one for Yakutsk. The Vicar Bishop Peter took up his residence at Sitka and the other at Yakutsk.

As an Archbishop this unusual man was not satisfied with teaching and preaching; he continued his mechanical occupation whenever he had an opportunity. History states that he made furniture for the priest's house at Kodiak as well as at Sitka. He had regular work shops in Sitka, Kodiak, Yakutsk and at Blagoveschensk, where he spent part of his afternoons planing, sawing, and hammering.

During his travels at sea, Archbishop Innocent took much interest in the navigation and courses of the ship. He studied all the observations taken by the captain and the mates and knowing his interest in this, the officers of the ship made no changes in the course without telling him about it and explaining the sailing directions on the charts. In this way the Archbishop acquired a very practical course in navigation.

In the narrative of H. T. Verechagin, one of his acolytes who made many trips with him along the Alaskan and Siberian coasts, we read: "Once, going through the straits along the Kurile islands at night, the ship was kept on a certain course during the whole night. In the morning a very heavy fog enveloped the ship and the shore was not visible. When the Archbishop awoke his first question was 'On what course is the ship sailing?' The Captain made some evasive answer and the Archbishop continued: 'Can you see the cliffs of such an island? We must be close to this island and it is very rocky and dangerous; there is also a very strong current here which you don't seem to take into consideration.' The Captain was somewhat hurt, but the Archbishop insisted that the ship should turn on another tack and the Captain was at last prevailed upon to turn the vessel. No sooner had he tacked ship than the fog began to clear; the cliffs and rocky shore appeared quite close to them just as the Archbishop had insisted and pointed out. Had the Captain continued a little longer on the first course, the ship would have been dashed upon the reefs."

He visited Sitka again in 1860 and while here he continued his work in bringing the Alaska diocese into efficient order. From here he again traveled over his immense ecclesiastical see; he preferred to give his personal attention to all the phases of his work rather than to entrust it to subordinates.

Finally on the 22nd of June, 1862, Archbishop Innocent arrived at Blagovestchensk for permanent residence there. In 1865 the Archbishop was called to St. Petersburg to be present at the session of the Holy Synod, of which he had been appointed a member. In October 1867 Metropolitan Philaret of Moscow died and in January of the next year Archbishop Innocent was made the Metropolitan of Moscow. In May, 1868, Metropolitan Innocent arrived at Moscow to take up his duties and here his great activities in the religious world of Russia began. The outstanding work as a Metropolitan was the establishment of Missionary Societies, the re-organization of schools and religious institutions.

At this time Metropolitan Innocent began to lose his eyesight; the constant travel over snowy wastes had its effect upon his eyes and gradually his vision dimmed and at last left him totally blind. This did not deter him from taking active part in the administration of the church affairs. Knowing the services of the church so well he continued to take his part in the celebration of the liturgy and other services; very often he read the Gospel at the services without being able to see the book.

Feeling that the end was coming, Metropolitan Innocent made his will in which one paragraph is of great significance to the Sitka Cathedral.*

Paragraph 6. ''Of the *Panageas* (An image worn around the neck by a bishop) that may remain after my death, send one, representing the annunciation, to the cathedral at Blagovestchensk and the other, representing the miraculous apparition of the Blessed Virgin, to the Cathedral at Sitka, Alaska.''

In 1868 certain sacred vessels and church paraphernalia of rare value were stolen by the soldiers then at Sitka. Later most of the items were recovered. In 1926, when the excavation for the new school building at Sitka was being made, one *panagea* and a few other church articles were dug up in the same place where the other articles had been found after the theft. The finder at first refused to return these rare articles to the church, but later was prevailed upon to sell them to the Cathedral and the writer is of the opinion that the *panagea* found is the identical one mentioned in the will of Metropolitan Innocent.

In 1871, March 17, Ambassador Constantine Katakuzin, writing from Washington to Metropolitan Innocent, among other things says: ''The Christianity and enlightment in Alaska, especially in the western portion, stands firm. The light of the Gospel, planted among them made them true Christians. This opinion was voiced in Congress where several of the members strongly criticised the Government for not doing its duty in looking after the moral and material condition of the natives of Alaska. 'Such was not the policy of the Russian Government,' said one of the Senators. 'The Russian Government and the Russian Clergy made Christians from savages; from ignorant people they made civilized beings; they built churches, established schools, and, even at the present time, the rays of Christianity, be it said to our shame, reach there not from Washington, but from St. Petersburg.' ''

Metropolitan Innocent was greatly depressed when first he lost his sight. Being a man who all his life was accustomed to activity this calamity was a severe blow to him. But like all great men he did not allow this to interfere with his work. He asked many times to be relieved of the post of Metropolitan of Moscow but always without avail.

On the 31st of March, 1879, ''the great pillar of Christianity ceased to exist,'' says his biographer; at 11 o'clock in the morning the great bell of Moscow announced the death of the greatest missionary Alaska had seen. Metropolitan Innocent had requested that no eulogies be said over his remains, saying, ''If a sermon is to be said, let this be your text: 'The steps of a man are ordered by the Lord.' (Psalm 37, v. 23.)''

---

*Page 677, ''Life of Innocent,'' by Ivan Barsukov.

AKATHIST HYMN TO ST. INNOCENT, APOSTLE TO AMERICA

*O Holy Fa*ther, Good *She*pherd of the Flock entrusted to *you* by the Lord!
You dedicated *all* your st*ren*gth and heart all your mind and *soul* to Christ!
In the re*mot*est re*g*ions you labored tirelessly without thought of earthly reward, for the sake of His *Ho*ly Ch*u*rch and the sal*va*tion of all.
We the re*ci*pients *of* your great spiritual legacy offer to you this h*ym*n of praise.
As you stand bef*ore* the T*hro*ne of the Lord of Glory, intercede for our land and its p*eo*ple!
That united in *One* Holy *Ort*hodox Church we may gratefully *sing* to you:
Rejoice O *Ho*ly *Fa*ther Metropolitan *In*nocent! Equal to the A*pos*tles and Enl*igh*tener of Al*as*ka.

1

O Holy Father Innocent! Your glory has shone from the Far Eastern lands to the Western World. From humble origins in a Siberian village you rose to world renown as a modern Apostle. The Lord chose you to bring the Orthodox Faith to the ancient Peoples of Alaska and Asia, who together with us honor you with these songs of praise:
Rejoice! Imitator of the Apostles and their Suc*ces*sor!
Rejoice! Evangelizer of the Arctic *Peo*ples!
Rejoice! Scholar and Teacher of the *A*leuts!
Rejoice! Illuminator of the Eskimos and *In*dians!
Rejoice! Humble genius whose footsteps were g*ui*ded by the Lord!
Rejoice! Visionary Architect of the Orthodox Church in A*mer*ica!
Rejoice! O Holy Father *In*nocent! Equal to the Apostles and Enlightener of A*las*ka!

2

You distinguished yourself as a young student, displaying your many interests and talents by excelling in your studies at home and in school. Your greatest joy was the service of God and His Holy Church. Your uncle instructed you in the ways of piety and Faith so that from an early age you sang to the Lord: ALLELUIA!
In your youth, the Lord prepared you for your lifetime of service by enabling you to study various disciplines. Remembering your dedication, we thankfully celebrate your memory:
Rejoice! your talents were employed in the s*er*vice of Christ!
Rejoice! your achievements inspire all who are fa*mil*iar with them!

Rejoice! Skilled craftsman, imitator of the Carpenter of *Naz*areth!
Rejoice! Clock-maker who proclaimed the T*ime*less One!
Rejoice! Your teachers marvelled at your in*tel*ligence!
Rejoice! Your spiritual children praise your hu*mil*ity!
Rejoice! O Holy Father In*no*cent! Equal to the Apostles and Enlightener of A*las*ka!

Completing your preparation at the seminary at Irkutsk, you accepted the Divine Call to the missionary frontier of Alaska. Together with your wife, the beloved Katherine, you set out on your Apostolic journey to Russian America, as you sang to the Lord: ALLELUIA!

As a newly-ordained priest you showed great determination in reaching your destination, 1,000 miles away, in the Bering Sea. You willingly forsook all for the sake of the Gospel of Christ, travelling for many months over frozen tundra and treacherous seas. Inspired by your dedication, we sing to you thus:

Rejoice! Apostle to A*mer*ica!
Rejoice! Heroic Founder of Orthodoxy in the *Wes*tern World!
Rejoice! Imitator of the Holy A*pos*tle Paul!
Rejoice! Courageous voyager on the *nor*thern seas!
Rejoice! your dedication equalled that of the A*pos*tles!
Rejoice! your perseverance was a Gift of the Holy *Spi*rit!
Rejoice! O Holy Father *Inn*ocent! Equal to the Apostles and Enlightener of A*las*ka!

Arriving at Unalaska, you rendered thanks to the Lord for your safe passage. Kneeling on the beach together with all those in your company, you praised God with the hymn: ALLELUIA!
Together with your tutor, the Aleut Chieftain Ivan, you studied the Native language and devised a writing system for it. You labored for many years, preparing the Word of God for publication in the Aleut tongue. You astounded the indigenous peoples with your ability to preach to them in their own language, thus enlightening them with the Light of Christian Truth. We glorify God for bringing you to our shores and honor your evangelical accomplishments:
Rejoice! Ennoblement of Ancient *Peo*ples!
Rejoice! Father of Learning in A*las*ka!
Rejoice! Teacher of Virtue and Di*vin*e Truth!
Rejoice! Catechist of those seeking R*igh*teousness!
Rejoice! your vision inspires all future *mis*sionaries!

Rejoice! your brilliance illumines the *arc*tic night!
Rejoice O Holy Father *Inn*ocent! Equal to the Apostles and Enlightener of Al*as*ka!

You travelled throughout the Aleutian region, braving storms and hostile seas in your efforts to evangelize your scattered flock. Warmed by your love for the Lord, you journeyed in your bidarka on the icy waves, softly singing to the Creator of all: ALLELUIA!

During the ten years you remained in the Aleutian Islands, you devoted much time and energy to the study of the land, people, and wildlife of the area. You kept careful records of your experiences and observations so that this heritage could be preserved for future generations. You opened schools for the Native children so that they could advance in the Knowledge of God and His Creation. Praising the Lord for His bounties, we offer a hymn to you:

Rejoice! Patient instructor of the *sim*ple and the wise!
Rejoice! Scholar and Teacher of the Aleutian l*an*guages!
Rejoice! Preserver of Alaska's ancient *her*itage!
Rejoice! Dispeller of the darkness of *ign*orance!
Rejoice! Perceptive observer of the wonders of Cr*eat*ion!
Rejoice! Messenger of the Good News of Sal*va*tion!
Rejoice! O Holy Father *Inn*ocent! Equal to the Apostles and Enlightener of A*las*ka!

Having created a written language for the Native people, you developed textbooks for them so that they could become literate. Reading the Word of God in their own tongue, and giving thanks to God, the Aleuts sang with joy: ALLELUIA!

O Holy Father, you travelled beyond the limits of your own extensive district into the land of the Eskimo people. You brought to the natives of Bristol Bay the sanctifying Grace of Holy Baptism. You made the Nushagak River a new Jordan for them, bringing Christianity to the northern shores of the Bering Sea, where you are remembered today with these words of praise:

Rejoice! Enlightener of the Eskimo *Nat*ion!
Rejoice! Sanctification of the *Nus*hagak!
Rejoice! Husbandman sent to the plentiful *har*vest!
Rejoice! Laborer in the *Vin*eyard of Christ!

Rejoice! Warrior clothed in the *arm*or of Truth!
Rejoice! Soldier armed with the Gospel of Peace and the s*wor*d of Prayer.
Rejoice! O Holy Father *Inn*ocent! Equal to the Apostles and Enlightener of A*las*ka!

Using your talents, you erected the first Orthodox Cathedral in the New World, designing the Temple and supervising its construction yourself. The Faithful celebrated the consecration of the new church, singing the hymn of Thanksgiving: ALLELUIA!

Transferring the center of your missionary activity to the City of New Archangel, you began anew the evangelization of the Tlingit People. You became proficient in their language and preached the Gospel in their villages, winning converts to Christ by your knowledge of medicine as well as theology. You admired the nobility of these proud warriors, who together with us offer these praises to you:

Rejoice! Teacher of the Tlingit *Ind*ians!
Rejoice! Physician of souls and *bod*ies!
Rejoice! Fearless apostle, pro*tec*ted by God!
Rejoice! Illuminator of the Northern *Peo*ples!
Rejoice! Mountain rising above the clouds of *er*ror!
Rejoice! Harbor, sheltering from t*re*acherous seas!
Rejoice! O Holy Father In*noc*ent! Equal to the Apostles and Enlightener of A*las*ka!

You were summoned to appear before the Holy Synod to present your many translations for ecclesiastical approval. You returned to your homeland by circumnavigating the globe; arriving at St. Petersburg you praised God in song: ALLELUIA!

Learning of your wife's repose during your absence, you prayerfully visited the Holy monasteries at Kiev and Zagorsk in order to discern the Lord's Will. The Emperor himself, impressed with your apostolic fervor and achievements, approved your elevation to the rank of bishop. Returning to Alaska, you were welcomed with these words:

Rejoice! You who took up the Cross and *fol*lowed Christ!
Rejoice! You who first brought the Joy of the Resurrection to A*las*ka!
Rejoice! You who were inspired by the heroic example of St. *Inn*ocent of Irkutsk!
Rejoice! You who promoted the apostolic labors of St. N*ich*olas of Japan!

Rejoice! You were among the first to ask the Elder Herman to intercede for you!
Rejoice! By his prayers, you arrived safely in Kodiak.
Rejoice! O Holy Father I*nn*ocent! Equal to the Apostles and Enlightener of A*las*ka!

As bishop of the Russian colony, you renewed your efforts to bring the Gospel to all Alaska. You opened a seminary in Sitka for the training of indigenous clergy and designed a new cathedral for the capital city. You also constructed the clock for the church bell-tower. When the Holy Temple was completed you sang out in gratitude to the Lord: ALLELUIA!

As over-seer of the huge diocese which included Eastern Siberia as well as Alaska, you dispatched priests to areas where no missionaries had ever gone. Your own son-in-law was assigned to the Nushagak, while your former student, Father Yakov, set out for the Yukon delta. Because of your great vision for the future of Orthodoxy in this land, we honor you with these hymns:

Rejoice! Good Shepherd of the *Arc*tic!
Rejoice! First Hierarch of A*mer*ica!
Rejoice! Our guide to the *Kin*gdom of God!
Rejoice! Benefactor of the n*ee*dy and oppressed!
Rejoice! Your foresight determined the growth of the Church in A*las*ka!
Rejoice! Your boundless energy established the True F*ai*th in the North!
Rejoice! O Holy Father *Inn*ocent! Equal to the Apostles and Enlightener of A*las*ka!

With characteristic enthusiasm you visited the peoples of the Amur Valley in Siberia and began yet again to study their languages and traditions. Together with the Aleuts and Tlingits they learned to praise the Almighty Creator with the song of Thanksgiving: ALLELUIA!

Transferring your headquarters to the Far East, you bid farewell to the New World and returned to the Old. Following the example you had set for them, the Native clergy of Alaska continued your work in America. Through them we have become your spiritual children and venerate your memory in these words:

Rejoice! Student of Alaskan languages and Teacher of the T*ru*e Word!
Rejoice! Preacher "in tongues" like the Apostles on P*en*tecost!
Rejoice! You published the Gospel in the Aleut l*an*guage!

Rejoice! you founded schools for the enlightenment of the Native P*eop*les!
Rejoice! you directed the evangelization of Alaska and Si*ber*ia!
Rejoice! you planted the seeds of the Orthodox Faith on A*meri*can soil!
Rejoice! O Holy Father *Inn*ocent! Equal to the Apostles and Enlightener of A*las*ka!

You spent your entire life laboring in remote regions for the propagation of the Holy Faith. In your later years you were called to yet another great task. You were elected Metropolitan of Moscow to succeed the venerable Philaret. As you journeyed across the frozen steppes of Asia en route to your enthronement, you sang in amazement to God: ALLELUIA!

You revitalized the missionary spirit of your homeland by organizing societies for the support of evangelical enterprises. You assisted your former flocks with your holy prayers and material aid. We who have benefited from these labors sing to you in gratitude:

Rejoice! You who were faithful in l*itt*le things!
Rejoice! You have been *se*t over much!
Rejoice! Rushing Wind dispelling the fog of ig*nor*ance and fear!
Rejoice! Mighty River watering the spiritual w*ild*erness!
Rejoice! Precious Vessel filled with the Holy *Spi*rit!
Rejoice! Adornment of the Church in the Old W*or*ld and the New!
Rejoice O Holy Father *Inn*ocent! Equal to the Apostles and Enlightener of A*las*ka!

With the same humility you exhibited throughout your earthly life, you asked that no eulogies be delivered at your burial. Instead, you requested an edifying sermon be preached for the benefit of all. Learning of your falling asleep, your spiritual children commended your soul to the Lord, singing: ALLELUIA!

The heirs of your spiritual legacy throughout the New World rejoice today at your glorification, O Holy Father. Asking for your prayers for the Church in America, we gather to celebrate your remarkable achievements with these words:

Rejoice! Inspiration of Orthodox pastors and *tea*chers!
Rejoice! Indicator of the Way to the Kingdom of *Hea*ven!
Rejoice! Faithful steward in the H*ous*ehold of Faith!
Rejoice! Far-sighted Champion of *Ort*hodoxy!
Rejoice! Loving Father of your spiritual C*hil*dren!

Rejoice! Intercessor for all who come to the *Or*thodox Faith!
Rejoice! O Holy Father *Inn*ocent! Equal to the Apostles and Enlightener of A*las*ka!

O Holy Father, Bishop Innocent! As we remember all the glorious deeds you so humbly accomplished, we are inspired by your vision, courage and perseverance. Pray therefore that we may be accounted worthy to continue your work in the New World, and to sing gratefully to the Lord: ALLELUIA! [3 times].

O Holy Hierarch and Father Innocent!
The Lord chose you and ordained you to go and bring forth much fruit in His New Vineyard, on the frontiers of Russia and America. You dedicated your life to building up the Body of Christ in the New World and the Old, and brought the Treasures of the Holy Apostolic Faith to Alaska and Siberia. We your spiritual children kneel before your holy ikon and ask you to intercede for the Holy Orthodox Church in your adopted and native lands. As you were humble and kind, help us by your prayers to be patient and generous. As you persevered under difficult circumstances in a remote and lonely region, strengthen us in our dedication to Christ and His Gospel. As you loved God and your flock and devoted your life in service to them, pray to Our Lord that our hearts may be filled with love for Him and our neighbor. You planted the seeds of the Orthodox Faith in Alaskan soil: implore the Lord that we may be accounted worthy to continue the work you so gloriously began, to bring the Light of Christ to every corner of America. You indicated the Way into the Kingdom of Heaven by your words and example: intercede for the salvation of all of us who venerate your holy memory.

That by your holy prayers we may become worthy of the precious spiritual heritage which God has entrusted to us through you, and sing eternally the praises of the Holy Consubstantial and Life-Creating Trinity, the Father and Creator who is without Beginning, the Son, Our Lord and Savior who became Man in order to sanctify and save us, and the Comforter, the Holy Spirit who enlightens and enlivens all, now and ever and unto ages of ages.

EXTRACTS FROM ORTHODOX FEAST DAY HYMNS (IN YUP'IK ESKIMO) TRANSCRIBED BY ESKIMO PRIEST, REV. MARTIN NICOLAI

[*Reprinted with permission from Rev. Martin Nicolai.*]

HERMAN-AQ ALASKARMIU

TROPAR TONE 7
NU-NA-NIR-QEL-RIA NEGEQUAM AGIA A-GA-YU-VIA KRIS-TUU -SSAM
CIU-LI-QAGG-LU-KI YUUT QILIIM A-NGA-YU-QAU-VIA-NUN.
ELIT-NAU-RIS-TA CALI APUUSTALAQ PI-CIUL-RIA-MEK UK -VE-LEK
KAI-GAL-RIA CA-LI I-KA-YUR-TIIT PIS-TAIL -NGUUT. KENEG-NAA
PI-CIUL-RIIM AGAYUVIIM A-ME-RI-CA - MI. NAN-RAU-MAL-
-RIA AATAQ HERMAN-AAQ A-LAS-KA-MI, A-GA-YUS-KUT

KRIS-TUU-SSA-MUN A-GA - YUT-MUN, A-NIR - TUUS-
- QELLU-KU A-NER-NER-PUT WANG - KU-TA.
NANRAUTII
NAN-RA-RAM-TEGGEN, NAN-RA-RAM -TEGGEN EL-PET.
NAN-RAU-MAL-RIA AA-TAQ HER-MAN-AAQ, CA-LI NAN-RAR-
- NAUR-PUT TAN-QIL-RIA EREN- -REN EL-PET, A-LER-
- QUAS-TIIT MA-NA-GGAT, CA-LI QA-LLA-TELL-GUT-KES-TIIT AN-GI-LAT.

TANQILRIA IAKUVAQ

TROPAR TONE 3
TAN-QIL-RIA APUUSTA-LAQ I-A-KU-VAQ, A-GA-YUS-KUT
WANGKUTA KUSGURTALRIAMUN A-GA- YUT- MUN. TA-MA-TEN
AU-GA-RII-CES-QELLU-KI A-SSIIL-NGUR-NEK, A-NER-NEM-
-TA WANG-KU-TA.

SELECTED BIBLIOGRAPHY

Adams, G.R. *Life on the Yukon, 1865–1867.* Kingston, Ont.: Limestone Press, 1982.

Afonsky, Bishop Gregory. *A History of the Orthodox Church in Alaska.* Kodiak: St. Herman of Alaska Seminary, 1977.

Arseniev, Nicholas. *Russian Piety.* Crestwood, N.Y.: St. Vladimir's Seminary (SVS) Press, 1977.

———. *Revelation of Life Eternal.* Crestwood, N.Y.: SVS Press, 1965.

Berkh, V.N. *A Chronological History of the Discovery of the Aleutian Islands.* Translated by Dimitri Krenov. Kingston, Ont.: Limestone Press, 1974.

Black, Lydia T. *Aleut Art.* Anchorage: Aleutian-Pribilof Island Association, 1982.

———. *Atkha: An Ethnohistory of the Western Aleutians.* Kingston, Ont.: Limestone Press, 1984.

———. *The Journals of Iakov Netsvetov: The Atkha Years.* Kingston, Ont.: Limestone Press, 1980.

———. *The Journals of Iakov Netsvetov: The Yukon Years.* Kingston, Ont.: Limestone Press, 1984.

Bria, Ion, ed. *Martyria/Mission.* Geneva: WCC Press, 1980.

Cabasilas, Nicholas. *The Life in Christ.* Crestwood, N.Y.: SVS Press, 1974.

Chetverikov, Sergei. *Starets Paisii Velichkovskii.* Belmont, Mass.: Nordland Publishing, 1980.

Chitty, Derwas. *The Desert A City.* Crestwood, N.Y.: SVS Press, 1966.

Colliander, Tito. *The Way of the Ascetics.* Crestwood, N.Y.: SVS Press, 1985.

Cracraft, James. *The Church Reform of Peter the Great.* London: Macmillan & Co. Ltd., 1971.

Cunningham, James. *A Vanquished Hope.* Crestwood, N.Y.: SVS Press, 1982.

Davydov, G.I. *Two Voyages to Russian America, 1802–1807*. Kingston, Ont.: Limestone Press, 1977.

Documents on the History of the Russian American Company. Translated by Ramsey, Marina. Kingston, Ont.: Limestone Press, 1976.

Elliot, H.W. *The Seal Islands*. Kingston, Ont.: Limestone Press, 1976.

Fedorova, S.G. *The Russian Population in Alaska and California*. Translated by Richard Pierce and Alton Donnelly. Kingston, Ont.: Limestone Press, 1973.

Fedotov, George. *St. Filipp: Metropolitan of Moscow*. Belmont, Mass.: Nordland Publishing, 1978.

———. *A Treasury of Russian Spirituality*. Belmont, Mass.: Nordland Publishing, 1975.

Florovsky, George. *Christianity and Culture*. Belmont, Mass.: Nordland Publishing, 1974.

———. *Creation and Redemption*. Belmont, Mass.: Nordland Publishing, 1976.

———. *Ways of Russian Theology*. Belmont, Mass.: Nordland Publishing, 1979.

Garrett, Paul D. *St. Innocent, Apostle to America*. Crestwood, N.Y.: SVS Press, 1979.

Gibson, James R. *Imperial Russia in Frontier America*. New York: Oxford University Press, 1976.

Golovin, P.N. *The End of Russian America*. Portland: Oregon Historical Society, 1979.

Gregorios, Paulos. *The Cosmic Man*. New Delhi: Sophia Publications, 1980.

———.*The Human Presence*. Geneva: WCC Press, 1978.

Gorodetzky, Nadejda. *Saint Tikhon of Zadonsk*. Crestwood, N.Y.: SVS Press, 1976.

Hopko, Thomas. *All the Fulness of God*. Crestwood, N.Y.: SVS Press, 1982.

———.Handbook on the Orthodox Faith: Department of Religious Education Orthodox Church in America, Syosset, N.Y. Volume I, Doctrine, 1971; Volume II, Worship, 1976; Volume III, Bible and Church History, 1979. Volume IV, Spirituality, 1976.

Huggins, Eli L. *Kodiak and Afognak Life, 1868–1870*. Kingston, Ont.: Limestone Press, 1981.

Jones, Dorothy. *A Century of Servitude: The Pribilof Islands under U.S. Rule*. Washington, D.C.: University of America Press, 1985.

Kadloubovsky, E., and G.E.H. Palmer, *Early Fathers from the Philokalia*. London: Faber & Faber, 1978.

———. *Writings from the Philokalia*. London: Faber & Faber, 1962.

Kesich, Veselin. *The First Day of the New Creation.* Crestwood, N.Y.: SVS Press, 1982.

Lossky, Vladimir. *In the Image and Likeness of God.* Crestwood, N.Y.: SVS Press, 1974.

———. *The Mystical Theology of the Eastern Church.* Crestwood, N.Y.: SVS Press, 1968.

———. *The Vision of God.* Crestwood, N.Y.: SVS Press, 1963.

Luibheid, Colm. *The Ladder of Divine Ascent.* Ramsey, N.J.: Paulist Press, 1982.

Macarius (Starets of Optino). *Russian Letters of Direction 1834–1860.* Crestwood, N.Y.: SVS Press, 1975.

Makarova, R.V. *Russians on the Pacific 1743–1799.* Kingston, Ont.: Limestone Press, 1975.

Meyendorff, John. *The Byzantine Legacy in the Orthodox Church.* Crestwood, N.Y.: SVS Press, 1982.

———. *Byzantine Theology.* New York: Fordham University Press, 1974.

———. *Catholicity and the Church.* Crestwood, N.Y.: SVS Press, 1983.

———. *Christ in Eastern Christian Thought.* Crestwood, N.Y.: SVS Press, 1969.

———. *Living Tradition.* Crestwood, N.Y.: SVS Press, 1978.

———. *St. Gregory Palamas and Orthodox Spirituality.* Crestwood, N.Y.: SVS Press, 1974.

———. *A Study in Gregory Palamas.* Crestwood, N.Y.: SVS Press, 1964.

Miller, D.H. *The Alaska Treaty.* Kingston, Ont.: Limestone Press, 1981.

Nichols, Robert L., and Theofanis G. Stavrou. *Russian Orthodoxy under the Old Regime.* Minneapolis: University of Minnesota Press, 1978.

Okun, S.B. *The Russian-American Company.* New York: Octagon Books, 1979.

Oswalt, Wendell. *Napaskiak, An Alaskan Eskimo Community.* Tucson: University of Arizona Press, 1963.

Ouspensky, Leonid, and Vladimir Lossky. *The Meaning of Icons* and *The Theology of the Icon.* Crestwood, N.Y.: SVS Press, 1978.

Pascal, Pierre. *The Religion of the Russian People.* Crestwood, N.Y.: SVS Press, 1976.

Pierce, Richard. *Alaskan Shipping 1867–1878.* Kingston, Ont.: Limestone Press, 1972.

———. *The Russian-American Company, Correspondence of the Governors: Communications Sent 1818.* Kingston, Ont.: Limestone Press, 1984.

———. *The Russian Orthodox Religious Mission in America 1794–1837.* Kingston, Ont.: Limestone Press, 1978.

———. *Russia's Hawaiian Adventure 1815–1817*. Kingston, Ont.: Limestone Press, 1976.

———, with Alton Donnelly, trans. and ed. *A History of the Russian American Company,* by P.A. Tikmenev. Seattle: University of Washington Press, 1978.

———, with George Lantzeff. *Eastward to Empire*. Montreal: McGill-Queens University Press, 1973.

Purmonen, Veikko. *Orthodoxy in Finland, Past and Present*. Kuopio: Orthodox Clergy Association, 1981.

Schmemann, Alexander. *For the Life of the World*. Crestwood, N.Y.: SVS Press, 1973.

———. *Great Lent*. Crestwood, N.Y.: SVS Press, 1969.

———. *Historical Road of Eastern Orthodoxy*. New York: Holt, Rinehart and Winston Co., 1966.

———. *Of Water and the Spirit*. Crestwood, N.Y.: SVS Press, 1974.

Shelikov, Gregory. *A Voyage to America 1783–1786*. Kingston, Ont.: Limestone Press, 1981.

Smith, Barbara S. *Orthodoxy and Native Americans: The Alaskan Mission*. Occasional Paper 1. Syosset, N.Y.: Orthodox Church in America, Historical Society, 1980.

Sophrony (Archimandrite). *Wisdom from Mount Athos: The Writings of Staretz Silouan 1866–1938*. Crestwood, N.Y.: SVS Press, 1975.

Teben'kov, M.D. *Atlas of the Northwest Coasts of America*. Kingston, Ont.: Limestone Press, 1981.

Tikhmenev, P.A. *A History of the Russian American Company*. Seattle: University of Washington Press, 1978.

Trubetskoy, Eugene. *Icons: Theology in Color*. Crestwood, N.Y.: SVS Press, 1973.

Veniaminov, Innocent. *Notes on the Unalaska District*. Translated by Lydia T. Black. Kingston, Ont.: Limestone Press, 1984.

Waddell, Helen. *The Desert Fathers*. Ann Arbor: University of Michigan Press, 1966.

Ware, Kallistos. *The Orthodox Church*. New York: Pelican Books, 1976.

———. *The Orthodox Way*. Crestwood, N.Y.: SVS Press, 1979.

Wrangell, Ferdinand P. *Russian America*. Kingston, Ont.: Limestone Press, 1980.

Zagoskin, Lavrentii A. *Travels in Russian America 1842–1844*. Edited by Henry N. Michel. Toronto: University of Toronto Press, 1967.

Zander, Valentine. *St. Seraphim of Sarov*. Crestwood, N.Y.: SVS Press, 1975.

Zernov, Nicholas. *The Russians and Their Church*. Crestwood, N.Y.: SVS Press, 1978.

APPENDIX

ALEUT AND CREOLE CHURCHMEN IN ALASKA:
NINETEENTH AND EARLY TWENTIETH CENTURIES

Name	Birth/Death	Education	Service (dates)
John S. Alexandroff	Kodiak	Kodiak	Reader: Afognak Teacher $10 per month (1894)
Nikifor Amkan	Bristol Bay (Yup'ik)	Unalaska	Choirmaster 1897 Priest for Kuskokwim (1905)
Nicholas E. Avakumov	Yukon 1888	Unalaska	Choirmaster, St. Michael (1908)
John Balashin	c. 1813–	Unalaska	Warden, Unalaska (1833–1857)
Andrew P. Batuyev	c. 1824–1853	Sitka	Cathedral Choir director and music instructor at Seminary (1846)

Nicholas Belkov	b. 1871	San Francisco and American Public School	Yukon Delta (1892)
Rev. Zachary N. Belkov	1838–1899	Sitka; San Francisco	Yukon (as priest) 1876–1897
Matthew Bereskin	c. 1880–1971	Unalaska	Choirleader Kuskokwim, (1906–1971)
Peter A. Bureniev	b. 1811	Unalaska	Songleader Unalaska, 1832–1836; Sitka, 1836–?
Alexander I. Burtzev	c. 1849	Irkutsk	Sitka (secretary) 1867; trans. to Amur district, 1868.
Gregory Chechenoff	c. 1846	Sitka	Choirleader 1865–1868
Subdeacon Nikanor S. Chernov		Yakutsk Sem.	Sitka 1867; Amur 1868
Subdeacon Nicholas P. Chichenoff	1795	unknown	Sitka (choir) 1824 Kodiak 1847–1860
Peter I. Chubarov	June 18, 1881	San Francisco St. Petersburg	Sitka, (Teacher) (1902) Unga (1904); Unalaska 1905
Alexander A. Demidov	1884 Kodiak	Kenai	Songleader Kenai 1906

Rev. Peter Dobrovolsky	1833	Sitka	ordained 1880 Atka 1881–1884; Kodiak 1884–1893
John Galaktionoff			Surgeon: Kodiak
Nicholas N. Goltava	1832	Sitka	Warden, Yukon 1848
John Ivanov	1823	Atka	Warden, Atka 1837
Makary A. Ivanov	1834	Nushagak	Songleader, Kenai 1852–1878
Archpriest Andrew P. Kashevarov	1863 Kodiak	San Francisco	Sitka, San Francisco; Teacher: 1881–1886; English Teacher, Sitka 1887; Tlingit School Teacher (Eng. & Music) 1889; Killisnoo, 1893; Priest 1904; Dean of Ak. Clergy 1909–; Archpriest 1917
Leonty Kashevarov	1882	St. Petersburg (1903)	Songleader, Unalaska
Rev. Nicholas P. Kashevarov	1859, Kodiak	San Francisco	Choirleader, Kodiak 1875; Priest, 1895; trans. to Nushagak 1900; Rector

Rev. Nicholas P. Kashevarov			Kodiak, 1900–1914?
Rev. Peter Kashevarov	b. 1828 (Kodiak?)	Sitka	Priest, Kodiak 1852–1879
Rev. Peter P. Kashevarov	1856	Kodiak, Sitka, San Francisco	Songleader, Belkovski 1875; Unalaska 1877; Yukon 1878; ordained deacon at Belkovski, 1882; Nushagak 1894; Kuskokwim 1894; Unalaska 1895; Priest: St. George Is. 1898–1915?
Vasily G. Kashevarov	1838	Yakutsk Sem.	Librarian Yakutsk 1863; Sitka 1863; Deacon, 1864–1866 at Tlingit School
Vasily P. Kashevarov	1868 Kodiak	San Francisco & US Gov't. school	Teacher, Unalaska 1888; Songleader, Yukon, 1893; Nushagak 1896; ordained Priest 1899; served Unalaska, 1899–1906, Nushagak, 1906—
Vladimir P. Kashevarov	1861 Kodiak		Songleader

Elia Katanook	Father was Tlingit	Sitka	Songleader, Juneau 1901
Siginis King	1879 Unalaska	Kodiak Parish and American schools	Songleader, Priest; Kodiak 1916
Gregory Kochergin	1897; St. Paul	San Francisco	Songleader 1897; Priest, Nushagak
Jacob Korchinsky	Kiev (not Creole)	Missionary on Kuskokwim/Yukon 1896–1897; possibly responsible for introduction of ''Slaviq'' (Kolyadi) folksongs.	
Alexander G. Kostygin	1827	Sitka	Warden Kodiak 1845; Songleader, Nushagak 1860–1864; returned to Kodiak
John Kozhevnikov	1861	Belkovsky	Warden, St. Michael 1886
Philip Kruikov	c. 1809–1843		Songleader Kodiak, 1828–1843
Nicholas K. Kugiakin	Belkovsky 1887		Songleader 1909
Michael V. Kukichook	(Yup'ik)	Unalaska School	Songleader, Kuskokwim 1902
Andrew K. Ladochnikov	1834–1901	Unalaska	Warden 1863; Unalaska Songleader, 1867–1894
John F. Ladygin	1824		Warden, Atka 1841
Constantine Larionoff	c. 1820 Kodiak	Kodiak	Warden, Kodiak

Vasily Larionoff	1877	Sitka Seminary	Songleader, Killisnoo 1894
Dimitri Lestenkof	c. 1862		Songleader, St. George 1884
Innocent M. Lestenkof	c. 1830–1895	Sitka Sem.	Atka Songleader 1846; Unalaska 1873; Belkovsky 1877; Unalaska 1879; ordained Priest for St. George 1880
Constantine Lukin	c. 1828 Kodiak	self-taught	Yukon teacher 1845; songleader Yukon 1848–1857?
Xenophont Malutin	Jan. 1890	Afognak School	Songleader Kodiak 1912
Emilian Molchanov	1822 (Tlingit mother)	Sitka	Warden Sitka 1837–1841; Nushagak 1841–?
Igor Netsvetov	c. 1770–1837		Administrator at Atka
Michael I. Netsvetov	1847	Yakutsk	Subdeacon, Sitka 1867; Teacher, Sitka 1869; Deacon 1873
Yakov (Jacob) G. Netsvetov	c. 1804 Atka	Irkutsk	Priest, Atka 1828; Yukon 1845; Sitka 1862

John E. Orlov	1859 Sitka	San Francisco	Songleader Yukon 1879; Priest 1891, Yukon; to St. Paul, 1902; to Tatitlik 1915; Killisnoo 1916
Vasily Orlov	c. 1839	Kenai	Warden, Nushagak 1860; Manager at N. 1863; Deacon 1880–1895
Alex. Petelin	1855 Kodiak	Kodiak	Songleader, Kodiak 1867; Nushagak, Teacher 1892; to Kodiak 1893; Priest at Sitka, 1905; to Afognak, 1905
Stephan Repin	1884 Unalaska	Unalaska	Songleader Unalaska 1899–
Nicholas S. Rysev	1828	Sitka	Warden, Kodiak 1873; Priest 1881; Unalaska 1884; St. Paul 1893; Sitka 1907; Unalaska 1908–1910; Killisnoo 1910–? Archpriest
George D. Salamatov	1846	tutored at Atka	Warden, Atka 1865–

Lauvrenty S. Salamatov	c. 1818–c. 1865	Atka	Songleader, Atka 1834; Priest 1843; Teacher 1849–1850
M. V. Salamatov	c. 1846	Yakutsk	Songleader, Sitka 1865; Songleader, Tlingit chapel 1867
Matrona Salamatov			Taught English at Belkovsky school 1887
Moses Salamatov	c. 1843	Sitka	Songleader, Sitka 1849–1869; Priest 1875 on Alaska Penn.; Belkovsky 1881
Vasily M. Shabalin	1826	Unalaska	Teacher, Unalaska 1842; Deacon 1863; Priest 1864; Atka 1865; Sitka 1869–1875.
Innocenty K. Shayashnikov	c. 1824	Atka	Songleader, Yukon 1845; Priest, Unalaska 1848; Missionary, Kuskokwim 1873; Yukon 1874; Unalaska 1883.

Paul K. Shayashnikov	(brother of Innocenty) b. 1834, St. Paul		Warden, St. Paul 1857–6 Songleader, Sitka 1867; Priest 1874
Zachary K. Shayashnikov			Songleader, Unalaska 1867; St. Paul 1875; Deacon 1882–1886
Tikhon Sheratine	1875, Afognak	San Francisco	Clerk for Northern Commerce Co. (at $25 mo.); songleader, Afognak 1896; teacher of Sergei Sheratine (+1984), his nephew.
Leonty I. Sivtsov	1866	Unalaska	Songleader, Unalaska 1895
Andrew P. Sizov	1811	Irkutsk	Teacher, Sitka 1836; Deacon/Priest, Sitka 1838; teacher, Unalaska 1841–;
Simeon Sokolov	1830		Warden, Sitka 1859–1861; Kodiak (tempr.) 1860
Nicholai S. Sorokovaikov	1847, Kodiak	Yakutsk	Songleader, Kurile Islands 1863; Kodiak 1864; Kenai 1875–

Stepan I. Sorkovaikov	c. 1824	Sitka	Warden, Sitka 1841; Songleader 1845–
Michael S. Stepanov	c. 1883	Sitka	Songleader and Teacher, Juneau 1906–
Zachary I. Tiankin	c. 1831–	Sitka	Warden, Sitka 1850–
Gerassim Zyrianov	c. 1817 Kodiak	Kodiak	Warden, Kodiak 1844–1846; Teacher 1845– (enrollment 21 Creole boys)

GLOSSARY

The derivation of some words is indicated by a capital letter in parentheses indicating the following languages:

(A) *Alutiiq* (the Alaskan Native language of Kodiak Island, the upper Alaska Peninsula, Prince William Sound, and the tip of the Kenai Peninsula)
(G) *Greek* (in some cases the original Greek endings -os or -ion are included in parentheses after the shortened Slavonic version, which usually dropped them; see, for example, akathist (os).
(OCS) *Old Church Slavonic* (the liturgical language of the Slavic Orthodox tradition)
(R) *Russian*
(U) *Unangan* (the Native Alaskan language of the Aleutian Archipelago and the lower Alaskan Peninsula)
(Y) *Yup'ik* (the Native Alaskan language of the Kvichak and Nushagak rivers and the Yukon-Kuskokwim Delta)

AGAYUN: (A and Y) Divinity, God. The Yup'ik words for "to pray, worship," "to make the sign of the cross," and "to be Christian," as well as "clergyman/priest" (*agayulirta*), Sunday (*Agayuneq*) and church (*agayuvik*), all derive from the same verb stem, *Agayu-*. Also ⟨A AND Y⟩, Name Days and Feast Days are called *Agayuneq* while the eve of any Feast or Sunday is referred to as *Maqineq* (derived from the verb stem *maqi-*, which means to take a steam bath); thus every Saturday is *Maqineq*.

AGUUGUX: (U) Divinity, God. Also: Aguugux-agunax, Birthgiver of God/Theotokos.

AKATHIST(OS) (G): Literally "no sitting"; a poetic hymn, usually celebrated as an addition to a Molieben or Matins service, praising a particular saint or meditating on a particular event in the life of Christ. In the Greek tradition, the Akathistos Hymn to the Theotokos is regularly celebrated on the Fridays of Great Lent. In Alaska, the Akathistos Hymn to St. Herman is sung in many parishes each week throughout the year.

AMVON (G): The raised area directly in front of the Royal Doors from which the Gospel is read, sermons preached, and official announcements made. The faithful receive Holy Communion at the Amvon as well.

ANTIMENS(ION) (G): Literally "in place of a table"; a rectangular cloth on which is depicted the descent from the Cross or burial of Christ, and often bordered by icons of the four evangelists, into which, in the Slav practice, are sewn relics of a saint, and always signed by the ruling bishop of a diocese or region, normally placed on the Altar Table. The antimens (Greek: Antimension) represents the celebrant's official permission to conduct services as authorized by the Church, and is therefore required for the celebration of the Divine Liturgy. The relics within the cloth (in the Russian tradition—in the Greek, the relics are sealed within the stone Altar Table itself) indicate that the Church is essentially people who are the Mystical Body of Christ, founded on the witness (martyria) of the apostles and saints throughout the ages.

APQAUQ/APQAUR- (A and Y) Sacramental Confession/to confess in the Sacrament of Penance.

ARCH—A prefix attached as an honorary distinction to clerical titles bishop, priest, or deacon, indicating long, faithful, meritorious service. In the Greek practice, Archbishop ranks above Metropolitan; in the Russian practice, Metropolitan ranks above Archbishop. Bishops are addressed "His Grace, the Right Reverend"; Archbishops, "His Eminence, the Most Reverend"; and the ruling Metropolitan of the Orthodox Church in America, "His Beatitude, the Most Blessed." Archpriests are addressed "the Very Reverend."

ARCHIMANDRITE: A monk who has been ordained to the priesthood and appointed the head of a group or community of monks.

AUGTUQ/AUGTURLUNI: (A and Y) Communion/to receive Communion.

AUTOCEPHALOUS (G): Literally self-headed; administratively self-governing. The term applies to fifteen autocephalous Orthodox Churches in the world, which share total doctrinal and liturgical unity but are locally administered. Thus, the "Greek Orthodox" or "Russian Orthodox" Churches are more accurately the Orthodox Church *in* Greece or *in* Russia. The fifteen autocephalous Churches are:
Constantinople (and various Orthodox communities scattered throughout the New World); Alexandria (and Africa); Antioch (and the Middle East); Sophia (and Bulgaria); Athens (Greece); Bucharest (Romania); Cyprus; Serbia; Poland; Czechoslovakia; Georgia; Albania; and America. Semi-independent or Autonomous Churches include the Churches of Japan, Finland, and Mount Sinai. The greatest mission fields for the

Orthodox Church are currently East and Central Africa, Australia, and North America.

BÁTIUSHKA (R): Familiar/affectionate title for a spiritual father or priest (the diminutive form, literally "little father"), the masculine counterpart of "Matushka."

BEMA/HIGH PLACE: The area in the sanctuary directly behind the Altar Table, to which the celebrants proceed to complete each entrance during Vespers and Divine Liturgy.

BOGORODITSA (OCS): Literally the one who gave birth to God; (G) "Theotokos" or (popularly) Bozhii Mater, meaning Mother of God, an ancient title dogmatically assigned to the Virgin Mary through whom the "Word Who was with God and was God" "became Flesh and dwelt among us." The title was devised not so much to glorify the Virgin as to defend and proclaim the doctrine of Christ's full and perfect Divinity and Humanity, for if He is not Fully God and Fully Man, our unity with God cannot be restored through Him, God remains inaccessible, and salvation, as unity with Him, is impossible.

BRIGHT WEEK: The week following Pascha (Easter), itself a celebration known as "Bright Night." Each weekday of Bright Week is celebrated as if it were a Sunday Liturgy, with special hymns indicative of the Paschal season.

BUZHIK/PUUSIQ: Native Alaskan term, derived from Slavonic *Bozhe,* vocative of *Bog* (God). The Alaskan term refers to any religious article, symbol, or even action—an icon, a cross, a prayer. Also: MALISS'AAQ (Y), MALISAQ (A), or KAMGALUX (U).

CHIEF: In the nineteenth century, the social and political leader and spokesman for a native village; at present, a catechist usually selected by the parish and confirmed by the priest and/or bishop to preach at Orthodox services. The chief and sometimes the starosta is usually vested in a *stichar* similar to the deacon's vestment after several satisfactory years of service as an honorary distinction. Many parishes have assistant or "second" starostas and chiefs who may also enjoy the privilege of wearing the stichar.

CHRISMATION: Anointing with Chrism/Confirmation; the mystery of personal sanctification usually administered immediately after baptism and conferring full membership in the Church. In cases where baptism was performed by a layperson, the anointing with chrism, a special perfumed oil prepared by the ranking bishop of each autocephalous church, completes the rite of Christian initiation. Signing the chest, forehead, eyes, ears, nose, lips, hands, and feet, the priest announces "The Seal of the Gift of the Holy Spirit" as the personal sanctification and dedication of the person and all his or her senses, as a unique child of God and member of the Body of Christ.

FORTY DAY PRAYERS/CHURCHING: A series of short prayers of blessing and dedication for a newborn child and its mother on the fortieth day after birth, or on whatever day the mother is sufficiently recuperated to resume her regular household and community functions. Other prayers in this cycle include the prayer for the first day after birth, and the rite of Naming, performed on the eighth day. The basis for these prayers is Old Testamental, following the example of Our Lord mentioned in Luke 2.

GREAT BLESSING OF WATER: A rite of sanctification performed on the eve and on the Feast of Epiphany (January 5–6) in commemoration of Christ's Baptism and the manifestation of the Holy Trinity at the Jordan, and the second theme in the Orthodox Baptismal rite. The importance of the ceremony lies in its extension of Christ's redemptive work to the entire creation, restoring and sanctifying the universe and renewing it as prophesied in Isaiah.

HESYCHASM: (G) Literally silence; the traditional monastic spirituality developed by Orthodox ascetics and articulated by St. Gregory Palamas (1296–1359). The basic precepts of this spiritual tradition include the accessibility of direct participation in God through His Energies, and the total inaccessibility of God in His Divine Nature. Human beings become all that they were created to be by becoming open to God by a deliberate redirection of their selfish egos and reorientation of their lives to God. This is accomplished primarily through incessant prayer, constant "remembrance of God" through repetition of the Jesus Prayer: "Lord Jesus Christ, Son of God, have mercy on me a sinner." Hesychia, and with it receptivity to the action/energy/grace of God, can be achieved only when the tumult of inner thoughts and passions has been silenced and all sinful actions permanently abandoned. The ultimate aim of the Christian life, union with God and transformation into a "new creation," is realized for the "pure in heart" for they shall "see God." The hesychast saints claim that their vision of light constitutes participation in the Uncreated Energies of God, and that the brightness that surrounds the saints and angelic hosts in heaven represents not a metaphorical but an ontological reality in which all Christians are called to share. Hesychasm also insists on sacramental realism (in the Reality of Christ's Presence in the Eucharistic Mysteries) as a primary means by which participation in Divine Life is open to all believers. In the fourteenth century, the Orthodox affirmed hesychasm as the official doctrine of the Church and renounced any definition of humanity as naturally autonomous from God.

HIERO- : A prefix attached to another ecclesiastical title such as monk, or deacon, to indicate that the person is an ordained monk. A hieromonk is therefore a priest-monk, a hierodeacon, a deacon-monk.

ICONOSTAS/IKONOSTASIS (G): A screen of icons which separates the nave or main body of the church building from the sanctuary at the eastern end of the Temple. It is pierced by three doorways, the northern and southern Deacons Doors, and the "Royal Doors," which open in the center and provide direct access to the Altar Table (Prestol'). On the left of the Royal Doors an icon of the Theotokos and Child is displayed, to commemorate the first Coming of Christ, and on the right, an icon of Christ "Pantocrator" (literally Ruler of All) to depict His Second Coming.

JULIAN CALENDAR: Also known as the "Old Calendar." The official twelve-month, 365¼ day solar calendar authorized by Julius Caesar, which differs from the astronomically more correct Gregorian Calendar, devised at the request of Pope Gregory in 1585, by a few minutes per year. However, in the course of two millennia, the discrepancy has become quite pronounced—a total of twelve days in the nineteenth and thirteen days in the twentieth century. Most Protestant and Orthodox countries resisted the change to the Gregorian calendar, primarily because of its association with Rome, for several centuries, but conservative forces within Slavic Orthodox Churches have forestalled adoption of the Gregorian calendar for the celebration of the fixed Feasts of the liturgical year to the present day. Thus, in Alaska, December 25, the Feast of the Nativity of Jesus Christ, arrives thirteen days later than the Gregorian December 25, placing Christmas on January 7. The calendars will diverge by another day in 2100 A.D. All the dates on Russian American documents are, of course, according to the Julian calendar, since the Gregorian calendar was not adopted in Russia until after the overthrow of the tsarist regime.

KADILO (R)/CENSER: A vessel used to burn charcoal and incense as was traditional in both Old Testamental worship and is described in Revelation as employed in the heavenly liturgy.

KAMGA- (U) Stem for many interrelated church terms such as *kamgax* (feast), *kamgaluq* (icon), *kamgadtix* (baptism), *kamgaasix* (prayer); from the verb *kamgal* (to pray). Similar to Alutiiq *puusiq* and Yup'ik *maliss'aaq*.

KAMILAVKA: A cylindrical hat in the Russian practice, traditionally worn by married clergy as an award bestowed by the diocesan bishop and by all tonsured monks who also wear a veil (*klobuk*) which drapes over the kamilavka and down the back, below the shoulders. In the Russian usage, married clergy wear colored kamilavki, monastics only black, and metropolitans white. In the Greek practice, married clergy wear black kamilavki (in Greek *kalummavkhion*) distinguished from the monastic style by a small brim around the top edge.

KASAAKAQ: (A) A Russian (as distinct from *Melikaansaaq*, "American"); (Y) (in some areas) a Caucasian.

KASS'ALUGPIAQ: (Y) (literally, "original Kassaq"), a Russian.

KAS'AQ (A): "Orthodox Priest"; KASS'AQ (Y) (in regions where Agayulirta is not commonly used) "Priest." Otherwise, a Caucausian.

KELISTAAQ (A)/KELISTAQ (Y): A cross or crucifix. Also: *Puusiq* or *maliss'aaq*.

KELUSSNAQ: Yup'ik term for godparent; derived from Russian (*kryostny*).

KRAASNAA (Q): Alutiiq term for godparent.

KUM/KUMA: A male (*kum*) or female (*kumaa*) church member related by sacramental ties, as members of two families, one of whom served as godparent at the baptism for a member of the other.

KUTYA: Sweetened cooked rice or wheat, sometimes decorated with raisins, brought to a *panakhida* as an offering in memory of the departed, symbolizing the seed, which "if it dies and is buried in the earth will bring forth fruit a hundred-fold," and therefor a sign of the Resurrection. Also called *panakhida* in Alutiiq.

MATUSHKA (R) (accent on the first syllable): Literally "little mother"; the popular Russian title for the wife of a priest. In Greek, *presbytera;* in Native Alaskan usage, often pronounced "matuusica."

MEMORIAL SATURDAY: Certain Saturdays of the year devoted to the remembrance of the departed who "lie asleep in the Lord" as Christ Himself "rested" in the tomb on the Seventh Day.

MOLIEBEN (OCS): An abbreviated Matins service usually sung as a special intercessory or thanksgiving service on certain civil or church holidays, or at the request of a member with a particular need. Moliebens are traditionally celebrated at civil New Year, special Thanksgiving Days, and for the health of the seriously ill, as well as before or after completing a particularly difficult or dangerous task or journey. A "Te Deum".

MYSTERION/MYSTERY (G): The Orthodox term for a sacrament. In the East they have never been numbered, classified, or analyzed for minimum standards of validity. Thus, while the Great Blessing of water, the tonsuring of a monk or nun, and the consecration of an icon or a church building as well as any service or prayer constitute sacramental actions, baptism and the Eucharist enjoy a definite preeminence as the source and basis for all other Mysteries. Under Latin influence in the late Middle Ages, Orthodox began listing "seven" sacraments, although this sort of classification has never been universally accepted by the entire Church.

PANAGIA (G): (Literally "Most Holy"; referring to the Theotokos, the Virgin Mary). A small icon of the Theotokos, usually set in precious metal and sometimes set in semi-precious or precious stones, worn by all bishops as a sign of their position.

PANAKHIDA/PARASTASIS: A special memorial service for one or more departed Orthodox Christians, often celebrated in the home during the burial rites, and again on the ninth, twentieth, and fortieth days following the death, as well as on the Name Day and anniversary of the death and on Memorial Saturdays during Great Lent. Also, in some Alutiiq communities, the *kutya*.

PASCHA: The central and most joyous Festival of the Orthodox liturgical year celebrated after the first day of spring, at the full moon following Jewish Pesach (Passover), from which the name derives. This Christian Passover, from "Death to Life and from Earth to Heaven," as one of the Paschal hymns proclaims, reveals in the course of the three days the eternal significance of the Death and Resurrection of Jesus Christ.

On Great and Holy Thursday Evening, the Matins service is punctuated by the reading of twelve Gospel lessons, after which the hymns comment on the events, as for example these verses sung after the sixth reading:

Today is hung upon the Tree
He who suspended the earth in the midst of the waters
A crown of thorns crowns Him
Who is the King of the Angels.
He who wrapped the heavens in clouds
Is wrapped with the purple of mockery.
He who freed Adam in the Jordan endures scourging.
The Son of the Virgin is transfixed with nails.
We venerate Thy Passion O Christ!
We venerate Thy Passion O Christ!
We venerate Thy Passion O Christ!
Show us also Thy Glorious Resurrection!

On Friday, the Hours are read, but there is no service from noon until three. Vespers of Great and Holy Friday, however, focus on the burial of Christ, with the *Plaschanitsa* (in Greek *Epitaphion*)—an icon of Christ's descent from the Cross embroidered or painted on a large cloth—carried in procession from the sanctuary, through the northern door of the iconostas and placed in a "tomb" in the center of the church. That evening, the faithful stand at the bier, lamenting and praising this ''Life-creating Death'' and carry the Shroud in procession outdoors, commemorating the descent of Christ's soul into Hades. Immediately upon reentering the church, the Prophecy of Ezekiel (chapter 37) is announced.

On the Great and Holy Sabbath, Liturgy begins with Vespers during which these hymns are sung:

Today Hell cries out groaning:
''I should not have accepted the Man born of Mary!
He came and destroyed my power.
He shattered the gates of brass
And now, as God, He raises those whom I had held captive!''
Glory to Thy Cross and Resurrection, O Lord!

Today Hell cries out groaning:
''My power has been trampled on!
The Shepherd has been crucified and raises Adam.
All those whom I had swallowed in my strength I have disgorged.
He who was crucified has cleared the tombs,
And the power of Death can not avail.''
Glory to Thy Cross and Resurrection, O Lord!

There follows the reading of fifteen Old Testament prophecies and events, reviewing the history of salvation and culminating in the reading of the first Resurrection Gospel, the final chapter of the Gospel of St. Matthew. This is done with the *plaschanitsa* still in the ''tomb'' and without singing any of the Paschal hymns. The faithful eagerly anticipate the fullness of the Paschal Feast, which begins at midnight, the time the Bridegroom comes. Holy Saturday is, each year, the ''icon'' in time, of the joyful expectation of the Coming of Christ that characterizes that Christian life in this world. The midnight Paschal Marriage Feast of the Bridegroom represents the culmination of the lenten fast and the three-day Pascha. Nothing in Christendom equals the beauty the Orthodox celebration of the ''Bright Night'' of the Resurrection.

PLASCHANITSA (OCS)/EPITAPHIOS (G): An icon resembling the Shroud of Turin (on which is depicted the Body of Christ prepared for burial), carried in procession on Great and Holy Friday to a tomb in the center of an Orthodox church at Vespers, and in procession (in commemoration of the Descent into Hades) at Matins, and close to midnight on Great and Holy Saturday, removed to the altar, where it remains from Pascha until the Feast of Ascension, forty days later.

POKLON (OCS): A prostration—kneeling and touching the forehead to the ground as an outward gesture of repentance. It is a regular feature of services throughout Great Lent, but expressly forbidden during the Paschal season.

PROKIMENON: An introductory Biblical verse, usually from the Psalms, chanted or sung before the reading of Scripture at Orthodox services. The "Gradual".

PROTO- : Literally "First"; an honorific title bestowed on presbyters or deacons, appointing them "first" among the priests or deacons in a particular region.

PROSKOMEDIA: The first part of the Divine Liturgy during which the priest prepares the *prosphora* by cutting the breads and arranging the particles on the diskos (Paten/plate) in remembrance of Christ, the Church triumphant (the saints) and the Church militant (the living and departed members of the local community).

PROSPHORA (G): (Literally "offering"). Bread made with water, yeast, and flour, stamped with a special seal and used for the celebration of the Divine Liturgy. The single large loaf (in the Greek practice) or the five smaller two-layered loaves (in the Russian usage) are ritually cut during the Proskomedia, and the remainder of each loaf is distributed to all those in attendance at the end of the Liturgy.

PSALOMSHCHIK: A chanter or reader whose function is to chant the appointed psalms, and in some communities to lead the choral responses. In villages without a resident priest, the reader is usually considered the leading parish officer. (Y) *Naaqista.*

RIASA: A black outer robe with wide sleeves worn by all monks and ordained clergy both in and out of church.

SELAVI (Q) (Y) derived from "Slava" (Glory)/STARRING: Native Alaskan term for traditional Julian Calendar Christmas, combining elements of Ukrainian/Russian Orthodox hymns and folk customs and traditional indigenous practices. A pinwheel-shaped "Star" representing the Star of Bethlehem, with an icon of the Nativity of Christ in the center, leads the procession of carolers from house to house where (1) in the Aleut regions, they sing Orthodox hymns and the traditional "Many Years," often greeted with a rifle salute; or (2) in some Yup'ik Eskimo regions, all are treated to a lavish three-course meal (with the elders and church functionaries dining first), and in some households adults are presented with small gifts; or (3) in other Yup'ik areas, each household presenting "to the Star" their major annual contribution to the parish the singers represent. Entire communities "follow the Star'' not only from house to house, but from village to village along the Nushagak and Kvichak Rivers, and in the Lake Clark/Iliamna Lake region. Also (A) *Slaawiq,* and by nonnative Alaskans often *Slavi.*

STAROSTA (R): The parish warden; chief assistant to the parish priest in administering the parish, and in Alaska, often a lifetime position. Responsibilities usually include maintenance of order in the nave—including attending to the lighting and extinguishing of candles, and other functions of an usher—as well as many practical administrative concerns of the local church.

STIKHERI/VERSES: A series of hymns prescribed for a particular feast or day of the liturgical year.

SUISTAAQ: from Slavonic *svezda* (star); an Alutiiq term specifically for the Christmas (pinwheel-style) star used at Selaviq.

TABLE OF OBLATION: A table arranged in the northeastern corner of the sanctuary on which the Proskomedia is performed. On it are stored the Chalice (Communion Cup), Diskos (Communion Plate or paten), Star (a four-pronged cross-shaped metal cover placed over the Gifts and later covered with a veil during the Proskomedia), Spear (a knife shaped like a lance, used to cut the prosphora), and Spoon (used in the Liturgy to administer the Consecrated Gifts to the laity).

TETRAPOD/Analogion (G)/analoy (R): Literally four-footed; special lectern-like stand on which an icon or sometimes the Gospel Book is displayed for veneration in the vestibule or nave of an Orthodox church.

THEOSIS (G): The eternal process by which a human being increasingly draws nearer to God and becomes like Him, participating through His Grace in the Divine Life of the Holy Trinity. Begun at baptism, the process of directing one's will and action toward fulfilling the teachings of the Gospel is a difficult one, requiring constant struggle. In the Kingdom, the process will continue, but without pain or suffering. Growth in God-likeness will then be the essence of eternal life and joy. The saints are depicted in traditional Orthodox iconograph as having been already transformed into a ''new creation.''

THRONE: The technical name for the Altar Table; also the seat of the bishop, in the Russian practice at the Bema; in the Greek practice a permanent and more elaborate canopied chair in the nave.

TRISAGION (G): Literally Thrice-Holy; the angelic hymn ''Holy God, Holy Might, Holy Immortal, have mercy on us!'' sung three times at the Divine Liturgy, Matins, and as the funeral processional hymn; also a series of prayers, beginning with the same hymn, and ending with the Lord's Prayer, with a short prayer to the Holy Trinity, preceded and followed by the exclamation ''Glory to the Father and to the Son and to the Holy Spirit, now and ever and unto ages of ages'' inserted in the middle, chanted at almost every Orthodox service, often several times at various points; also in some Orthodox traditions, the name for a short memorial service (*Parastas/Panakhida*).

TROPAR(ION): In modern Orthodox liturgical terminology, the theme hymn for a particular celebration, usually sung at Vespers, Matins, and the Liturgy on that day, and in the case of major feasts, repeated for from one to eight days thereafter at every service. The Paschal Tropar, ''Christ is Risen from the Dead trampling down Death by Death and upon those in the tombs bestowing Life'' begins all services during the forty-day Paschal season.

WIIRPAQ/VERBA: Pussywillow branches, often decorated with home-made paper flowers used as a substitute for palms on Palm Sunday. In some villages, the multicolored branches are inserted into a special pole in the center of the nave, constituting an entire ''tree'' at Vespers on the eve of the Feast.

INDEXES

TO INTRODUCTION

INDEX TO TEXTS